AF758214

Global Economic Prospects

A World Bank Group Flagship Report

JUNE 2026

Global Economic Prospects

WORLD BANK GROUP

© 2026 International Bank for Reconstruction and Development / The World Bank
1818 H Street NW, Washington, DC 20433
Telephone: 202-473-1000; Internet: www.worldbank.org

Some rights reserved

1 2 3 4 29 28 27 26

This work is a product of the staff of The World Bank with external contributions. The findings, interpretations, and conclusions expressed in this work do not necessarily reflect the views of The World Bank, its Board of Executive Directors, or the governments they represent. The World Bank does not guarantee the accuracy, completeness, or currency of the data included in this work and does not assume responsibility for any errors, omissions, or discrepancies in the information, or liability with respect to the use of or failure to use the information, methods, processes, or conclusions set forth. The boundaries, colors, denominations, links/footnotes, and other information shown in this work do not imply any judgment on the part of The World Bank concerning the legal status of any territory or the endorsement or acceptance of such boundaries. The citation of works authored by others does not mean the World Bank endorses the views expressed by those authors or the content of their works.

Nothing herein shall constitute or be construed or considered to be a limitation upon or waiver of the privileges and immunities of The World Bank, all of which are specifically reserved.

Rights and Permissions

This work is available under the Creative Commons Attribution 3.0 IGO license (CC BY 3.0 IGO) http://creativecommons.org/licenses/by/3.0/igo. Under the Creative Commons Attribution license, you are free to copy, distribute, transmit, and adapt this work, including for commercial purposes, under the following conditions:

Attribution—Please cite the work as follows: World Bank. 2026. *Global Economic Prospects, June 2026.* Washington, DC: World Bank. License: Creative Commons Attribution CC BY 3.0 IGO

Translations—If you create a translation of this work, please add the following disclaimer along with the attribution: *This translation was not created by The World Bank and should not be considered an official World Bank translation. The World Bank shall not be liable for any content or error in this translation.*

Adaptations—If you create an adaptation of this work, please add the following disclaimer along with the attribution: *This is an adaptation of an original work by The World Bank. Views and opinions expressed in the adaptation are the sole responsibility of the author or authors of the adaptation and are not endorsed by The World Bank.*

Third-party content—The World Bank does not necessarily own each component of the content contained within the work. The World Bank therefore does not warrant that the use of any third-party-owned individual component or part contained in the work will not infringe on the rights of those third parties. The risk of claims resulting from such infringement rests solely with you. If you wish to reuse a component of the work, it is your responsibility to determine whether permission is needed for that reuse and to obtain permission from the copyright owner. Examples of components can include, but are not limited to, tables, figures, or images.

All queries on rights and licenses should be addressed to World Bank Publications, The World Bank Group, 1818 H Street NW, Washington, DC 20433, USA; e-mail: pubrights@worldbank.org.

ISSN: 1014-8906

ISBN (paper): 978-1-4648-2315-2

ISBN (electronic): 978-1-4648-2349-7

DOI: 10.1596/978-1-4648-2315-2

Cover design: Bill Pragluski, Critical Stages LLC.

Library of Congress Control Number: 2026915397.

The cutoff date for the data used in the report was June 2, 2026.

Summary of Contents

Contents

Figures

Figures

Tables

Acknowledgments

This World Bank Group Flagship Report is a product of the Prospects Group in the Development Economics (DEC) Vice Presidency. The project was managed by M. Ayhan Kose and Carlos Arteta, under the general guidance of Indermit Gill.

Dana Vorisek contributed to the coordination of the report and oversaw the analytical work on fiscal policy in commodity exporters. The report was prepared by a team that included Marie Albert, Francisco Arroyo Marioli, Mirco Balatti, Tommy Chrimes, Reina Eskimez, Bram Gootjes, Steven Kamin, Phil Kenworthy, Gitanjali Kumar, Mathilde Lebrand, Jiwon Lee, Dawit Mekonnen, Alen Mulabdic, Edoardo Palombo, Nikita Perevalov, Franz Ulrich Ruch, Peter Selcuk, Shijie Shi, Kersten Stamm, Naotaka Sugawara, Takuma Tanaka, Neha Varma, and Garima Vasishtha.

Main research assistance was provided by Emma Caillet, Sergiu Dinu, Jiayue Fan, Mario Guillen Salvatore, Rafaela Martinho Henriques, Shiya Luo, Maria Hazel Macadangdang, Celine Papageorgiou, Vasiliki Papagianni, Juan Felipe Serrano Ariza, Kaltrina Temaj, and Chao Wang. Additional research assistance was provided by Nikita Makarenko and Sadhna Naik. Modeling and data work was provided by Vasiliki Papagianni and Shijie Shi.

Adriana Maximiliano handled design and production. Graeme Littler produced the online products, with assistance from the Open Knowledge Repository, and provided editorial support, with contributions from Adriana Maximiliano and Michael Harrup. Joe Rebello managed communications and media outreach with a team that included Kristen Milhollin and Leslie Yun, with support from the World Bank's media and digital communications teams.

Regional projections and write-ups were produced in coordination with country teams, country directors, and the offices of the regional chief economists.

Many reviewers provided extensive feedback. The report also benefited from comments and suggestions by World Bank Group staff, and from Executive Directors in their discussion of the report on June 2, 2026. However, the forecasts and analysis are those of the World Bank Group staff and should not be attributed to Executive Directors or their national authorities. The Prospects Group gratefully acknowledges financial support from the Government of Japan, provided through the Policy and Human Resources Development (PHRD) Fund, for some of the analytical work in the report.

Foreword

Barring a miracle, the 2020s will prove to be what their ominous opening foreshadowed: a lost decade—not just for a couple of outliers, but for dozens of developing economies. Amid one of the densest clusters of global shocks since the 1970s, nearly one out of every two developing economies has failed since 2019 to advance on the most rudimentary promise of development: narrowing the income gap with the world's most prosperous economies. For light at the end of the tunnel, you'd have to look to the 2030s.

That new decade is an eyeblink away—and it offers a historic opportunity the world cannot afford to squander. As this report makes clear, the losses of the 2020s have been stark. Global growth this year will slump to its weakest pace outside of outright recession in close to 20 years—a meager 2.5 percent. By the end of 2026, one-quarter of developing economies, one-third of low-income economies, and half of fragile and conflict-affected economies will be poorer than they were in 2019 on the eve of the COVID-19 crisis. Among the 24 poorest economies, 19 still depend on foreign assistance for their food supplies, but the world has seldom been in a less charitable mood than it is today. Government debt in developing economies has surged to all-time highs, meanwhile, and private investment growth in the 2020s has more than halved relative to the 2010s.

Yet on the horizon are three pockets of opportunity that could make the 2030s a golden era for job creation and growth. The first is impossible to miss: the rapid adoption of artificial intelligence (AI), even if it failed to live up to the hype, would by most accounts still boost global productivity rates above the paltry average of the 2020s. But if it is managed well, if its potential for good is maximized, our estimates suggest that global growth in the 2030s would surpass the average of the 2000s. AI would, in short, usher in the world's most prosperous decade since the 1970s.

The second is energy security. The two major conflicts of this decade have concentrated the minds of policymakers. Clean energy now accounts for two-thirds of all global investment in energy. In 2025, global investment in clean energy reached a record $2.2 trillion, eclipsing fossil fuels by a wide margin. Over the past five years, most of the increase in clean-energy spending—as much as 70 percent—has been attributable to net importers of fossil fuels aiming to bolster energy security. Clean energy, in short, is now as much a national security imperative as it is a priority for global development. That convergence, if it holds, could speed up economic growth in developing economies—by creating jobs, expanding access to affordable power, and making them more resilient to future shocks.

The third is regional trade. Globalization might have lost its luster in some parts of the world, but regional trade is on the upswing. The number of regional trade agreements has surged over the 2020s, rising from slightly more than 300 in 2020 to nearly 400 today. Collectively, these agreements now account for 60 percent of global trade, up from 40 percent in 1990. That makes them a potent complement to the global rules-based system, given its diminished state. Regional trade is increasingly binding developing economies together—and bringing a much-needed measure of predictability, not just through tariffs but also through clear rules on investment, standards, and services.

Realizing these opportunities will not be easy. AI, for example, depends on digital infrastructure, computing capacity, and technical expertise—resources still concentrated in richer economies. Developing economies account for less than one-quarter of global data-center capacity; the world's 24 poorest economies account for less than one-tenth of 1 percent. AI's leading models, moreover, suffer from a major blind spot: the languages of roughly half the world's people remain poorly represented in the data that trains the models. Unless such gaps are closed, the AI revolution could widen rather than narrow the gap between rich and poor countries.

Similar gaps exist in energy and trade. Since 2022, higher borrowing costs, rising inflation, and difficulties in connecting new renewable projects to electricity grids have slowed the pace of growth in clean energy investment. Such investment, moreover, has remained uneven. China, for example, accounts for nearly a third of the global share. But smaller economies struggling with high debt and tight government budgets, especially in Sub-Saharan Africa, have had a hard time mobilizing the capital necessary for clean-energy infrastructure. In the area of regional trade, developing economies still have significant gains to be reaped: they could trade much more with nearby economies, for example, if they cut red tape at borders, harmonized rules, and made it easier for firms—especially small businesses—to obtain financing. At the same time, investment treaties should shift from simply protecting investors toward making investment happen while advancing overall development and sustainability goals.

All of this, moreover, must happen while governments manage the immediate fallout of the conflict in the Middle East and return to the unfinished work of economic repair. Debt must come down. Inflation must stay contained. Food insecurity must recede. And countries must return to putting in place the pre-requisites for sustained job creation and rising living standards: stronger infrastructure, healthier and better-skilled workers, a regulatory environment that rewards investment, and deeper pools of private capital. Few challenges in modern times have required this degree of sustained global coordination and support.

The World Bank Group was created for exactly such a moment. In response to the historic setbacks of the 2020s, we responded on a historic scale: during the five-year period that ended June 30, 2025, we provided more in financing commitments to help developing countries than in any previous five-year period in our history. Today, we are helping developing economies confront the Middle East shock by providing immediate liquidity—up to $25 billion through existing instruments—to help them cope. We are bringing additional resources to bear by reprioritizing projects already in the pipeline. And we stand ready to do more if needed: if the conflict and economic fallout persist, World Bank Group financing could be increased to $80 to $100 billion over 15 months.

The first half of the 2020s are now behind us, and it is possible that this decade might already be lost. But the 2030s are not. The economic forces now gathering—AI, energy transformation, and deeper regional integration—are powerful enough to unlock transformative progress in the next decade. Seizing that potential, however, will require immense preparation, and it must begin now.

Indermit Gill
Senior Vice President and Chief Economist
The World Bank Group

Executive Summary

The global economy is facing another major shock. The conflict in the Middle East has triggered sharp increases in energy prices, renewed inflationary pressures, and fueled expectations of tighter monetary policy. Global growth is projected to slow to 2.5 percent in 2026, from 2.9 percent in 2025—the lowest rate since the COVID-19 pandemic—amid weaker prospects for economies dependent on energy imports and those directly affected by hostilities. Activity is expected to firm in 2027–28 as energy supplies recover, monetary easing resumes, and trade strengthens.

Growth in emerging market and developing economies (EMDEs) is expected to slow to 3.6 percent this year. For all EMDE regions, growth this year is forecast to be weaker than in 2025. Per capita income growth in EMDEs is projected to slow in 2026 to its weakest pace since the pandemic. The level of per capita income across EMDEs excluding China and India, relative to advanced economies, is not expected to return to the pre-pandemic level until after 2028, implying nearly a decade of lost income convergence.

Risks to the outlook remain skewed to the downside. A renewed escalation of hostilities or more prolonged disruptions to commodity flows could further raise commodity prices, intensify inflationary pressures and food insecurity, trigger financial stress, and lower growth. If energy supply disruptions prove more severe than assumed and are accompanied by substantial financial stress, global growth could fall to just 1.3 percent in 2026. Persistent trade policy uncertainty, geopolitical strains, and weather-related shocks also pose material risks. On the upside, broader investment in and adoption of artificial intelligence (AI) could lift activity.

Policy action is critical to address ongoing challenges. Enhanced global cooperation is needed to safeguard energy and food security, bolster the trading system, and advance the energy transition. Domestically, policy makers will need to balance controlling inflation with supporting activity, strengthen fiscal sustainability, and maintain financial stability. Slower growth prospects translate into reduced investment, constrained hiring, and tighter fiscal space, compounding the challenge of creating jobs in EMDEs with growing workforces in an era of potentially transformative change linked to AI. Meeting this challenge will require a concerted agenda centered on the conditions for job creation: investing in physical, human, and digital capital; fostering a business-friendly environment; and mobilizing private investment.

In addition to the global and regional outlooks, this edition of *Global Economic Prospects* features two analytical chapters. One chapter examines the impact of government debt on interest rates. Another chapter considers the challenges of fiscal policy in commodity-exporting EMDEs.

A Rising Challenge: Sovereign Debt Levels and Interest Rates in EMDEs. Rising government debt poses a key challenge for EMDEs, as it leads to higher interest rates, higher debt-service payments, and a greater likelihood of debt distress. Debt levels are positively associated with dollar-denominated sovereign bond spreads and domestic-currency government bond yields. The relationship with rising debt is non-linear: the increases in spreads or yields associated with increases in debt-to-GDP ratios are greater the higher the debt-to-GDP ratio.

The increase in EMDE debt-to-GDP ratios since 2010 is associated with increases in sovereign spreads and domestic-currency yields of about 110 and 30 basis points, respectively. Rising debt in advanced economies, by pushing up yields in those economies, has added further to the increase in EMDE interest rates. With EMDE government debt at historically high levels, additional borrowing may lead to progressively larger increases in interest rates. Rising debt has led to even larger increases in interest rates in countries with a history of default, low credit ratings, frontier market status, heavy reliance on short-term debt, and weak governance.

These findings underscore the importance of strengthening fiscal positions. This can be achieved through stronger domestic revenue mobilization, more efficient public spending, improved debt management, support for domestic debt market development, and, where appropriate, debt-for-development swaps. By helping contain borrowing costs and preserve fiscal space, these measures can also support the infrastructure, services, and private investment needed for long-term growth and job creation.

Navigating Volatility: Fiscal Policy and Commodity Price Swings. Large commodity market disruptions—most recently triggered by the conflict in the Middle East—have brought renewed attention to the persistent fiscal challenges faced by commodity-exporting EMDEs. Since 2000, fiscal positions in these economies have generally been weaker than those in other EMDEs, reflecting lower and more volatile revenues, commodity price swings, and limited buffer accumulation in good times.

Government debt across EMDEs has risen since the global financial crisis, but commodity exporters are especially vulnerable. A 1 percent increase in commodity prices raises both revenues and primary spending in commodity exporters by about 0.4 percent after five years, suggesting that revenue windfalls are gradually spent rather than saved. Fiscal positions over commodity price cycles vary across exporters of different commodities. Primary balances in energy and metal exporters strengthen during booms and worsen in slumps, mainly as a result of revenue swings, while primary spending remains broadly contained; debt ratios fall in booms and rise in slumps. In contrast, agricultural exporters increase spending in booms, offsetting revenue gains and leading to more lasting debt accumulation.

Although sovereign wealth funds (SWFs) and fiscal rules have helped smooth spending over commodity cycles in some countries, they offer limited protection amid intensifying spending pressures after commodity shocks. Policy implications point to an integrated approach combining credible fiscal rules, well-governed SWFs, independent fiscal councils, strengthened debt management, revenue diversification, and robust institutions. Together, such reforms are critical to enhancing fiscal resilience, reducing volatility, supporting sustainable and inclusive growth, and boosting job creation.

Abbreviations

AE	advanced economy
AI	artificial intelligence
ASEAN	Association of Southeast Asian Nations
CPI	consumer price index
EAP	East Asia and Pacific
ECA	Europe and Central Asia
EMBI	J.P. Morgan Emerging Markets Bond Index
EMBIG	J.P. Morgan Emerging Markets Bond Index Global
EMDEs	emerging market and developing economies
FAO	Food and Agriculture Organization of the United Nations
FCS	fragile and conflict-affected situations
FDI	foreign direct investment
FY	fiscal year
GCC	Gulf Cooperation Council
GDP	gross domestic product
GNFS	goods and nonfactor services
ICRG	International Country Risk Guide
ICT	information and communications technology
IMF	International Monetary Fund
LAC	Latin America and the Caribbean
LIC	low-income country
LNG	liquefied natural gas
MNA	Middle East, North Africa, Afghanistan, and Pakistan
ODA	official development assistance
OECD	Organisation for Economic Co-operation and Development
PDM	public debt management
PMI	purchasing managers' index
PPP	public-private partnership
RTA	regional trade agreement
SAR	South Asia
SOE	state-owned enterprise
SSA	Sub-Saharan Africa
SWF	sovereign wealth fund
TFP	total factor productivity
UNCTAD	United Nations Conference on Trade and Development
USMCA	United States-Mexico-Canada Agreement
VIX	Chicago Board Options Exchange Volatility Index
WEO	*World Economic Outlook*

CHAPTER 1

GLOBAL OUTLOOK

The global economy is facing another major shock. The conflict in the Middle East has triggered sharp increases in energy prices, renewed inflationary pressures, and fueled expectations of tighter monetary policy. Global growth is projected to slow from 2.9 percent in 2025 to 2.5 percent in 2026—the lowest rate since the COVID-19 pandemic—amid weaker prospects for economies dependent on energy imports and those directly affected by hostilities. Activity is expected to firm in 2027–28 as energy supplies recover, monetary easing resumes, and trade strengthens. Risks to the outlook remain skewed to the downside. A renewed escalation of hostilities or more prolonged disruptions to commodity flows could further raise commodity prices, intensify inflationary pressures and food insecurity, trigger financial stress, and lower growth. If energy supply disruptions prove to be more severe than assumed and are accompanied by substantial financial stress, global growth could fall to just 1.3 percent in 2026. Persistent trade policy uncertainty, geopolitical strains, and weather-related shocks also pose material risks. On the upside, a broadening of artificial intelligence (AI)-related investment and its adoption could lift activity. Policy action is critical to address ongoing challenges. Enhanced global cooperation is needed to safeguard energy and food security, bolster the trading system, and advance the energy transition. Domestically, policy makers will need to balance controlling inflation with supporting activity, strengthen fiscal sustainability, and maintain financial stability. Slower growth prospects translate into reduced investment, constrained hiring, and tighter fiscal space, compounding the challenge of creating jobs in EMDEs with growing workforces in an era of potentially transformative change linked to AI. Meeting this challenge will require a concerted agenda centered on the conditions for job creation: investing in physical, human, and digital capital; fostering a business-friendly environment; and mobilizing private investment.

Summary

The global economic outlook has shifted markedly as the conflict in the Middle East has generated major disruptions in energy markets. Before the outbreak of the conflict, global activity seemed to be on a firm footing, supported by strong growth in some major economies and better-than-expected global trade, amid robust growth in artificial intelligence (AI)-related technology exports and a slight decline in tariff levels. The conflict, however, has led to a marked deterioration in the global outlook, with about two-thirds of economies around the world facing weaker growth prospects (figure 1.1.A).

Disruptions to flows of energy and other commodity supplies from the Gulf region have led to sharp commodity price increases (figure 1.1.B). Overall, commodity prices are expected to rise by 22 percent in 2026, in contrast to the 7 percent decline expected in January. This reflects a baseline assumption that shipping through the Strait of Hormuz remains severely disrupted through July, with shipping volumes haltingly resuming thereafter, and approaching pre-conflict levels by the end of the year. These disruptions are projected to keep energy prices elevated, with the Brent crude oil price averaging $94/barrel (bbl) in 2026, an increase of 36 percent over 2025 and more than 50 percent above the January projection. European natural gas prices are anticipated to rise about 30 percent in 2026, on tightened liquefied natural gas (LNG) availability globally. The conflict has also severely disrupted global fertilizer trade, triggering sharp price increases that reflect the Gulf's large share of global fertilizer exports and the surge in natural gas prices, a key input for nitrogen fertilizers.

While conflict-related disruptions are weighing on commodity trade flows, an improved trade policy environment and buoyant AI-related investment provide countervailing support to global trade (figure 1.1.C). This is in part attributable to a slight decline in U.S. tariffs following a U.S. Supreme Court ruling that struck down tariffs imposed on international economic emergency grounds, alongside trade liberalization efforts by other countries.

The increase in commodity prices has led to a notable resurgence of inflationary pressures. Headline inflation has picked up in both advanced

Note: This chapter was prepared by Carlos Arteta, Nikita Perevalov, Peter Selcuk, Phil Kenworthy, Jiwon Lee, and Garima Vasishtha, with contributions from Gitanjali Kumar, Neha Varma, Mirco Balatti, and Alen Mulabdic, and inputs from Dawit Mekonnen, Edoardo Palombo, Shijie Shi, Naotaka Sugawara, and Takuma Tanaka.

TABLE 1.1 Real GDP [1]

(Percent change from previous year unless indicated otherwise)

	2023	2024	2025e	2026f	2027f	2028f	Percentage-point differences from January 2026 projections: 2026f	Percentage-point differences from January 2026 projections: 2027f
World	**2.8**	**2.9**	**2.9**	**2.5**	**2.8**	**2.8**	**-0.1**	**0.1**
Advanced economies	**1.6**	**1.8**	**1.8**	**1.5**	**1.8**	**1.7**	**-0.1**	**0.2**
United States	2.9	2.8	2.1	2.2	2.1	2.0	0.0	0.2
Euro area	0.5	1.0	1.4	0.8	1.3	1.3	-0.1	0.1
Japan	0.7	-0.2	1.1	0.7	0.9	0.8	-0.1	0.1
Emerging market and developing economies	**4.3**	**4.4**	**4.4**	**3.6**	**4.2**	**4.1**	**-0.4**	**0.1**
East Asia and Pacific	5.2	5.0	5.0	4.2	4.4	4.3	-0.2	0.1
China	5.4	5.0	5.0	4.2	4.3	4.2	-0.2	0.1
Indonesia	5.0	5.0	5.1	5.0	5.2	5.2	0.0	0.0
Thailand	2.2	2.9	2.4	1.7	2.1	2.4	-0.1	-0.4
Europe and Central Asia	3.6	3.9	2.5	2.1	2.3	2.6	-0.3	-0.4
Russian Federation	4.1	4.9	1.0	0.8	0.7	0.7	0.0	-0.3
Türkiye	5.0	3.3	3.6	2.8	3.7	4.3	-0.9	-0.7
Poland	0.2	3.2	3.6	3.1	2.6	2.9	-0.1	-0.3
Latin America and the Caribbean	2.3	2.3	2.3	2.2	2.5	2.6	-0.1	-0.1
Brazil	3.2	3.4	2.3	1.9	2.0	2.2	-0.1	-0.3
Mexico	3.1	1.4	0.6	1.3	1.7	1.9	0.0	-0.1
Argentina	-1.9	-1.3	4.4	3.6	3.7	3.5	-0.4	-0.3
Middle East, North Africa, Afghanistan, and Pakistan	2.0	2.9	4.0	1.6	5.0	4.0	-2.7	0.7
Saudi Arabia	0.5	2.6	4.5	3.1	4.9	3.7	-1.2	0.5
United Arab Emirates	4.3	6.6	6.2	2.4	4.1	4.2	-2.6	-1.0
Egypt, Arab Rep. [2]	3.8	2.4	4.4	4.6	4.0	4.6	0.3	-0.8
South Asia	6.6	6.8	7.0	6.3	6.9	7.1	0.1	0.4
India [2]	7.2	7.1	7.7	6.6	7.2	7.0	0.1	0.6
Bangladesh [2]	5.8	4.2	3.5	3.8	4.6	5.5	-0.8	-1.5
Sri Lanka	-2.0	5.0	5.0	3.6	3.8	3.9	0.1	0.7
Sub-Saharan Africa	3.0	3.8	4.1	4.0	4.4	4.5	-0.3	-0.1
Nigeria	3.3	4.1	4.0	4.1	4.2	4.3	-0.3	-0.2
South Africa	0.8	0.5	1.1	1.0	1.5	1.7	-0.4	0.0
Ethiopia [2]	7.2	8.1	9.2	8.0	6.9	8.4	0.9	-0.8
Memorandum items:								
Real GDP [1]								
High-income countries	1.7	1.9	1.9	1.5	1.9	1.8	-0.2	0.1
Middle-income countries	4.7	4.5	4.6	3.9	4.3	4.3	-0.3	0.0
Low-income countries	1.2	3.7	5.0	5.4	5.6	5.4	-0.3	0.0
EMDEs excluding China	3.6	4.0	3.9	3.2	4.1	4.1	-0.6	0.1
Commodity-exporting EMDEs	2.9	3.5	3.3	2.4	3.5	3.3	-0.9	0.1
Commodity-importing EMDEs	5.0	4.8	4.8	4.2	4.5	4.5	-0.2	0.1
Commodity-importing EMDEs excluding China	4.3	4.5	4.5	4.1	4.7	5.0	-0.2	0.0
EM7	5.2	4.9	4.6	3.9	4.2	4.2	-0.2	0.1
World (PPP weights) [3]	3.2	3.4	3.5	2.9	3.4	3.4	-0.3	0.1
World trade volume [4]	**0.4**	**3.8**	**4.8**	**2.9**	**3.3**	**3.1**	**0.7**	**0.6**
							Level differences from January 2026 projections	
Commodity prices [5]								
WBG commodity price index	108.0	105.1	98.4	119.8	104.5	96.4	28.9	10.4
Energy index	106.9	101.5	90.0	119.6	98.4	85.9	39.7	13.5
Oil (US$ per barrel)	82.6	80.7	69.0	94.0	76.0	65.0	34.0	11.0
Non-energy index	110.2	112.5	115.4	120.2	116.7	117.7	7.1	4.0

Source: World Bank.

Note: e = estimate; f = forecast. EM7 = Brazil, China, India, Indonesia, Mexico, the Russian Federation, and Türkiye; WBG = World Bank Group. World Bank forecasts are frequently updated based on new information. Consequently, projections presented here may differ from those contained in other World Bank documents, even if basic assessments of countries' prospects do not differ at any given date. For the definition of EMDEs, developing countries, commodity exporters, and commodity importers, please refer to table 1.2. The World Bank is currently not publishing economic output, income, or growth data for República Bolivariana de Venezuela owing to lack of reliable data of adequate quality. República Bolivariana de Venezuela is excluded from cross-country macroeconomic aggregates.

1. Headline aggregate growth rates are calculated using GDP weights at average 2010-19 prices and market exchange rates.

2. GDP growth rates are on a fiscal year (FY) basis. Aggregates that include these countries are calculated using data compiled on a calendar year basis. For India, the column for 2023 refers to FY2023/24. For Bangladesh, and the Arab Republic of Egypt, and Ethiopia, the column for 2023 refers to FY2022/23.

3. World growth rates are calculated using average 2010-19 purchasing power parity (PPP) weights, which attribute a greater share of global GDP to emerging market and developing economies (EMDEs) than market exchange rates.

4. World trade volume of goods and nonfactor services.

5. Indexes are expressed in nominal U.S. dollars (2010 = 100). Oil refers to the Brent crude oil benchmark. For weights and composition of indexes, refer to https://worldbank.org/commodities.

economies and emerging market and developing economies (EMDEs), though the impact was attenuated somewhat by the introduction of fuel subsidies and price caps in some economies. In addition, core inflation has firmed across many EMDEs and in some large economies. As a result, headline inflation expectations have risen broadly (figure 1.1.D).

The sharp escalation in geopolitical stress also resulted in elevated volatility across financial markets. Concerns about inflationary pressures have pushed up bond yields as well as breakeven rates of inflation in major advanced economies, and expectations of near-term monetary policy easing have dissipated. In addition, equity markets weakened in the initial weeks of the conflict but many have mostly recovered following the cease-fire, largely as a result of AI optimism. Across EMDEs, equity prices declined, bond yields increased, and currencies came under pressure amid capital outflows, with only a partial recovery for some commodity importers after hostilities eased (figure 1.1.E). In contrast, financial conditions in energy-exporting EMDEs outside the Middle East, and other EMDEs with improved policy frameworks and substantial buffers, have recovered more quickly.

In this context, global growth is forecast to slow this year to 2.5 percent, the lowest rate since the COVID-19 pandemic, as higher energy prices, rising inflation, tighter monetary conditions, and weaker trade weigh on activity. The expected deceleration is driven by slowing growth in advanced economies and EMDEs reliant on imported energy, as well as sharply weaker exports in economies in the Middle East directly exposed to the conflict (figure 1.1.F). Global growth is envisaged to pick up to 2.8 percent on average in 2027–28 as energy prices moderate, financial conditions ease, and trade recovers.

Growth in advanced economies is forecast to slow this year, to 1.5 percent, from 1.8 percent in 2025, mainly due to the impact of substantially higher energy prices. The United States—a large oil producer—is proving resilient to the disruptions in global energy markets, with the adverse impacts of the conflict expected to be offset by fiscal easing and continued AI-related investment.

FIGURE 1.1 Global economic prospects

Global growth is expected to slow in 2026, with growth downgraded relative to January in nearly two-thirds of economies. This mainly reflects sharp disruptions in key commodity markets caused by the conflict in the Middle East. The conflict's impact on global trade has partly been offset by robust AI-related investment. Consensus inflation expectations picked up notably following the surge in energy prices. Local-currency bond yields and external bond spreads remained higher in commodity importers, reflecting more adverse impacts of the conflict. Against this backdrop, global growth is forecast to decelerate to 2.5 percent in 2026, down from 2.9 percent in 2025, with notably weaker prospects in EMDEs.

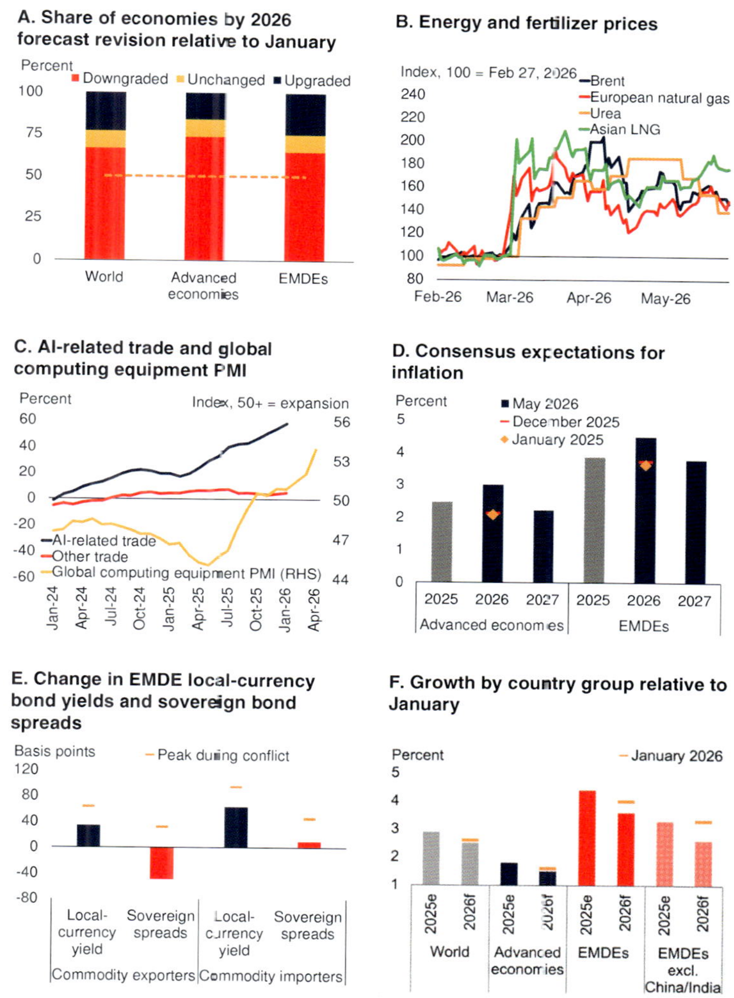

Sources: Bloomberg; Consensus Economics; Haver Analytics; J.P. Morgan; UN Comtrade; World Bank.

Note: e = estimate; f = forecast. AI = artificial intelligence; EMDEs = emerging market and developing economies; excl. = excluding; LNG = liquefied natural gas; PMI = purchasing managers' index (readings above/below 50 indicate expansion/contraction); RHS = right-hand scale. Aggregates use real U.S. dollar GDP weights at average 2010-19 prices and market exchange rates.

A. The share of economies by group and type of forecast revision in the current edition of the *Global Economic Prospects* report compared to the January 2026 report. The dashed line shows 50 percent.

B. Daily prices for Brent spot, European natural gas, and weekly prices of urea, indexed to 100 on February 27, the last market day before the onset of the Middle East conflict. Last observation is May 29, 2026.

C. Five-month averages of (1) year-on-year growth in nominal global goods imports, and (2) PMI for global computing equipment. AI-related trade includes 13 HS 6-digit product codes. Last observation is January 2026 (trade) and April 2026 (PMI). Sample includes 48 countries.

D. Median headline consumer price index inflation expectations for 35 advanced economies and up to 53 EMDEs from Consensus Economics surveys.

E. Changes in average local-currency bond yields and foreign-currency sovereign bond spreads across 20 and 63 EMDEs, respectively, before (January 2–February 26) and after (February 27–June 2) the start of the conflict this year.

F. Projected annual GDP growth by group from the current (bars) and January 2026 (yellow) editions of the *Global Economic Prospects* report.

FIGURE 1.2 Global risks and policy challenges

EMDEs excluding China and India are facing almost a full decade of lost convergence with advanced economy income levels. A further surge in energy prices, especially if exacerbated by financial market stress, could further reduce growth and raise inflation this year. On the upside, higher productivity related to AI adoption could raise trend global growth. Policymakers need to take coordinated efforts to mitigate the threat of a rise in food insecurity in the context of the conflict in the Middle East. Rising EMDE government debt levels may push up interest rates, diverting resources away from development priorities. Domestically, the implementation of structural reforms could substantially boost private investment.

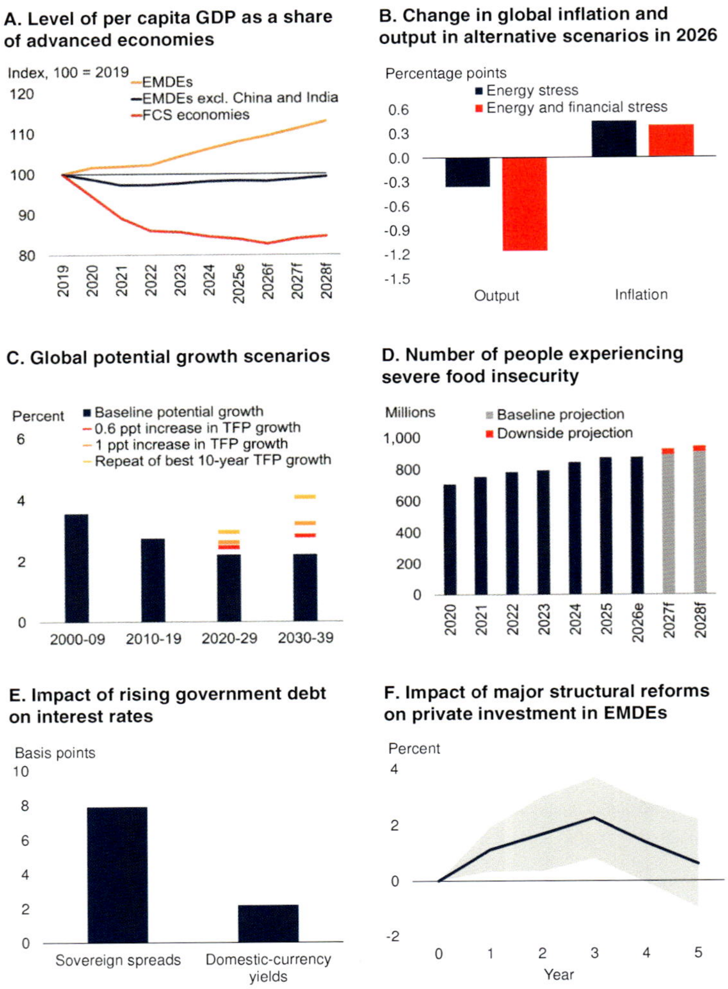

Sources: Adarov (2025); Kose and Ohnsorge (2024); Oxford Economics; UN World Population Prospects (database); World Bank; World Food Security Outlook (database).

Note: e = estimate; f = forecast. AI = artificial intelligence; EMDEs = emerging market and developing economies; excl. = excluding; FCS = fragile and conflict-affected situations; TFP = total factor productivity. The FCS country group is based on current World Bank FCS classification.

A. Lines show per capita GDP by country groups as a share of advanced economies', indexed to 2019 = 100. GDP per capita is aggregated GDP (weighted by real U.S. dollar GDP at average 2010–19 prices and market exchange rates) divided by the respective population.

B. Panel shows the deviation of aggregate inflation and output in scenarios produced using Oxford Economics' Global Economic Model.

C. Averages, weighted by gross domestic product (GDP), of production function-based estimates of potential growth. Sample includes 31 advanced economies and 52 EMDEs. Markers show the predicted impact of each scenario on global potential growth.

D. Population facing severe food insecurity (blue bars). Gray (gray plus red) bars show the World Food Security Outlook's April 2026 baseline (downside) projection for 152 EMDEs excluding China.

E. Panel shows the estimated effect on interest rates of a one-percentage-point rise in the government debt-to-GDP ratio, based on a linear panel data regression.

F. Line shows the cumulative increase in private investment following reforms to domestic and external financing, trade, and product market. Gray shading shows 90 percent confidence bands.

Growth in the euro area is projected to face somewhat greater headwinds due to the region's reliance on natural gas and oil imports, but nevertheless the outlook remains only slightly weaker than January forecasts following better-than-anticipated data in late 2025 and a solid start to 2026. Growth in advanced economies is expected to edge up to 1.7 percent in 2027–28 as energy prices decline, inflation pressures subside, monetary conditions ease, and uncertainty recedes.

Growth in EMDEs is anticipated to decelerate to 3.6 percent in 2026—0.4 percentage point below January projections. The expected near-term deceleration across EMDEs depends on their degree of exposure to the conflict and its associated disruptions, with growth in those economies directly affected by hostilities tumbling from 3.9 percent in 2025 to close to zero in 2026. Over 2027–28, lower energy prices, renewed monetary easing, and a recovery in trade are envisaged to underpin a broad-based pickup in activity, with growth rebounding to 4.2 percent over 2027–28. The outlook for low-income countries (LICs) has also deteriorated notably, with the conflict amplifying pre-existing vulnerabilities, including food insecurity, elevated inflation, constrained fiscal space, and weak policy buffers. In addition, beyond the human toll, the recent Ebola outbreak may weigh on activity in some large LIC economies.

In per capita terms, growth in EMDEs in 2026 is projected to slow to its weakest pace since the pandemic, with the conflict and lingering disruptions impacting EMDEs to varying degrees. In EMDEs excluding China and India, subdued per capita income growth is expected to lead to nearly a decade of lost income convergence with advanced economies by 2028 (figure 1.2.A). Weaker growth prospects, combined with constrained fiscal space and declining official development assistance (ODA), are stripping away critical buffers for the most vulnerable countries, widening existing development gaps and exacerbating food insecurity and poverty, especially in LICs and economies in fragile and conflict-affected situations (FCS).

The outlook is subject to substantial downside risks. In particular, a further surge in energy prices and a sharper acceleration in inflation could weigh on global growth, with the impact potentially amplified by financial market stress. Specifically, if energy supply disruptions prove more severe than currently assumed and are accompanied by substantial financial stress, global growth could fall to just 1.3 percent in 2026, and inflation would rise to 4.4 percent (figure 1.2.B).

Growth could also be weaker if trade tensions and trade policy uncertainty escalate, or if global financial conditions tighten in response to rising inflationary pressures or heightened fiscal concerns in major economies, or if equity market valuations decline, especially in the technology sector. In addition, activity could be disrupted by the rising frequency of weather related natural disasters with worsening economic impacts.

On the upside, increased spending on AI-related investment that broadens across geographies and lifts exports of countries embedded in AI supply chains could boost global growth in the short run. In the longer term, higher productivity related to effective AI adoption could raise trend global growth, including through the adoption of small-AI solutions in EMDEs (box 1.1; figure 1.2.C).

Global policy action is essential to confront continued challenges. The conflict in the Middle East is likely to exacerbate food insecurity, warranting coordinated global action to bolster emergency food aid mechanisms and establish humanitarian corridors to prevent further deterioration (figure 1.2.D). Global cooperation is also needed to bolster multilateral trading arrangements, deepen and diversify trade partnerships, and modernize cross-border investment frameworks, alongside efforts to enhance supply chain finance to ease liquidity constraints and reduce nontariff barriers within regional value chains. Additionally, accelerating the energy transition is key to addressing environmental and energy security challenges. Clean energy investment has risen significantly, but its rate of growth has slowed in recent years.

At the national level, EMDE central banks will need to carefully calibrate their policy stance to guard against inflation becoming entrenched while limiting the drag on growth, alongside heightening vigilance to financial stability risks amid renewed market volatility and shifts in risk appetite. EMDE fiscal policy makers face mounting challenges as elevated debt and borrowing costs, along with new pressures—including those related to spending on security needs and higher energy prices—are increasingly constraining fiscal space. In particular, rising debt burdens increase borrowing costs and further erode fiscal space (chapter 3; figure 1.2.E). This in turn constrains resources for infrastructure, public services, and other investments needed to support private sector growth and job creation. Lower and more volatile revenues, sharp commodity price swings, and limited buffer accumulation during good times create especially difficult fiscal policy challenges for commodity-exporting EMDEs (chapter 4). Weak revenue mobilization, particularly in LICs, where refinancing risks and interest burdens have increased, is adding to debt sustainability concerns.

EMDEs face a major jobs challenge as 1.2 billion young people are expected to reach working age by 2035. The jobs imperative cuts across the broader policy agenda, particularly at a time when the global economy finds itself at another difficult juncture. Headwinds stemming from conflict-related disruptions, higher borrowing costs, heightened uncertainty, and constrained fiscal space, will have a direct bearing on EMDEs' ability to increase investment and productivity in job-rich sectors and create employment. These challenges come as the effects of generative AI technologies on labor markets are still unfolding and likely to be uneven across EMDEs.

In response, policy action must be calibrated not only to stabilize the near-term outlook, but also to lay the structural foundations for sustained growth. EMDEs can tackle these challenges through a steadfast commitment to the fundamentals of long-term growth and job creation: greater food and energy security, better foundational infrastructure, practical diffusion of technology, and openness to trade and diversification, all underpinned by fiscal discipline, strong institutions, enabling regulation, investment in human

BOX 1.1 How much will AI affect global growth?

Artificial intelligence (AI) has emerged as a potential catalyst for economic growth at a time when the global economy is experiencing a structural slowdown. In the near term, AI is likely to boost growth mainly through higher investment, especially in advanced economies. Over the medium term, however, its most important contribution would come from faster productivity growth. Yet estimates of the productivity impact of AI vary widely, from modest gains to transformative effects. Illustrative scenarios suggest that these differences could lead to markedly different growth paths. Under optimistic assumptions about AI's productivity effects, growth in the 2030s could exceed the average recorded in the 2000s, making the decade the strongest period of global growth since the 1970s. Under less optimistic assumptions, however, the gains would be considerably smaller. The growth benefits of AI are also likely to vary across countries, depending on digital infrastructure, human capital, regulatory frameworks, and the speed and breadth of adoption. They may also play out differently in advanced economies and emerging market and developing economies. Ultimately, the extent to which AI reshapes global growth will depend on the scale and persistence of the productivity improvements it generates and on whether countries can build the conditions needed to capture them.

The impact of artificial intelligence (AI) on economic growth has become one of the central economic debates of our time. At stake is not only the future trajectory of growth, but also outcomes for labor and product markets and income distribution within and across countries. The debate also has important financial and macroeconomic implications: expectations of large growth gains have already fueled investment in AI-related sectors in several economies and pushed valuations of AI linked firms to record highs, raising concerns about an equity bubble. At the same time, emerging market and developing economies (EMDEs) that cannot adopt AI widely risk falling further behind.

The debate about the economic effects of AI comes at a time when potential growth—the maximum sustainable rate of expansion without generating inflationary pressures—has been slowing for more than two decades. If the trends of the past two decades persist, global potential growth is expected to fall to a three-decade low in the 2020s. It has already declined from 3.6 percent per year in the 2000s to 2.8 percent in the 2010s and is projected to fall further to about 2.2 percent this decade (figure B1.1.1.A; Kose and Ohnsorge 2024).

The slowdown is even more pronounced in EMDEs where potential growth is expected to fall from 5.9 percent in 2000–09 to 4.1 percent in 2020–29. It has also been broad-based: during the 2010s, potential growth declined in 54 percent of EMDEs, accounting for 76 percent of total EMDE GDP (figure B1.1.1.B). The slowdown reflects weakening contributions from the main drivers of growth, including total factor productivity (TFP), investment, and labor force expansion (Adarov 2025; Dieppe 2021).

This is why much of the debate centers on whether AI can meaningfully raise economy-wide productivity growth over the next decade and beyond. The structural decline in TFP growth has played a major role in weakening potential growth, accounting for more than 40 percent of the slowdown. Global productivity growth fell from about 1.4 percent per year in the 2000s to 1.1 percent in the 2010s and, absent a major technological shift, is expected to average about 0.8 percent this decade (figure B1.1.1.C). If AI generates sustained productivity gains, it could alter the trajectory of global growth and materially improve long-term income and welfare outcomes.

Drawing on the rapidly growing literature on the impact of AI on productivity and illustrative scenarios, this box addresses three questions: (1) How large could AI's impact on productivity growth be? (2) Could AI reverse the slowdown in global potential growth? (3) What will determine whether countries can capture the benefits of AI?

From task-level gains to economy-wide productivity

Estimating the impact of AI on aggregate productivity depends on several key assumptions: the share of tasks exposed to AI, the productivity gains in those tasks, their value-added share in the economy, the speed and breadth of adoption, and whether AI generates a one-time improvement or sustained productivity growth. Differences in these assumptions explain much of the wide divergence in estimates.

Note: This box was prepared by M. Ayhan Kose and Kersten Stamm.

BOX 1.1 How much will AI affect global growth? (*continued*)

FIGURE B1.1.1 AI, productivity, and potential growth

The global economy has been experiencing a prolonged and broad-based slowdown in potential growth, which is expected to continue. This slowdown reflects weakness across all major drivers of growth, including TFP. AI could become a catalyst for faster productivity growth, but its impact remains highly uncertain. Moreover, economies that lack the physical, digital, and institutional foundations needed to benefit from AI risk being left behind. An illustrative scenario shows that AI-driven productivity gains could significantly alter global growth trajectories.

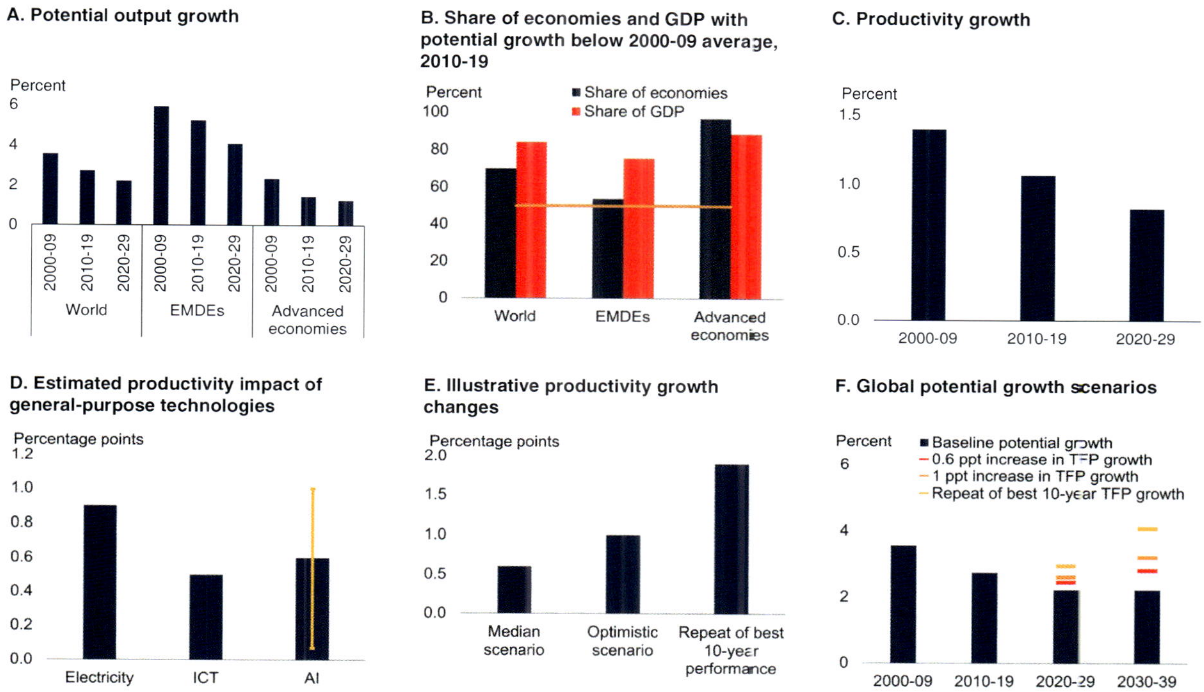

Sources: Aghion and Bunel (2024); Kose and Ohnsorge (2024); UN World Population Prospects (database); World Bank.

Note: AI = artificial intelligence; EMDEs = emerging market and developing economies; ICT = information and communications technologies; TFP = total factor productivity. "Productivity" refers to TFP. Data for 2022 and later years are projections.

A.C.F. Averages, weighted by gross domestic product (GDP), of production function-based estimates of potential growth. Sample includes 31 advanced economies and 52 EMDEs.

B. Number of economies with potential growth in 2010-19 below their 2000–09 average and their share of global or group GDP. Horizontal line indicates 50 percent. Sample includes 31 advanced economies and 52 EMDEs for 2000–19.

C. Bars show GDP-weighted averages of estimated, potential TFP growth, by decade.

D. Bars show the impact of the electricity and ICT revolutions on productivity growth in Europe and the U.S., respectively, taken from Aghion and Bunel (2024). Labor productivity estimates were converted to TFP estimates assuming a capital share of one-third. For the impact of AI, the bar shows the median impact estimated in the literature for the United States, and the whisker shows the range of estimates. The impacts for the electricity and ICT revolutions apply to a period of 12 years each. The estimated impact of AI generally spans a period of 10 years in the literature.

E. Bars show global TFP growth increase in each scenario.

F. Markers show the predicted impact of each scenario on global potential growth.

Most studies focus on the United States and other advanced economies, with limited analysis of EMDEs. This gap is important because the potential growth implications of AI may differ substantially in economies with weaker digital infrastructure and skills, and lower exposure of jobs to AI. These economies may also have more limited scope to adopt existing AI solutions without significant customization, particularly those trained on English-language data sets in advanced economies (World Bank 2025a).

Evidence of AI's productivity effects is most directly observed at the task level, where findings remain mixed. AI appears to raise productivity in many information-

BOX 1.1 How much will AI affect global growth? (*continued*)

processing and cognitive tasks, with some estimates suggesting gains of 50 percent or more. It may also benefit less experienced or lower-performing workers in some occupations, narrowing performance gaps (Appel et al. 2026; Imas 2026). This evidence is not limited to workers in advanced economies. For example, customer-support agents with access to AI assistance in the Philippines increased their productivity by 15 percent, on average (Brynjolfsson, Li, and Raymond 2025).

However, adoption remains concentrated among highly educated white-collar professionals, particularly managers and knowledge workers. In some cases, expert users see limited or even negative productivity effects. These findings suggest that gains vary widely across occupations and depend critically on how AI is integrated into workflows.

Translating task-level improvements into economy-wide productivity gains depends on the extent of adoption across firms and the share of tasks that can benefit from AI. While some firms may realize efficiency gains quickly, broader sector-wide effects depend on organizational change, skill adaptation, complementary investment, and supportive regulation. Without these adjustments, aggregate productivity gains may remain modest even if task-level improvements are substantial.

As a result, estimates of AI's productivity impact span a wide range (figure B1.1.1.D). Most U.S.-based studies assume a one-time boost to productivity that unfolds over roughly a decade. Optimistic estimates suggest that productivity growth could rise by about 1 percentage point per year, assuming continued improvements in AI capabilities, broad adoption across firms, and widespread benefits for workers (Briggs and Kodnani 2023). The most transformative projections also emphasize AI's potential to spur innovation by accelerating scientific discovery and process improvements (Baily, Brynjolfsson, and Korinek 2023). More cautious assessments argue that automating complex tasks will prove difficult and estimate gains of only about 0.07 percentage point per year (Acemoglu 2025).

History can also offer a guide to what to expect from the emergence of a new general-purpose technology, such as electricity and the dynamo in the 1920s, or information and communications technology (ICT) in the 1990s and 2000s. In Europe, electrification eventually may have added around 0.9 percentage point to annual productivity growth once widely adopted, although the transition took decades because factories had to be redesigned and complementary infrastructure installed. By contrast, the ICT revolution diffused more rapidly and contributed about 0.5 percentage point to annual productivity growth (Aghion and Bunel 2024).

Illustrative growth scenarios

Given the wide range of productivity estimates, the impact of AI on economic growth remains highly uncertain (Cunningham 2025). Using the productivity estimates above, illustrative scenarios show how AI could affect potential growth over the next decade through the productivity channel. For transparency and analytical clarity, these scenarios use a standard production function framework in which changes in TFP are directly reflected in output (Kose and Ohnsorge 2024). This simple exercise abstracts from adoption dynamics, cross-country spillovers, investment needs, labor market adjustments, and broader demand and supply responses, which could either amplify or dampen the effects of AI on potential growth.

In the baseline scenario, global productivity growth averages about 0.8 percent per year in the 2020s and 2030s, reflecting the slowdown observed since the 2000s. Relative to this baseline, three illustrative scenarios assume progressively stronger AI effects beginning in 2026 and continuing through 2039 (figure B1.1.1.E). The first scenario assumes a 0.6 percentage point annual increase in productivity growth, corresponding to the midpoint of estimates in the literature. The second assumes a 1 percentage point increase, reflecting more optimistic projections. The third assumes that widespread AI adoption leads to a transformative repeat of the historically strongest 10-year productivity growth rate observed across economies, implying global productivity growth of about 2.7 percent per year. These scenarios apply common productivity assumptions across country groups and therefore should be interpreted as illustrative upper-bound exercises.

These scenarios suggest that AI-driven productivity gains could significantly alter global growth trajectories, although outcomes vary widely (figure B1.1.1.F). Under the transformative scenario, the slowdown in global potential growth could be reversed: growth in the 2030s would exceed the average recorded in the 2000s, making the decade the strongest period of global growth

BOX 1.1 How much will AI affect global growth? (*continued*)

FIGURE B1.1.2 An enabling environment for AI

Countries lacking an AI-enabling ecosystem risk falling further behind in reaping the benefits of AI. AI preparedness, a measure that captures physical and digital infrastructure, human capital, and the regulatory and institutional environment, is much lower in EMDEs than in advanced economies. The impact of AI on employment will also depend on ICT-related human capital. In EMDEs, the share of individuals using the internet or with above-basic ICT skills is lower than in advanced economies.

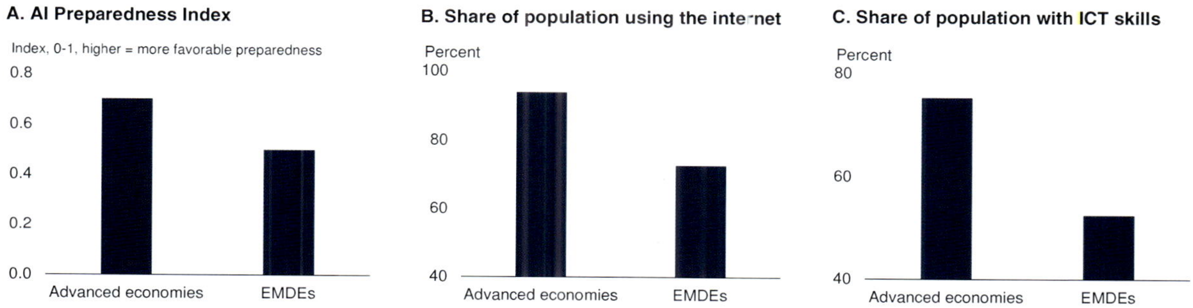

Sources: Cazzaniga et al. (2024); ITU DataHub (database); World Bank.

Note: AI = artificial intelligence; EMDEs = emerging market and developing economies; ICT = information and communications technologies.

A. Panel shows scores on the AI Preparedness Index (AIPI) as of 2023 by Cazzaniga et al. (2024), covering 174 economies. Higher values represent more favorable AI preparedness. Country groups are as defined by the International Monetary Fund and aggregated using averages.

B. Bars show the median share of individuals using the internet in advanced economies and EMDEs. Sample includes 37 advanced economies and 154 EMDEs using the latest available data for each economy.

C. Bars show the median share of individuals with above-basic ICT skills in advanced economies and EMDEs. Sample includes 21 advanced economies and 16 EMDEs using the latest available data for each economy. Above-basic ICT skill level is defined as an individual having done more than one of a list of ICT-related activities in the past three months.

since the 1970s, driven largely by gains in advanced economies. The least optimistic scenario would also raise growth in this decade and the next, but would fall short of returning growth to its 2000s average.

These global growth scenarios mask substantial heterogeneity across country groups and assume similar productivity gains in EMDEs and advanced economies. This assumption is especially optimistic for EMDEs. Their slowdown in potential growth has been more pronounced than in advanced economies, and their ability to adopt and benefit from AI may be more limited without significant policy intervention. As a result, a return to previous growth rates would be an inherently more ambitious outcome for these economies.

Capturing the benefits of AI

Understanding how countries at different levels of development can prepare for and harness AI is a critical priority. Countries lacking digital infrastructure, human capital, or supportive regulatory frameworks risk falling further behind in reaping the benefits of AI. AI preparedness, a measure that captures physical and digital infrastructure, human capital, and the regulatory and institutional environment, is much lower in EMDEs than in advanced economies (figure B1.1.2.A; Cazzaniga et al. 2024). Few studies estimate the impact of AI on productivity growth in EMDEs, but those that do generally find that productivity gains will be much lower in these economies than in advanced economies (Briggs and Kodnani 2023; Cerutti et al. 2025).

Effective use of AI also relies on an enabling ecosystem. Yet, as of mid-2025, EMDEs accounted for less than one-quarter of global data center capacity. The share in low-income countries (LICs) was less than 0.1 percent. Similarly, middle-income countries account for 40 percent of global ChatGPT usage whereas LICs account for less than 1 percent (World Bank 2025a). As of 2022, only one in four individuals in LICs used the internet, and the share of internet users is much lower in EMDEs than in advanced economies (figure B1.1.2.B; World Bank 2024a, 2026a).

Harnessing the benefits of AI in EMDEs will also require AI ecosystems and solutions that differ from those

BOX 1.1 How much will AI affect global growth? (*continued*)

in advanced economies. Beyond digital infrastructure and human capital, localized AI solutions require training data that reflect country circumstances and local languages, models that are accessible on mobile devices and can operate with limited connectivity, and a vibrant start-up sector that can adapt existing models to new use cases (World Bank 2025a). One example is "small AI": solutions that prioritize efficiency and localized autonomy, and do not require the same up-front investment as the leading frontier models (Kim and Qiang 2025). Such solutions could help smallholder farmers identify crop diseases and time fertilizer applications through chat apps, deliver customized tutoring to students, or support health care in remote areas.

Even with more localized solutions, the diffusion of AI remains highly uncertain. Less than one-fifth of firms in the United States are using AI, and estimates of the productivity gains of AI are thus based on early-adopter firms and may not generalize broadly (Kolko 2026). There is a large gap across studies about the share of tasks that will become more productive with AI, a combination of exposure to AI and the successful adoption of AI for these tasks. For the United States, estimates of this share in studies range from 5 percent to 15 percent. For EMDEs, this share is likely lower than in advanced economies (Acemoglu 2025; Briggs and Kodnani 2023; Cazzaniga et al. 2024).

Managing risks and labor-market transitions

Even if AI raises productivity in some tasks, aggregate gains may be constrained if large parts of the economy remain difficult to automate. As AI lowers the relative cost of rapidly improving sectors, a growing share of spending and employment may shift toward non-automated sectors where productivity growth is slower and relative costs rise, a phenomenon known as Baumol's growth disease (Aghion, Jones, and Jones 2017; Filippucci et al. 2025).

Beyond productivity growth, AI could reshape labor markets and income distributions within and across countries. The scope of disruption and opportunity differs sharply by level of development: about 60 percent of jobs in advanced economies are exposed to AI, compared with 40 percent in EMDEs and just 26 percent in LICs (Cazzaniga et al. 2024). Historical evidence suggests that, with the right policies, labor-augmenting technologies can raise labor demand even as automation displaces certain tasks (Autor et al. 2024). Early evidence that combines the share of tasks that could see a boost in productivity from AI with observed AI utilization for these tasks indicates that AI exposure may slow hiring in some entry-level positions, while the potential productivity gains from AI appear to rise along the income distribution (Massenkoff and McCrory 2026).

The employment impact of AI also depends on labor supply constraints. Job vacancies for workers with AI skills are rising faster in EMDEs than in advanced economies yet only a small share of workers in EMDEs have above-basic digital skills (figure B1.1.2.C; World Bank 2025a). The net impact on employment, wages, and inequality remains uncertain and will depend on how quickly workers acquire new skills, how easily they move across tasks and occupations, and how effectively policies support the transition. Beyond direct employment effects, workers may also benefit from AI through better matching in the labor market, improved market access for entrepreneurs, and more effective government services (Nayyar et al. 2024).

For EMDEs, the policy priority is therefore not only to expand digital infrastructure, but also to build complementary capabilities: digital skills, adaptable regulatory frameworks, local data ecosystems, competitive start-up environments, and social protection systems that help workers adjust.

Looking forward

AI could offer a path to reversing the prolonged slowdown in global growth, but only if productivity gains are large, persistent, and widely diffused. At this pivotal moment, policy and investment choices will determine whether it becomes a broad-based driver of growth or a narrowly concentrated efficiency tool. Capitalizing on AI's potential will require careful policy choices and planning—including those around innovation, regulation, data privacy, and digital infrastructure—that evolve with technological advances and shape the employment effects of structural change (World Bank 2024b). If AI becomes a transformative general-purpose technology, historical experience suggests that its broader economic effects are likely to unfold gradually, and projections of AI-driven growth should therefore be interpreted with caution.

BOX 1.1 How much will AI affect global growth? (*continued*)

The brief analysis in this box also shows that several areas require further research to better understand AI's long-term economic impact. A key question is how micro-level productivity gains translate into macroeconomic outcomes through diffusion, complementary investments, general equilibrium effects, and AI-driven innovation in scientific discovery and processes. Its employment effects remain highly uncertain. Finally, more analysis is needed on EMDEs, where AI's growth benefits may be constrained by gaps in digital infrastructure, human capital, regulatory frameworks, and the availability of off-the-shelf AI solutions trained on local data and context (World Bank 2026a, forthcoming).

capital, and the catalytic role of private capital mobilization. In particular, countries need to reverse the decline in private investment, which has been on a downward trend since the 2000s. In this context, a comprehensive set of structural reforms could help policymakers boost private investment substantially (box 1.2; figure 1.2.F).

Against this background, the World Bank Group is assisting EMDEs in confronting the near-term impact of the conflict in the Middle East using a three-part plan. First, it is providing immediate liquidity. Using instruments such as the Crisis Preparedness and Response Toolkit, countries can now draw on prearranged contingent financing, existing project balances, and fast-disbursing instruments—and they can move quickly without new approvals. This can provide clients with between $20 and $25 billion of support to respond quickly to the stresses caused by the conflict. The immediate response includes protecting poor and vulnerable people through social safety nets and targeted transfers, supporting fiscal needs of governments, providing working capital and liquidity support for firms and farms, maintaining access to critical imports and trade finance, and reducing the risk of financial sector distress.

Second, the World Bank is reprioritizing projects already in the pipeline. The World Bank Group will reorient parts of its portfolio and pipeline to support the crisis response as needed, while staying anchored in medium-term development priorities. This could expand available resources by $50 to $60 billion over the next six months. Third, it is scaling up the balance sheet if needed. The World Bank Group has the headroom to increase support through new financing, guarantees, private sector support and, if needed, the use of crisis buffers and front-loading. If the conflict and economic fallout persist, this financing could be increased to $80 to $100 billion over 15 months.

Global context

The conflict in the Middle East is affecting the global economic context through several distinct transmission channels. Global trade flows, particularly for energy, have been disrupted, with the near cessation of shipping through the Strait of Hormuz. Severe disruptions are expected to last through July, easing gradually in subsequent months. Reduced flows of commodities from the Gulf region have pushed energy prices sharply higher, contributing to increased cost pressures and heightened consumer inflation. Against the backdrop of intensifying inflationary pressures, global monetary conditions are expected to tighten.

Global trade

Following the U.S. Supreme Court ruling striking down the use of tariffs on international economic emergency grounds, the U.S. administration introduced a temporary 10 percent tariff surcharge under a different law, set to expire in late July. Together with sector- and country-specific measures, the U.S. effective tariff rate has declined slightly, to about 12 percent from about 14 percent earlier this year. While trade policy uncertainty remains elevated, several initiatives are expected to support trade growth and diversification. They include recent free trade agreements

FIGURE 1.3 Global trade

Although global trade is set to slow in 2026—reflecting a reversal of front-loading activity, lagged effects of tariffs, and disruptions related to the conflict in the Middle East—goods trade is still expected to be supported by continued strong demand for AI-related products. Despite this slowdown, trade growth is projected to be stronger than previously anticipated, reflecting continued resilience.

A. AI-related trade and global computing equipment PMI

B. Global trade growth

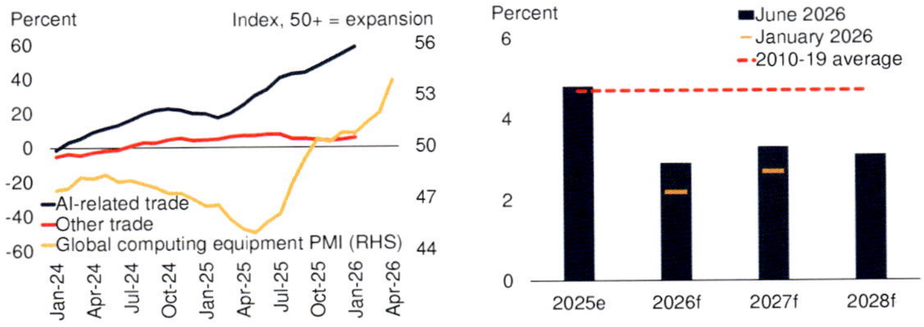

Sources: Haver Analytics; UN Comtrade; World Bank.

Note: e = estimate; f = forecast. AI = artificial intelligence; PMI = purchasing managers' index; RHS = right-hand scale; WTO = World Trade Organization.

A. Five-month averages of (1) year-on-year growth in nominal global goods imports, and (2) PMI for global computing equipment. AI-related trade includes 13 HS 6-digit product codes. Last observation is January 2026 (trade) and April 2026 (PMI). Sample includes 48 countries.

B. Trade is measured as the average of export and import volumes. "June 2026" and "January 2026" refer to the forecasts in the associated editions of the *Global Economic Prospects* report.

between the European Union and Mercosur, India, and Australia respectively, and between the United Kingdom and India. They also include unilateral market access initiatives such as China's zero-tariff treatment for African countries and the U.S. reauthorization of the African Growth and Opportunity Act.

Despite these supporting factors, growth in global goods and services trade is projected to decelerate from 4.8 percent in 2025 to 2.9 percent in 2026, reflecting a reversal of the earlier front-loading activity in anticipation of higher trade barriers; the delayed impact of tariffs; and the effects of the conflict in the Middle East, including disruptions related to the closure of the Strait of Hormuz. Partially offsetting these headwinds, goods trade is envisaged to be supported by continued robust demand for AI-related products (figure 1.3.A). Meanwhile, services trade growth is set to ease, in part reflecting rising travel and transport costs due to higher fuel prices. Compared with previous projections, however, trade growth in 2026 is 0.7 percentage point higher, reflecting continued resilience, strong AI-related activity, lower global tariffs, and recent trade agreements. Global trade growth is then projected to firm to an average of 3.2 percent in 2027–28, broadly in line with global output, as the adverse effects of tariffs and policy uncertainty ease (figure 1.3.B). Tariff rates in effect as of mid-May 2026 are assumed to prevail throughout the forecast period.

The trade outlook remains subject to substantial downside risks. A re-escalation of the conflict in the Middle East and increased geopolitical tensions could further disrupt goods trade logistics, including maritime and air transport. Uncertainty about the safety of key shipping routes, together with higher fuel prices, could raise shipping costs and weigh on goods trade (Brancaccio, Kalouptsidi, and Papageorgiou 2023; von Below and Vézina 2016). In addition, prolonged geopolitical stress could lead to sharp declines in services trade, particularly tourism (Mulabdic and Yotov 2025). A renewed escalation of trade tensions, potentially extending to third countries and involving secondary sanctions—measures targeting firms or countries trading with sanctioned entities—as well as uncertainty around previously concluded trade agreements, could further dampen trade growth prospects.

Commodity markets

The near halt of shipping through the Strait of Hormuz has triggered enormous disruptions in commodity markets—particularly crude oil, LNG, and fertilizers—since early March (figure 1.4.A). Amid large price swings reflecting geopolitical shifts, spot Brent crude, European natural gas, and urea prices in April averaged 80, 31, and 106 percent above their January levels, respectively. The outlook remains highly sensitive to the duration and intensity of these disruptions. The baseline assumes the most acute phase of disruptions ends in July, with shipping volumes through the Strait of Hormuz returning near pre-conflict levels by the end of 2026.

More prolonged impediments to shipping would imply materially higher prices for key commodities than assumed in the baseline, with broader spillovers to inflation and economic activity. In particular, market stress and disorderly price surges could emerge if crude oil and oil products inventories are drawn down to critical levels. Any reversal of recent increases in oil exports from producers outside the Gulf region could accelerate this process. Moreover, further damage to oil and gas infrastructure in the Middle East could keep energy prices higher in the medium term, even when acute disruptions abate.

Against this backdrop, average commodity prices are projected to rise by about 22 percent in 2026, a sharp reversal from the 7 percent decline anticipated in January, driven mainly by the surge in energy prices (figure 1.4.B). Brent crude oil is forecast to average $94/bbl in 2026, $34 higher than projected in January, reflecting unprecedentedly large oil supply disruptions that are expected to ease gradually in the second half of this year. Average natural gas prices are also projected to rise in 2026, by a sharp 30 percent in Europe, but only 2 percent in the United States. These forecasts reflect markedly tighter global LNG availability that raises wholesale natural gas prices in East Asia, Europe, and other gas-importing regions.

Price pressures extend beyond energy. Industrial metal prices are expected to increase by about 18 percent in 2026 on tighter supply conditions and firm demand, including from the energy transition, electrification, and data center infrastructure. The average price of precious metals could be about 42 percent higher than last year, supported by strong safe-haven demand. Fertilizer and food markets are also affected. Pre-conflict, economies in the Gulf region supplied about 20 percent of urea and diammonium phosphate (DAP) fertilizer exports, as well as extensive inputs for fertilizer production. Average fertilizer prices are therefore expected to climb by 38 percent this year. Even so, food commodity prices are expected to firm by only 3 percent in the baseline, owing to ample recent grain production globally.

The conflict nonetheless poses significant food security risks. It directly threatens food security in the Middle East by disrupting food imports in the Gulf region, raising domestic food inflation as supplies are rerouted through longer and more costly overland channels. More broadly, a longer-than-anticipated trough in Middle East exports would further lift agricultural input costs and raise

FIGURE 1.4 Commodity markets

The Middle East conflict and its effects on shipping triggered major disruptions in commodity markets, particularly for oil, liquefied natural gas, and fertilizer. Commodity prices are expected to rise by about 22 percent on average in 2026, a sharp reversal from the decline previously anticipated.

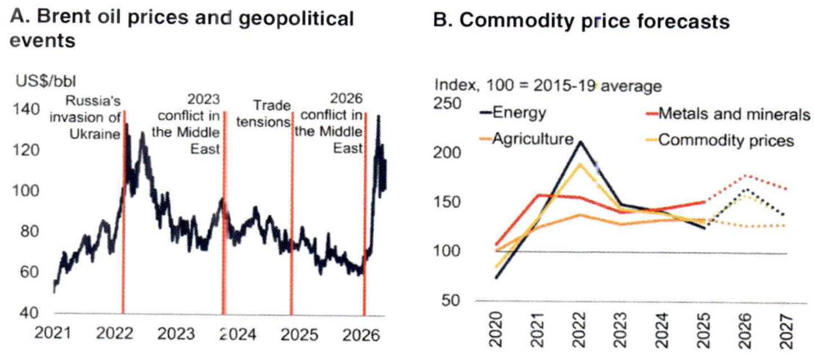

Sources: U.S. Energy Information Administration; World Bank.

A. bbl = barrel. Daily data. Last observation is May 26, 2026. Vertical lines indicate geopolitical events.

B. Commodity prices line refers to the World Bank commodity price index, excluding precious metals. Dashed lines indicate forecasts for 2026–27 as of June 2, 2026.

the risk of reduced fertilizer use, weaker crop yields, and higher food prices. Under adverse scenarios, up to an additional 70 million people could face acute hunger and food insecurity over the forecast period (World Food Security Outlook 2026). Beyond developments in the Middle East, the possible emergence of El Niño weather conditions could push food prices above current expectations.

Global inflation

Before the onset of the conflict in the Middle East, global headline and core inflation had remained broadly stable, albeit above pre-pandemic levels and with notable cross-country differences. However, with the interruption of the supply of crucial commodities, particularly oil and natural gas, as well as broader disruptions to global supply chains, global headline inflation picked up, driven by higher input costs and consumer energy prices despite the introduction of fuel subsidies and price caps in some economies (figure 1.5.A). In the United States, this pickup occurred against a backdrop of the passthrough of tariff costs to consumer prices (Cavallo, Llamas, and Vazquez 2025).

Although the impact of higher energy prices on core inflation has been subdued so far, underlying

FIGURE 1.5 Global inflation and financial developments

The interruption of supplies of crucial energy commodities has led to a pickup in headline inflation worldwide. Consensus forecasts indicate that inflation is expected to edge up in 2026 across advanced economies and EMDEs as a result of the conflict. Rising energy prices have also driven up bond yields and breakeven inflation rates in advanced economies, particularly in Europe. In EMDEs, local-currency bond yields increased and bond spreads on foreign-currency-denominated debt widened as a result of the conflict and remain higher for commodity importers.

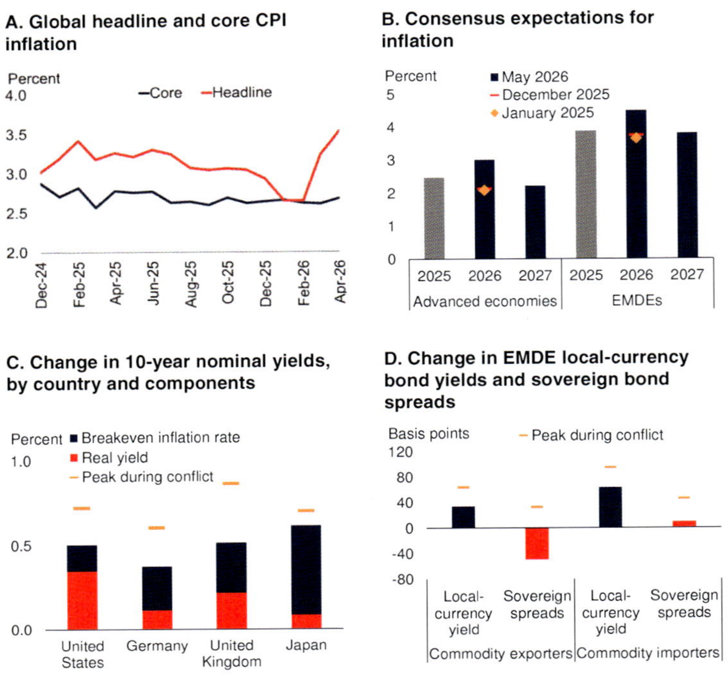

Sources: Bloomberg; Consensus Economics; Haver Analytics; J.P.Morgan; World Bank.

Note: CPI = consumer price index; EMDEs = emerging market and developing economies.

A. Panel shows median year-on-year CPI inflation reading from a sample of up to 136 countries. Last observation is April 2026.

B. Median headline CPI inflation expectations for 35 advanced economies and up to 53 EMDEs from Consensus Economics surveys in the respective months of 2025 and 2026.

C. 10-year nominal yields by country, decomposed into real yields and breakeven inflation rates, changes and peak changes since February 27, 2026. Last observation is May 28, 2026.

D. Changes in average local-currency bond yields and foreign-currency sovereign bond spreads across 20 and 63 EMDEs, respectively, before (January 2–February 26) and after (February 27–June 2) the start of the conflict this year.

price pressures persist, with about one-fourth of economies seeing accelerating core prices amid some impact on producer costs and transportation prices. This increase is a notable challenge for a relatively high share of economies, particularly EMDEs, where core inflation is already elevated relative to headline targets.

Surveys of professional forecasters indicate that CPI inflation is projected to edge up in 2026 across advanced economies and EMDEs on the back of higher energy prices (figure 1.5.B). In contrast, the increase for 2027 has been modest, suggesting that headline inflation is expected to moderate due to abating energy price pressures as the conflict winds down and central banks keep monetary policy more restrictive than previously envisaged. The concentration of higher inflation projections in the near term suggests that survey respondents anticipate conflict-driven inflationary pressures to be temporary, indicating that overall expectations remain well anchored.

In all, global headline inflation is projected to pick up to 4 percent this year, with advanced economies and EMDEs seeing headline inflation rise due to increases in energy costs. Global inflation is expected to moderate to 3.1 percent next year as the average crude price declines from $94/bbl in 2026 to $76/bbl in 2027, consistent with the baseline assumption that the current conflict in the Middle East subsides, energy supplies through the Strait of Hormuz resume after July, and energy production curtailed earlier in the conflict gradually recovers. Core inflation is assumed to be relatively stable amid anchored medium-term inflation expectations. Nevertheless, the inflation outlook remains highly uncertain because of the intensity and duration of the commodity market disruption.

Global financial developments

After easing substantially in the second half of last year, global financial conditions tightened following the onset of the conflict in the Middle East. Risk appetite recovered as the ceasefire began, and financial market volatility, which had been elevated across asset classes, receded. However, given heightened uncertainty about how the conflict will proceed, conditions remain tighter than before the conflict for some economies as investors continue to evaluate the impact on inflation and growth.

Concerns about rising inflation due to higher commodity prices and energy supply disruptions have pushed up bond yields as well as breakeven rates of inflation in major advanced economies, especially in Europe (figure 1.5.C). Expectations for central bank policy easing in major economies have dissipated, with the possibility of rate hikes in the euro area and the United Kingdom in the near term, while the U.S. Federal Reserve is now envisaged to raise its policy rate by late 2026 or early 2027. Correspondingly, the U.S. dollar index is higher than its pre-conflict level.

The broader risk-off sentiment in financial markets affected equity markets to varying degrees. In the United States, conflict-related risk aversion added to investor worries about the size of AI investments relative to their payoffs and the potential for AI to replace certain business models. However, equity prices bounced back to reach all-time highs after the ceasefire, driven by strong earnings and renewed optimism about AI, despite uncertainty about the resolution of the conflict. Equity markets elsewhere experienced larger declines reflecting the greater impact of the conflict on growth and inflation, especially for energy importers, and the recovery has been more sluggish in some cases. High-yield corporate bond spreads widened at the start of the conflict, in both the United States and the euro area, but have recovered since as risk sentiment improved.

In EMDEs, financial conditions initially tightened, with only a partial recovery for some commodity importers after the ceasefire. Investors have differentiated across EMDEs based on their energy exposure and ability to adjust to the shock, which is reflected across asset classes. While bond spreads on foreign-currency-denominated debt widened and local-currency bond yields increased during the conflict, the changes were more pronounced for commodity importers, especially where the rise in oil prices could strain fiscal positions and exacerbate inflation (figure 1.5.D). Deteriorating risk sentiment also led to equity price declines, portfolio outflows from EMDEs, and currency depreciation, leading some authorities to intervene in foreign exchange markets to alleviate pressures. Sovereign debt issuance by EMDEs slowed amid higher market volatility. However, equity markets, portfolio flows, and issuance rebounced strongly as risk appetite recovered, despite uncertainty regarding the duration of the conflict and its impact. Energy exporters outside the Middle East and EMDEs with improved policy frameworks and substantial buffers have benefited the most. However, higher borrowing costs are set to put pressure on rising sovereign debt burdens, and issuance is expected to moderate if geopolitical uncertainty persists.

Major economies: Recent developments and outlook

Advanced economies

Economic activity in advanced economies turned out to be better than expected last year, with a less pronounced drag from trade policy shifts. This year, growth is projected to slow to 1.5 percent, owing to the impact of higher energy prices and inflation, constrained energy supplies, and tighter monetary conditions following the outbreak of the conflict in the Middle East. Over 2027–28, energy supplies are anticipated to recover, inflation and uncertainty are expected to recede, and financial conditions are envisaged to ease, supporting a pickup in growth to an average of 1.7 percent.

In the **United States**, private domestic demand continued to expand at a steady pace in early 2026, supported by generally robust AI-related investment and resilient consumer spending, with additional tax breaks that came into effect earlier this year boosting household incomes. Despite resilient activity, U.S. consumer sentiment remained downbeat amid rising inflation expectations. Since the outbreak of the conflict, the spike in energy prices has sent U.S. consumer prices on a steep upward path, leading market participants to begin pricing modest monetary tightening over the remainder of the year.

Going forward, the U.S. near-term outlook will hinge, on the one hand, on developments in the Middle East conflict, along with the attendant geopolitical and policy uncertainty, and, on the other, on continued AI-related investment. Tighter monetary conditions in response to rising consumer inflation are expected to dampen private consumption, with the drag likely to be concentrated among higher-income households. The latter have accounted for a sizable share of consumption growth and are particularly sensitive to fluctuations in financial markets (figure 1.6.A).

On the business side, investment spending is set to continue along a two-track path. Investment in non-technology sectors is expected to remain lackluster, dampened by uncertainty and high energy costs. In contrast, spending on AI-related

FIGURE 1.6 Major economies: Recent developments and outlook

In the United States, tighter monetary conditions and heightened policy and geopolitical uncertainty are expected to weigh on spending, particularly by higher-income households, which have been driving U.S. consumption. Nevertheless, spending on AI-related technology is envisaged to remain robust, as large technology companies continue to invest in computing equipment to power AI models. In the euro area, growth is projected to slow, with the spike in energy prices causing consumer confidence to record its largest decline since Russia's invasion of Ukraine. In China, consumer confidence remains subdued amid the ongoing adjustment in the property sector and a soft labor market.

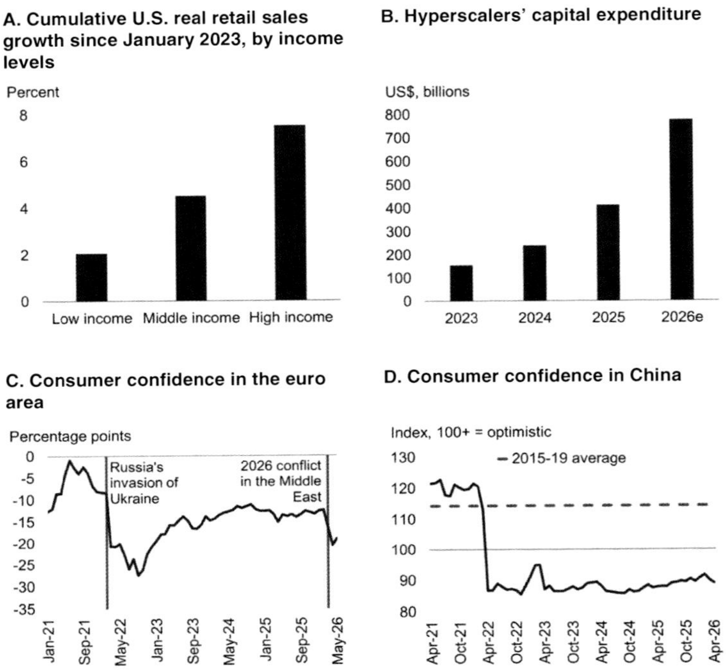

Sources: Bloomberg; Eurostat; Federal Reserve Bank of New York; Haver Analytics; World Bank.
Note: e = estimate. AI = artificial intelligence.
A. "Low income" refers to income below $40K, "middle income" refers to income from $40K to $125K, and "high income" refers to income above $125K. Cumulative growth between January 2023 and April 2026. Real retail spending excludes autos.
B. Bars show annual total hyperscalers' capital expenditure for five companies (Amazon, Google, Meta, Microsoft, and Oracle). 2026e data are based on company announcements through May.
C. Blue line shows the euro area consumer confidence indicator (percent balance of respondents reporting an increase less those reporting a decrease). Vertical lines indicate geopolitical events. Last observation is May 2026.
D. Blue line shows the monthly consumer confidence index in China, with values over 100 representing optimistic confidence. Red dashed line shows the average between 2015–19. Last observation is April 2026.

technology is anticipated to remain robust, as large technology companies continue to invest in computing equipment to power AI tools (figure 1.6.B). Technology investment is expected to remain high, even as its growth is envisaged to gradually slow in 2027–28, with its contribution to overall output growth continuing to be mitigated by its relatively high import content.

In all, U.S. growth is projected to average 2.2 percent in 2026, as expected in January, with the impact of the conflict offsetting the stronger underlying trend growth in consumption and robust AI-related investment spending. Nevertheless, tighter monetary conditions, higher consumer energy prices, and still-elevated uncertainty are anticipated to progressively weigh on growth over the course of the year. In 2027–28, growth is expected to ease to 2.1 percent, in line with estimates of potential growth over the next few years, as investment in data center capacity begins to stabilize at elevated levels, while consumption spending eases in line with weaker nominal income growth, even as inflation recedes and monetary conditions ease.

In the **euro area**, the sharp increase in energy prices is expected to have a notable impact on growth. Following better-than-expected activity in several large economies in late 2025, accompanied by buoyant consumer and business sentiment and a strong labor market in early 2026, activity deteriorated with the outbreak of hostilities in the Middle East in March. The headline services sector PMI fell sharply, while the European Commission's consumer confidence indicator recorded its largest one-month decline in March since the Russian Federation's invasion of Ukraine in February 2022 and has since remained subdued (figure 1.6.C). While the headline manufacturing PMI continued to remain firmly in expansionary territory through April and May, subindexes related to input price pressures and delivery times deteriorated.

In all, growth in the euro area is projected to slow to 0.8 percent in 2026, slightly weaker than January forecasts, as the negative effects of higher energy prices more than offset the positive effects of firmer activity at the turn of the year and lower U.S. tariffs on euro area exports. Elevated energy prices are expected to restrain consumption and investment, with the impact on the euro area amplified compared to some other advanced economies, reflecting its dependence on energy imports. The baseline outlook is also predicated on tighter euro area monetary conditions in 2026 amid rising inflation.

Growth in the euro area is expected to recover to 1.3 percent over 2027–28, slightly outpacing estimates of potential growth, led by a firming of domestic demand against a backdrop of declining energy prices. Rising fiscal support and investment, particularly in Germany, are also anticipated to further underpin activity, alongside a resumption of monetary easing, recovering real incomes, and improving confidence. Net exports are also envisaged to contribute more positively to growth over the next two years, as global activity strengthens and trade firms with progress on several trade agreements since late 2025, including with India.

In Japan, rising energy prices are expected to weigh on near-term growth, more than offsetting additional fiscal support. Growth is projected to decelerate to 0.7 percent in 2026 from 1.1 percent in 2025, mainly reflecting slowing consumption and exports. Over 2027–28, growth is anticipated to pick up to an average of 0.8 percent as domestic demand improves amid easing inflation and rising wages.

China

China's growth continued at a solid pace in early 2026, with policy stimulus supporting consumption and infrastructure investment. Export growth remained robust, boosted by technology-related demand. Higher producer price inflation was largely driven by the increase in commodity prices due to the conflict. Meanwhile, the adjustment in the property sector continued, with modest improvements in large cities.

Growth is projected to decelerate to 4.2 percent in 2026, with consumption growth weighed down by the ongoing property sector adjustment, a soft labor market, and subdued consumer confidence (figure 1.6.D). In the near term, the impact of the conflict in the Middle East will be cushioned by several factors, including substantial oil reserves, a high share of renewable energy, and very low inflation. Caps on fuel prices are set to limit the pass-through of higher energy prices to households. Export growth is expected to moderate relative to 2025, owing to the fading of front-loading and weaker external demand this year, although it will be partly supported by lower U.S. tariffs and the continued strength in technology-related exports. The fiscal impulse from the announced measures is expected to be positive, albeit somewhat smaller compared to last year. Fiscal stimulus remains heavily focused on investment, with an incremental increase in support for household consumption.

Growth is expected to edge up to 4.3 percent on average in 2027–28, as energy prices ease while diminishing returns to capital, high debt, and demographic pressures continue to lower China's potential growth.[1] As exports ease, medium-term policy priorities are expected to provide an incremental boost to consumption and lead to productivity gains from digital and industrial innovation.

Emerging market and developing economies

Recent developments

Before the onset of the conflict in the Middle East, activity in EMDEs remained solid in early 2026. Retail sales and services activity had continued to expand, while manufacturing and services activity had improved. The disruption in energy supplies and sharp increase in energy prices caused by the conflict have dampened confidence and weakened broader economic activity. Indeed, since the start of the conflict, both the headline manufacturing and services PMIs have deteriorated across EMDEs, albeit to varying degrees.

In EMDEs directly affected by the conflict, the composite PMI fell steeply in March, reaching the lowest point since the pandemic, suggesting that activity has decelerated sharply, before partially rebounding in April (figure 1.7.A). In the Gulf region, conflict-related disruptions to oil and natural gas production and exports led to a pronounced contraction in the energy sector. Outside of the energy sector, activity stalled as the security situation deteriorated, with both services and non-energy industrial activity coming to a halt amid a surge in outward flows of workers and declining visitor arrivals. Sharply lower confidence

[1] Debt refers to aggregate non-financial sector debt as measured by total social financing (excluding equity).

FIGURE 1.7 Recent developments in emerging market and developing economies

Following the onset of the conflict in the Middle East, EMDEs directly affected by hostilities have experienced a sharp deceleration in activity, with the slowdown being less severe elsewhere. Despite the energy shock, EMDEs integrated into AI and digital equipment supply chains have continued to see steady export growth, against a backdrop of strong AI-related investment in advanced economies, particularly the United States.

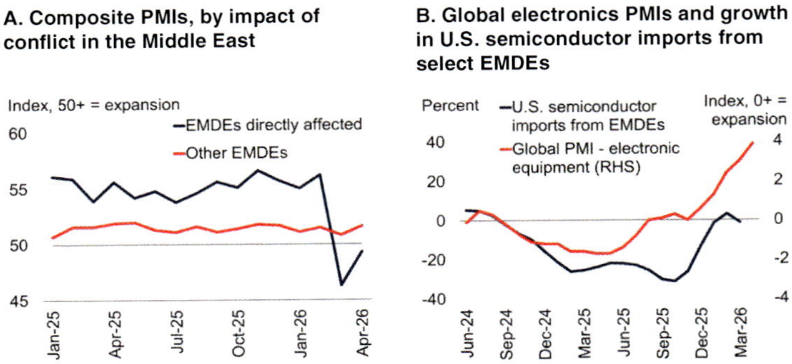

Sources: Haver Analytics; United States International Trade Commission (USITC); World Bank.
Note: EMDEs = emerging market and developing economies; PMI = purchasing managers' index; RHS = right-hand scale.
A. Red (blue) line shows a simple average of 5 (13) EMDEs directly (not directly) affected by the conflict in the Middle East. Readings above (below) 50 indicate expansion (contraction). Last observation is April 2026.
B. Blue line shows a three-month moving average of year-on-year growth in U.S. semiconductor imports from China, Indonesia, Malaysia, the Philippines, Thailand, and Viet Nam. Red line shows the three-month moving average of global electronic equipment PMI. Readings above (below) zero indicate expansion (contraction). Monthly readings are recentered at 0, the expansionary threshold. Last observation is March 2026 for U.S. semiconductor imports and April 2026 for PMI.

indicators suggest that both consumption and investment are set to slow significantly in these economies this year.

In EMDEs not directly affected by the conflict, activity also appears to have slowed but to a much lesser degree. Indicators of consumption, including retail sales growth, consumer confidence, and services sector PMIs, have deteriorated somewhat since February. However, these indicators continue to remain broadly supportive despite the surge in energy prices and moves to ration energy supplies in some economies. Business confidence has also eased in parallel to softening but still-expansionary headline manufacturing PMIs. Although, a deterioration in PMI subindices tied to input prices and employment since late 2025 suggests that activity may slow.

For EMDEs excluding China, trade growth has softened, following a pullback in U.S. imports in the second half of 2025. Nevertheless, some EMDEs—particularly those in the East Asia and Pacific (EAP) region that are integrated into AI-related supply chains—have continued to record steady export growth, with strong demand linked to sustained investment in digital and AI-related equipment, especially in the United States, supporting activity (figure 1.7.B).

EMDE outlook

Overall, growth in EMDEs is projected to slow to 3.6 percent this year, reflecting the drag from the conflict and higher energy prices, tighter monetary conditions, heightened geopolitical strains, weaker global trade growth, and ongoing trade policy uncertainty in some regions (World Bank 2026b, 2026c). Over 2027–28, growth across EMDEs is expected to rebound to an average of 4.2 percent. At the aggregate level, the EMDE outlook continues to reflect developments in China, given its large weight in the group. As China's growth gradually moderates, this mechanically lowers medium-term growth for EMDEs as a whole. Nevertheless, the recovery over 2027–28 is expected to be broad-based, with growth accelerating in about 70 percent of EMDEs. Excluding China, growth in EMDEs is forecast to decelerate from 3.9 percent in 2025 to 3.2 percent in 2026, before strengthening to an average of 4.1 percent over 2027–28.

Growth prospects in 2026 for EMDEs as a whole have been revised down by 0.4 percentage point relative to January, mainly reflecting the adverse effects of the conflict. These effects are expected to be highly uneven across EMDE regions (Chapter 2). Economic activity is estimated to be severely disrupted in some economies in the Middle East, following the destruction and disruptions suffered because of the conflict. That said, some factors are providing partial positive offsets. These include broadly resilient activity in early 2026; lower effective tariffs; positive spillovers from large AI-related investments in advanced economies, particularly to the EAP region; and China's relative insulation from energy supply disruptions.

With EMDE governments' capacity to respond to higher energy prices constrained by limited fiscal space, owing to elevated debt levels and tighter monetary conditions, adjustment to the energy shock has relied partly on non-fiscal measures, including promoting remote work, public transport, and fuel conservation. As a result, fiscal policy is expected to modestly weigh on growth, or at best be neutral, in most EMDEs. Over most of 2026, tighter monetary conditions amid higher inflation relative to late 2025 are anticipated to restrain activity. Nonetheless, over 2027–28, monetary conditions are envisaged to ease against a backdrop of lower energy prices and fading uncertainty, supporting activity.

Commodity-exporting economies are forecast to see the most pronounced slowdown among EMDEs, with growth slowing to 2.4 percent in 2026, 0.9 percentage point weaker than anticipated in January, before rebounding to 3.4 percent on average over 2027–28 (figure 1.8.A). This dynamic is largely driven by energy-exporting EMDEs in the Gulf region that are directly affected by the conflict.[2]

Activity in EMDEs directly affected by the conflict is forecast to decelerate sharply, with growth tumbling from 3.9 percent in 2025 to 0.2 percent in 2026, the slowest pace since the pandemic, reflecting severe disruptions and damage to infrastructure, which will weigh on energy production and export volumes, and other non-energy-sector activity more broadly. Average growth in these economies is expected to recover to 5.0 percent over 2027–28, partly reflecting reconstruction spending. Nevertheless, these EMDEs are likely to face lasting adverse effects due to the conflict, with output levels projected to be about 4 percent lower by the end of 2028 than envisaged in January (figure 1.8.B). In contrast, forecasts for growth in energy-exporting EMDEs not directly affected by the conflict are broadly unchanged from January, as the temporary boost from higher energy prices this year is anticipated to provide only modest overall support to activity, somewhat offset by tighter monetary conditions and higher uncertainty.

The deceleration in growth in commodity-importing EMDEs excluding China is expected to be less severe, with growth softening to 4.1 percent in 2026, about 0.2 percentage point weaker than forecast in January, before it picks up to an average of 4.8 percent over 2027–28. The slowdown in 2026 reflects the dampening effects of higher energy prices, elevated uncertainty, and tighter monetary conditions on investment, and to a lesser extent private consumption, despite a modest increase in government consumption compared to January in some economies (figure 1.8.C). Over 2027–28, moderating energy prices, rising real incomes, improving confidence, and the resumption of monetary easing are expected to support a pickup in both consumption and investment. Strengthening external demand, including for AI-related equipment, and a recovery in global trade beginning later in 2026 are anticipated to boost net exports.

The adverse effects of higher energy prices are expected to be more pronounced in the roughly one-quarter of EMDEs with weak sovereign creditworthiness—many of them energy importers (figure 1.8.D). Elevated energy and commodity prices have put pressure on exchange rates, particularly in commodity importers, and are likely to widen current account and fiscal deficits (Lebrand, Vasishtha, and Yilmazkuday 2024). In weakly rated EMDEs, these effects are anticipated to weigh more heavily on financial conditions and borrowing costs, leading to larger negative impacts on activity and confidence (IMF 2024). Indeed, among these economies, the largest downward revisions to growth forecasts are concentrated in energy importers. Such dynamics may exacerbate pre-existing imbalances and raise sovereign spreads, increasing the risk of balance-of-payments or fiscal crises, further weighing on fiscal sustainability.

LICs outlook

In low-income countries (LICs), the conflict in the Middle East is dampening growth, heightening fiscal pressures, and threatening food security (box 2.1). Higher global energy, fertilizer, and food prices; elevated uncertainty; and weaker external demand are disproportionately affecting LICs, most of which are net importers of energy and food. These shocks compound ongoing headwinds, including persistent fragility and insecurity,

[2] EMDEs directly affected by the conflict include Bahrain, Iraq, Kuwait, Qatar, Saudi Arabia, and the United Arab Emirates. Associated growth forecasts for this group of economies exclude the Islamic Republic of Iran and Lebanon because of a high degree of uncertainty.

BOX 1.2 Unlocking private investment

Against a backdrop of weak output growth, mounting fiscal pressures, declining aid flows, and persistent structural challenges, private investment has a pivotal role to play in unlocking durable growth and job creation in emerging market and developing economies. Yet despite its importance, private investment growth has trended downward since the 2000s. Firms cite a range of constraints, notably persistent infrastructure gaps, high risk and uncertainty, and limited access to finance. Recent overlapping crises and elevated uncertainty make it even more important to design policies that accelerate private investment growth. Case studies show that sustained increases in private investment are possible, but policies need to reflect country circumstances. Foundational infrastructure and a business-friendly environment are essential building blocks. Access to finance, whether domestic or external, is crucial for firms to grow and create jobs. Comprehensive reform packages that combine infrastructure, finance, regulatory, and institutional reforms tend to deliver the strongest impacts.

Investment is pivotal to development progress, underpinning durable growth and job creation prospects. Yet investment growth, both public and private, in emerging and developing economies (EMDEs) has been on a prolonged declining path. This slowdown has contributed to weakening output growth and slowing development progress (Adarov 2025; Kose and Ohnsorge 2024; Mahler et al. 2026). Overlapping shocks have contributed to historically high levels of uncertainty and strained fiscal positions, which may both weigh further on investment at a time when EMDEs face a multitude of development challenges, including an unprecedented demographic wave. Looking ahead, a record 1.2 billion young people in EMDEs are set to reach working age over the next decade. Boosting investment will be crucial to efforts to create sufficient job opportunities, particularly in rapidly growing urban areas where most employment is generated (Baker et al. 2023). Most of this investment will need to come from the private sector. Mobilizing private capital to reinvigorate investment growth should therefore be a priority for policy makers.

Against that backdrop, this box examines three main questions: (1) How has private investment growth in EMDEs evolved over recent history? (2) What are the key constraints to private investment growth? and (3) What policies can promote private investment growth?

Trends and developments in private investment

Globally, both public and private investment growth have been on a broad-based slowing trend since the 2000s (Adarov and Stamm 2025). In EMDEs, private investment growth over the first half of the 2020s has averaged 2.7 percent a year: less than half the 7 percent average of the 2010s, and about one-quarter of the 10.8 percent average seen over the 2000s (figure B1.2.1.A). Beyond these aggregate headlines, the slowdown in private investment growth over time has been broad-based across EMDEs. The slowdown appears particularly sharp because of dynamics in China, which recorded very strong private investment growth in the 2000s that subsequently decelerated significantly through the 2010s and into the 2020s.

The overlapping crises of recent years—including the pandemic, conflicts, and global inflationary pressures—are casting a further shadow over the outlook for private investment. Investment growth in EMDEs was already weak heading into the pandemic. The subsequent recovery was weaker than the recovery which followed the 2009 global recession after the financial crisis (figure B1.2.1.B). Even excluding 2020 (the year when the COVID-19 shock hit the global economy, prompting a contraction in private investment), or the subsequent year, annual private investment growth in the early 2020s has been weaker than the 2010–19 average. The weak recovery in private investment reflects several factors. Uncertainty, which was already persistently high, has risen further in the first half of 2026, including in response to conflict in the Middle East. Policy makers face pressure to respond to these crises. A cycle of global monetary tightening in response to higher inflation has increased borrowing costs for EMDEs. Debt levels and debt servicing costs have both risen as a share of GDP in EMDEs. Fiscal pressures can be exacerbated by high debt burdens. Low-income countries (LICs) in particular are vulnerable: not one is at low risk of debt distress (Mawejje 2025).

Beyond the short term, the implications of lower private investment growth are stark. Slow-moving structural forces can have profound implications for living

Note: This box was prepared by Tommy Chrimes, Kersten Stamm, and Mathilde Lebrand.

BOX 1.2 Unlocking private investment (*continued*)

FIGURE B1.2.1 Investment trends in EMDEs

Private investment growth has been on a declining trend since the 2000s. The recovery in private investment following the COVID-19 pandemic was weaker than that following the global financial crisis. Since 2000, EMDEs that have achieved higher rates of private investment growth have also tended to deliver higher employment growth.

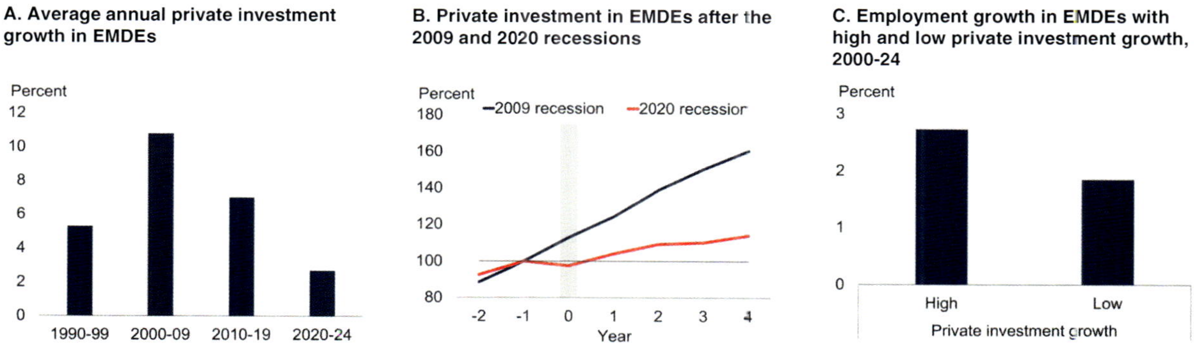

Sources: Haver Analytics; ILOSTAT (database); World Development Indicators (database); World Bank.
Note: EMDEs = emerging market and developing economies. Sample includes up to 36 EMDEs in any year.
A. Bars show average annual investment growth for EMDEs.
B. Investment is indexed to 100 in the year before the global recession; 0 indicates the year of the global recession (2009 or 2020).
C. Bars show group medians of annual employment growth. "Low" and "high" indicate annual private investment growth in the bottom and top third of the distribution of private investment growth, respectively. Sample of 44 EMDEs, covering the period from 2000 to 2024.

standards. How these shifts play out and the ability of countries to adapt to them depend in part on investment. Demographics is one such trend. For EMDEs as a group, the projected number of young people reaching working age over the next decade will be unprecedented (Chrimes, Kose, and Stamm 2026). On a per capita basis, investment in EMDEs excluding China remains low relative to advanced economies, with no upward trend in the ratio so far this century. Reinvigorating private investment growth will be important everywhere, and particularly in capital-poor EMDEs with rapidly growing populations.

Higher private investment growth over time is also associated with higher employment growth. Over the period between 2000 and 2024, the median economy which ranked in the top third of EMDEs for private investment growth typically recorded annual employment growth of 2.7 percent—almost 50 percent higher than the equivalent EMDE in the bottom third for private investment growth, where employment growth averaged less than 1.9 percent (figure B1.2.1.C). Moreover, in a fast-changing economic environment amid technological change, equipping workers for better-paid jobs will likely require higher investment growth, and much of this will need to come from the private sector.

Constraints to private investment

Private investment hinges on risk-adjusted returns and the capacity to finance and execute viable projects, and is shaped both by investment-specific constraints (such as infrastructure and financing frictions) and broader macroeconomic conditions, including sovereign risk and global financing conditions (Chrimes, Lebrand, and Mawejje 2025).

An important concern is elevated risk and uncertainty, which are high in EMDEs, and in LICs in particular. Country risk is substantially higher in LICs, which have a much larger concentration of high- and very high-risk economies, in contrast to advanced economies that are predominantly low risk (figure B1.2.2.A). At the same time, global geopolitical risk has risen sharply in recent years, reaching levels comparable to or above earlier peaks over the past four decades (figure B1.2.2.B). High levels of uncertainty complicate investment decisions, increasing the return that investors require before committing capital, and can have a chilling effect on private investment, especially long-term investment

BOX 1.2 Unlocking private investment (*continued*)

commitments. Recent overlapping shocks, including the pandemic, conflicts, and global inflation, have raised uncertainty and contributed to higher interest rates, which in turn increase the cost of finance and weigh on investment.

A weak business environment can raise operating costs, increase uncertainty, and reduce the reliability of future production and sales, holding back private investment. Surveys highlight access to finance and crime or political instability as prominent obstacles faced by firms operating in EMDEs, while firms in LICs also often point to infrastructure-related constraints (figure B1.2.2.C). Access to reliable electricity is an important infrastructure gap, with almost half of firms in the median LIC reporting access to electricity as a major constraint (figure B1.2.2.D). Tax and tax administration also add complexities to investment decisions. Many firms in EMDEs report tax administration as a major obstacle, reflecting high compliance costs and uncertainty created by limited regulatory clarity, cumbersome procedures, and inconsistent implementation.

Limited access to finance can inhibit firms from undertaking otherwise viable projects. A sizable share of firms in EMDEs report finance as an obstacle, and the incidence is higher in LICs than in other EMDEs and advanced economies (figure B1.2.2.E). Financing constraints are often compounded by shallow financial markets and limited financial development (figure B1.2.2.F). In EMDEs, the mismatch between the long-term capital requirements of many investment projects and the short-term nature of available bank financing is larger than in advanced economies.

Policies to promote private investment

Efforts to boost private investment need to address country-specific constraints, often with a particular focus on risk, infrastructure gaps, and financing frictions, and potentially requiring the strengthening of macroeconomic and institutional fundamentals. Policy measures include public investment in foundational infrastructure that crowds in private investment; strong economic fundamentals such as sound fiscal, monetary, and financial policies coupled with strong institutions and well-designed regulations; and policies that enhance access to finance for firms (Chrimes, Lebrand, and Mawejje 2025). Effective reform packages can help create conditions for strong domestic and foreign private sector investment. Policies may also address market failures or alleviate other specific constraints. The optimal policy package will depend on country circumstances, including institutional capacity for implementation, and alignment with broader policy objectives.

Infrastructure to underpin private investment

Well-functioning foundational infrastructure is an important building block for sustained private sector investment and long-run growth. Reliable transportation, affordable energy, and strong digital connectivity help firms connect to markets. Recent evidence also suggests that targeted equity investment in EMDE infrastructure can deliver competitive returns, underscoring the potential for infrastructure to support both development outcomes and private investment opportunities (Chari, Henry, and Mauro 2025).

In EMDEs with sufficient fiscal space and efficient government spending, public investment can crowd in private investment (figure B1.2.3.A; Straub et al. 2026; World Bank 2024c). Social rates of return on infrastructure investment in EMDEs can be high, though this varies depending on country circumstances (Chari, Henry, and Picardo 2025; Gardner and Henry 2023). Steps to enhance the reliability of electricity supply have supported foreign direct investment (FDI) in Sub-Saharan Africa, especially when complemented with other infrastructure such as digital connectivity and roads (Mensah 2024; Mensah and Traore 2024). In many EMDEs, urban policies, particularly those related to land use, housing, municipal finance, and urban infrastructure, also play a critical role in shaping private investment, given that most private-sector activity is concentrated in cities (Baker et al. 2023).

Policies can incentivize private investment in foundational infrastructure under the right conditions. Policy options to incentivize private sector participation in infrastructure investment include effective and independent regulation, setting cost-reflective tariffs for services, and shifting from broad subsidies to target interventions that do not distort competition (Kessides 2005). Public-private partnerships (PPPs) can crowd in private investment by pooling capital for large projects, improving risk sharing, and reducing entry risks. They can be complemented by risk-mitigation instruments

BOX 1.2 Unlocking private investment (*continued*)

such as guarantees and blended finance. Effective PPP design and regulation, however, require significant institutional capacity (Cull et al. 2024; Fabre and Straub 2023).

An investment-friendly business environment

Improving the investment climate and undertaking structural reforms coupled with well-functioning institutions are important underpinnings for private investment (Chrimes, Lebrand, and Mawejje 2025; Development Committee 2026). In EMDEs, reform spurts that improved an economy's investment climate, for example by establishing enforceable property rights and minimizing expropriation risk, have led to sustained increases in private investment. Furthermore, in EMDEs, major structural reforms, including strengthening the domestic financial sector or boosting competition, led to a statistically significant 2.2 percent increase in private investment three years after the reforms were implemented (figure B1.2.3.B). An investor-friendly business environment, underpinned by high institutional quality, is also a catalyst for attracting FDI. Reforms that substantially raise institutional quality are associated with a significant and large boost to FDI inflows (figure B1.2.3.C; Adarov and Pallan 2025).

Micro, small, and medium-sized enterprises represent the majority of businesses in EMDEs but face constraints that vary widely across firm size and maturity. Lowering the cost of doing business—including by strengthening insolvency regimes, credit information systems, and financial regulation—can help close financing gaps and support firm growth. Policy priorities vary across firms, ranging from easing entry and compliance for smaller firms to expanding access to finance, land, and capital markets for larger and growing firms (Carvajal and Didier 2024; Development Committee 2026).

Well-functioning financial markets

Policies that enhance firms' access to financing, deepen and improve the efficiency of capital markets, and boost access to credit and local-currency financing can support private investment. Key measures include boosting access to external finance and removing constraints to sustainable capital flows, developing digital infrastructure that allows small firms and financial institutions to participate in financial markets, and strengthening contract enforcement to help lower collateral demands (United Nations 2022).

In EMDEs, financial institutions generally provide a smaller share of private sector credit than in advanced economies, particularly for longer-term loans. Establishing credit-reporting frameworks that reduce information asymmetries between firms and lenders, establishing licensing frameworks for nonbank financial institutions such as microfinance lenders, and scaling up guarantee schemes to address high perceived risk can all crowd in additional private capital (Carvajal and Didier 2024). Furthermore, well-functioning local-currency debt and equity markets can help attract large institutional investors in economies with underdeveloped financial markets. In EMDEs that saw capital market deepening over the past three decades, productive firms were able to access new sources of financing and boost investment (figure B1.2.3.D; Meh and Schmukler 2025).

Country-specific context and reform combinations

Comprehensive reform packages, especially when coupled with strong institutions, can spark private investment accelerations: periods of sustained and relatively rapid private investment growth. During these acceleration periods, private investment growth typically reached 11 percent per year, while output growth increased by 2 percentage points compared to other years, and total factor productivity growth tripled from 0.5 percent per year to 1.6 percent per year (figure B1.2.3.E). These accelerations often followed or coincided with reforms that improved institutions, stabilized the macroeconomy (supported, for example, by fiscal consolidation and inflation targeting), and eased cross-border trade and financial flows. Such reforms have tended to be particularly effective when combined in coherent and well-sequenced packages (figure B1.2.3.F; Chrimes, Lebrand, and Mawejje 2025).

Policies to boost private investment should be tailored to country-specific circumstances and priorities. Governments with the greatest needs often lack the technical and administrative capacity to address them, especially in LICs and FCS economies. Building stronger implementation capabilities is a gradual process that often depends on greater international support. In

BOX 1.2 Unlocking private investment (*continued*)

FIGURE B1.2.2 Constraints to private investment

Country risk is high in EMDEs, and in LICs in particular, while globally, uncertainty has spiked in recent years and remains elevated. Firms in EMDEs report a range of obstacles, with access to finance an important common theme, and electricity access a concern in the majority of LICs. Financial development is also lower in EMDEs, and in LICs in particular.

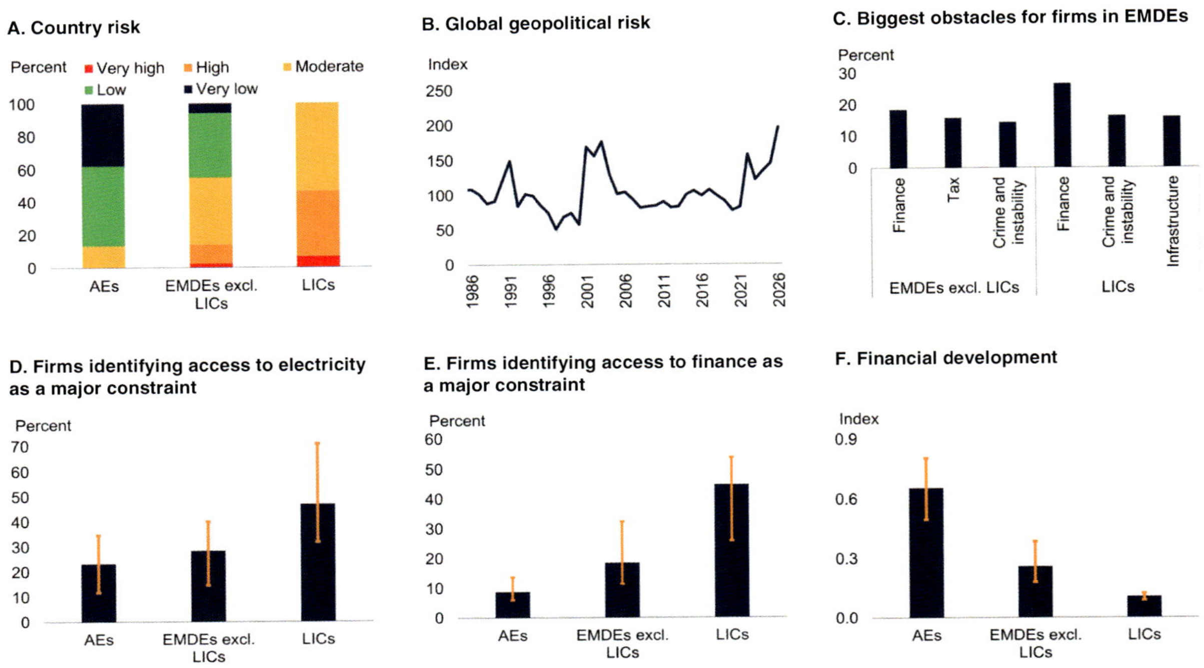

Sources: Caldara and Iacoviello (2022); International Monetary Fund, Financial Development Index; PRS Group, International Country Risk Guide (ICRG) (database); World Bank Enterprise Surveys; World Bank.

Note: AEs = advanced economies; EMDEs = emerging market and developing economies; excl. = excluding; LICs = low-income countries.

A. Share of economies, by risk category. Based on the ICRG composite index, as of February 2026. The index aggregates financial, economic, and political risks, and ranges between 0 and 100. Sample includes 34 AEs and 73 EMDEs, of which 14 are LICs.

B. Geopolitical Risk Index from Caldara and Iacoviello (2022). The index is available at monthly frequency; observations are averaged to the annual level. Data downloaded on April 21, 2026. Higher values imply greater levels of geopolitical risk.

C. Panel shows the top three obstacles cited by firms as per Enterprise Surveys, using the latest available year for each economy. Bars show averages for the indicated country groups, based on up to 128 EMDEs, including 23 LICs. "Infrastructure" combines firms naming electricity and transportation; "Taxation" combines tax administration and tax rates; "Crime/instability" combines crime, theft, disorder, and political instability; and "Labor" combines an inadequately educated workforce and labor regulations. Percentages reflect the share of firms in each country identifying that combined category as their single biggest obstacle.

D.E. Blue bars show the median share of firms identifying access to electricity (D) or access to finance (E) as a major constraint as per Enterprise Surveys, using the latest available year for each economy. Orange whiskers show the interquartile range. Sample includes up to 23 AEs and 128 EMDEs, of which 23 are LICs.

F. Blue bars show the median financial development index for each country category. Orange whiskers show the interquartile range. Based on 2021 data for 34 AEs and 130 EMDEs, of which 22 are LICs. Each indicator within the index is normalized between 0 and 1. The highest value of a given variable across time and countries is equal to one; all other values are measured relative to this maximum. Data are winsorized at the 5th and 95th percentiles to temper the effects of extreme outliers.

addition, well-planned reform agendas require commitment and patience and are often more effective when they fit into existing frameworks (Acemoglu, Johnson, and Robinson 2001).

Private Investment Accelerations: Case Studies

The policy challenges may seem daunting, but history offers many examples of countries that have successfully boosted private investment growth (Chrimes, Lebrand, and Mawejje 2025; Stamm and Yu 2024). For example:

- **Colombia** saw an investment acceleration between 2001 and 2007, with private investment growing at 12.2 percent on average over this period. This acceleration followed a difficult period of macroeconomic performance and was preceded by a set of significant stabilizing macroeconomic reforms, including the adoption of a floating exchange rate and inflation targeting, the strengthening of central bank independence, and improved government finances supported by tax

BOX 1.2 Unlocking private investment (*continued*)

FIGURE B1.2.3 Policies to promote private investment

A rise in public investment typically results in an increase in private investment several years later. Major structural reforms also have a positive impact on private investment. At the firm level, stock or bond issuance is associated with more physical capital and higher employment one year on. During private investment accelerations, output rises, and TFP growth surges. Packages of reforms are more likely to trigger private investment accelerations.

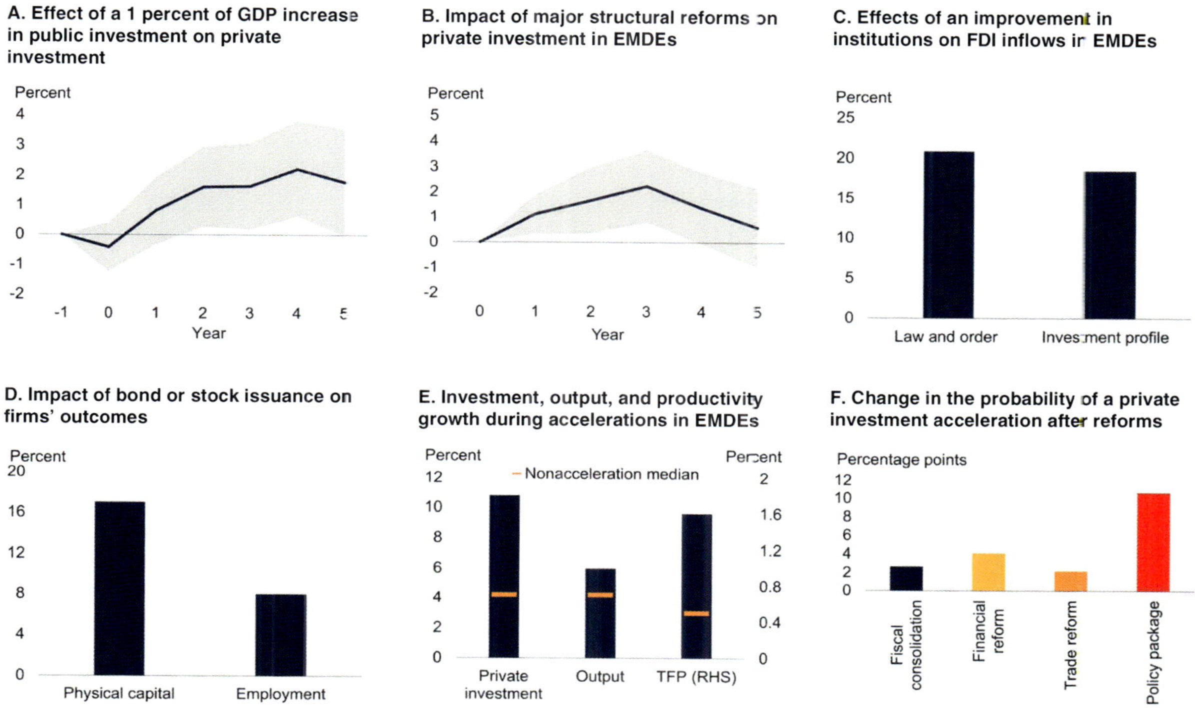

Sources: Adarov (2025); Alesina et al. (2024); Chinn and Ito (2008); Feenstra, Inklaar, and Timmer (2015); Haver Analytics; Investment and Capital Stock Dataset (IMF 2021); Meh and Schmukler (2025); PRS Group, International Country Risk Guide (ICRG) (database); Stamm and Yu (2024); World Development Indicators (database); World Bank.

Note: AEs = advanced economies; EMDEs = emerging market and developing economies; FDI = foreign direct investment; LICs = low-income countries; RHS = right-hand scale; TFP = total factor productivity.

A. Panel shows cumulative response to a shock in year *t* relative to year *t* = -1; *t* = 0 is the year of the shock. Shaded areas indicate 90 percent confidence bands. Sample includes up to 129 EMDEs.

B. Line shows the cumulative increase in private investment, in percent, following a reform. The shaded area shows 90 percent confidence bands. The reform indicator is the average sum of domestic and external financing, trade, and product market reform indicators. Sample includes 61 EMDEs.

C. Bars show marginal effects on FDI inflows of an increase from the sample median to the top quartile of ICRG law and order and investment profile indexes, based on gravity model estimates.

D. Bars show the change in physical capital and employment one year after issuance of bonds or stocks in capital markets in a global sample, taken from Meh and Schmukler (2025).

E. Bars and markers show medians. Sample includes 68 EMDEs, spanning 85 private investment accelerations in EMDEs and 155 in total between 1960 and 2019. Identification of episodes follows Stamm and Yu (2024).

F. Sample includes 68 EMDEs and 35 AEs, spanning 155 private investment accelerations (85 in EMDEs). Bars show the increase in the probability of a private investment acceleration following an improvement in economic policy by 1 standard deviation. Right bar shows the increase when all economic policies are improved.

reforms. In addition, there were enhancements to domestic financial markets, as well as reforms to enhance the business environment. Macroeconomic reform, structural measures, and relative political stability may all have helped set the stage for higher private investment.

- **India** experienced an investment acceleration between 1994 and 1999, and again between 2004 and 2012, with private investment growing faster than public investment in both cases. These acceleration phases followed on from a range of liberalizing reforms to trade and the capital account

BOX 1.2 Unlocking private investment (*continued*)

in the 1990s. Many public sector monopolies were also dismantled, creating opportunities for the private sector and opening international trade and investment.

- **The Republic of Korea** had investment acceleration periods from 1985 to 1996, and again from 1999 to 2007, with private investment growth 8.3 percentage points higher on average during these episodes (although the period in between saw a recession linked to the Asian financial crisis). Macroeconomic stabilization policies and comprehensive reforms to liberalize trade, capital markets, and foreign investment supported these surges in investment, delivered as part of a wider long-term growth strategy.

- **Türkiye** saw an investment acceleration between 2003 and 2008 (recording double-digit private investment growth on a per capita basis) and another between 2010 and 2014 (albeit with more modest private investment growth). Macroeconomic stabilization, including in response to the 2000–01 economic crisis, together with structural reforms including trade liberalization, financial sector strengthening, and labor and product market reforms, helped underpin the initial acceleration episode.

Conclusion

Private investment is central to delivering sustained output growth and job creation, which in turn underpin development prospects. Yet even as investment needs rise, and with many EMDEs facing a backdrop of demographic pressures and a major jobs challenge, private investment growth has slowed. Case studies highlight that addressing constraints to private sector investment is possible but requires concerted policy action. Effective strengthening of macroeconomic stability is a common enabling factor. Ensuring that foundational infrastructure is in place to support private sector expansion and advancing structural reforms to improve the business environment and facilitate the development of well-functioning financial markets are important contributors. Coherent and coordinated reforms, tailored to country circumstances, increase the likelihood of a sustained boost in private investment. The extent to which policy makers can reverse weakening private investment growth and sustainably mobilize private capital will be pivotal in shaping job creation and development outcomes in the years ahead.

sharp declines in ODA, and constrained fiscal space, which continue to weigh on investment and medium-term growth (Chapter 3; OECD 2026a).

In all, the challenging global environment will likely hurt living standards in LICs, with the effects of the conflict leading to a downgrade in LICs' growth by 0.3 percentage point to 5.4 percent in 2026, offsetting positive factors such as reduced internal hostilities, better-than-expected agricultural output, and resilient global trade. Growth forecasts are projected to diverge between LICs in FCS and other LICs. Growth in LICs in FCS is projected at 4.9 percent in 2026, a downgrade of 0.1 percentage point, which assumes that improvements in security conditions in some economies offset substantially weaker growth in others. Meanwhile, growth in LICs not in FCS, many of which tend to be more reliant on food and energy imports, has been downgraded by 0.4 percentage point to 6.3 percent in 2026. Over 2027–28, growth across LICs is anticipated to firm slightly, to an average of 5.5 percent, as the impact of the conflict abates and trade and external demand pick up.

The outlook for LICs remains uncertain, and risks are tilted to the downside. A prolonged or escalating Middle East conflict represents the key near-term risk, with the potential to further raise energy and food prices, intensify inflationary pressures, and strain already limited fiscal space. Should the recent Ebola outbreak in the Democratic Republic of Congo and Uganda worsen, it could further intensify already fragile public health and humanitarian situations, as well as damage economic activity. Such shocks could exacerbate food security through higher prices, weaker growth, and eroding real incomes, especially for vulnerable households. They would also further compound existing vulnerabilities, including slow progress on debt restructuring, delayed structural reforms, domestic conflict, and exposure to weather-related shocks.

Per capita income growth

Against a backdrop of sharply higher energy prices, development progress in many EMDEs is slowing, with mounting pressures on living standards and poverty reduction. The capacity of many governments to respond remains constrained: fiscal space in many vulnerable country groups was already depleted by the pandemic, and declining ODA is compounding these pressures further. Net ODA fell by 23 percent in 2025 in real terms—the largest annual drop on record—and is expected to decline further, stripping away one of the last remaining buffers that countries depend on to sustain schools, health care, and food assistance programs (OECD 2026a). For the most vulnerable populations, this erosion of public services translates into higher risks of child malnutrition, maternal mortality, and other preventable health outcomes associated with rising poverty (da Silva et al. 2026).

In 2026, per capita income growth in EMDEs is projected to slow by 0.7 percentage point to 2.7 percent—the weakest pace since the pandemic—in part due to eroding purchasing power as households face higher fuel and food prices. With China and India excluded, EMDE per capita income growth is anticipated to fall to 1.3 percent, with many economies in the Middle East, North Africa, Afghanistan, and Pakistan (MNA) region suffering a sharp decline. The slowdown is expected to be even more pronounced in FCS economies, many of which are LICs, where per capita income growth is projected to decelerate to about zero percent in 2026. Over 2027–28, average per capita income growth is projected to recover to 3.2 percent across EMDEs, 2.1 percent in EMDEs excluding China and India, and 2.7 percent in FCS economies.

Nevertheless, the recovery over 2027–28 is anticipated to be uneven across and within countries, and unlikely to be sufficient to reverse the deterioration in living standards already underway. The level of per capita income across EMDEs excluding China and India, relative to

FIGURE 1.8 Outlook for emerging market and developing economies

The EMDE outlook has deteriorated, reflecting headwinds from higher energy prices, elevated uncertainty, and tighter monetary conditions. EMDEs directly affected by the conflict in the Middle East are expected to face the sharpest slowdown, due to the destruction of energy infrastructure and the disruption of energy exports, leading to protracted output losses. By contrast, the moderation in commodity-importing EMDEs excluding China is expected to be less pronounced. The adverse effects of the conflict are envisaged to be more pronounced in the roughly one-quarter of EMDEs with weak sovereign-credit ratings, as higher commodity prices add to already strained financial positions.

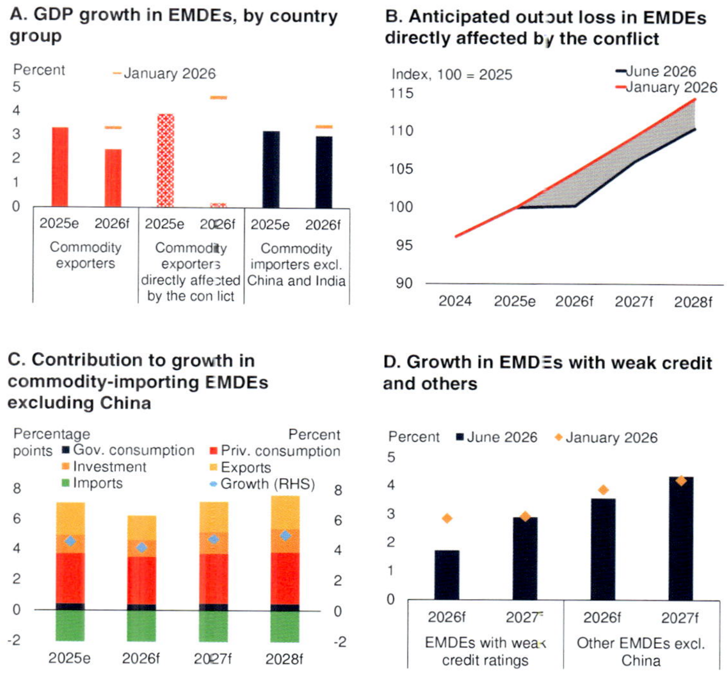

Sources: Moody's Analytics; World Bank.

Note: e = estimate; f = forecast. EMDEs = emerging market and developing economies; excl. = excluding; Gov. = government; Priv. = private; RHS = right-hand scale.

A. Panel shows projected annual GDP growth by group. Aggregate growth rates are calculated using GDP weights at average 2010–19 prices and market exchange rates. Bars show the projected growth rate reported in the current edition of the *Global Economic Prospects* report; yellow markers show the projected growth rate in the January 2026 report.

B.D. "June 2026" and "January 2026" refer to the forecasts in the associated editions of the *Global Economic Prospects* report.

B. Panel shows the level of real GDP indexed to 100 in 2025. The January and June 2026 projections use country-level forecasts for six EMDEs directly affected by the conflict in the Middle East. For the January 2026 projection, the trend for 2028 was extended using 2027 growth rates. Shaded area indicates output loss. EMDEs directly affected by the conflict include Bahrain, Iraq, Kuwait, Qatar, Saudi Arabia, and the United Arab Emirates. Associated growth forecasts for this group of economies exclude the Islamic Republic of Iran and Lebanon because of a high degree of uncertainty.

C. Panel shows the projected annual GDP growth and contributions of subcomponents. Discrepancies between GDP growth and the sum of its components are explained by inventories and statistical residuals.

D. Blue bars (red markers) represent forecasted growth by country group. The weak credit ratings sample includes up to 26 EMDEs with sovereign bond rating grades at CCC+/Caa1 and below.

advanced economies, is not expected to return to the pre-pandemic level until after 2028, implying nearly a decade of lost income convergence (figure 1.9.A). Prospects are particularly bleak for FCS economies, where per capita income is projected

FIGURE 1.9 Per capita income growth

Prospects for per capita income convergence remain weak, pointing to nearly a decade of lost ground for EMDEs. Reflecting both the lingering effects of conflict and subdued growth, per capita income levels in EMDEs excluding China and India are not expected to regain their 2019 relative position compared with advanced economies before 2028. The outlook is particularly challenging for economies in fragile and conflict-affected situations (FCS), where setbacks to convergence are projected to be even more pronounced. With income growth prospects remaining weak and food and fertilizer price pressures related to the conflict rising, food insecurity is set to intensify, potentially reaching a new high.

A. Level of per capita GDP as a share of advanced economies

B. Number of people experiencing severe food insecurity

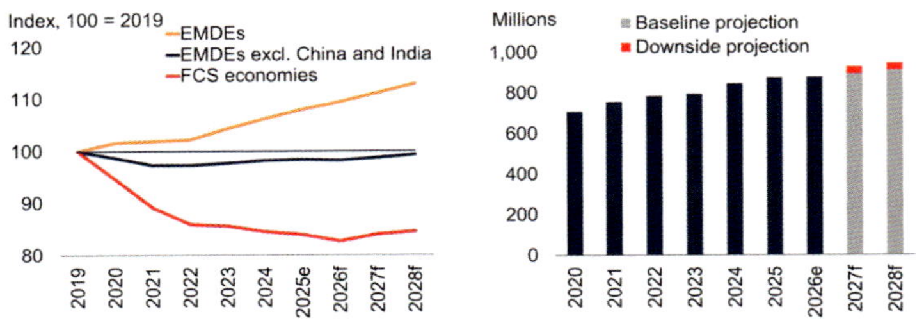

Sources: UN World Population Prospects (database); World Bank; World Food Security Outlook (database).

Note: e = estimate; f = forecast. EMDEs = emerging market and developing economies; excl. = excluding; FCS = fragile and conflict-affected situations. The FCS country group is based on the current World Bank FCS classification.

A. Lines show per capita GDP by country groups as a share of advanced economies' per capita GDP, indexed to 2019 = 100. GDP per capita is calculated as aggregated GDP divided by the aggregate population and aggregated by country group using real U.S. dollar GDP weights at average 2010–19 prices and market exchange rates.

B. Blue bars show the population facing severe food insecurity. Gray (gray plus red) bars show the World Food Security Outlook's baseline (downside) projection as of April 2026 for 152 EMDEs excluding China.

to remain more than 15 percent below 2019 levels relative to advanced economies by 2028.

These pressures are further undermining efforts to reduce food insecurity and poverty. Amid the lingering effects of the pandemic and several major conflicts, the number of people facing severe food insecurity in EMDEs excluding China rose by around 220 million between 2019 and 2025. This total could rise by a further 35 to 70 million by the end of 2028, as the conflict in the Middle East intensifies an already acute global food crisis in the context of growing food and fertilizer price pressures (figure 1.9.B; World Food Security Outlook 2026). Extreme poverty also remains well above pre-pandemic levels in vulnerable countries and is set to worsen: based on pre-conflict estimates, nearly 60 percent of the population in LICs and about 40 percent in FCS economies are projected to live in extreme poverty by end–2026 (World Bank 2026d).

Global outlook and risks

Global growth is expected to decelerate this year to 2.5 percent as conflict-related energy supply disruptions, higher energy prices, and tighter monetary conditions weigh on growth in advanced economies and EMDEs. In addition, economies directly affected by the conflict are seeing significant and broad disruptions to energy production. Despite the already downbeat outlook, risks are tilted firmly to the downside (figure 1.10.A). Weaker growth outcomes could result if the conflict or its aftermath evolves such that disruptions to global commodity flows are more severe or protracted than envisaged in the baseline. This could reflect increasing conflict-related damage to essential energy production infrastructure, or prolonged impediments to shipping from the Middle East. These or other triggers could also give rise to a sharp tightening of financial conditions, which would undercut global demand.

Risks to the outlook

Downside risks

Prolonged or escalating geopolitical stress

The conflict in the Middle East has led to closures of crucial shipping routes and extensive economic disruptions, including attacks on critical infrastructure in the region (figure 1.10.B). Adverse global consequences are mounting amid sharply higher oil, natural gas, and fertilizer prices and spreading shortages of fuel and various industrial inputs. The baseline assumes a relatively short-lived spell of acute disruptions to commodity production and trade in the Gulf region, with economic consequences outside the Middle East limited to a spell of elevated inflation and reduced activity.

However, a range of considerably more adverse outcomes is possible, with major implications for commodity markets, activity, and inflation globally. A resumption of hostilities could result in more damage to essential energy infrastructure, curtailing oil, LNG, and fertilizer supplies over the medium term and driving prices persistently higher. In addition, shipping in the Middle East could be impaired for an extended period, also resulting in lasting commodity price increases and prolonged uncertainty. Beyond the region directly affected by the conflict, large net energy importers, especially those with fragile sovereign balance sheets, would see a further weakening in the growth outlook.

More broadly, the conflict in the Middle East is the latest in a series of large geopolitical shocks that have roiled the world economy over the 2020s, with geopolitical tensions rising unabated. Against this backdrop, the potential for further geopolitical ruptures in the next few years cannot be discounted, raising the possibility of further disruptive supply shocks. As the effects of these events compound over time, escalating geopolitical stress may weaken international trade and financial integration, weighing on business sentiment, investment, and ultimately productivity globally.

Tighter global financial conditions

Generally benign financial conditions and buoyant investor sentiment were key to supporting growth last year, offsetting some of the adverse impacts of trade policy shifts. At the outset of the conflict in the Middle East, financial conditions tightened, as risk-off sentiment took hold in financial markets, although conditions eased following the implementation of the ceasefire.

An additional sharp tightening in financial conditions remains a substantial risk. Rising global inflationary pressures driven by energy price increases could lead to expectations of higher policy rates and even higher bond yields (figure 1.10.C). Fiscal vulnerabilities in major economies could become more pronounced amid elevated public debt levels and large fiscal deficits, potentially pushing up term premiums and leading to disorderly movements in bond markets.

Moreover, periodic bouts of financial market volatility in response to conflict-related developments could lead to a broader retrenchment in risk appetite and a reassessment of asset prices. This may include equity valuations of AI-focused companies in the context of so-far-limited productivity gains despite substantial investments in computing power. Broad-based declines in equity markets and higher yields would dampen business investment and consumption.

Resurgent trade tensions and trade policy uncertainty

Even as trade tensions have abated somewhat following the U.S Supreme Court ruling, uncertainty around trade policy remains elevated for several reasons. First, the U.S. administration signaled its intent to reinstate tariffs using a different legal basis, which is likely to introduce further uncertainty around the exact levels of tariffs imposed on particular products and countries. Second, elevated geopolitical tensions and competition for markets and strategic resources among major economies are likely to continue to spill over into international trade relations, resulting in further trade policy uncertainty.

A resurgence of trade barriers, compounded by heightened uncertainty, threatens to undermine business confidence and stifle investment, particularly within sectors integrated into global supply chains. Given that investment-related goods possess a high import content, such constraints further diminish international trade volumes. These shifts are likely to disproportionately affect the economic growth of jurisdictions implementing these barriers, as well as export-dependent EMDEs. Furthermore, the long-term persistence of trade restrictions may impede productivity growth by obstructing the international diffusion of technological advancements.

Weather-related natural disasters

The rising frequency and intensity of natural disasters pose growing risks to lives, livelihoods, and the global economy and are expected to intensify further with global warming (figure 1.10.D). Global temperatures are continuing to rise, setting the stage for further increases in the incidence of weather-related disasters, including in the context of more severe El Niño weather events. Beyond the tragic losses of life, extreme weather events generate immediate economic losses by damaging physical capital and generating disruptions to labor markets and economic activity more broadly. Although estimates of their economic costs vary, ample evidence shows that such events significantly depress economic performance on impact and leave output on a persistently lower trend (Cavallo, Becerra, and Acevedo 2022).

FIGURE 1.10 Risks to the outlook

Risks are tilted firmly to the downside, largely because of the possibility of the prolongation or escalation of the conflict in the Middle East, which has already led to closures of crucial shipping routes and economic disruptions. Rising global inflationary pressures driven by high energy prices could lead to expectations of higher policy rates and even higher bond yields. The rising frequency and intensity of natural disasters pose growing risks to lives, livelihoods, and the global economy. A downside scenario that includes further energy market stress would raise global inflation by 0.5 percentage point in 2026 relative to the baseline and lower growth by up to 0.4 percentage point. An even more adverse scenario that also includes financial stress would result in markedly weaker growth.

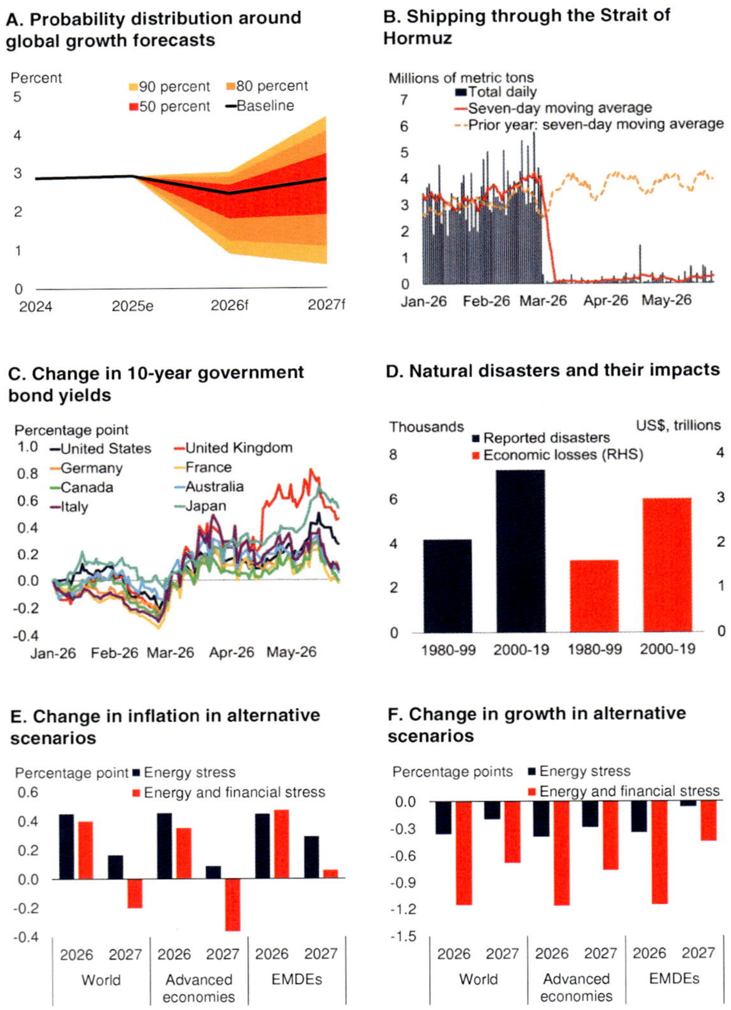

Sources: Arslanalp, Koepke, and Verschuur (2021); Bloomberg; Consensus Economics; Goldman Sachs; Haver Analytics; IMF PortWatch; Ohnsorge, Stocker, and Some (2016); Oxford Economics; CRED and UNDRR (2020); World Bank.

Note: e = estimate; f = forecast. EMDEs = emerging market and developing economies; RHS = right-hand scale.

A. Probabilities use the range and skewness implied by oil and equity price derivatives, and term spread forecasts. Values for 2026-27 use 6-month- and 18-month-ahead forecast distributions, with data up to May 29, 2026.

B. Panel shows the estimated trade volume carried by ships transiting through the Strait of Hormuz through May 24, 2026.

C. Panel shows the change in 10-year government bond yields since January 5, 2026. Last observation is May 29, 2026.

D. Panel shows the number of reported disaster events and total economic losses from 1980 to 1999, and 2000 to 2019. Refer to the human costs of disasters (UNDRR 2020).

E.F. Panel shows the deviation of aggregate inflation (panel E) and growth (panel F) in scenarios produced using Oxford Economics' Global Economic Model.

Weather-related disasters can weaken investment, reduce trend productivity growth, hinder human capital accumulation, and compound food insecurity.

These risks are particularly acute in EMDEs, which are more exposed to extreme events and often constrained by limited institutional capacity (Bettin, Jallow, and Zazzaro 2024). The impact of extreme weather events can be mitigated by introducing early-warning systems, raising preparedness at relevant government agencies, and designing effective safety nets.

In the aftermath of natural disasters, governments of affected countries are faced with an urgent need to provide humanitarian assistance and begin reconstruction, which can impose substantial fiscal costs. The ongoing decline in foreign aid for the most vulnerable countries and the increasing difficulty in mobilizing international support in the context of burgeoning geopolitical tensions could leave economies impacted by natural disasters in weak fiscal positions and could hinder support to affected populations.

Growth outcomes under alternative downside scenarios

In the baseline, the most acute supply disruptions related to the conflict in the Middle East end relatively soon, even if global economic activity decelerates notably this year. The crystallization of downside risks could result in a markedly steeper decline in global growth. The most prominent downside risks are quantified in two graduated scenarios using a global macroeconomic model.[3]

Energy stress scenario

If the Strait of Hormuz is effectively closed to shipping for longer than assumed in the baseline, or if energy production capacity in the Middle East is further degraded, energy prices may far exceed the baseline projections. In this scenario of further energy stress, the Strait does not meaning-

[3] These simulations are conducted using the Oxford Economics Global Economic Model, a semi-structural macroeconomic projection model that includes 188 individual country blocks in its extended version, available at quarterly or annual frequencies (Oxford Economics 2019).

fully reopen until the fourth quarter of 2026, with shipping volumes gradually recovering through the first quarter of 2027. In addition, there is a medium-term reduction of at most 4 percent in global oil supply capacity. Increased energy supply stress causes the Brent oil price to surge anew in the second half of the year, averaging $115/bbl in 2026 and remaining elevated well into 2027. Amid prolonged LNG scarcity, natural gas prices would also far exceed the baseline projections, with additional upward pressure on prices for coal as a substitute for natural gas.

The direct effects of the energy price shock alone would substantially increase inflation and curb real income growth and global demand in 2026. In addition, extensive disruptions to fertilizer trade and generally more expensive production inputs would increase cost-push pressures for food and other essentials. With oil inventories rapidly depleting, balancing global oil markets would require oil and oil products consumption to fall via potentially disruptive channels, with reverberations through global supply chains. Given the extent and duration of price pressures, major central banks would likely raise policy rates this year, also weighing on growth.

In all, GDP-weighted global inflation would be expected to average 4.5 percent in 2026—exceeding the baseline by about 0.5 percentage point (figure 1.10.E). Global GDP growth would fall to 2.1 percent this year, 0.4 percentage point below the baseline, with EMDE growth 0.3 percentage point lower than in the baseline (figure 1.10.F). The impacts of the shock would be pronounced in both EMDE commodity importers and, because of the protracted trough in Gulf-region exports, some key EMDE commodity exporters.

Energy and financial stress scenario

In the energy and financial stress scenario, risk appetite in financial markets is severely undermined by the outsized energy shock outlined in the scenario above. As a result, the renewed surge in oil prices—to an average of $115/bbl this year—is accompanied by a sharp fall in global equity prices, sustained increases in equity market volatility, and a persistent decline in consumer and business confidence. Alongside this, corporate bond spreads would likely widen, with the U.S. dollar strengthening. Pervasive risk-off sentiment and current account pressures in energy importers could induce capital flight, driving EMDE risk premiums higher.

The combined effects of energy market stress and widespread financial strains would result in much weaker growth outcomes than in the baseline scenario. If equity market volatility (proxied by the Chicago Board Options Exchange Volatility Index, or VIX index) were to approach its 2020 peak in mid-2026 before gradually normalizing, accompanying the steep increase in oil prices and trough in confidence, global GDP growth would fall to just 1.3 percent in 2026, undershooting the baseline by 1.2 percentage point.

Compared with the energy stress scenario, the addition of financial stress would reduce growth in EMDEs by a further 0.9 percentage point in 2026, to 1.2 percentage point below the baseline, leaving growth at just 2.4 percent this year. Global inflation would be slightly lower than in the energy stress scenario, reflecting softer demand, but still 0.4 percentage point higher than in the baseline in 2026.

Upside risk

Technology-led investment and productivity gains

Despite subdued private investment across EMDEs as a group, growth in AI has heralded a boom in private investment in some economies and led to spillovers through increased trade in related goods. As the race to build superior AI technology continues, the corresponding investment in areas such as software, ICT equipment, and data centers may broaden to more geographies. Demand for upstream commodities and components could strengthen further, lifting exports in a wide range of economies that are directly or indirectly embedded in AI-related supply chains.

Over the medium to long term, the expanding use of AI may raise productivity in an increasing number of economies and trigger broader technological breakthroughs, supporting growth and productivity globally. Even for EMDEs where full-scale AI adoption remains out of reach, small-AI solutions—for example, task-specific applications that run on local devices with little or no internet connectivity—can help deliver meaningful productivity gains (World Bank 2026e).

Nevertheless, any productivity gains from AI adoption may be limited in some EMDEs on account of adjustment costs or slow diffusion because of inadequate digital infrastructure and an inadequate AI ecosystem. In addition, the impact on overall growth could be offset by potential labor displacement in some sectors.

Policy challenges

Policy makers face formidable challenges. Stronger global cooperation is needed to mitigate food insecurity and deepen trade amid geopolitical strains, as well as advance the energy transition. Domestically, EMDE central banks need to balance price stability with support to growth while managing currency pressures and financial volatility. On the fiscal side, higher energy costs and tighter monetary conditions are increasing deficits and debt, particularly in commodity exporters where fiscal policy is constrained by reliance on resource revenues and weak tax systems. At the same time, rapid population growth and technological change are intensifying the jobs challenge in EMDEs. Subdued private investment is further limiting job creation and constraining long-term growth.

Key global challenges

Mitigating food insecurity amid geopolitical stress

Even prior to the Middle East conflict, food insecurity was rising. As of 2025, the share of the global population in severe food insecurity stood at about 12 percent, roughly 2 percentage points above the pre-pandemic level in 2019 (UN World Population Prospects 2024; World Food Security Outlook 2026). The increase was concentrated in FCS economies, especially many of those still below their pre-pandemic income levels as a result of higher incidence of conflict and more frequent natural disasters.

The conflict is likely to further exacerbate the challenge of food insecurity. Higher shipping costs and longer travel routes for a significant volume of food aid intensify the financing strains on international aid organizations, many of which have faced funding cuts (WFP 2026). Reduced fertilizer use in the current planting season because of higher fertilizer prices could result in lower crop yields and tighter food supplies in the second half of 2026 and into 2027. Sub-Saharan Africa (SSA) and lower-income economies in Asia are particularly vulnerable, given their heavy reliance on energy and fertilizer imports and as planting seasons in many cases coincide with the period of elevated input costs. The possible emergence of strong El Niño weather conditions in the second half of 2026 could further strain agricultural supplies.

Coordinated global action is critical to mitigating these challenges. To address the urgent needs of countries most adversely affected by conflict-related disruptions, global policy makers need a clear roadmap to bolster emergency food aid mechanisms alongside efforts to establish humanitarian corridors to facilitate the movement of aid and commercial fertilizers.

Over the longer term, shoring up food security will require sustained investment across several fronts. These include scaling up sustainable and resilient agriculture, expanding rural infrastructure such as storage facilities and last-mile transport networks, diversifying supply sources of fertilizers, and deploying robust early warning systems for extreme weather. International partners and development institutions can play a critical role by increasing concessional financing while actively de-risking private investment through blended finance structures and guarantees, alongside the provision of technical assistance, particularly in FCS economies where food insecurity is most acute and institutional capacity is often most constrained.

Diversifying and deepening trade and economic partnerships

Amid heightened trade tensions and geopolitical strains, concerted efforts are needed to bolster a predictable multilateral trading system. Clear multilateral rules, such as the most-favored-nation principle, serve a crucial role by providing a stable, nondiscriminatory framework for trade negotiations among countries (Staiger 2026). Such a framework facilitates large-scale as well as deep trade agreements that address a wide range of issues, including harmonizing regulations and protecting intellectual property, which are increasingly important to support the fast-growing digital and services sectors.

With multilateralism facing greater challenges, regional trade agreements (RTAs) have emerged as important complements to the broader rules-based trading system. The share of global trade taking place among members of RTAs rose from about 40 percent in 1990 to over 60 percent by 2025 (figure 1.11.A). RTAs can support diversification across partners and products, reducing reliance on narrow export bases. Significant untapped opportunities remain in intraregional trade, which could be unlocked by lowering nontariff barriers and improving border procedures. Realizing further gains will also require narrowing trade finance gaps, including by strengthening the supply chain finance ecosystem to ease liquidity constraints and support participation by small- and medium-sized enterprises (IFC 2021).

In tandem, international investment frameworks need to be modernized to support deeper economic partnerships, such as the reform of the International Investment Agreement regime toward treaties that are more balanced, targeted, and aligned with sustainable development goals. Notably, dedicated and extensive investment facilitation provisions are now being embedded in major regional trade and investment agreements, such as the Regional Comprehensive Economic Partnership and the European Union-Mercosur Partnership Agreement.

Supporting the energy transition

Promoting energy diversification, with renewables rising as a share of the energy mix, is key to addressing environmental challenges while strengthening the global economy's resilience to future energy shocks. A more diversified energy mix can enhance economic stability, and countries should adopt a tailored approach that helps address immediate energy constraints while balancing longer-term structural requirements. In particular, diversification can reduce exposure to energy price fluctuations, reinforce energy independence, and enhance resilience to growing environmental risks (IMF 2026a). As a key pillar of the energy transition, global clean energy investment has increased significantly, surpassing investment in fossil fuels over the last decade and reaching an estimated $2.2 trillion last year, led by investments in renewable power as well as energy efficiency and end-use electrification. Nearly 70 percent of the increased spending on clean energy over the past five years has been from net-fossil-fuel importers seeking to strengthen energy security (IEA 2025).

Nevertheless, the pace of clean energy investment growth has slowed, from a peak of 17 percent in 2022 to an estimated 6 percent in 2025 (figure 1.11.B). Higher borrowing costs and inflationary pressures in recent years, infrastructure bottlenecks in connecting renewable energy projects to grids, and policy shifts have contributed to this slowdown (IEA 2026). Moreover, clean energy invest-

FIGURE 1.11 Global policy challenges

Amid heightened trade barriers and geopolitical strains, regional trade agreements (RTAs) have emerged as key complements to the global rules-based system The share of global trade within these agreements increased from about 40 percent in 1990 to more than 60 percent by 2025. Meanwhile, accelerating the energy transition is key to addressing environmental and energy security challenges. Although clean energy investment growth experienced a marked increase after the pandemic—especially investment in renewable power as well as energy efficiency and electrification—the pace of growth has slowed in recent years.

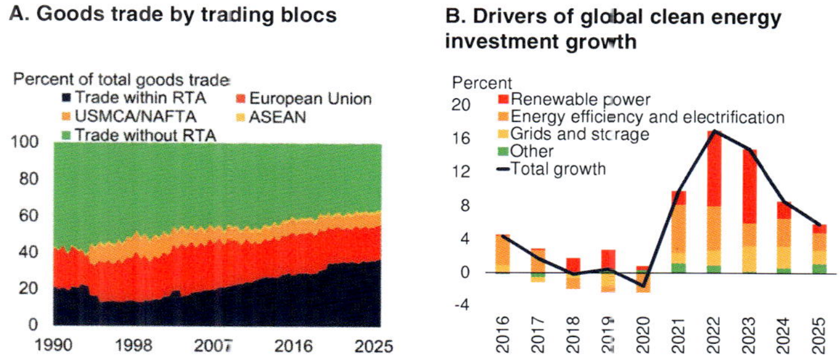

Sources: Egger and Larch (2008); International Energy Agency; IMF International Merchandise Trade Statistics (IMTS); World Bank.

Note: ASEAN = Association of Southeast Asian Nations; NAFTA = North American Free Trade Agreement; RTA = regional trade agreement; USMCA = United States–Mexico–Canada Agreement.

A. Panel shows the shares of nominal trade among countries that are members of different RTA blocs and among country pairs without trade agreements ("Trade without RTA"). "Trade within RTA" refers to trade within RTAs other than the European Union, USMCA/NAFTA, and ASEAN. Last observation is 2025Q4.

B. Line shows global investment growth in clean energy. Bars show the contributions to growth of clean energy subcomponents. "Other" includes low-emission fuels and nuclear and other clean power. 2025 values are estimated.

ment remains unevenly distributed. While some large EMDEs have made significant progress in recent years, including China, which accounts for almost one-third of the global clean energy investment share, smaller EMDEs—especially those in SSA—face challenges in mobilizing capital for clean energy infrastructure. The conflict in the Middle East reinforces the urgency to diversify energy sources.

The global policy community can support the transition by expanding development finance and improving access to affordable capital, particularly in EMDEs where high upfront costs and financing constraints remain major barriers (World Bank 2023). This includes scaling up concessional financing, strengthening domestic financial systems, and supporting the development of energy infrastructure such as grids and storage to facilitate the effective integration of renewable capacity. International organizations can also help mobilize private capital by reducing investment risk, including through mechanisms such as blended finance.

EMDE monetary and financial policy challenges

EMDE central banks face a difficult balancing act as they assess the conflict's implications for commodity and financial markets, inflation, and growth, especially given the rising share of EMDEs with above-target inflation (figure 1.12.A). Many will need to balance support for economic activity and tolerance for higher headline inflation against the risk of a de-anchoring of inflation expectations, as excessive easing could erode credibility. In EMDEs facing currency depreciation pressures, these trade-offs can be compounded by the risk of imported inflation. Clear communication of central banks' risk management approach and contingent policy responses can support policy transmission and limit disruptive movements in interest rate risk premiums (Cieslak, Hansen, and Pang 2025).

Central banks will also need to monitor the uncertain implications of the ongoing AI expansion for inflation and monetary policy (figure 1.12.B). In the near term, AI-driven investment is expected to support activity in economies where rapid adoption is concentrated. Investment in AI is boosting demand for semiconductors, energy, and other key inputs, supporting exports in various EMDEs while adding to broader cost pressures. Over the medium term, AI-related productivity gains may exert downward pressures on prices in some EMDEs as adoption becomes more widespread. Uneven AI adoption across countries could generate divergent productivity dynamics, terms-of-trade shocks, and headwinds for EMDEs that export business services. These effects will need to be incorporated into central bank projections and risk assessments for inflation, economic activity, and labor markets.

Recent financial market volatility underscores the need for prudential authorities to remain attentive to financial stability risks from sharp asset repricing or abrupt shifts in risk appetite. Heightened uncertainty and geopolitical stress could trigger capital outflows and exert pressure on EMDE currencies, underscoring the importance of adequate foreign reserves buffers (Rodnyansky, Timmer, and Yago 2026). This warrants close vigilance, underpinned by sound prudential standards and robust supervision of financial institutions (including nonbanks) to minimize the impact of adverse shocks, sovereign-bank nexus risks, as well as AI-related cybersecurity risks to financial systems.

EMDE fiscal policy challenges

The conflict in the Middle East is adding to fiscal pressures in EMDEs, particularly in energy importers, as higher energy prices prompt fiscal support measures and tighter monetary conditions raise debt-servicing costs. In some MNA economies, repairing damaged infrastructure and sustaining military defense systems are adding further strain to public finances (World Bank 2026f). Fiscal deficits in EMDEs are expected to widen in 2026, especially among energy importers, where median deficits are projected to rise to 3.5 percent of GDP before easing only modestly thereafter (figure 1.12.C). Against this backdrop, in EMDEs excluding China, government debt as a ratio of GDP is projected to continue rising. Higher debt-service burdens are increasingly diverting resources away from infrastructure, public services, and other development priorities needed to support private sector growth and job creation. When debt levels are high, borrowing costs tend to rise disproportionately, having the potential to push debt-service costs above the returns to public investment and underscoring the urgent need to mobilize private investment (figure 1.12.D; chapter 3).

LICs faced rising debt vulnerabilities even before the conflict, as debt had shifted toward greater reliance on non-concessional and short-term borrowing. Interest payments on total public debt in LICs have more than doubled over the past decade (IMF and World Bank 2025). Refinancing risks are also rising, with roughly half of LICs' outstanding sovereign bonds scheduled to mature by 2028 (OECD 2026b).

Rebuilding fiscal space and catalyzing private investment and job creation require stronger domestic revenue mobilization and more effective public spending. Broadening the tax base, strengthening tax administration, reducing exemptions, and selectively increasing tax rates can help raise government revenues (IMF and World Bank 2024a). This is particularly relevant for commodity-exporting EMDEs, especially energy exporters, where reliance on resource revenues has contributed to fiscal procyclicality and heightened debt vulnerabilities following adverse commodity price shocks (figure 1.12.E; chapter 4). Reducing informality and supporting formal job creation can also expand the tax base, while selective excise taxes on products with adverse health impacts could raise additional revenues and help reduce future health-related fiscal pressures. On the expenditure side, improving the efficiency of government services, consolidating spending, and replacing broad-based subsidies with better-targeted support for vulnerable populations can free up fiscal resources.

Institutional reforms can further strengthen fiscal credibility and sustainability. Medium-term budget frameworks, fiscal rules, and independent fiscal councils can help anchor fiscal policy and lower debt-servicing costs. Many commodity exporters have adopted a combination of fiscal

FIGURE 1.12 EMDE monetary and fiscal policy challenges

EMDE central banks face a delicate policy trade-off as energy price pressures mount and the share of economies with above-target inflation rises. Uncertainty about the AI boom's impact on inflation adds further complications. Recent geopolitical tensions are compounding fiscal pressures across EMDEs. Fiscal deficits are expected to widen further, with the increase driven by high debt-servicing costs. Rising EMDE government debt levels may push up interest rates, crowding out resources for public investment and broader development priorities. Boosting domestic revenue mobilization is a key priority, particularly in energy exporters. Many commodity exporters use a combination of fiscal rules, SWFs, and fiscal councils to manage revenue volatility.

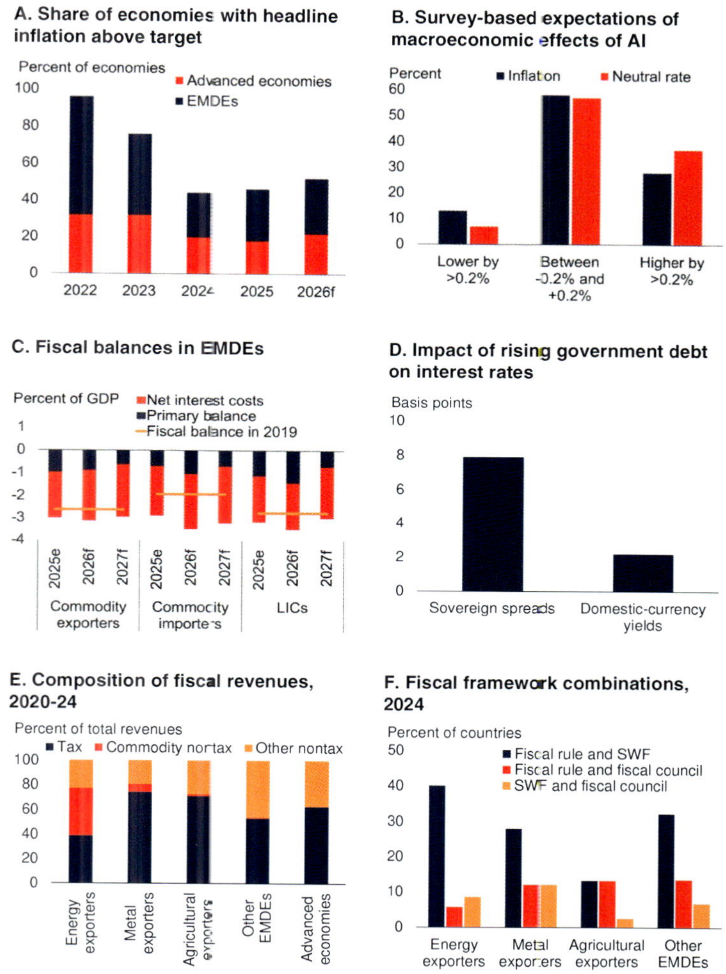

Sources: Alonso et al. (2025); Consensus Economics; Financial Times-Chicago Booth survey; Global SWF (database); Haver Analytics; International Monetary Fund (IMF); World Bank; Zhang (2025).

Note: e = estimate; f = forecast. AI = artificial intelligence; EMDEs = emerging market and developing economies; LICs = low-income countries; SWF = sovereign wealth fund.

A. Bars show the share of economies with headline inflation above target, based on average monthly year-on-year inflation. 2026 data are from May 2026 Consensus Economics surveys. Sample includes 16 advanced economies and 34 EMDEs.

B. Bars show the share of responses to the Financial Times-Chicago Booth survey on the likely effects of the AI boom on Personal Consumption Expenditure (PCE) inflation and the neutral real interest rate over the next two years. Numbers may not sum to 100 because of rounding.

C. Median fiscal balance for up to 152 EMDEs, by country group. Horizontal lines represent the pre-pandemic (2019) fiscal balance. Data are from the IMF's *World Economic Outlook* (April 2026).

D. Panel shows the estimated effect on interest rates of a one-percentage-point rise in the government debt-to-GDP ratio, based on a linear panel data regression.

E. Sample includes 90 commodity-exporting EMDEs (34 for energy, 22 for metals, and 34 for agriculture), 58 other EMDEs, and 38 advanced economies. Commodity nontax revenues include direct revenue from extractive activities. Other nontax revenues include social contributions, grants, and other miscellaneous types of revenue.

F. Sample of EMDEs includes 35 energy exporters, 24 metal exporters, 35 agricultural exporters, and 59 other EMDEs.

rules, sovereign wealth funds, and fiscal councils to manage the complex fiscal challenges stemming from commodity revenue volatility (figure 1.12.F). Strengthening debt management, including extending debt maturities and improving debt transparency, can also help mitigate rollover risks and safeguard fiscal sustainability (World Bank 2025b).

Because these efforts take time to yield results, they will need to be complemented by concessional financing and continued progress in debt restructuring frameworks, including through the G20 Common Framework for countries in or at high risk of debt distress (IMF 2025, 2026b; IMF, World Bank, and G20 Presidency 2026). In some cases, debt-for-development swaps could create fiscal space for growth-enhancing investments while supporting debt sustainability (IMF and World Bank 2024b).[4] In the near term, fiscal responses to elevated energy costs stemming from the conflict should be temporary and well-targeted to vulnerable households and viable firms.

EMDE structural policy challenges

Creating jobs amid evolving AI impacts and subdued private investment

EMDEs face a historic jobs challenge, with an estimated 1.2 billion young people entering working age over the next decade. At the same time, the labor market effects of generative AI technologies are still unfolding, posing both risks and opportunities of varying degrees depending on whether AI complements or substitutes for workers. Subdued private investment in many EMDEs further constrains firm expansion and the creation of new businesses, and thus job creation capacity.

Most EMDEs currently have a smaller share of jobs potentially affected by generative AI than high-income countries, mainly reflecting differences in industrial structure (Cazzaniga et al. 2024; figure 1.13.A). This lowers the risk of labor dislocations in EMDEs, but it could also slow the diffusion of AI that could support growth and employment. Countries with substantial business services export sectors risk larger indirect disruptions if these tasks are handled by AI. Meanwhile, global AI-related demand could lift employment in some EMDEs through supply-chain linkages, depending on the labor intensity of the affected sectors. As such, the net impact of AI on tradable goods and services sectors across EMDEs is likely to be uneven. A widening digital divide risks constraining growth and job creation in some EMDEs, particularly LICs that already lag in exports of digitally deliverable services—the fastest-growing segment of global trade in middle-income EMDEs over the last decade (figure 1.13.B).

Tackling the jobs challenge requires progress along three mutually reinforcing pillars: (1) investing in physical and human capital; (2) fostering a business-friendly regulatory and legal environment; and (3) mobilizing private capital and investment. This includes scaling up investment in reliable electricity, transport, and digital connectivity, including broadband, mobile networks, and digital public infrastructure (World Bank 2025a; 2025c). Such investments would lower production costs, improve reliability, and facilitate firms' access to suppliers and markets, thereby supporting firm formation and growth. Better infrastructure can also crowd in private investment by improving returns and reducing risks for firms, generating further employment.

EMDEs will equally need to invest in digital skills and broader reskilling programs, particularly for women, youth, and marginalized groups facing affordability and physical infrastructure constraints, restrictive social norms, and low digital literacy (World Bank 2025a, 2025d). Such investments also support broader private sector development, enabling job creation beyond AI-intensive sectors. Small AI solutions that are task-specific applications on local devices can be complementary to EMDE workers and can support growth in job-rich sectors, such as agribusiness, healthcare, tourism, value-added manufacturing, and infrastructure and energy (Dixit and Gill 2023; World Bank 2026e).

[4] Debt-for-development swaps replace existing sovereign debt with arrangements linked to spending commitments for specific development goals, such as nature conservation, climate action, education, or nutrition. For details, refer to the Global Hub on Debt for Development Swaps.

EMDEs also need to strengthen regulatory and institutional frameworks. Greater policy clarity and more predictable regulation can reduce uncertainty, fostering firm entry and encouraging private investment, with substantial improvements in institutional quality being associated with a significant and large boost to foreign direct investment inflows. More broadly, a strong business climate—underpinned by appropriate land use policies, effective contract enforcement, and sound macroeconomic policies—supports sustained private sector expansion and employment growth. Improving access to finance, including local-currency financing, through deeper and more efficient capital markets, particularly for small and medium-sized enterprises, can support private investment, ease constraints on firm entry and expansion, and in turn drive growth and employment at scale.

Bolstering energy security

Energy security has become an urgent priority in the context of geopolitical conflicts in recent years, including the conflict in the Middle East. Many energy-importing EMDEs remain structurally vulnerable on account of heavy reliance on a narrow set of energy sources and supply routes, exposing these economies to supply disruptions and price volatility that feed into inflation, current account pressures, and tighter fiscal space. Prolonged price surges can also weigh on productivity, particularly in energy-intensive sectors where energy and capital are strong complements (André et al. 2023).

Diversifying the domestic energy mix and improving energy efficiency can help dampen exposure to global energy price shocks. Robust legal and regulatory frameworks, particularly around land use for renewable generation and transmission infrastructure, as well as well-structured risk mitigation instruments and public-private partnerships can reduce private sector investment costs and spur investment in modernizing grid infrastructure (World Bank 2024d).

FIGURE 1.13 EMDE structural policy challenges

About 1.2 billion youth will reach working age in EMDEs over the next decade, alongside the direct and indirect effects of AI technologies that are still emerging and pose both risks and opportunities for EMDE labor markets to varying degrees. The share of jobs potentially exposed to AI declines with country income levels, which may insulate some EMDEs from large labor market dislocations but increases the risks of slower pro-growth diffusion of AI and a widening digital divide. The most vulnerable EMDEs already trail well behind in exports of digitally deliverable services, which has been the fastest growing segment of global trade over the past decade.

A. Share of jobs facing different degrees of exposure to generative AI

B. Average annual growth of exports, 2015–24

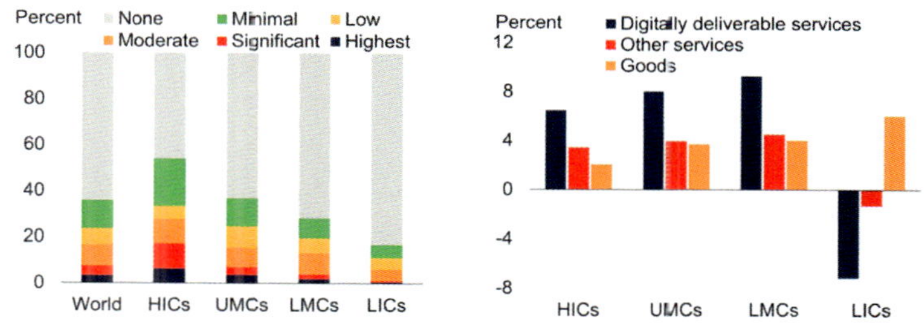

Sources: Gmyrek et al. (2025); UNCTAD; World Bank.

Note: AI = artificial intelligence; EMDEs = emerging market and developing economies; HICs = high-income countries; LICs = low-income countries; LMCs = lower-middle income countries; UMCs = upper-middle income countries.

A. Panel shows occupational exposure to generative AI by share of employment and country income group. The "minimal" ("highest") level of exposure to AI refers to an occupation with a greater (lower) share of tasks that have low (highest) variability. "None" refers to occupations where AI currently has no observable potential to automate tasks.

B. Panel shows the compound annual growth rates of digitally deliverable services exports, other services exports, and goods exports.

Competitive procurement mechanisms, such as auctions and tenders, can mobilize private financing for renewables at scale and in a cost-efficient manner, though careful design is needed to avoid delays or undersubscription (del Río and Kiefer 2023). Phasing out fossil fuel subsidies and implementing taxes for carbon-intensive practices can further incentivize investment in cleaner and more energy-efficient technologies. Decentralized renewable energy solutions, such as standalone off-grid solar solutions or small-scale grid-connected distributed generation, offer cost-effective means to improve energy access in economies with limited grid capacity and in remote areas (Diallo and Moussa 2020; IEA et al. 2024; Wagner et al. 2021; World Bank 2024e).

TABLE 1.2 Emerging market and developing economies[1]

Commodity exporters[2]		Commodity importers[3]	
Algeria*	Lao PDR	Afghanistan	Somalia, Fed. Rep.
Angola*	Liberia	Albania	Sri Lanka
Argentina	Libya*	Antigua and Barbuda	St. Kitts and Nevis
Armenia	Madagascar	Bahamas, The	St. Lucia
Azerbaijan*	Malawi	Bangladesh	St. Vincent and the Grenadines
Bahrain*	Mali	Barbados	Syrian Arab Republic
Belize	Mauritania	Belarus	Thailand
Benin	Mongolia	Bosnia and Herzegovina	Tonga
Bhutan*	Mozambique	Cambodia	Tunisia
Bolivia*	Myanmar*	China	Türkiye
Botswana	Namibia	Djibouti	Tuvalu
Brazil	Nicaragua	Dominica	Vanuatu
Burkina Faso	Niger	Dominican Republic	Viet Nam
Burundi	Nigeria*	Egypt, Arab Rep.	
Cabo Verde	Oman*	El Salvador	
Cameroon*	Papua New Guinea	Eswatini	
Central African Republic	Paraguay	Georgia	
Chad*	Peru	Grenada	
Chile	Qatar*	Haiti	
Colombia*	Russian Federation*	Hungary	
Comoros	Rwanda	India	
Congo, Dem. Rep.	São Tomé and Príncipe	Jamaica	
Congo, Rep.*	Saudi Arabia*	Jordan	
Costa Rica	Senegal	Kiribati	
Côte d'Ivoire	Seychelles	Lebanon	
Ecuador*	Sierra Leone	Lesotho	
Equatorial Guinea*	Solomon Islands	Malaysia	
Eritrea	South Africa	Maldives	
Ethiopia	South Sudan*	Marshall Islands	
Fiji	Sudan	Mauritius	
Gabon*	Suriname	Mexico	
Gambia, The	Tajikistan	Micronesia, Fed. Sts.	
Ghana*	Tanzania	Moldova	
Guatemala	Timor-Leste*	Montenegro	
Guinea	Togo	Morocco	
Guinea-Bissau	Trinidad and Tobago*	Nauru	
Guyana*	Turkmenistan*	Nepal	
Honduras	Uganda	North Macedonia	
Indonesia*	Ukraine	Pakistan	
Iran, Islamic Rep.*	United Arab Emirates*	Palau	
Iraq*	Uruguay	Panama	
Kazakhstan*	Uzbekistan	Philippines	
Kenya	West Bank and Gaza	Poland	
Kosovo	Yemen, Rep.*	Romania	
Kuwait*	Zambia	Samoa	
Kyrgyz Republic	Zimbabwe	Serbia	

* Energy exporters.

1. Emerging market and developing economies (EMDEs) include all those that are not classified as advanced economies and for which growth data are published for this report. Dependent territories are excluded. Advanced economies include Australia; Austria; Belgium; Bulgaria; Canada; Croatia; Cyprus; Czechia; Denmark; Estonia; Finland; France; Germany; Greece; Hong Kong SAR, China; Iceland; Ireland; Israel; Italy; Japan; the Republic of Korea; Latvia; Lithuania; Luxembourg; Malta; the Netherlands; New Zealand; Norway; Portugal; Singapore; the Slovak Republic; Slovenia; Spain; Sweden; Switzerland; the United Kingdom; and the United States.

2. An economy is defined as commodity exporter when, on average in 2017-19, either (1) total commodities exports accounted for 30 percent or more of total exports or (2) exports of any single commodity accounted for 20 percent or more of total exports. Economies for which these thresholds were met as a result of re-exports were excluded. When data were not available, judgment was used. This taxonomy results in the classification of some well-diversified economies as importers, even if they are exporters of certain commodities (for example, Mexico).

3. Commodity importers are EMDEs not classified as commodity exporters.

References

Acemoglu, D. 2025. "The Simple Macroeconomics of AI." *Economic Policy* 40 (121): 13–58.

Acemoglu, D., S. Johnson, and J. A. Robinson. 2001. "The Colonial Origins of Comparative Development: An Empirical Investigation." *American Economic Review* 91 (5): 1369–401.

Adarov, A., ed. 2025. *Accelerating Investment: Challenges and Policies.* Washington, DC: World Bank.

Adarov, A., and H. Pallan. 2025. "Foreign Direct Investment in Retreat: Policies to Turn the Tide." In *Accelerating Investment: Challenges and Policies,* edited by A. Adarov. Washington, DC: World Bank.

Adarov, A., and K. Stamm. 2025. "Investment Trends, Structures, and Drivers in EMDEs." In *Accelerating Investment: Challenges and Policies,* edited by A. Adarov, 53–93. Washington, DC: World Bank.

Alesina, A., D. Furceri, J. D. Ostry, C. Papageorgiou, and D. P. Quinn. 2024. "Structural Reforms and Elections: Evidence from a World-Wide New Dataset." *Journal of the European Economic Association* 22 (4): 1936-80.

André, C., H. Costa, L. Demmou, and G. Franco. 2023. "Rising Energy Prices and Productivity: Short-Run Pain, Long-Term Gain?" OECD Economics Department Working Papers 1755, Organisation for Economic Co-operation and Development, Paris.

Aghion, P., B. F. Jones, and C. I. Jones. 2017. "Artificial Intelligence and Economic Growth." NBER Working Paper 23928, National Bureau of Economic Research, Cambridge, MA.

Aghion, P., and S. Bunel. 2024. "AI and Growth: Where Do We Stand?" Mimeo. https://www.frbsf.org/wp-content/uploads/AI-and-Growth-Aghion-Bunel.pdf.

World Food Security Outlook (database). Accessed May 28, 2026. World Bank. https://microdata.worldbank.org/catalog/6103.

Appel, R., M. Massenkoff, P. McCrory, M. McCain, R. Heller, T. Neylon, and A. Tamkin. 2026. "The Anthropic Economic Index Report: Economic Primitives." Anthropic.

Arslanalp, S., R. Koepke, and J. Verschuur. 2021. "Tracking Trade from Space: An Application to Pacific Island Countries." IMF Working Paper 21/225, International Monetary Fund, Washington, DC.

Autor, D., C. Chin, A. Salomons, and B. Seegmiller. 2024. "New Frontiers: The Origins and Content of New Work, 1940-2018." *Quarterly Journal of Economics* 139 (3): 1399–465.

Baily, M., E. Brynjolfsson, and A. Korinek. 2023. *Machines of Mind: The Case for an AI-Powered Productivity Boom.* Washington, DC: Brookings Institution.

Baker, J., N. Choi, M. Gonzalez-Schuler, and D. Sivaev. 2023. "Cities, Jobs, and Local Economic Development: A Guidance Note for Task Teams." Guidance Note, World Bank, Washington, DC.

Bettin, G., A. Jallow, and A. Zazzaro. 2024. "Responding to Natural Disasters: What Do Monthly Remittance Data Tell Us?" *Journal of Development Economics* 174 (May): 103413.

Brancaccio, G., M. Kalouptsidi, and T. Papageorgiou. 2023. "The Impact of Oil Prices on World Trade." *Review of International Economics* 31 (2): 444–63.

Briggs, J., and D. Kodnani. 2023. "The Potentially Large Effects of Artificial Intelligence on Economic Growth." *Goldman Sachs Global Economics Analyst,* March 26.

Brynjolfsson, E., D. Li, and L. Raymond. 2025. "Generative AI at Work." *Quarterly Journal of Economics* 140 (2): 889–942.

Caldara, D., and M. Iacoviello. 2022. "Measuring Geopolitical Risk." *American Economic Review* 112 (4): 1194–225.

Carvajal, A., and T. Didier. 2024. *Boosting SME Finance for Growth: The Case for More Effective Support Policies.* Washington, DC: World Bank.

Cavallo, A., P. Llamas, and F. Vazquez. 2025. "Tracking the Short-Run Price Impact of U.S. Tariffs." NBER Working Paper 34496, National Bureau of Economic Research, Cambridge, MA

Cavallo, E. A., O. Becerra, and L. Acevedo. 2022. "The Impact of Natural Disasters on Economic Growth." In Handbook on the Economics of Disasters, edited by M. Skidmore. Cheltenham, U.K.: Edward Elgar Publishing.

Cazzaniga, M., F. Jaumotte, L. Li, G. Melina, A. J. Panton, C. Pizzinelli, E. J. Rockall, et al. 2024. "Gen-AI: Artificial Intelligence and the Future of Work." IMF Staff Discussion Note 24/001, International Monetary Fund, Washington, DC.

Cerutti, E. M., A. I. Garcia Pascual, Y. Kido, L. Li, G. Melina, M. Mendes Tavares, and P. Wingender. 2025. "The Global Impact of AI: Mind the Gap." IMF Working Paper 25/76, International Monetary Fund, Washington, DC.

Chari, A., P. Henry, and P. Mauro. 2025. "Financial Returns to Equity Investments in Infrastructure in Emerging Markets and Developing Economies." Research Note, International Finance Corporation, Washington, DC.

Chari, A., P. Henry, and P. Picardo. 2025. "The Social Rate of Return on Road Infrastructure Investments." NBER Working Paper 34501, National Bureau of Economic Research, Cambridge, MA.

Chinn, M., and H. Ito. 2008. "A New Measure of Financial Openness." *Journal of Comparative Policy Analysis* 10 (3): 309-22.

Chrimes, T., M. Lebrand, and J. Mawejje. 2025. "Reinvigorating Private Investment: Policy Options." In *Accelerating Investment: Challenges and Policies,* edited by A. Adarov. Washington, DC: World Bank.

Chrimes, T., M. A. Kose, and K. Stamm. 2026. "The Global Jobs Challenge." *World Bank Group Brief.* World Bank, Washington, DC.

Cieslak, A., S. Hansen, and H. Pang. 2025. "Risk Management in Monetary Policy: A Review with Asset Pricing Implications." SSRN Working Paper 5718588.

Cull, R., I. Gill, A. Pedraza, C. Ruiz-Ortega, and F. Zeni. 2024. "Mobilizing Private Capital for the Sustainable Development Goals." Policy Research Working Paper 10838, World Bank, Washington, DC.

Cunningham, T. 2025. "Forecasts of AI & Economic Growth." https://tecunningham.github.io/posts/2025-10-19-forecasts-of-AI-growth.html.

CRED (Centre for Research on the Epidemiology of Disasters) and UNDRR (United Nations Office for Disaster Risk Reduction). 2020. *Human Cost of Disasters: An Overview of the Last 20 Years 2000-2019.* United Nations Office for Disaster Risk Reduction.

De Haan, J., K. Stamm, and S. Yu. 2025. "The Magic of Investment Accelerations." In *Accelerating Investment: Challenges and Policies,* edited by A. Adarov. Washington, DC: World Bank.

da Silva, A. F., R. V. R. Anderle, G. Barreix Sibils, L. de Oliveira Ferreira de Sales, D. Pena, C. Monti, et al. 2026. "Impact of Two Decades of Humanitarian and Development Assistance and the Projected Mortality Consequences of Current Defunding to 2030: Retrospective Evaluation and Forecasting Analysis." *Lancet Global Health* 14 (5): E690–E701.

del Río, P., and C. P. Kiefer. 2023. "Academic Research on Renewable Electricity Auctions: Taking Stock and Looking Forward." *Energy Policy* 173 (February): 113305.

Development Committee. 2026. *Creating the Enabling Environment for More and Better-Paid Jobs.* Washington, DC: World Bank.

Diallo, A., and R. K. Moussa. 2020. "The Effects of Solar Home System on Welfare in Off-Grid Areas: Evidence from Côte d'Ivoire." *Energy* 194 (March): 116835.

Dieppe, A., ed. 2021. *Global Productivity: Trends, Drivers, and Policies.* Washington, DC: World Bank.

Dixit, S., and I. Gill. 2023. "AI, the New Wingman of Development." World Bank, Washington, DC.

Egger, P., and M. Larch. 2008. "Interdependent Preferential Trade Agreement Memberships: An Empirical Analysis." *Journal of International Economics* 76 (2): 384–99.

Fabre, A., and S. Straub. 2023. "The Impact of Public-Private Partnerships (PPPs) in Infrastructure, Health, and Education." *Journal of Economic Literature* 61 (3): 655–715.

Feenstra, R., R. Inklaar, and M. Timmer. 2015. "The Next Generation of the Penn World Table." *American Economic Review* 105 (10): 3150–82.

Filippucci, F., P. Gal, K. Laengle, M. Schief, and F. Unsal. 2025. "Opportunities and Risks of Artificial Intelligence for Productivity." Organisation for Economic Co-operation and Development, Paris.

Gardner, C., and P. Henry. 2023. "The Global Infrastructure Gap: Potential, Perils, and a Framework for Distinction." *Journal of Economic Literature* 61 (4): 1318–58.

Gmyrek, P., J. Berg, K. Kamiński, F. Konopczyński, A. Ładna, B. Nafradi, K. Rosłaniec, and M. Troszyński. 2025. "Generative AI and Jobs: A Refined Global Index of Occupational Exposure," ILO Working Paper 140, International Labour Organization, Geneva.

IEA (International Energy Agency). 2025. *World Energy Investment 2025.* Paris: International Energy Agency.

IEA (International Energy Agency). 2026. *World Energy Investment 2026.* Paris: International Energy Agency.

IEA, IRENA, UNSD, World Bank, and WHO. 2024. *Tracking SDG 7: The Energy Progress Report.* Washington, DC: World Bank.

IFC (International Finance Corporation). 2021. *Supply Chain Finance by Development Banks and Public Entities.* Washington, DC: World Bank Group.

Imas, A. 2026. "What Is the Impact of AI on Productivity? Reconciling the Micro and the Macro Evidence." *Ghosts of Electricity* (Substack). https://aleximas.substack.com/p/what-is-the-impact-of-ai-on-productivity.

IMF (International Monetary Fund). 2021. "Investment and Capital Stock Dataset." Macroeconomic and Financial Data. International Monetary Fund.

IMF (International Monetary Fund). 2024. "Navigating the Tides of Commodity Prices." *External Sector Report 2024.* International Monetary Fund, Washington, DC.

IMF (International Monetary Fund). 2025. "Debt Vulnerabilities and Financing Challenges in Emerging Markets and Developing Economies: An Overview of Key Data." International Monetary Fund, Washington, DC.

IMF (International Monetary Fund). 2026a. *World Economic Outlook: Global Economy in the Shadow of War.* April. Washington, DC: International Monetary Fund.

IMF (International Monetary Fund). 2026b. "Global Prospects and Policies." In *World Economic Outlook: Global Economy in the Shadow of War.* April. Washington, DC: International Monetary Fund.

IMF (International Monetary Fund) and World Bank. 2024a. *Stepping Up Domestic Resource Mobilization: A New Joint Initiative from the IMF and the World Bank.* Washington, DC: International Monetary Fund.

IMF (International Monetary Fund) and World Bank. 2024b. *Debt for Development Swaps: An Approach Framework.* Washington, DC: International Monetary Fund.

IMF (International Monetary Fund) and World Bank. 2025. "Debt Vulnerabilities in Low-Income Countries: Recent Developments and Trends." International Monetary Fund, Washington, DC.

IMF (International Monetary Fund), World Bank, and G20 Presidency. 2026. *Global Sovereign Debt Roundtable: 6th Co-Chairs Progress Re-*

port. Washington, DC: International Monetary Fund.

International Country Risk Guide (database). PRS Group. Accessed May 28, 2025. https://www.prsgroup.com/explore-our-products/icrg/.

Investment and Capital Stock Dataset (database). International Monetary Fund. Accessed May 28, 2025. https://data.imf.org/Datasets/ICSD.

ITU DataHub (database). International Telecommunication Union. Accessed May 28, 2025. https://datahub.itu.int/.

Kessides, I. 2005. "Infrastructure Privatization and Regulation: Promises and Perils." *World Bank Research Observer* 20 (1): 81–108.

Kim, S., and C. Z. Qiang. 2025. "Small AI, Big Impact: Harnessing Artificial Intelligence for Development." *Voices* (blog), September 10. https://blogs.worldbank.org/en/voices/small-ai-big-impact-harnessing-artificial-intelligence-for-development.

Kolko, J. 2026. "Research on AI and the Labor Market Is Still in the First Inning." Brookings Institution, March 10. https://brookings.edu/articles/research-on-ai-and-the-labor-market-is-still-in-the-first-inning/.

Kose, A. M., and F. Ohnsorge, eds. 2024. *Falling Long-Term Growth Prospects: Trends, Expectations, and Policies.* Washington, DC: World Bank.

Kose, A. M., S. Kurlat, F. Ohnsorge, and N. Sugawara. 2022. "A Cross-Country Database of Fiscal Space." *Journal of International Money and Finance* 128: 102682.

Lebrand, M., G. Vasishtha, and H. Yilmazkuday. 2024. "Energy Price Shocks and Current Account Balances: Evidence from Emerging Market and Developing Economies." *Energy Economics* 129 (January): 107201.

Mahler, D., U. Serajuddin, D. Wadwha, and N. Yonzan. 2026. "The World Is Developing at Its Slowest Pace in 75 Years." Policy Research Working Paper 11350, World Bank, Washington, DC.

Massenkoff, M., and P. McCrory. 2026. "Labor Market Impacts of AI: A New Measure and Early Evidence." Anthropic.

Mawejje, J. 2025. *Fiscal Vulnerabilities in Low-Income Countries: Evolution, Drivers, and Policies.* Washington, DC: World Bank.

Meh, C. A., and S. Schmukler, eds. 2025. *Financing Firm Growth: The Role of Capital Markets in Low- and Middle-Income Countries.* Washington, DC: International Finance Corporation.

Mensah, J. 2024. "Jobs! Electricity Shortages and Unemployment in Africa." *Journal of Development Economics* 167 (March): 103231.

Mensah, J., and N. Traore. 2024. "Infrastructure Quality and FDI Inflows: Evidence from the Arrival of High-Speed Internet in Africa." *World Bank Economic Review* 38 (1): 1–23.

Mulabdic, A., and Y. Yotov. 2025. "Geopolitical Risks and Trade." Policy Research Working Paper 11219, World Bank, Washington, DC.

Nayyar, G., R. Pleninger, D. Vorisek, and S. Yu. 2024. "Digitalization and Inclusive Growth: A Review of the Evidence." Policy Research Working Paper 10941, World Bank, Washington, DC.

Ohnsorge, F., M. Stocker, and M. Y. Some. 2016. "Quantifying Uncertainties in Global Growth Forecasts." Policy Research Working Paper 7770, World Bank, Washington, DC.

OECD (Organisation for Economic Co-operation and Development). 2026a. "International Aid Fell Sharply in 2025, Says OECD." Organisation for Economic Co-operation and Development, Paris.

OECD (Organisation for Economic Co-operation and Development). 2026b. *Global Debt Report 2026: Sustaining Debt Market Resilience Under Growing Pressure.* Organisation for Economic Co-operation and Development, Paris.

Oxford Economics. 2019. "Global Economic Model." Oxford Economics, Oxford, U.K.

Rodnyansky, A., Y. Timmer, and N. Yago. 2026. "Intervening Against the Fed." *Journal of Financial Economics* 179 (May): 104265.

Staiger, R. 2026. "The Value of the WTO: An Economics Viewpoint in Six Instalments." *WTO Blog,* March 9. https://www.wto.org/english/news_e/news26_e/blgrs_09mar26_311_e.htm.

Stamm, K., and S. Yu. 2024. "The Magic of Investment Accelerations." In *Global Economic Prospects*, 97-147. January. Washington, DC: World Bank.

Straub, S., H. He, Y. Li, X. Lyu, J. Steinbuks, E. Vergara Cobos, C. Dann, M. García-Santana, and H. Selod. 2026. *Infrastructure Foundations: From Current Assets to Future Growth.* Washington, DC: World Bank.

United Nations. 2022. *Financing for Sustainable Development Report 2022.* New York: United Nations.

UN World Population Prospects (database). United Nations. Accessed May 28, 2026. https://population.un.org/wpp/.

Von Below, D., and P.-L. Vézina. 2016. "The Trade Consequences of Pricey Oil." *IMF Economic Review* 64 (2): 303-18.

Wagner, N., M. Rieger, A. S. Bedi, J. Vermeulen, and B. A. Demena. 2021. "The Impact of Off-Grid Solar Home Systems in Kenya on Energy Consumption and Expenditures." *Energy Economics* 99 (July): 105314.

WFP (World Food Programme). 2026. "Projected Increase in Acute Food Insecurity due to the Middle East Conflict." World Food Programme, Rome.

World Development Indicators (database). Accessed May 28, 2026. World Bank, Washington, DC.

World Bank. 2023. "Scaling Up to Phase Down: Financing Energy Transition in Developing Countries." World Bank. https://worldbank.org/en/news/press-release/2023/04/20/scaling-up-to-phase-down-financing-energy-transition-in-developing-countries.

World Bank. 2024a. *Digital Progress and Trends Report 2023.* Washington, DC: World Bank.

World Bank. 2024b. *Global Trends in AI Governance: Evolving Country Approaches.* Washington, DC: World Bank.

World Bank. 2024c. *Global Economic Prospects.* June. Washington, DC: World Bank.

World Bank. 2024d. *The Critical Link: Empowering Utilities for the Energy Transition.* Washington, DC: World Bank.

World Bank. 2024e. *Off-Grid Solar Market Trends Report 2024: Outlook.* Washington, DC: World Bank.

World Bank. 2025a. *Digital Progress and Trends Report 2025: Strengthening AI Foundations.* Washington, DC: World Bank.

World Bank. 2025b. *Radical Debt Transparency.* Washington, DC: World Bank.

World Bank. 2025c. *Digital Public Infrastructure and Development: A World Bank Group Approach.* Washington, DC: World Bank.

World Bank. 2025d. *What Works to Advance Women's Digital Literacy? A Review of Good Practices and Programs.* Washington, DC: World Bank.

World Bank. 2026a. *Global Economic Prospects.* January. Washington, DC: World Bank.

World Bank. 2026b. *East Asia and Pacific Economic Update: Industrial Policy in the Digital Age.* April. World Bank.

World Bank. 2026c. *Latin America and Caribbean Economic Update: Revisiting Industrial Policy—Strategic Options for Today.* April. Washington, DC: World Bank.

World Bank. 2026d. *March 2026 Update to the Poverty and Inequality Platform.* Washington, DC: World Bank.

World Bank. 2026e. "Small AI, Big Impact." *World Bank Brief.* https://www.worldbank.org/en/topic/digital/brief/small-ai-big-impact.

World Bank. 2026f. *Middle East, North Africa, Afghanistan & Pakistan Economic Update: Challenges of Conflict and Industrial Policies for Development.* April. Washington, DC: World Bank.

World Bank. Forthcoming. *World Development Report 2026: Decoding AI for Development.* Washington, DC: World Bank.

World Bank Enterprise Surveys (database). World Bank. Accessed May 28, 2025. https://enterprisesurveys.org.

World Food Security Outlook (database). Accessed May 28, 2026. Washington, DC: World Bank. https://microdata.worldbank.org/index.php/catalog/6103.

Zhang, Z. 2025. "Inflation Targets, Bands, and Track Records: A Dataset of Inflation Targeting Countries." *Data in Brief* 61: 111753.

CHAPTER 2

REGIONAL OUTLOOKS

The conflict in the Middle East is affecting emerging market and developing economy (EMDE) regions to varying degrees through commodity prices, trade, inflation, and tighter monetary conditions. The largest effects are occurring in the economies directly impacted by hostilities in that region. However, for all regions, growth in 2026 is now projected to be slower than in 2025 and has been downgraded relative to January for most regions. Outside of the Middle East, the impact on growth and inflation is expected to be larger for net energy importers, particularly those dependent on imports from the Middle East, although the impact may be cushioned by strategic reserves and policy buffers in some cases. As governments take action to mitigate the effects of the conflict, fiscal positions are likely to worsen; moreover, lower-income countries are particularly at risk of rising food insecurity. Constrained fiscal space will put pressure on the ability of EMDEs, especially the most vulnerable, to create jobs. On the assumption that the peak disruptions from the conflict end in July, recoveries are projected across all regions for 2027–28, driven by declining energy prices and the rebound in global trade and activity. Risks to the growth outlook for all EMDE regions are tilted to the downside and include an intensification of the conflict, protracted disruptions in commodity markets, tighter financial conditions, persistently elevated trade policy uncertainty, and severe weather-related shocks.

Recent developments

Growth. Growth was broadly resilient across emerging market and developing economy (EMDE) regions in early 2026 but has become increasingly uneven since the outbreak of the conflict in the Middle East. Activity in much of the Middle East, North Africa, Afghanistan, and Pakistan (MNA) region has been significantly disrupted. Elsewhere, elevated energy prices and heightened uncertainty have weighed on activity in some regions, although some commodity exporters have benefited from higher commodity prices across regions.

In MNA, high-frequency data indicate that conflict-related disruptions in economies directly affected have weighed on growth, with purchasing managers' indexes (PMIs) indicating a decline in private sector activity. Even in other MNA economies, growth has slowed amid rising energy and input costs and logistics disruptions. Growth in other regions has been relatively more robust. In East Asia and Pacific (EAP) and South Asia (SAR), although growth has slowed somewhat, it has been supported by strong exports and resilient consumption (figure 2.1.A). In Europe and Central Asia (ECA), activity has softened this year amid deteriorating confidence, while growth has been uneven across Latin America and the Caribbean (LAC), reflecting divergent monetary policies and commodity exposure. In Sub-Saharan Africa (SSA), after being buoyed in 2025 by higher non-energy commodity prices, growth has remained resilient despite higher energy prices and geopolitical uncertainty.

Inflation and financial indicators. Inflation generally moderated before the conflict but was uneven across regions (figure 2.1.B). Inflation was within or near official target ranges in many economies in EAP and SAR, but was elevated in several economies in ECA, LAC, and MNA. Since the outbreak of the conflict, inflation has picked up in most regions because of the surge in energy prices. Currency depreciations have added to price pressures in many cases, particularly for vulnerable energy importers. Correspondingly, local-currency bond yields remain elevated, reflecting expectations of tighter monetary policy. A few economies in ECA, SSA, and Asia have already raised policy rates in response to conflict-related inflation.

Trade. Despite elevated trade policy uncertainty, international trade has been broadly resilient. Reductions in U.S. import tariffs since 2025 have helped soften the headwinds from higher energy costs and supply disruptions. In MNA, however, conflict-related damages have weighed heavily on trade flows and logistics in some economies. EAP continues to benefit from strong artificial intelligence (AI)-related export demand, while improved trade conditions—including trade agreements with major partners—have supported exports in LAC and SSA.

Note: This chapter was prepared by Gitanjali Kumar, Marie Albert, Francisco Arroyo Marioli, Jiwon Lee, Edoardo Palombo, Shijie Shi, and Naotaka Sugawara.

Outlook

Growth. Growth is forecast to slow across all regions in 2026, largely owing to the fallout from the conflict in the Middle East, the slowdown in trade, and the tightening of monetary conditions (figure 2.1.C). The increase in energy prices arising from the conflict will adversely affect net energy importers, particularly those that source their imports from the Middle East. The impact may be softened for some economies that have strategic reserves and policy buffers. Net energy exporters not involved in the conflict are likely to benefit from higher energy prices, although they will face higher inflationary pressures and slower global growth. Interruptions to the production of oil, gas, and related products, disruptions to shipping, and damage to critical infrastructure in the countries directly affected by hostilities will have adverse indirect effects on trade, activity, and inflation across all regions this year.

Growth is projected to firm in all regions over 2027–28, on the assumption that peak disruptions from the conflict end in July with a gradual recovery in shipping volumes by end-2026. The projected recoveries are mainly shaped by the assumed post-conflict decline in energy prices and the rebound in global trade. In EAP, SAR, and SSA, solid growth of investment and exports, as well as structural reforms in some economies, are expected to contribute positively to the outlook. Elevated geopolitical and trade policy uncertainty, however, continue to act as a drag. SAR is expected to remain the strongest-performing EMDE region in 2026 and over the forecast horizon, anchored by India's robust growth.

In 2026, the worst-affected region is MNA, where a number of economies have been directly involved in the conflict. In addition to the human toll, damage to critical energy infrastructure and disruptions to trade and investment will contribute to a sharp slowdown in growth in the region from 3.9 percent in 2025 to 1.6 percent in 2026—a downward revision of 2.7 percentage points from January. Among other regions, those dominated by energy importers that rely heavily on imports of oil and gas from the Middle East will be most affected. This is particularly the case for economies in EAP and SAR with limited buffers. By contrast, economies in LAC and SSA import relatively little fuel from MNA and are therefore likely to be less affected (figure 2.1.D; World Bank 2026a). Within EAP, however, China is relatively insulated because of its large petroleum reserves and high share of renewable energy. In ECA, growth is expected to slow not only in energy importers but also in the Russian Federation, the region's largest energy exporter, as higher oil revenues are set to be directed toward a reduction of the fiscal deficit. The region is facing another large energy shock after being severely impacted by Russia's invasion of Ukraine.

Inflation and monetary policy. Similarly, the pass-through of higher energy prices to inflation will differ across regions depending on the food- and energy-intensity of consumption baskets, initial levels of inflation and inflation expectations, and domestic price caps and subsidies. Higher fuel, food, and fertilizer costs are envisaged to add significantly to headline consumer inflation in the near term in MNA and SAR and keep food inflation elevated in ECA and LAC (figure 2.1.E). In contrast, inflationary pressures in EAP are expected to remain relatively contained, supported partly by low initial inflation, particularly in China. Central banks across regions are likely to maintain tighter policy stances and may choose to either look through or react to short-term inflationary pressures, depending on the proximity of current inflation to its target and the risk of de-anchoring inflation expectations. Monetary policy is likely to be particularly restrictive in LAC, where inflation is structurally higher.

Tighter domestic monetary conditions and higher borrowing costs are expected to weigh on growth, particularly for energy-importing EMDEs in EAP, SAR, and SSA. In addition, tighter monetary policy in advanced economies could generate capital outflows, especially from vulnerable EMDEs in EAP, SAR, and MNA, putting additional pressure on currencies, inflation, and borrowing costs, and further weighing on investment and growth.

Trade. Trade prospects for 2026 are being shaped by higher energy prices and shipping disruptions, lower U.S. import tariffs, progress on trade agreements, and continuing elevated trade policy uncertainty. Trade in MNA will continue to be severely disrupted by infrastructure damage and the cessation of flows through key waterways this year. In EAP, export growth is projected to moderate owing to slowing global demand and the easing of front-loading ahead of U.S. tariff increases, partially offset by continued strong demand for electronics and semiconductors. In ECA, the euro area slowdown is expected to weigh on manufacturing exports. In LAC, the upcoming United States–Mexico–Canada Agreement (USMCA) renegotiation will keep uncertainty elevated for Mexico, while the broader region is likely to benefit from higher commodity prices. Similarly, in SSA, trade prospects are closely tied to commodity exports, with intraregional trade agreements and lower Chinese and U.S. tariffs providing additional support.

Energy exporters not directly affected by the conflict will benefit from the rise in energy prices, notably through improved current account balances, while energy importers' trade deficits are set to widen, provided shipping disruptions are short-lived. The conflict is also reducing remittance flows, particularly in MNA, SAR, and some economies in EAP. Higher jet fuel costs and damage to aviation infrastructure in some economies in MNA are expected to slow tourism. Over 2027–28, trade growth is anticipated to recover across regions as commodity prices normalize and global growth rebounds.

Fiscal policy. Fiscal policy prospects vary across regions, and the conflict is likely to put pressure on fiscal positions in many cases. Economies in MNA most affected by the conflict will suffer the largest fiscal costs, owing to lower oil revenues and the destruction of assets in the near term, and reconstruction costs thereafter. Energy-exporting economies not directly affected by the conflict will benefit from higher revenues, although lower growth might constrain fiscal consolidation efforts. Fiscal positions are likely to worsen in regions dominated by energy importers, such as EAP and SAR. In SSA, given elevated public debt levels and cuts to official development assistance (ODA), rising borrowing costs are likely to pressure fiscal positions despite improvements made in recent years, limiting governments' ability to support at-risk populations.

FIGURE 2.1 Recent developments and outlook

The Middle East conflict has weighed heavily on activity in MNA and has slowed growth momentum elsewhere. Higher energy prices due to the conflict have pushed up inflation across regions. Growth is projected to weaken in all regions in 2026, especially MNA. Apart from MNA, EAP and SAR are more exposed to the current shock because of their heavier reliance on oil and gas imports from the Middle East. Food inflation is set to rise, posing challenges for central banks in regions where it was already elevated, such as ECA and LAC. Fiscal positions across regions will be affected by governments' policy responses to the crisis.

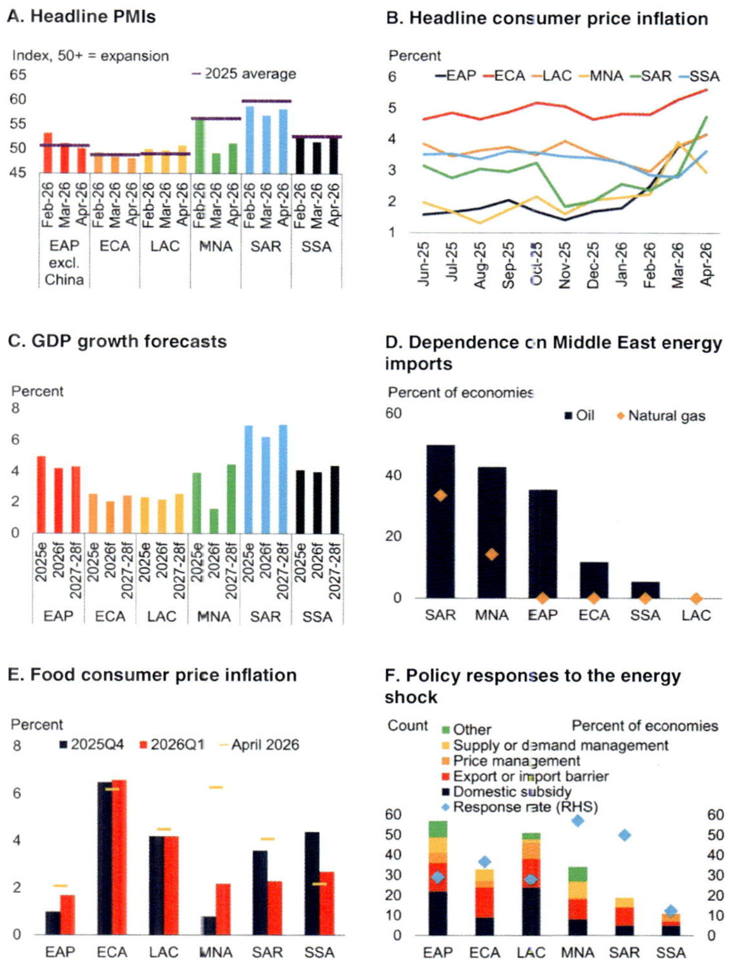

Sources: Gaulier and Zignago (2010); Haver Analytics; Global Trade Alert; World Bank.

Note: e = estimate; f = forecast. EAP = East Asia and Pacific; ECA = Europe and Central Asia; EMDEs = emerging market and developing economies; excl. = excluding; LAC = Latin America and the Caribbean; MNA = Middle East, North Africa, Afghanistan, and Pakistan; PMI = purchasing managers' index; RHS = right-hand scale; SAR = South Asia; SSA = Sub-Saharan Africa.

A. Bars show 2025 GDP-weighted average composite or manufacturing PMIs by region. PMI readings above (below) 50 indicate expansion (contraction). Horizontal lines represent the 2025 monthly average. Sample includes 6 EMDEs in EAP excluding China, 5 in ECA, 3 in LAC, 6 in MNA, 1 in SAR (India), and 7 in SSA. Last observation is April 2026.

B. Year-on-year regional median headline inflation. Sample includes up to 11 EMDEs in EAP, 20 in ECA, 22 in LAC, 15 in MNA, 4 in SAR, and 26 in SSA. Last observation is April 2026.

C. GDP-weighted aggregate growth rates at average 2010–19 prices and market exchange rates. Growth rates for 2027–28 are annual averages.

D. Middle East includes Bahrain, the Islamic Republic of Iran, Iraq, Kuwait, Qatar, Saudi Arabia, and the United Arab Emirates. Bars (markers) show the share of economies by region that sourced more than 30 percent of their oil (natural gas) imports from the Middle East in 2023. Sample includes 108 (89) EMDEs for oil (natural gas).

E. Quarterly averages of regional medians monthly year-on-year food inflation. Sample includes up to 8 EMDEs in EAP, 18 in ECA, 20 in LAC, 16 in MNA, 3 in SAR, and 24 in SSA. Last observation is April 2026.

F. Total count of policy response type to the energy shock, by region. Sample includes 9 EMDEs in EAP, 11 in ECA, 12 in LAC, 12 in MNA, 3 in SAR, and 6 in SSA. Markers show the percentage of countries in each region with at least one response. Last observation is May 29, 2026.

FIGURE 2.2 Risks

SSA, which already has the highest incidence of food insecurity, is also the region most at risk of it rising further on account of the conflict. Higher borrowing costs could create fiscal stress, particularly in the regions where government debt is high, such as EAP, LAC, and SAR. Extreme weather events in EMDEs have become more frequent, particularly in EAP. AI adoption rates increased across all regions in the second half of 2025, but widening disparities across regions could deepen gaps in productivity.

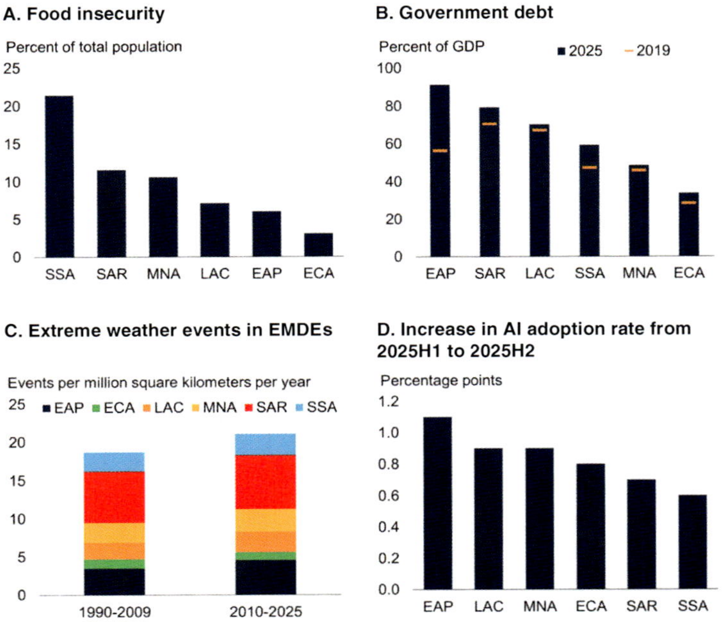

Sources: EM-DAT (database); Food and Agriculture Organization of the United Nations (FAO); Kose et al. (2022); Misra et al. (2025); World Bank; World Food Security Outlook (database).

Note: AI = artificial intelligence; EAP = East Asia and Pacific; ECA = Europe and Central Asia; EMDEs = emerging market and developing economies; LAC = Latin America and the Caribbean; MNA = Middle East, North Africa, Afghanistan, and Pakistan; SAR = South Asia; SSA = Sub-Saharan Africa.

A. Prevalence of severe food insecurity in the total population (percent, three-year centered average). Values represent the regional median. Data are 2026 estimates.

B. Aggregates are computed as weighted averages using GDP in U.S. dollars as weights, based on data for up to 151 EMDEs (24 in EAP, 22 in ECA, 33 in LAC, 19 in MNA, 6 in SAR, and 47 in SSA).

C. Simple average of the number of events per million square kilometers per year over the specified time periods. Storms, droughts, floods, and extreme heat episodes are classified as extreme weather events. Sample includes up to 123 EMDEs (21 in EAP, 18 in ECA, 28 in LAC, 13 in MNA, 6 in SAR, and 47 in SSA).

D. Figure shows the median percentage point increase in the share of the working-age population using AI tools between the first and second halves of 2025 in each region. The Microsoft AI Diffusion Index tracks AI usage penetration—the share of a country's working-age population that actively uses AI tools. Since the data are derived primarily from Microsoft products, the index may underestimate usage in areas where Microsoft has low market share. Sample includes up to 11 EMDEs in EAP, 19 in ECA, 23 in LAC, 17 in MNA, 4 in SAR, and 41 in SSA.

Governments across all regions have implemented a range of measures to cushion the impact on economies and households, ranging from price caps and fuel subsidies, which will have high fiscal costs, to rationing and trade barriers, where fiscal space is constrained (figure 2.1.F; Global Trade Alert 2026). Select energy importers in EAP (the Philippines and Viet Nam) have responded heavily, while economies in LAC with already high inflation (Brazil and Mexico) have also implemented several measures, with responses in both regions skewed toward domestic subsidies. Trade barriers have been used across most regions.

Per capita income. Real per capita income convergence with advanced economies is set to stall in 2026–28 in LAC, MNA, and SSA, with gaps projected to widen in 2026 and narrow gradually thereafter, leaving them larger in 2028 than in 2019. Subdued per capita income growth is expected to slow poverty reduction, particularly in SSA and MNA. By 2028, the share of the population living in extreme poverty is envisaged to be nearly 40 percent in SSA and about 14 percent in MNA, where it would remain above its 2019 level. Convergence is expected to proceed at a moderate pace in ECA and remain relatively solid in EAP and SAR.

Jobs challenge. Over the longer term, job creation is a pressing issue for all EMDE regions. Between 2025 and 2035, about 1.2 billion young people in EMDEs will reach working age, with the largest increases in SSA, followed by SAR and EAP (Chrimes et al. 2026). The jobs context, however, differs among regions. High youth unemployment characterizes EAP, while female labor force participation is the lowest in MNA. ECA faces a combination of an aging population and slow productivity growth. In LAC, job creation is also held back by constraints on entrepreneurial quality, barriers to firm growth, and broader structural impediments. Low-skilled jobs prevail in SAR, leaving workers exposed to automation, while SSA will see the largest rise in working-age population. The challenge of generating enough employment will be compounded by slower global growth and tight fiscal space amid technological change and geopolitical tensions.

Risks

Risks to the outlook remain tilted to the downside across all EMDE regions and have increased with the Middle East conflict. Even if the conflict soon ends, uncertainty about the duration and severity of economic disruptions remains.

A renewed escalation of hostilities would generally worsen outcomes for energy prices, inflation, and growth across EMDEs, as discussed in Chapter 1. MNA would be affected most directly, but EAP, ECA, and SAR, would also be vulnerable, given their exposure to energy supply disruptions. Higher fertilizer and food prices, together with raised energy and transport costs, would particularly hurt lower-income households because of the outsized weight of these essentials in their consumption baskets and a general lack of financial buffers. This risks a further rise in poverty and food insecurity, particularly in SSA and low-income countries (LICs), where high food-import dependence coincides with an already large share of the population facing food insecurity (figure 2.2.A and box 2.1).

Persistently higher energy and food prices would increase the risk of second-round effects on prices and wages, particularly where inflation is already elevated, which could de-anchor inflation expectations and constrain policy responses. Remittances and tourism would decline further, especially in MNA and SAR, if geopolitical tensions persist.

A more prolonged reduction in energy supplies and a further rise in prices would reduce risk appetite, potentially resulting in increased capital outflows, added pressure on currencies, and higher sovereign bond yields across EMDE regions. Higher borrowing costs would especially strain economies with larger government debt burdens, particularly in EAP, LAC, and SAR (figure 2.2.B). Fiscal vulnerabilities would also rise if persistently higher fuel prices led governments to increase subsidies. In SSA, the deterioration of fiscal balances could be magnified by further declines in ODA. Worsening external balances in commodity -importing economies could lead to currency pressures, particularly where international reserves are limited, putting additional upward pressure on inflation.

A deeper retrenchment in risk appetite could also trigger financial stress through interactions with AI-related vulnerabilities in equity markets. Economies where there have been large equity market gains driven by optimism about AI—particularly the United States and some economies in East Asia—will be especially vulnerable to a repricing of assets if investors become more skeptical about the payoffs from AI-related investments. Spillovers from associated declines in global equity markets would be especially large in EAP and SAR, where trade and investment are more heavily linked to AI developments. Sharply tighter global financial conditions would weigh on investment and growth across regions.

Another downside risk to trade and growth in some regions is a further escalation in trade tensions amid ongoing investigations into trade practices. The upcoming USMCA negotiations present a heightened risk of dampening exports and investment for Mexico. Persistent trade policy uncertainty also poses a challenge for EAP, where favorable U.S. import tariff differentials relative to China and sector-specific exemptions have been important drivers of export growth and trade reallocation in several economies over the past year. Should tariff rates rise again, there could be significant adjustments in value chains across EAP.

The increasing frequency of extreme weather events, such as droughts, floods, and storms, has the potential to dampen growth across regions and affect agricultural output. EAP, LAC, and SSA remain particularly vulnerable (figure 2.2.C). Last year, extreme weather events attributable to La Niña conditions led to lower growth in many economies, especially in EAP and SAR. Disruptive weather could emerge again with the transition to El Niño patterns later in 2026. Small states and economies in SSA that have limited buffers and insurance mechanisms are the most vulnerable, facing threats to agricultural output, energy generation, and the potential for intensified food insecurity.

On the upside, advances in AI are boosting investment, particularly in advanced economies, and lifting exports as well as raising demand for critical materials in regions such as EAP and SSA (World Bank 2026b, 2026c). In addition, faster AI diffusion can raise productivity, particularly in EAP and ECA, which are more prepared to reap the gains from AI adoption (World Bank 2026d). However, with many economies lacking the capacity and skills to capture the productivity gains from AI, its diffusion has been quite uneven (figure 2.2.D). Further, the employment impact of AI across regions remains uncertain. The extent of labor market disruption depends not only on the share of tasks that can be augmented by AI, but also on labor supply constraints as workers must acquire the skills necessary to leverage AI effectively (box 1.1).

BOX 2.1 Low-income countries: Recent developments and outlook

The Middle East conflict has exacerbated challenges for low-income countries (LICs). Growth in this group is now expected to reach 5.4 percent in 2026, 0.3 percentage point lower than previous forecasts. Downgrades across LICs generally reflect the impact of the conflict, which more than offsets support from solid domestic demand and commodity exports. Growth is projected to edge up to an average of 5.5 percent a year in 2027–28 as domestic drivers return to the fore. Although real GDP per capita is envisaged to firm, gains are expected to be uneven across countries and, in many cases, insufficient for rapid poverty reduction. Risks to the outlook are predominantly on the downside, including a prolonged conflict in the Middle East that would further raise energy and fertilizer prices and worsen food insecurity. A wider spread of the recent Ebola outbreak would significantly worsen humanitarian conditions and weigh on economic activity. Additionally, tighter financial conditions, weaker global activity, weather-related shocks, and a slower energy transition could all hinder LICs' growth. If downside risks materialize, economic and humanitarian costs would be amplified, particularly in economies in fragile and conflict-affected situations, given their limited policy buffers and declining donor aid.

Recent developments

Growth in low-income countries (LICs) firmed to 5 percent in 2025 from 3.7 percent in 2024, reflecting easing violent conflict in some economies in fragile and conflict-affected situations (FCS), moderating inflation, stronger agricultural output in some economies following favorable weather, and higher prices for certain non-oil commodities such as coffee, gold, and other precious metals. Last year, a significantly more muted recovery in conflict-affected Sudan and a recession in Mozambique offset strong growth in agricultural commodity exporters such as Chad, Rwanda, and Uganda, supported in part by strong harvests. Eastern Africa's recovery from drought improved agricultural output and lowered food inflation, boosting real incomes and consumption. At the same time, higher precious metal prices benefited industrial commodity exporters such as Burkina Faso, the Democratic Republic of Congo, and Niger.

Conflict-related violence in LICs in FCS decreased at the end of 2025 and in early 2026, reflecting reduced hostilities in Sudan, although humanitarian conditions remained severe (figure B2.1.1.A). Growth in FCS LICs firmed to 4.3 percent in 2025, though slightly below the January forecast. This was driven by growth in the Democratic Republic of Congo, which slowed for the third consecutive year, reflecting moderating mining activity amid intensified conflict and tighter fiscal conditions. However, activity was stronger than previously expected in other economies in FCS, such as Burkina Faso, Chad, and Niger.

Note: This box was prepared by Edoardo Palombo.

Among LICs not in FCS, growth edged up to 5.9 percent in 2025, supported by robust domestic demand, resilient export performance, and moderating inflation. In Uganda, growth picked up to 6.3 percent, bolstered by recovering household consumption, increased government spending, solid investment growth, and buoyant coffee exports. In Rwanda, growth rebounded to 9.4 percent—the highest among LICs in 2025—reflecting solid investment and stronger-than-expected industrial performance, alongside robust agricultural output and increased export earnings supported by higher coffee prices.

At the start of 2026, disinflation in LICs continued, with median year-over-year headline consumer price inflation falling to 3.5 percent in March from an average of 6.1 percent in 2025 (figure B2.1.1.B). Disinflation, driven mainly by easing food price inflation amid strong agricultural harvests, was widespread, with inflation slowing in more than two-thirds of LICs. However, in April, headline and food inflation increased once again as evidence of the impact of the conflict in the Middle East, through higher energy and food prices, emerged. This suggests that the disinflation trend may have already reversed, particularly because food and energy account for a larger share of household consumption baskets in LICs than in other emerging market and developing economies.

In May 2026, the Democratic Republic of the Congo and, to a smaller extent, Uganda experienced the onset of the third-largest Ebola outbreak on record, adding pressure to humanitarian and public health conditions in two of the largest LIC economies, especially amid the recent drop in official development assistance (ODA) flows (figure B2.1.1.C). As of early June, there have been almost 1,000 suspected cases and between 220 and

BOX 2.1 Low-income countries: Recent developments and outlook (*continued*)

FIGURE B2.1.1 LICs: Recent developments

In LICs, conflict-related violence had eased by the turn of the year, supporting a gradual pickup in activity in some economies in fragile and conflict-affected situations. However, insecurity remains uneven across economies and elevated in some cases. Disinflation continued into early 2026, with median headline inflation declining amid easing food price pressures following improved harvests. The ongoing conflict in the Middle East has contributed to heightened volatility in energy and food markets, increased prices, and additional fiscal pressures, further exacerbating food insecurity for vulnerable populations. The largest LIC economies have recently recorded the third-largest Ebola outbreak in history; although less fatal than earlier episodes, it exhibited rapid transmission and remains without a broadly available vaccine.

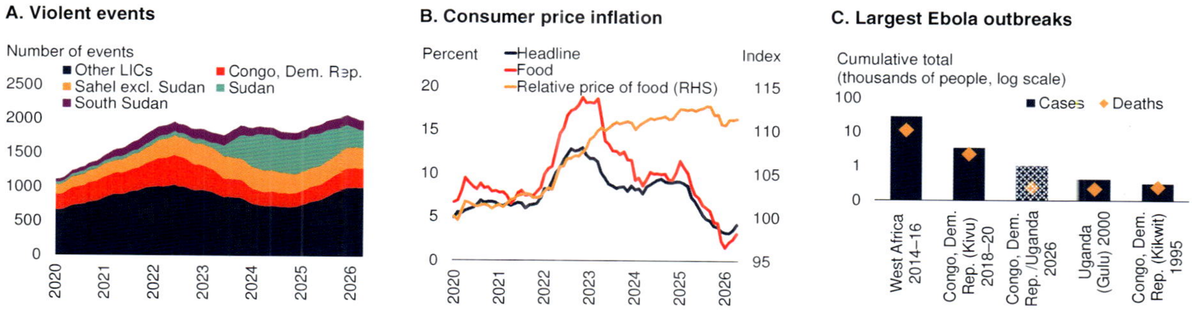

Sources: ACLED (database); CDC; Haver Analytics; World Food Security Outlook (database); WHO; World Bank.

Note: excl. = excluding; LICs = low-income countries; RHS = right-hand scale.

A. Twelve-month moving average; violent events include battles, explosions, violence against civilians, and riots. Last observation is April 2026. Sample includes up to 21 LICs, of which 6 are Sahel countries.

B. Median increases in year-over-year consumer prices. Sample includes up to 21 LICs for headline inflation and up to 19 LICs for food inflation. Last observation is April 2026. Relative food price index is calculated as food inflation relative to headline inflation.

C. Blue bars represent the cumulative number of cases of Ebola, with the yellow markers denoting the respective cumulative number of deaths for each outbreak. Shaded bar and marker represent suspected cases and deaths for the Ebola outbreak in the DRC and Uganda, declared on May 17, 2026, and the last observation is as of May 29, 2026. Outbreaks are ordered by total number of cases.

350 suspected deaths (CDC 2026). The outbreak has spread rapidly, in part because it is caused by the Bundibugyo strain—against which there is yet no approved vaccine—and because it has also affected urban areas, increasing the risk of broader transmission.

Food insecurity, especially in LICs in FCS, has remained well above pre-pandemic averages, exacerbated by conflict, weather-related shocks, natural disasters, and population displacement (FAO et al. 2025). It is estimated that 19 of the 24 LICs still require external assistance with food supplies (FAO 2026).

Amid elevated global economic and geopolitical uncertainty, monetary policy in LICs remained cautious in the first half of 2026. In some economies, such as the Democratic Republic of Congo and Mozambique, central banks continued to lower policy rates. In others, including Rwanda, rates were raised amid rising inflationary pressures driven by domestic increases in energy and food costs. Declining risk appetite, mainly stemming from the conflict, also tightened monetary conditions across LICs, contributing to currency depreciation in some cases and reducing the scope for interest rate cuts.

Outlook

Growth in LICs is expected to reach 5.4 percent in 2026, 0.3 percentage point below previous expectations, reflecting the intensification of challenges associated with the Middle East conflict. Downgrades across LICs generally reflect the impact of the conflict, which offsets support from robust domestic demand and solid commodity exports (figure B2.1.2.A). Growth is projected to edge up to an average of 5.5 percent a year in 2027–28 as domestic drivers return to the fore. These projections assume that security situations do not deteriorate, that debt crises are avoided, that natural disasters have limited effects, and that continued institutional reforms occur across key LICs.

The conflict has worsened the outlook for most LICs by driving up energy prices, causing fuel shortages,

BOX 2.1 Low-income countries: Recent developments and outlook (*continued*)

FIGURE B2.1.2 LICs: Outlook and risks

Although growth in LICs is expected to rise in 2026–28, forecasts have been downgraded following a deterioration in the global environment due to the conflict in the Middle East. The conflict has raised energy prices and increased volatility in fertilizer and food markets, creating renewed inflationary and fiscal pressures for net importers and heightening food security risks. Exposure is greatest in economies with high oil import dependence, limited international reserves, and elevated debt burdens.

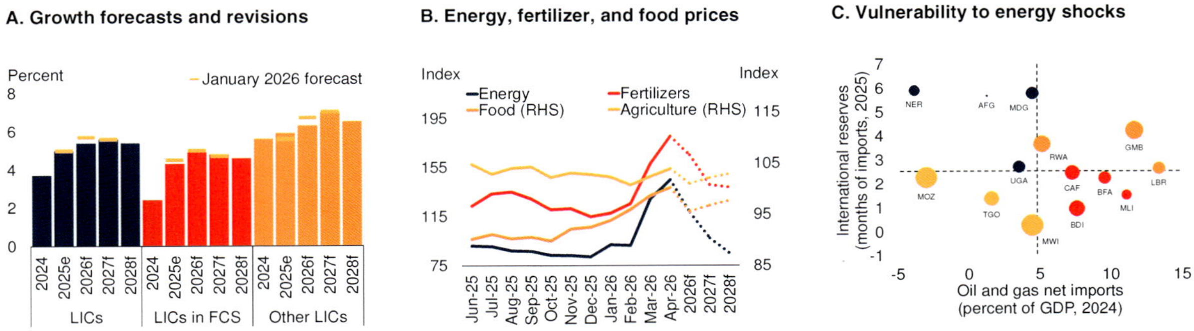

Sources: FAO; Haver Analytics; World Bank.

Note: e = estimate; f = forecast. AFG = Afghanistan; BDI = Burundi; BFA = Burkina Faso; CAF = Central African Republic; FCS = fragile and conflict-affected situations; GMB = The Gambia; LBR = Liberia; LICs = low-income countries; MDG = Madagascar; MLI = Mali; MOZ = Mozambique; MWI = Malawi; NER = Niger; RHS = right-hand scale; RWA = Rwanda; TGO = Togo; UGA = Uganda.

A. Projected annual GDP growth by group from the current (bars) and January 2026 (orange) edition of the *Global Economic Prospects* report. Sample includes 21 LICs.

B. Indexes are set to 100 as of January 2024. Dotted lines represent forecasts. Last monthly observation is April 2026.

C. Diameter of the bubbles proportionally represents government gross debt as a percent of GDP in 2025. Horizontal dashed line represents the average number of months of reserves, while the vertical dashed line represents the average oil and gas imports share of GDP.

reducing fertilizer supply, and increasing inflation (figure B2.1.2.B). While a few oil-exporting LICs may benefit temporarily from higher energy prices, most LICs are energy importers and thus face negative impacts. Heightened inflation may prompt central banks to tighten policy, further slowing growth, especially in countries with limited fiscal space. Increased import bills and currency depreciation will erode real incomes and domestic demand, disproportionately affecting vulnerable households. Food prices are expected to rise modestly in 2026, with the impact of higher fertilizer costs felt more fully in the following harvest season. The effect will vary by country depending on fertilizer reliance and farmers' ability to adjust input use or crop choice.

Despite global headwinds, growth in LICs in FCS is forecast to rise from 4.3 percent in 2025 to 4.9 percent in 2026 before moderating to an annual average of 4.7 percent in 2027–28. These projections mask a diversity of prospects across countries; while growth in most LICs in FCS is projected to slow in 2026, a substantial recovery is still projected for South Sudan, supported by the resumption of oil exports and base effects. At the same time, Sudan's rebound continues with returning displaced populations and easing supply constraints—though both countries still face severe humanitarian challenges. Growth in the Democratic Republic of Congo is set to slow for the fourth consecutive year, despite the boost from higher metal prices and stronger exports to China. Afghanistan's improved growth projections are overshadowed by persistent conflict, insecurity, limited external financing, and a severe humanitarian crisis.

Growth in LICs not in FCS is projected to firm from 5.9 percent in 2025 to 6.3 percent in 2026, and then to an average of 6.8 percent a year over 2027–28. The overall acceleration largely reflects strengthening growth in Uganda, driven by oil-related investment, robust domestic demand, solid export performance, and the anticipated start of oil production in late 2026. Excluding Uganda, growth in LICs not in FCS is expected to average 5.2 percent in 2026–28. Growth in

BOX 2.1 Low-income countries: Recent developments and outlook (*continued*)

TABLE B2.1.1 Low-income country forecasts[a]

(Real GDP growth at market prices in percent, unless indicated otherwise)

	2023	2024	2025e	2026f	2027f	2028f	Percentage-point differences from January 2026 projections: 2026f	Percentage-point differences from January 2026 projections: 2027f
Low-income countries, GDP[b]	**1.2**	**3.7**	**5.0**	**5.4**	**5.6**	**5.4**	**-0.3**	**0.0**
GDP per capita (U.S. dollars)	-1.5	0.9	2.1	2.6	2.8	2.6	-0.2	0.0
Afghanistan [c d]	2.3	1.9	4.8	4.0	3.9	3.8	0.2	0.4
Burkina Faso	3.0	4.8	5.3	4.9	5.8	5.5	0.0	0.7
Burundi	2.7	4.1	4.0	4.1	4.8	4.9	-0.8	-0.7
Central African Republic	0.7	1.5	4.5	2.3	3.1	3.2	-0.7	0.0
Chad	4.0	5.0	5.6	5.2	5.3	5.3	1.5	1.2
Congo, Dem. Rep.	8.6	6.1	5.5	5.2	5.1	5.1	0.1	-0.2
Eritrea	2.6	2.9	3.2	3.5	3.6	3.6	0.0	0.0
Gambia, The	5.9	5.6	5.9	5.3	5.2	5.2	-0.2	-0.1
Guinea-Bissau	5.3	4.1	5.8	4.8	4.9	5.0	-0.4	-0.3
Liberia	4.7	4.0	5.1	5.0	5.4	5.6	-0.4	-0.2
Madagascar	4.2	4.3	3.0	3.8	4.5	4.4	-0.2	0.1
Malawi	1.9	1.7	1.9	2.3	2.7	3.0	-0.3	-0.4
Mali	4.5	4.7	4.1	5.0	5.2	5.3	0.0	0.2
Mozambique	5.5	2.1	-0.5	0.9	1.6	2.5	-1.9	-1.9
Niger	2.6	8.3	7.0	6.7	6.4	6.1	0.0	-0.2
Rwanda	8.6	7.2	9.4	7.2	7.6	7.3	0.0	0.0
Sierra Leone	5.7	4.4	4.5	4.0	4.7	4.6	-0.4	0.1
Somalia, Fed. Rep.	4.2	4.1	3.0	2.8	3.1	3.5	-0.7	-0.4
South Sudan [d]	-1.3	-7.4	-7.7	20.3	2.4	2.9	-28.5	1.6
Sudan	-29.4	-14.0	3.1	5.5	4.4	2.6	0.4	0.7
Syrian Arab Republic [c e]	0.3	0.9	2.0	..	..	..	..	..
Togo	6.2	6.5	5.9	5.0	5.8	6.2	-0.4	0.2
Uganda [d]	5.3	6.1	6.3	6.8	8.5	8.1	0.4	-1.3
Yemen, Rep. [c]	-2.0	-1.5	-1.5	-0.5	1.6	..	-0.5	..

Source: World Bank.

Note: e = estimate; f = forecast. World Bank forecasts are frequently updated based on new information and changing (global) circumstances. Consequently, projections presented here may differ from those contained in other Bank documents, even if basic assessments of countries' prospects do not significantly differ at any given moment in time.

a. The Democratic People's Republic of Korea is not projected on account of data limitations.

b. Aggregate growth rates are calculated using GDP weights at average 2010-19 prices and market exchange rates. Data for the Syrian Arab Republic and the Republic of Yemen are excluded.

c. Forecasts for the Syrian Arab Republic (beyond 2025) and the Republic of Yemen (beyond 2027) are excluded because of a high degree of uncertainty

d. GDP growth rates are on a fiscal-year basis. For example, the column for 2023 refers to FY2022/23.

e. Growth estimates for 2025 range between 2.0–4.0 percent.

Rwanda is projected to moderate in 2026 before strengthening over the medium term, supported by expanding agricultural production and exports.

Real per capita GDP growth in LICs is forecast to increase from 2.1 percent in 2025 to an average of 2.7 percent a year over 2026–28. However, these gains are expected to be unevenly distributed, with much of the increase concentrated in the largest LICs. On average, per capita growth remains insufficient to reduce poverty to achieve development goals, especially amid rising food prices that disproportionately affect vulnerable households. Sluggish growth in living standards will be compounded by demographic pressures, as roughly 20 percent of the current LIC population is set to reach working age within the next decade, creating an urgent need for job creation (World Bank 2025a).

Fiscal space in LICs remains constrained by high public debt and limited access to financing. LICs' government debt-to-GDP ratios are projected to decline but remain above 60 percent through 2028, with primary surpluses helping to reduce debt burdens. Still, high interest payments and reduced ODA inflows are impeding

BOX 2.1 Low-income countries: Recent developments and outlook (*continued*)

faster progress. Higher energy prices resulting from the Middle East conflict are expected to further strain public finances, particularly in countries that maintain sizable fuel subsidies. ODA inflows may decline further than projected because of the strain from the energy shock and other spending priorities in advanced economies (OECD 2025). Ultimately, the G20 Common Framework provides a multilateral mechanism for debt restructuring should countries' debt burdens become unsustainable. However, debt relief alone is insufficient to address debt sustainability issues and must be accompanied by sound macroeconomic and structural reforms.

Risks

The outlook for LICs remains highly uncertain, and risks to the growth projections are tilted to the downside. A re-escalation of the Middle East conflict represents the key near-term risk. It could significantly reduce global oil and gas supplies, disrupt trade, drive up energy and food prices, intensify inflationary pressures, and strain already-limited fiscal space. Net energy importers with heavy reliance on oil imports, limited international reserves, and constrained fiscal space are especially vulnerable (figure B2.1.2.C). Heightened geopolitical uncertainty may also tighten global financial conditions, limit LICs' access to external financing, and worsen debt vulnerabilities, further dampening growth.

Food insecurity, already at record levels, is set to increase further because of the conflict. Risks would be amplified if the conflict worsens, as disruptions to key shipping routes and higher fertilizer prices would exacerbate supply bottlenecks and raise import prices. Higher food prices and slower income growth would place particular strain on vulnerable households' access to food. The effects will likely become more apparent in subsequent years, as this year's harvests are mostly unaffected and farmers may delay fertilizer purchases until prices stabilize (figure B2.1.2.B).

The recent Ebola outbreak is an additional downside risk to the outlook for LICs, especially because it is affecting the Democratic Republic of the Congo and Uganda, two of the largest LIC economies. Beyond the direct human toll, Ebola outbreaks can impose sizable macroeconomic costs by disrupting mobility, trade, labor supply, and confidence, while also straining already weak health systems and public finances. Even localized outbreaks can weigh on growth through fear-driven declines in activity and cross-border spillovers, suggesting that a worsening outbreak in eastern Africa could further weaken LIC growth (World Bank 2014). The outbreak comes at a time of already elevated humanitarian needs, while recent cuts in ODA risk reversing two decades of progress in reducing preventable mortality (da Silva et al. 2026; OECD 2025).

Weather-related risks also continue to interact with other LIC-specific vulnerabilities, potentially worsening food insecurity and conflict in fragile LICs, slowing poverty reduction, and undermining long-term development (UNU-CPR 2025). Concurrently, a potentially severe El Niño in the second half of 2026 could further strain food production and amplify food insecurity in Southern African LICs.

Another downside risk is that the security situations of several LICs in FCS deteriorate. The unexpected persistence or intensification of conflicts—notably in Burkina Faso, the Democratic Republic of Congo, Mali, Niger, South Sudan, and Sudan—would undermine growth, macroeconomic stability, fiscal balances, and humanitarian outcomes. Insecurity and conflict disrupt production, trade, and aid delivery; weaken investor confidence; and exacerbate food insecurity. Deteriorating terms of trade can also increase conflict by reducing aggregate income, creating a cycle of economic decline and rising conflict (Leepipatpiboon, Castrovillari, and Mineyama 2023).

Upside risks to the growth projections include stronger-than-expected spillovers from the energy transition and AI-related investment, through higher prices and demand for related critical minerals, which could boost external demand (IEA 2025; UNCTAD 2025). Favorable trade policy developments in trading partners—beyond the recent lowering of effective U.S. tariffs on most LICs through the extension of the African Growth and Opportunity Act to 2026 and the elimination of Chinese tariffs on imports from most African economies—could also strengthen export performance and accelerate trade integration. Nonetheless, this upside risk remains contingent on investor sentiment and policy changes that support energy and AI-related investments.

East Asia and Pacific

Recent developments

Economic activity in the EAP region remained resilient in early 2026, despite signs of spillovers from the conflict in the Middle East through higher inflation. In China, growth continued at a solid pace, with policy stimulus supporting consumption and infrastructure investment. Export performance remained robust, boosted by technology-related exports, while exports of consumer goods remained muted. Import growth was elevated, also underpinned by high-tech intermediate inputs, although shipping disruptions from the conflict weighed heavily on energy imports. Rising input costs were a primary driver of substantially higher producer price inflation, with limited increases in headline consumer price inflation. The property sector adjustment continued, with modest improvements in large cities.

Elsewhere in EAP, growth proved robust in early 2026, even with higher energy prices and input costs. Indicators of consumption growth, such as retail sales and consumer confidence, held steady. Moreover, demand for AI-related products supported strong industrial production and export growth, particularly in Malaysia, the Philippines, Thailand, and Viet Nam. Tourist arrivals recovered to pre-pandemic levels in some countries, but slower outbound tourism from China hampered the rebound in others, with the conflict further dampening tourist activity.

Financial conditions across the region tightened at the onset of the conflict. Currencies depreciated, equity markets declined, and local-currency bond yields rose, especially in Indonesia, the Philippines, and Thailand, with only a partial recovery after the ceasefire. Higher energy prices and conflict-related supply disruptions led to higher inflation, posing a challenge for some energy-importing economies where inflation was already elevated, such as Myanmar and Viet Nam. Many governments have taken action to cushion the impact on households either by absorbing higher costs through subsidies or managing energy demand through rationing where fiscal space is constrained.

Outlook

Growth in EAP is projected to moderate to 4.2 percent in 2026 from 5 percent in 2025, reflecting the impact of the conflict as well as China's outlook (figure 2.3.A; table 2.1). China's deceleration this year stems from subdued domestic demand amid low consumer confidence, the continued property sector adjustment, and a soft labor market. In parallel, export growth is expected to ease relative to 2025 because of weaker external demand this year, with some offset from lower U.S. import tariffs and continued strength in technology-related exports. In the near term, the growth impact of the conflict is expected to be cushioned by China's substantial oil reserves, its high share of renewable energy, and low inflation. In addition, the government has capped fuel prices, limiting the pass-through of higher global prices to households. Growth is expected to edge up to 4.3 percent in 2027–28, as energy prices ease while diminishing marginal returns to capital, high debt, and population aging continue to lower China's potential growth.[1] In the medium term, as export growth slows, policies are expected to provide an incremental boost to consumption and lead to productivity gains from digital and industrial innovation.

In EAP excluding China, growth is expected to slow to 4.4 percent in 2026 from 4.8 percent in 2025, as the conflict disrupts supply and weighs on demand through higher energy prices, elevated uncertainty, and, in some cases, tighter financial conditions. Export growth will be dampened by weaker external demand, the fading of front-loading ahead of U.S. tariff hikes that have now been lowered, and reduced U.S. tariff advantages relative to China. Continued strong demand for electronics and semiconductors is expected to provide a partial offset, although uncertainty remains about tariff exemptions and the availability of inputs, such as helium and sulfur, for these sectors (figure 2.3 B).

The effects of the conflict will vary among the economies in the region, depending on the size

[1] Debt refers to aggregate non-financial sector debt as measured by total social financing (excluding equity).

FIGURE 2.3 EAP: Outlook

Growth in EAP is projected to moderate to 4.3 percent over 2026–28, on average, largely reflecting China's outlook, given its sizable weight in the region. Excluding China, growth is set to recover after the 2026 slowdown induced by the conflict in the Middle East. Continued momentum in electronics exports is expected to buoy export growth in the region. However, most economies in the region are energy importers and are dependent on supplies from the Middle East, making them vulnerable to adverse impacts of the conflict. While inflation has been low in major EAP economies, higher food inflation could pose a challenge for some central banks and vulnerable households.

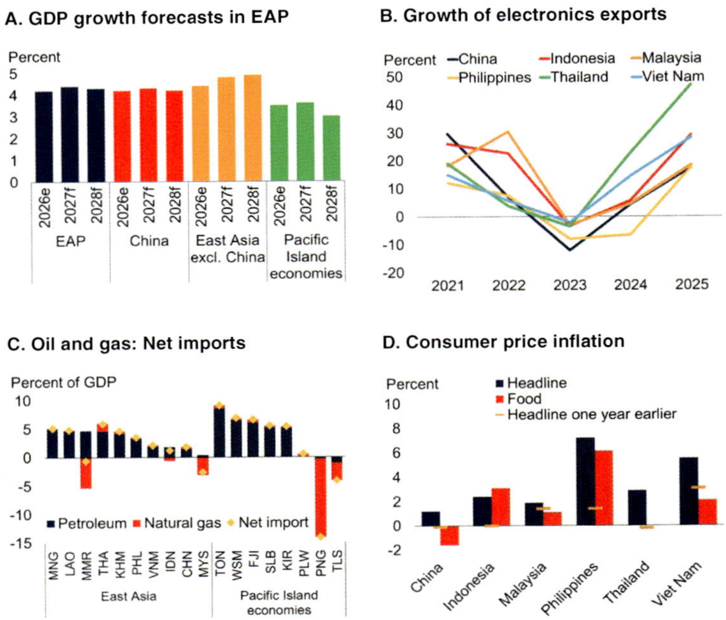

Sources: Haver Analytics; UN Comtrade; World Bank.

Note: e = estimate; f = forecast. CHN = China; EAP = East Asia and Pacific; excl. = excluding; FJI = Fiji; IDN = Indonesia; KHM = Cambodia; KIR = Kiribati; LAO = Lao PDR; MMR = Myanmar; MNG = Mongolia; MYS = Malaysia; PHL = Philippines; PLW = Palau; PNG = Papua New Guinea; SLB = Solomon Islands; THA = Thailand; TLS = Timor-Leste; TON = Tonga; VNM = Viet Nam; WSM = Samoa.

A. Annual real GDP growth. Projections for 2027 and 2028 are from the World Bank. Aggregate growth rates are calculated using average 2010–19 GDP weights and market exchange rates.

B. Year-on-year growth of electronics exports in major EAP economies.

C. Petroleum includes both crude and refined products. Simple average of net imports is calculated for 2014–24.

D. Year-on-year consumer price and food inflation rates. Last observation is April 2026.

and direction of their energy trade, their strategic petroleum reserves, and the policy buffers available (figure 2.3.C). In general, low inflation in major EAP economies and well-anchored inflation expectations provide central banks with the flexibility to look through the short-term increase in inflation. However, central banks, especially those that target headline inflation, could face a greater challenge if food price inflation rises markedly (figure 2.3.D). High energy and transportation prices are likely to dampen consumption and industrial production. Tourism would also suffer if shortages of jet fuel arise or households delay travel. Fiscal positions will come under pressure, especially for energy importers like the Philippines and Thailand, and Pacific Island nations such as Fiji, Tonga, and Vanuatu. In addition, the burden of declining remittances and higher food costs will be acutely felt by lower-income households. Net energy exporters like Malaysia and Papua New Guinea are likely to benefit from the improved terms of trade, although they will face higher inflation and slower global growth.

Growth in EAP excluding China is forecast to improve to 4.9 percent in 2027–28 as geopolitical uncertainty dissipates, energy prices settle, and demand improves. Public investment is expected to recuperate in the Philippines, and Indonesia's growth will be supported by state-led investment initiatives. Activity in Cambodia, Thailand, and Viet Nam is projected to rebound strongly as the global environment stabilizes (table 2.2). While AI-related investment and trade have picked up in the region, the diffusion of AI remains limited and uneven, creating challenges for productivity growth and job creation (World Bank 2026b).

In the Pacific Island economies, growth is expected to slow to 3.5 percent in 2026 and to 3.3 percent in 2027–28, on average, as tourism-led growth slows in Fiji and activity in the resource sector normalizes in Papua New Guinea. In the rest of the subregion, higher energy prices and shipping disruptions are leading to higher food, electricity, and transport costs, which will weigh on consumption, investment, and fiscal balances as financial buffers remain limited (World Bank 2026e).

TABLE 2.1 East Asia and Pacific forecast summary

(Real GDP growth at market prices in percent, unless indicated otherwise)

	2023	2024	2025e	2026f	2027f	2028f	Percentage-point differences from January 2026 projections: 2026f	2027f
EMDE EAP, GDP [1]	**5.2**	**5.0**	**5.0**	**4.2**	**4.4**	**4.3**	**-0.2**	**0.1**
GDP per capita (U.S. dollars)	5.1	4.9	4.9	4.1	4.3	4.3	-0.2	0.1
(Average including economies that report expenditure components in national accounts) [2]								
EMDE EAP, GDP [2]	5.3	5.0	5.0	4.2	4.4	4.3	-0.2	0.1
Private consumption	8.1	5.2	4.7	4.5	4.7	5.0	-0.4	-0.1
Public consumption	6.6	1.4	4.7	4.7	4.6	4.7	0.3	0.5
Fixed investment	4.4	3.2	2.5	2.3	3.0	3.1	-1.1	-0.8
Exports, GNFS [3]	0.0	12.7	9.8	6.2	5.5	4.9	2.5	2.3
Imports, GNFS [3]	2.0	8.1	4.4	4.0	4.5	4.7	1.3	1.4
Net exports, contribution to growth	-0.4	1.3	1.5	0.3	0.5	0.3	0.4	0.3
Memo items: GDP								
EAP excluding China	4.4	4.9	4.8	4.4	4.8	4.9	-0.1	0.1
Pacific Island Economies [4]	4.6	3.8	4.9	3.5	3.6	3.0	0.1	0.6

Source: World Bank.

Note: e = estimate; f = forecast. EMDE = emerging market and developing economy. World Bank forecasts are frequently updated based on new information and changing global circumstances. Consequently, projections presented here may differ from those in other World Bank documents, even if basic assessments of countries' prospects do not differ at any given moment in time.

1. GDP and expenditure components are measured in average 2010–19 prices and market exchange rates. Excludes the Democratic People's Republic of Korea and dependent territories.

2. Subregion aggregate excludes the Democratic People's Republic of Korea, dependent territories, Fiji, Kiribati, the Marshall Islands, the Federated States of Micronesia, Myanmar, Palau, Papua New Guinea, Samoa, Timor-Leste, Tonga, Tuvalu, and Vanuatu, for which data limitations prevent the forecasting of GDP components.

3. Exports and imports of goods and nonfactor services (GNFS).

4. Includes Fiji, Kiribati, the Marshall Islands, the Federated States of Micronesia, Nauru, Palau, Papua New Guinea, Samoa, the Solomon Islands, Tonga, Tuvalu, and Vanuatu.

TABLE 2.2 East Asia and Pacific economy forecasts [1]

(Real GDP growth at market prices in percent, unless indicated otherwise)

	2023	2024	2025e	2026f	2027f	2028f	Percentage-point differences from January 2026 projections: 2026f	2027f
Cambodia	5.0	6.0	5.3	3.9	4.9	5.1	-0.4	-0.2
China	5.4	5.0	5.0	4.2	4.3	4.2	-0.2	0.1
Fiji	9.4	3.5	3.2	2.7	3.2	3.3	-0.3	0.1
Indonesia	5.0	5.0	5.1	5.0	5.2	5.2	0.0	0.0
Kiribati	3.3	4.6	4.3	3.1	2.4	2.2	-0.1	-0.1
Lao PDR	3.7	4.1	4.8	3.8	3.7	3.7	-0.2	-0.2
Malaysia	3.5	5.1	5.2	4.4	4.4	4.1	0.3	0.4
Marshall Islands [2]	-4.0	3.0	2.5	2.0	2.4	1.9	-2.1	0.0
Micronesia, Fed. Sts. [2]	1.1	2.3	1.1	0.8	1.3	1.4	-0.7	0.5
Mongolia	7.2	5.1	6.9	5.0	5.5	5.5	-0.6	0.0
Myanmar [2,3]	1.0	-1.0	-2.0	2.0	..	..	-1.0	..
Nauru [2]	0.6	1.6	2.1	1.9	1.9	1.8	0.0	0.0
Palau [2]	1.2	12.0	6.7	3.0	2.7	2.6	-0.5	0.0
Papua New Guinea	3.8	3.9	5.6	3.8	3.8	3.1	0.3	0.7
Philippines	5.5	5.7	4.4	3.7	5.6	5.6	-1.6	0.2
Samoa [2]	15.2	4.8	4.2	4.0	3.3	2.4	-0.4	0.0
Solomon Islands	2.8	3.0	3.6	2.9	3.2	3.2	0.3	0.4
Thailand	2.2	2.9	2.4	1.7	2.1	2.4	-0.1	-0.4
Timor-Leste	2.4	4.3	4.5	4.1	4.0	4.0	0.7	0.2
Tonga [2]	2.1	2.1	2.7	2.0	1.8	1.5	-0.3	0.0
Tuvalu	4.0	3.1	3.0	2.5	2.7	2.3	-0.1	0.0
Vanuatu	2.1	0.9	1.7	2.3	2.7	2.3	-0.5	0.0
Viet Nam	5.0	7.0	8.0	6.8	7.1	7.4	0.5	0.4

Source: World Bank.

Note: e = estimate; f = forecast. World Bank forecasts are frequently updated based on new information and changing global circumstances. Consequently, projections presented here may differ from those in other World Bank documents, even if basic assessments of countries' prospects do not significantly differ at any given moment in time.

1. Data are based on GDP measured in average 2010–19 prices and market exchange rates.

2. Values for Timor-Leste represent non-oil GDP. For the following countries, values correspond to the fiscal year: the Marshall Islands, the Federated States of Micronesia, and Palau (October 1–September 30); Myanmar (April 1–March 31); and Nauru, Samoa, and Tonga (July 1–June 30).

3. Data for Myanmar beyond 2026 (which corresponds to the year ending March 2027) are excluded because of a high degree of uncertainty.

Europe and Central Asia

Recent developments

Growth in Europe and Central Asia (ECA) slowed to 2.5 percent in 2025, driven by softening domestic demand—particularly in the Russian Federation due to weaker fiscal stimulus and tight monetary policy. Excluding Russia and Türkiye, regional growth edged up to 3.4 percent, with Central Asia remaining the fastest-growing subregion (World Bank 2026f).

Data for early 2026 point to moderation in ECA growth momentum amid some tightening of financial conditions following the outbreak of the conflict in the Middle East, with pressures on equities, sovereign spreads, and currencies (figure 2.4.A). Disinflation has stalled, as inflation picked up following the rise in energy prices due to the conflict (World Bank 2026a). Median headline inflation rates increased above 5 percent in recent months, remaining above pre-pandemic levels and central bank targets in most countries. Inflation has been highest in Türkiye and Central Asia, and lowest in Central Europe and the Western Balkans. In this context, the scope for further monetary policy easing has narrowed. These developments point to a more challenging macroeconomic outlook.

Outlook

Growth in ECA is projected to decelerate further, to 2.1 percent in 2026, weakening in about 70 percent of economies, before picking up to 2.4 percent by 2027–28 (figure 2.4.B; tables 2.3 and 2.4). Slowing growth is expected to weigh on labor markets, dampening job creation in the near term, against a backdrop of ongoing demographic pressures. Excluding Russia and Türkiye, regional growth is projected to remain comparatively resilient, moderating to 2.8 percent in 2026 before firming to 3.1 percent by 2027–28. The baseline assumes that the most acute phase of commodity trade disruptions ends in July, with shipping volumes through the Strait of Hormuz recovering in the second half of the year, allowing energy supplies to gradually return close to pre-conflict levels. Higher oil prices, with elevated trade and geopolitical uncertainty, have led to downward revisions to 2026 growth projections since January for most commodity importers, outweighing limited upward revisions for commodity exporters.

Most ECA economies are net energy importers and are expected to face headwinds from higher commodity prices in 2026. Since January, the largest downward revisions have been in Romania, Türkiye, Moldova and Ukraine, largely driven by the commodity price shock, alongside country-specific developments. In Ukraine, earlier electricity and gas supply disruptions due to targeted attacks are also expected to weigh on activity in the context of Russia's invasion. Growth for commodity exporters is envisaged to slow in 2026 and remain subdued in 2027–28, although higher commodity prices are expected to support export revenues in energy exporters, including Azerbaijan, Kazakhstan, and Turkmenistan, and metals exporters. In Russia, the impact of the conflict in the Middle East on activity is anticipated to be contained. Oil revenue gains—estimated at about 1.5 percent of 2025 GDP for each $10 per barrel increase in oil prices (EBRD 2026)—are envisaged to be mainly directed toward fiscal consolidation, amid fiscal and financial pressures.

Domestic demand is expected to remain the primary driver of regional growth, though it is likely to be constrained in 2026 by elevated energy prices, which raise inflation and erode real incomes, and by tighter financial conditions. A gradual recovery is anticipated as commodity price pressures ease. Net exports are projected to continue to weigh on growth amid the euro area slowdown, before gradually strengthening in 2027–28 alongside its recovery.

Inflation is set to rise in 2026, driven by higher energy and food prices, before moderating over 2027–28 as commodity price pressures ease. The pass-through from energy prices to inflation is expected to be stronger in energy importers with large consumer price index energy weights, such as Armenia, Georgia, and Serbia. Indirect effects via upward pressures on input costs are also likely to be more pronounced in economies with greater fertilizer import dependence, including Moldova, Romania, and most Western Balkans countries (figure 2.4.C). Against this backdrop, monetary policy is envisaged to remain restrictive amid persistent inflation pressures, notably in Türkiye.

Fiscal policy is expected to be broadly supportive of growth in most economies over 2026–28. Fiscal deficits are projected to remain elevated amid persistent spending pressures, including defense spending and temporary economic measures, such as domestic subsidies and price management measures, to cushion the impact of higher energy prices (figures 2.4.D and 2.4.E). Limited fiscal space, particularly in Montenegro, Romania, and Ukraine, will likely constrain authorities' ability to absorb this shock. Upcoming elections in many countries add uncertainty to the fiscal outlook. Energy exporters stand apart, with stronger hydrocarbon revenues aiding consolidation efforts. The median public debt across the region is projected to increase to about 40 percent of GDP by 2027.

External balances among energy-importing economies are anticipated to weaken in 2026, reflecting higher energy costs and softer external demand due mainly to the euro area slowdown. Elevated energy prices are likely to weigh most heavily on Armenia, Georgia, Moldova, and Türkiye, where net energy imports exceed 70 percent of domestic energy use (figure 2.4.F). Economies with already-large current account deficits, notably Moldova, Montenegro, and Ukraine, remain particularly vulnerable to deteriorations in their terms of trade. Slower euro area growth is likely to weigh on manufacturing exports, particularly in Central Europe and the Western Balkans. Energy exporters, by contrast, are expected to record stronger current account positions. These external pressures are set to ease in 2027–28, supported by softer commodity prices and a gradual recovery in the euro area.

External balances will also be shaped by tourism, remittances, and ongoing structural trade shifts. Tourism is envisaged to moderate compared with the post-pandemic rebound, while remittance inflows—after surging following Russia's invasion and supporting consumption, especially in Central Asia—are expected to stabilize amid weaker growth in Russia. The Carbon Border Adjustment Mechanism is also expected to gradually reshape trade patterns in the Western Balkans, affecting the composition and competitiveness of carbon-intensive exports to the European Union.

FIGURE 2.4 ECA: Recent developments and outlook

Following the outbreak of the conflict in the Middle East, financial conditions in ECA tightened. Growth in the region is projected to slow to 2.1 percent in 2026, with mostly downward revisions for commodity importers. The energy price shock arising from the conflict is expected to increase inflation and weaken fiscal positions, as economic measures to limit its impact add to fiscal pressures. External balances in energy-importing economies are projected to deteriorate, particularly in economies with large current account deficits and high energy import dependence.

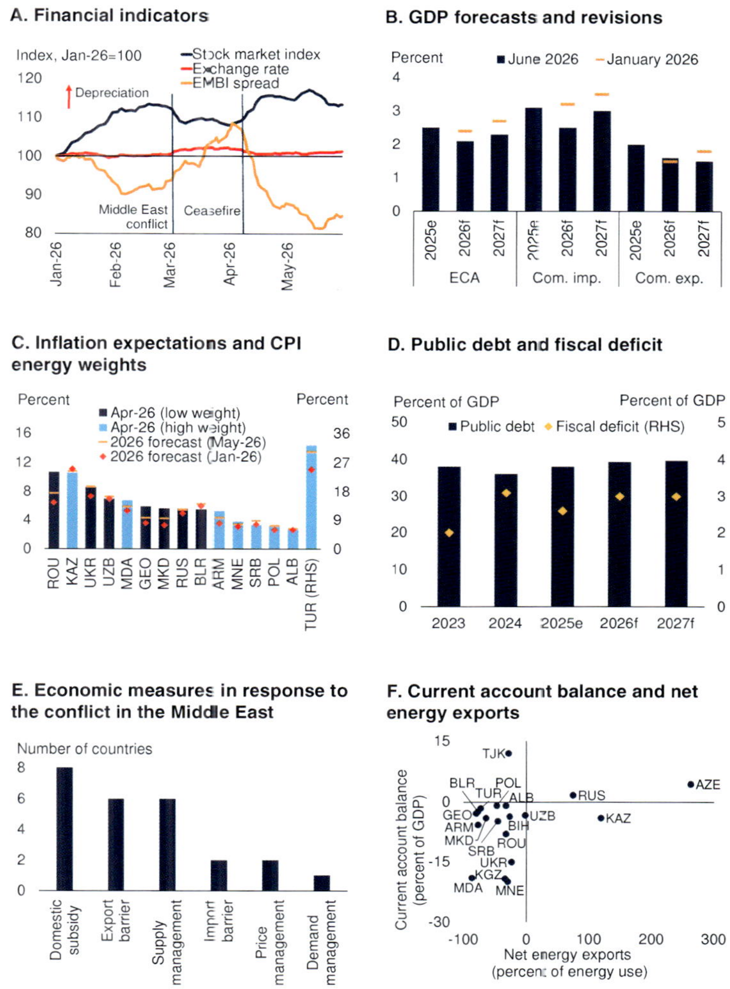

Sources: Consensus Economics; Global Trade Alert; Haver Analytics; International Monetary Fund; J.P. Morgan; Macro Poverty Outlook (database); World Bank.

Note: ALB = Albania; ARM = Armenia; AZE = Azerbaijan; BIH = Bosnia and Herzegovina; BLR = Belarus; Com. exp. = ECA commodity-exporting economies; Com. imp. = ECA commodity-importing economies; CPI = consumer price index; e = estimate; ECA = Europe and Central Asia; EMBI = Emerging Market Bond Index; f = forecast; GEO = Georgia; KAZ = Kazakhstan; KGZ = Kyrgyz Republic; MDA = Moldova; MKD = North Macedonia; MNE = Montenegro; POL = Poland; RHS = right-hand scale; ROU = Romania; RUS = Russian Federation; SRB = Serbia; TJK = Tajikistan; TUR = Türkiye; UKR = Ukraine; UZB = Uzbekistan.

A. Data are daily averages, based on a sample of up to 21 economies. Last observation is May 27, 2026.

B. GDP growth forecasts reported in the January 2026 and June 2026 editions of the *Global Economic Prospects* report.

C. Bars represent April 2026 headline inflation. Diamonds and dashes show 2026 year-on-year inflation expectations from the May and January 2026 Consensus Economics surveys. Dark and light blue bars indicate economies with CPI housing and energy weights below and above the ECA median.

D. Bars and diamonds represent ECA median gross public debt and fiscal deficit in percent of GDP.

E. Bars show the number of ECA economies by economic measures implemented in response to the conflict in the Middle East. Last observation is May 29, 2026.

F. Current account balance data are for 2025. Net energy export data are for 2022.

TABLE 2.3 Europe and Central Asia forecast summary

(Real GDP growth at market prices in percent, unless indicated otherwise)

	2023	2024	2025e	2026f	2027f	2028f	Percentage-point differences from January 2026 projections: 2026f	2027f
EMDE ECA, GDP [1]	**3.6**	**3.9**	**2.5**	**2.1**	**2.3**	**2.6**	**-0.3**	**-0.4**
GDP per capita (U.S. dollars)	4.0	3.8	2.3	1.9	2.2	2.5	-0.3	-0.4
(Average including economies that report expenditure components in national accounts) [2]								
EMDE ECA, GDP [2]	3.5	3.8	2.2	1.8	2.1	2.4	-0.4	-0.4
Private consumption	5.7	4.9	3.2	2.8	2.9	3.1	0.3	0.1
Public consumption	3.6	3.2	2.2	1.4	1.2	1.5	-0.7	-0.5
Fixed investment	11.0	2.2	2.1	1.0	1.3	1.8	-2.5	-2.0
Exports, GNFS [3]	0.6	0.9	1.2	1.7	2.4	2.6	0.5	-0.2
Imports, GNFS [3]	7.8	1.3	3.6	3.1	3.0	3.3	0.4	-0.6
Net exports, contribution to growth	-2.5	-0.1	-0.9	-0.5	-0.3	-0.3	0.0	0.1
Memo items: GDP								
ECA excl. Russian Federation and Türkiye	2.2	3.3	3.4	2.8	3.0	3.2	-0.3	-0.1
ECA plus Bulgaria and Croatia	3.6	3.9	2.5	2.1	2.3	2.6	-0.3	-0.4
Commodity exporters [4]	4.3	4.9	2.0	1.6	1.5	1.6	0.1	-0.3
Commodity importers [5]	3.0	3.0	3.1	2.5	3.0	3.5	-0.7	-0.5
Central Europe [6]	0.5	2.3	2.5	2.2	2.4	2.7	-0.5	-0.2
Central Europe plus Bulgaria and Croatia	0.8	2.4	2.6	2.3	2.4	2.7	-0.4	-0.3
Western Balkans [7]	3.8	3.6	2.6	2.9	3.2	3.7	-0.2	-0.1
Eastern Europe [8]	4.7	3.4	1.7	1.2	2.8	3.1	-0.6	0.0
South Caucasus [9]	4.0	5.8	3.9	3.4	3.4	3.2	0.1	0.3
Central Asia [10]	5.7	5.8	7.1	5.2	4.8	4.6	0.2	0.2

Source: World Bank.

Note: e = estimate; f = forecast. EMDE = emerging market and developing economy. World Bank forecasts are frequently updated based on new information and changing global circumstances. Consequently, projections presented here may differ from those in other World Bank documents, even if basic assessments of countries' prospects do not differ at any given moment in time. Since joining the euro area—Croatia on January 1, 2023, and Bulgaria on January 1, 2026—both countries have been added to the euro area aggregate and removed from the ECA aggregate in all tables to avoid double counting. Aggregates exclude Turkmenistan.

1. GDP and expenditure components are measured in average 2010–19 prices and market exchange rates, thus aggregates presented here may differ from other World Bank documents.
2. Aggregates presented here exclude Azerbaijan, Bosnia and Herzegovina, Kazakhstan, Kosovo, the Kyrgyz Republic, Montenegro, Serbia, Tajikistan, Turkmenistan, and Uzbekistan.
3. Exports and imports of goods and nonfactor services (GNFS).
4. Includes Armenia, Azerbaijan, Kazakhstan, the Kyrgyz Republic, Kosovo, the Russian Federation, Tajikistan, Ukraine, and Uzbekistan.
5. Includes Albania, Belarus, Bosnia and Herzegovina, Georgia, Hungary, Moldova, Montenegro, North Macedonia, Poland, Romania, Serbia, and Türkiye.
6. Includes Hungary, Poland, and Romania.
7. Includes Albania, Bosnia and Herzegovina, Kosovo, Montenegro, North Macedonia, and Serbia.
8. Includes Belarus, Moldova, and Ukraine.
9. Includes Armenia, Azerbaijan, and Georgia.
10. Includes Kazakhstan, the Kyrgyz Republic, Tajikistan, and Uzbekistan.

TABLE 2.4 Europe and Central Asia economy forecasts [1]

(Real GDP growth at market prices in percent, unless indicated otherwise)

	2023	2024	2025e	2026f	2027f	2028f	Percentage-point differences from January 2026 projections: 2026f	2027f
Albania	4.0	4.0	3.8	3.4	3.7	3.6	-0.1	0.2
Armenia	8.3	5.9	7.1	5.3	5.1	5.0	0.4	0.4
Azerbaijan	1.4	4.2	1.4	2.0	1.8	1.8	0.2	0.1
Belarus	4.1	4.3	1.3	1.1	0.8	0.7	-0.2	0.0
Bosnia and Herzegovina [2]	2.0	3.2	2.1	2.5	3.0	3.2	-0.5	-0.2
Bulgaria	1.7	3.4	3.1	2.6	2.9	3.0	-0.3	-0.2
Croatia	3.8	3.8	3.4	2.4	2.3	2.3	-0.5	-0.4
Georgia	7.8	9.7	7.5	5.0	5.5	5.0	-0.5	0.5
Kazakhstan	5.1	5.0	6.5	4.6	3.9	3.5	0.1	0.0
Kosovo	4.1	4.6	3.6	3.7	3.9	4.0	-0.1	0.0
Kyrgyz Republic	9.0	11.5	11.1	6.1	5.8	6.1	-0.4	-1.0
Moldova	1.2	0.3	2.4	1.9	2.9	3.2	-0.8	-0.9
Montenegro	6.5	3.2	2.7	2.9	3.1	3.1	-0.3	-0.1
North Macedonia	2.6	3.0	3.5	2.9	3.0	3.0	-0.1	0.0
Poland	0.2	3.2	3.6	3.1	2.6	2.9	-0.1	-0.3
Romania	2.3	0.9	0.7	0.0	1.7	2.0	-1.3	-0.2
Russian Federation	4.1	4.9	1.0	0.8	0.7	0.7	0.0	-0.3
Serbia	3.7	3.9	2.0	2.7	3.0	4.0	-0.3	-0.2
Tajikistan	8.3	8.4	8.4	6.5	5.0	4.8	0.3	0.3
Türkiye	5.0	3.3	3.6	2.8	3.7	4.3	-0.9	-0.7
Turkmenistan [3]	6.3	6.3	6.3	..	..	..	..	..
Ukraine	5.5	3.2	1.8	1.2	4.0	4.5	-0.8	0.0
Uzbekistan	6.3	6.7	7.7	6.4	6.7	6.8	0.4	0.8

Source: World Bank.

Note: e = estimate; f = forecast. World Bank forecasts are frequently updated based on new information and changing global circumstances. Consequently, projections presented here may differ from those in other World Bank documents, even if basic assessments of countries' prospects do not significantly differ at any given moment in time.

1. Data are based on GDP measured in average 2010–19 prices and market exchange rates, unless indicated otherwise.
2. GDP growth rate at constant prices is based on production approach.
3. Macroeconomic projections for Turkmenistan are not currently included, pending further alignment of data with international statistical practices.

Latin America and the Caribbean

Recent developments

Economic conditions in Latin America and the Caribbean (LAC) this year have been shaped by the conflict in the Middle East and heightened global uncertainty. Higher and more volatile global energy prices have raised inflation in some cases, leading to tighter monetary policy. However, the conflict has had only a moderate impact through financial channels, as sovereign spreads and exchange rates across major LAC economies remain broadly stable (figure 2.5.A). This is due in part to the net energy exporter status of several major LAC economies, which provides greater resilience to external shocks, as well as debt profiles composed of local-currency debt, reducing their vulnerability to exchange rate fluctuations.

Inflation continued to ease across much of the region in early 2026 prior to the escalation of the conflict, but progress with disinflation slowed in some cases and diverged further across countries thereafter, contributing to increasingly differentiated monetary policy paths (figure 2.5.B). Disinflation has stalled amid renewed energy-related pressures in Brazil and still-elevated core inflation in Mexico. Meanwhile inflationary pressures had already been strengthening in Colombia prior to the conflict, prompting tighter policy. In contrast, core inflation has remained close to targets in Chile and Peru despite the energy shock, allowing easing to continue, and declined sharply in Argentina following earlier stabilization measures, although monetary conditions remain restrictive.

Growth has shown uneven momentum across the region. Growth firmed in early 2026 in several South American economies, partly reflecting positive carryover from late 2025, although it moderated in Argentina amid still-tight monetary conditions. By contrast, economic activity in Mexico contracted amid weaker external demand and elevated trade policy uncertainty (figure 2.5.C).

Export performance has remained resilient, particularly among commodity and energy exporters such as Brazil, Colombia, Ecuador, and Guyana, reflecting favorable oil price developments. Trade conditions have also provided some support: lower U.S. tariffs have modestly improved the near-term outlook for regional exports, while the entry into force of the trade agreement between the European Union and the Southern Common Market (MERCOSUR) has strengthened market access and reduced trade-related uncertainty for exporters (Fitzgerald, Haller, and Yedid-Levi 2024; Kohn et al. 2024).

Outlook

Growth in LAC is projected to slow to 2.2 percent in 2026, reflecting still-weak domestic demand as well as weaker global growth, before strengthening gradually over 2027–28 to an average of 2.5 percent, as monetary policy eases and global conditions improve (table 2.5). The projected slowdown in 2026 is associated with softer growth in private consumption and exports relative to 2025, owing to weaker global growth and stricter monetary conditions. Investment is expected to be an important driver of the medium-term recovery, accelerating over 2027–28 as monetary easing gains traction and trade policy uncertainty abates.

Among net energy exporters, higher energy prices will support export revenues and external balances. In Argentina, growth is projected to remain relatively strong and roughly steady, at 3.6 percent over 2026-28, supported by exports but constrained by tight monetary and fiscal policies domestically. In Brazil, growth is projected to slow to 1.9 percent in 2026 amid lower consumption growth, before strengthening to 2.1 percent on average in 2027-28, as continuing disinflation allows monetary policy easing. In Colombia, growth is forecast to slow to 2.3 percent in 2026, with higher oil prices supporting incomes but inflationary pressures delaying monetary easing.

Mexico's exposure to the energy price shock is limited, given its broadly balanced energy trade position and fiscal efforts to contain its impact. Its economic prospects are shaped mainly by domestic demand and external trade conditions, particularly with respect to the United States and the USMCA revision. Growth is projected to pick up to 1.3 percent in 2026 and strengthen further to an average of 1.8 percent in 2027–28, as investment recovers and external demand stabilizes.

For net energy importers, higher oil prices will raise import costs and inflationary pressures. However, some economies, such as Chile and Peru, will partially benefit from elevated metals prices, which are expected to support export earnings and fiscal revenues (figure 2.5.D).

In Central America, where most economies are net energy importers, higher global oil prices are expected to weigh on activity through higher import costs, inflationary pressures, and weaker real incomes. These headwinds are partly mitigated by resilient remittance inflows and relatively stable domestic demand, but the subregion remains vulnerable to slower external demand and tighter external financing conditions following the conflict.

In the Caribbean, most economies are net energy importers and remain exposed to higher fuel costs, which are expected to add to price pressures and erode real incomes. Nevertheless, activity in the subregion is projected to strengthen, supported by a continued recovery in services, particularly tourism, as well as robust domestic demand. Growth is projected to reach 2.5 percent in 2026 and average about 3.9 percent in 2027–28. In Guyana, growth is expected to remain exceptionally strong as oil production continues to expand.

Despite broadly stable unemployment rates, labor market challenges persist across the region, reflecting weak formal job creation, high informality, and modest income growth, which continue to weigh on productivity, consumption, and poverty reduction (Loungani, Luttini, and Pallan 2025; World Bank 2026g). These constraints are compounded by tight fiscal positions in many economies. Elevated debt levels and high interest burdens limit the scope for countercyclical policies and targeted labor market support, making it more difficult to translate growth into better jobs and sustained income gains.

FIGURE 2.5 LAC: Recent developments and outlook

Financial markets in LAC have remained broadly stable in recent months, indicating limited spillovers from the Middle East conflict. Monetary policy paths have diverged further as central banks respond to country-specific inflation dynamics. Growth momentum at the start of 2026 has been uneven across major economies, reflecting differences in carryover and domestic conditions. The oil shock has generated differentiated terms-of-trade effects, benefiting net oil exporters, while high metals prices have more than offset the adverse effects of higher oil prices in some oil-importing economies.

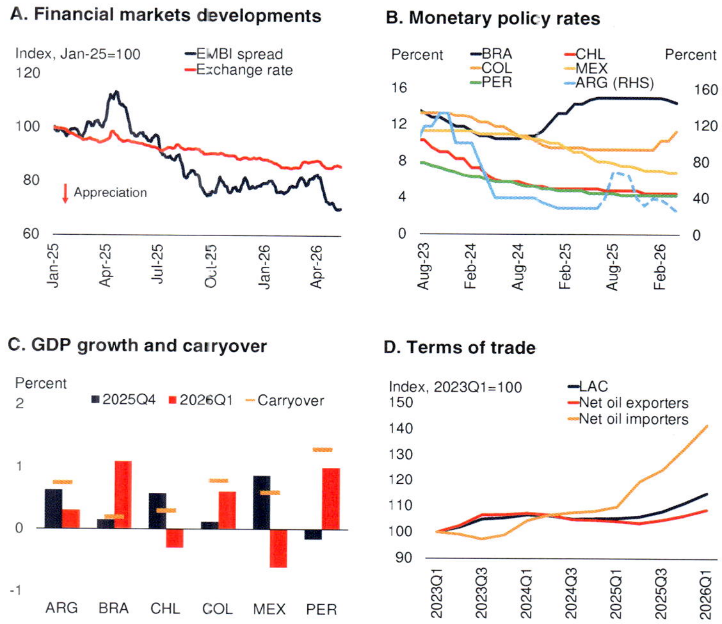

Sources: Banco Central de la República Argentina; Haver Analytics; J.P. Morgan; World Bank.

Note: ARG = Argentina; BRA = Brazil; CHL = Chile; COL = Colombia; EMBI = Emerging Market Bond Index; LAC = Latin America and the Caribbean; MEX = Mexico; PER = Peru RHS = right-hand scale.

A. Lines denote average LAC EMBI spread and exchange rate indexes. A decrease in the exchange rate indicates an appreciation of the domestic currency against the U.S. dollar. Sample includes Brazil, Chile, Colombia, Mexico, and Peru. Last observation is May 29, 2026.

B. End-of-period interest rates. Dashed line denotes the TAMAR rate in pesos at private banks because Argentina no longer formally sets a monetary policy rate. The TAMAR rate is the weighted average interest rate by amount of wholesale fixed-term deposits in pesos, from 30 to 35 days, constituted in the set of financial institutions in Argentina. Last observation is April 2026.

C. Carryover assumes that real GDP remains at its 2025Q4 level throughout 2026. It is computed as the percentage difference between 2025Q4 real GDP and the average level of real GDP in 2025. For Argentina, 2026Q1 GDP growth is calculated as the percentage change in average monthly GDP in Q1 relative to Q4.

D. LAC indicates the weighted average of terms-of-trade indexes for Argentina, Brazil, Chile, Colombia, Mexico, and Peru, using total goods trade as weights. Net oil importers are Chile and Peru. Net oil exporters are Argentina, Brazil, Colombia, and Mexico. Last observation is 2026Q1.

TABLE 2.5 Latin America and the Caribbean forecast summary

(Real GDP growth at market prices in percent, unless indicated otherwise)

	2023	2024	2025e	2026f	2027f	2028f	Percentage-point differences from January 2026 projections: 2026f	2027f
EMDE LAC, GDP [1]	**2.3**	**2.3**	**2.3**	**2.2**	**2.5**	**2.6**	**-0.1**	**-0.1**
GDP per capita (U.S. dollars)	1.6	1.6	1.6	1.5	1.8	2.0	-0.1	-0.1
(Average including economies that report expenditure components in national accounts) [2]								
EMDE LAC, GDP [2]	2.3	2.2	2.3	2.1	2.3	2.5	-0.1	-0.2
Private consumption	2.5	3.0	2.3	2.0	2.2	2.5	-0.3	-0.3
Public consumption	3.1	1.6	2.2	1.5	1.0	0.7	-0.2	-0.2
Fixed investment	1.8	2.5	1.9	1.6	3.3	3.6	-1.2	0.4
Exports, GNFS [3]	-0.5	4.1	5.9	4.0	4.4	4.6	1.3	1.1
Imports, GNFS [3]	0.4	4.7	6.0	3.2	4.3	4.4	0.4	1.2
Net exports, contribution to growth	-0.2	-0.2	-0.2	0.1	-0.1	0.0	0.2	-0.1
Memo items: GDP								
South America [4]	1.8	2.4	2.7	2.2	2.4	2.5	-0.2	-0.1
Central America [5]	4.8	3.5	4.3	3.6	3.7	3.8	0.0	0.0
Caribbean excluding Guyana [6]	1.9	3.2	1.5	2.5	3.7	4.0	-0.4	0.0

Source: World Bank.

Note: e = estimate; f = forecast. EMDE = emerging market and developing economy. World Bank forecasts are frequently updated based on new information and changing global circumstances. Consequently, projections presented here may differ from those in other World Bank documents, even if basic assessments of countries' prospects do not differ at any given moment in time. The World Bank is currently not publishing economic output, income, or growth data for República Bolivariana de Venezuela owing to a lack of reliable data of adequate quality. República Bolivariana de Venezuela is excluded from cross-country macroeconomic aggregates.

1. GDP and expenditure components are measured in average 2010–19 prices and market exchange rates.

2. Aggregate includes all countries in notes 4, 5, and 6, plus Mexico, but excludes Antigua and Barbuda, Barbados, Dominica, Grenada, Guyana, Haiti, St. Kitts and Nevis, St. Lucia, St. Vincent and the Grenadines, and Suriname.

3. Exports and imports of goods and nonfactor services (GNFS).

4. Includes Argentina, Bolivia, Brazil, Chile, Colombia, Ecuador, Paraguay, Peru, and Uruguay.

5. Includes Costa Rica, El Salvador, Guatemala, Honduras, Nicaragua, and Panama.

6. Includes Antigua and Barbuda, The Bahamas, Barbados, Belize, Dominica, the Dominican Republic, Grenada, Haiti, Jamaica, St. Kitts and Nevis, St. Lucia, St. Vincent and the Grenadines, Suriname, and Trinidad and Tobago.

TABLE 2.6 Latin America and the Caribbean economy forecasts[1]

(Real GDP growth at market prices in percent, unless indicated otherwise)

							Percentage-point differences from January 2026 projections	
	2023	2024	2025e	2026f	2027f	2028f	2026f	2027f
Argentina	-1.9	-1.3	4.4	3.6	3.7	3.5	-0.4	-0.3
Bahamas, The	3.0	3.4	2.8	2.2	1.9	1.8	0.1	0.1
Barbados	1.8	3.4	2.7	2.7	3.0	3.1	0.7	1.0
Belize	0.5	3.5	1.5	2.4	2.2	2.2	0.0	0.0
Bolivia	2.5	-1.1	-1.6	-3.2	4.0	3.2	-2.1	5.5
Brazil	3.2	3.4	2.3	1.9	2.0	2.2	-0.1	-0.3
Chile	0.7	2.8	2.5	2.1	2.5	2.3	-0.1	0.4
Colombia	0.8	1.5	2.6	2.3	2.4	2.7	-0.3	-0.4
Costa Rica	4.8	4.1	4.6	3.5	3.6	3.7	-0.1	-0.1
Dominica	3.7	2.1	3.1	2.8	2.9	2.8	-0.2	0.0
Dominican Republic	2.2	5.0	2.1	3.6	4.4	4.5	-0.9	-0.1
Ecuador	2.0	-2.0	3.7	2.5	2.5	2.5	0.5	0.1
El Salvador	3.4	2.6	3.9	3.2	3.0	3.1	0.2	0.0
Grenada	4.5	3.3	4.5	3.1	3.0	2.9	-0.2	0.0
Guatemala	3.5	3.7	4.2	3.7	3.8	3.8	0.0	0.1
Guyana	33.8	43.8	15.4	16.3	23.5	21.2	-3.3	1.6
Haiti [2]	-1.9	-4.2	-2.7	0.6	1.9	2.2	-1.4	-0.6
Honduras	3.6	3.6	3.8	3.4	3.7	3.8	-0.1	0.0
Jamaica	2.7	-0.5	-0.4	-1.0	3.2	1.6	1.3	-0.5
Mexico	3.1	1.4	0.6	1.3	1.7	1.9	0.0	-0.1
Nicaragua	4.4	3.6	4.9	3.4	3.4	3.3	0.4	0.4
Panama	7.4	2.9	4.4	3.9	4.1	4.1	-0.2	0.0
Paraguay	5.3	4.7	6.6	4.4	4.2	4.0	0.5	0.3
Peru	-0.4	3.5	3.4	2.7	2.8	2.8	0.2	0.3
St. Lucia	3.3	4.7	1.3	1.9	1.8	1.7	-0.1	-0.3
St. Vincent and the Grenadines	5.3	4.1	3.6	3.0	3.1	2.9	0.1	0.4
Suriname	2.4	1.7	1.8	4.0	4.5	20.5	0.5	0.8
Trinidad and Tobago	1.5	2.5	0.8	0.7	3.2	3.5	0.4	0.7
Uruguay	0.8	3.3	1.8	1.6	1.9	2.1	-0.6	-0.3

Source: World Bank.

Note: e = estimate; f = forecast. World Bank forecasts are frequently updated based on new information and changing global circumstances. Consequently, projections presented here may differ from those in other World Bank documents, even if basic assessments of countries' prospects do not significantly differ at any given moment in time.

1. Data are based on GDP measured in average 2010–19 prices and market exchange rates.

2. GDP is based on fiscal year, which runs from October to September of next year.

Middle East, North Africa, Afghanistan, and Pakistan

Recent developments

The conflict in the Middle East has had severe direct effects on economies in the MNA region. In addition to humanitarian losses, these impacts include a slump in economic activity and increased inflationary pressures due to higher energy and food prices, as well as a rise in transportation costs. While ceasefire agreements have at times eased fears of further escalation, uncertainty associated with the conflict remains high.

Among hydrocarbon exporters, the conflict has exacerbated already-weakened economic activity in the Islamic Republic of Iran, following intensified sanctions and heightened social unrest. Limited ship transit through the Strait of Hormuz and the destruction of energy-related infrastructure have significantly disrupted oil and natural gas production in other hydrocarbon exporters, including Iraq and Gulf Cooperation Council (GCC) countries. In some economies, non-hydrocarbon activity has remained soft, alongside tight financial conditions.

The conflict has also had repercussions for hydrocarbon importers, with higher energy and input costs and shipping disruptions weighing on activity. In some economies, worsened security conditions have led to currency depreciations, capital outflows, and reduced tourist arrivals. To combat supply shortages and price hikes, several economies have implemented energy-saving measures and increased subsidies.

Geopolitical tensions have been heightened across economies in fragile and conflict-affected situations (FCS), including Afghanistan, Lebanon, and the Republic of Yemen. In West Bank and Gaza, the October 2025 ceasefire opened a fragile window for stabilization of the economy, following unprecedented losses, with Gaza facing near total destruction of physical infrastructure and significant recovery needs. Economic activity remains markedly below pre-October 2023 levels amid severe labor market dislocation (World Bank 2026h).

Outlook

With forecasts for the Islamic Republic of Iran excluded because of exceptionally high uncertainty, growth in MNA is expected to weaken to 1.6 percent in 2026, from 4 percent in 2025, reflecting the adverse effects of the regional conflict (table 2.7). This represents a 2.7-percentage-point downgrade from the January projection. Assuming disruptions from the conflict taper off by the end of this year, growth in the region is projected to recover to an average of 4.5 percent over 2027–28. However, the outlook is subject to significant uncertainty.

Growth in hydrocarbon exporters in the Middle East is set to slow to 0.3 percent in 2026, with the projection downgraded by 4.3 percentage points since January (figure 2.6.A). This reflects significant declines in hydrocarbon production, alongside disruptions to trade, foreign investment, and services activity, including tourism and aviation. Inflation is forecast to pick up, partly as a result of higher food import prices, with a rise in shipping costs (figure 2.6.B). Hydrocarbon prices will also be higher, but the materialization of such benefits—particularly on the fiscal front—faces heightened uncertainty on account of increasing spending pressures in several economies, especially on defense.

Across these economies, the effects of the conflict are expected to vary depending on the extent of damage, the degree of exposure to hostilities, and the strength of policy buffers.

The sharp slowdowns projected for Iraq, Kuwait, and Qatar will be associated with worsening fiscal and current account balances stemming from declines in hydrocarbon revenues and, in some cases, increases in military spending (table 2.8). In contrast, the deceleration in growth is expected to be moderate in Oman, which is less exposed to the conflict primarily because its major ports are located outside the Strait of Hormuz. The weakening of growth is anticipated to be less pronounced in Saudi Arabia, mainly reflecting the ability to reroute oil exports through the East-West pipeline (World Bank 2026i).

The strengthening of growth in hydrocarbon exporters in the Middle East over 2027–28 will be supported by a recovery in hydrocarbon output, including infrastructure investment, alongside the steady expansion of non-hydrocarbon activity. As trade activity returns with lower cost pressures, inflation is projected to recede. Current account surpluses are forecast to shrink, with declines in energy prices (figure 2.6.C). In contrast, the expected improvement in fiscal balances reflects an increase in hydrocarbon production and revenues outpacing expenditure growth (figure 2.6.D).

Forecasts for 2026 have been upgraded since January for hydrocarbon exporters not directly involved in the conflict—namely, Algeria and Libya—primarily because of higher energy prices. Besides, a rise in hydrocarbon prices will improve fiscal and external balances in 2026, before they worsen amid the price decline over 2027–28.

Among hydrocarbon importers, growth is also set to slow in 2026, reflecting higher hydrocarbon prices, disruptions to shipping and tourism, and weaker remittances. Primary surpluses are anticipated to shrink in 2026, partly reflecting increases in subsidies and other social protection measures in several economies. In Djibouti, amid limited access to external financing, revenues are projected to moderate with lower donor grants (World Bank 2026j). Higher import prices and lower remittance inflows are expected to contribute to widening current account deficits in 2026, although higher fertilizer prices are likely to provide a partial offset for Jordan and Morocco through stronger export revenues.

Growth in hydrocarbon importers is forecast to recover in 2027–28, supported by lower energy prices and recoveries in shipping, tourism, and remittances. Waning inflationary pressures will lead to monetary policy easing, which should support activity. Primary surpluses are projected to widen with fiscal consolidation efforts, notably in the Arab Republic of Egypt, Pakistan, and Tunisia. However, job creation will likely remain subdued over the forecast horizon, partly reflecting weak labor market conditions and structural rigidities, with limited female labor force participation.

The outlook for economies in FCS in the region remains subdued and highly uncertain. The conflict is projected to weigh on activity,

FIGURE 2.6 MNA: Outlook

A sharp decline in activity among hydrocarbon exporters in the Middle East this year will be accompanied by rising inflation due to higher food prices and shipping costs. This should be followed by a rebound in growth over 2027–28, assuming the effects of the conflict wane. Higher hydrocarbon prices in 2026 are projected to benefit hydrocarbon exporters in North Africa, with improvements in their fiscal and current account positions. Growth in hydrocarbon importers is also expected to slow in 2026 amid higher energy prices, disruptions to shipping and tourism, and weaker remittances, before strengthening in 2027–28 alongside easing inflationary pressures.

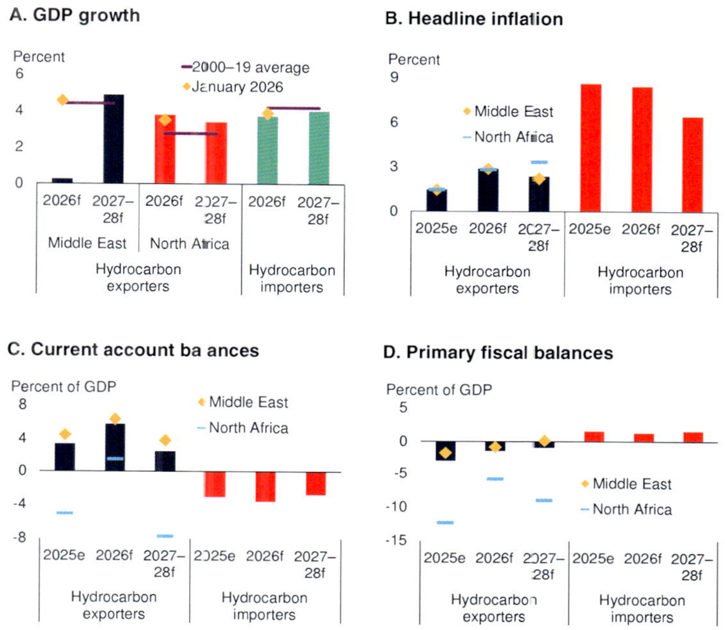

Source: World Bank.

Note: e = estimate; f = forecast. MNA = Middle East, North Africa, Afghanistan, and Pakistan. Forecasts for 2027–28 are shown as averages over the two years.

A. Aggregates are calculated as weighted averages, using GDP at average 2010–19 prices and market exchange rates as weights. Diamonds for January 2026 refer to rates computed with data in the January 2026 edition of the *Global Economic Prospects* report.

B. Aggregates are calculated as weighted geometric averages, using nominal GDP in U.S. dollars as weights.

C.D. Aggregates are calculated as weighted averages, using nominal GDP in U.S. dollars as weights.

particularly exports and tourism, and worsen food insecurity in Lebanon and the Syrian Arab Republic. A recovery in West Bank and Gaza will depend on the continuation of the ceasefire, while growth in Afghanistan hinges on improved absorption of returnees into the labor market (World Bank 2026k). In the Republic of Yemen, growth is forecast to remain subdued, reflecting persistent domestic unrest, institutional fragmentation, and the impacts of the conflict in the Middle East, including higher energy and food prices and worsened food insecurity (World Bank 2026l).

TABLE 2.7 Middle East, North Africa, Afghanistan, and Pakistan forecast summary

(Real GDP growth at market prices in percent, unless indicated otherwise)

	2023	2024	2025e	2026f	2027f	2028f	Percentage-point differences from January 2026 projections: 2026f	2027f
EMDE MNA, GDP [1]	**2.0**	**2.9**	**4.0**	**1.6**	**5.0**	**4.0**	**-2.7**	**0.7**
GDP per capita (U.S. dollars)	0.1	1.1	2.3	0.0	3.4	2.4	-2.6	0.7
(Average including economies that report expenditure components in national accounts) [2]								
EMDE MNA, GDP [2]	1.6	2.2	3.7	2.0	5.2	3.8	-2.1	1.2
Private consumption	5.1	5.0	4.9	4.3	4.3	4.4	0.1	0.3
Public consumption	3.1	2.5	3.3	2.6	3.0	2.9	-0.1	0.2
Fixed investment	1.8	4.9	2.6	3.5	4.3	5.7	-2.2	-2.7
Exports, GNFS	1.0	1.4	3.5	-0.5	9.8	5.7	-7.9	2.7
Imports, GNFS	7.8	6.9	6.1	3.5	6.8	7.2	-4.1	-1.0
Net exports, contribution to growth	-2.0	-1.8	-0.9	-1.4	0.8	-0.7	-1.3	1.1
Memo items: GDP								
Hydrocarbon exporters [3]	1.9	2.9	4.0	0.7	5.5	3.9	-3.8	1.1
GCC [4]	1.4	3.3	4.5	1.3	5.2	4.0	-3.1	0.6
Non-GCC [5]	3.5	1.2	2.0	-1.6	6.8	3.5	-6.4	3.2
Hydrocarbon importers [6]	2.2	3.0	3.9	3.7	3.9	4.1	-0.2	-0.2

Source: World Bank.

Note: e = estimate; f = forecast. EMDE = emerging market and developing economy; GCC = Gulf Cooperation Council; GNFS = goods and non-factor services; MNA = Middle East, North Africa, Afghanistan, and Pakistan. World Bank forecasts are frequently updated based on new information and changing global circumstances. Consequently, projections presented here may differ from those in other World Bank documents, even if basic assessments of countries' prospects do not differ at any given moment in time.

1. GDP and expenditure components are measured in average 2010–19 prices and market exchange rates. Excludes the Islamic Republic of Iran, Lebanon, the Syrian Arab Republic, and the Republic of Yemen because of the high degree of uncertainty. Aggregated growth rates based on data in the January 2026 edition of the *Global Economic Prospects* report are recomputed by excluding data for the Islamic Republic of Iran and therefore do not necessarily match those reported in the January 2026 publication.

2. Aggregate includes all economies in notes 3 and 6 except Jordan, Qatar, and the United Arab Emirates.

3. Algeria, Bahrain, Iraq, Kuwait, Libya, Oman, Qatar, Saudi Arabia, and the United Arab Emirates.

4. Bahrain, Kuwait, Oman, Qatar, Saudi Arabia, and the United Arab Emirates.

5. Algeria, Iraq, and Libya.

6. Afghanistan, Djibouti, the Arab Republic of Egypt, Jordan, Morocco, Pakistan, Tunisia, and West Bank and Gaza.

TABLE 2.8 Middle East, North Africa, Afghanistan, and Pakistan economy forecasts

(Real GDP growth at market prices in percent, unless indicated otherwise)

	2023	2024	2025e	2026f	2027f	2028f	Percentage-point differences from January 2026 projections: 2026f	2027f
Calendar-year basis								
Algeria	4.1	3.7	3.8	3.7	3.1	3.1	0.2	-0.2
Bahrain	3.9	2.9	3.5	1.3	2.8	3.1	-1.8	-0.1
Djibouti	6.8	7.0	6.5	5.9	6.3	6.5	-0.2	0.3
Iraq [1]	0.5	-1.5	-2.2	-8.9	12.2	3.5	-15.4	8.4
Jordan	3.1	2.6	2.8	2.7	2.9	3.0	-0.1	0.1
Kuwait	-1.6	-1.5	2.6	-6.4	13.5	2.8	-9.0	11.0
Lebanon [2]	-0.5	-5.2	4.2	..	..	..	..	..
Libya	10.2	1.9	13.4	4.5	4.0	6.0	1.0	0.1
Morocco	3.7	3.8	4.7	4.2	4.0	4.3	-0.2	-0.4
Oman	1.2	1.7	2.6	2.4	3.0	3.4	-1.2	-1.0
Qatar	1.2	3.0	3.0	-5.7	5.7	6.4	-11.0	-1.1
Saudi Arabia	0.5	2.6	4.5	3.1	4.9	3.7	-1.2	0.5
Syrian Arab Republic [2,3]	0.3	0.9	2.0	..	..	..	..	..
Tunisia	0.2	1.6	2.5	2.5	2.3	2.3	0.0	0.1
United Arab Emirates	4.3	6.6	6.2	2.4	4.1	4.2	-2.6	-1.0
West Bank and Gaza	-1.0	-22.9	4.1	4.5	11.3	9.1	-0.6	-0.3
Yemen, Rep. [2]	-2.0	-1.5	-1.5	-0.5	1.6	..	-0.5	..
Fiscal-year basis [4]	**2023/24**	**2024/25**	**2025/26e**	**2026/27f**	**2027/28f**	**2028/29f**	**2026/27f**	**2027/28f**
Afghanistan	2.3	1.9	4.8	4.0	3.9	3.8	0.2	0.4
Iran, Islamic Rep. [2]	5.3	3.7	-2.8	..	..	..	..	..
	2022/23	**2023/24**	**2024/25**	**2025/26e**	**2026/27f**	**2027/28f**	**2025/26e**	**2026/27f**
Egypt, Arab Rep.	3.8	2.4	4.4	4.6	4.0	4.6	0.3	-0.8
Pakistan [1]	-0.2	2.6	3.1	3.0	3.2	3.7	0.0	-0.2

Source: World Bank.

Note: e = estimate; f = forecast. World Bank forecasts are frequently updated based on new information and changing global circumstances. Consequently, projections presented here may differ from those in other World Bank documents, even if basic assessments of economies' prospects do not significantly differ at any given moment in time.

1. Data are reported on a factor cost basis.

2. Forecasts for the Islamic Republic of Iran (beyond FY2025/26), Lebanon (beyond 2025), the Syrian Arab Republic (beyond 2025), and the Republic of Yemen (beyond 2027) are excluded because of a high degree of uncertainty.

3. Growth estimate for 2025 ranges between 2.0 and 4.0 percent.

4. Fiscal year runs from March 21 to March 20 in Afghanistan and the Islamic Republic of Iran; and from July 1 to June 30 in the Arab Republic of Egypt and Pakistan.

South Asia

Recent developments

The disruptions to commodity markets and international trade resulting from the conflict in the Middle East have led to shortages of energy and agricultural products and put upward pressure on energy and food prices in SAR. Inflation has still generally remained within or below central banks' target ranges. In Bangladesh, however, inflation has stayed elevated, alongside tight monetary policy. In addition, monetary policy in Sri Lanka was tightened at the end of May to tame inflationary pressures.

Although financial conditions in the region eased somewhat following the de-escalation in hostilities, they remain tighter than before the conflict in several countries, with some currencies under pressure. Receipts of remittances have declined in many countries, particularly from GCC countries, and disruptions to tourism have also worsened fiscal and external imbalances, including in Maldives.

Despite heightened uncertainty related to the conflict, economic activity in India remained robust early this year, supported by resilient domestic demand. Private consumption, particularly in rural areas, has been strong, with urban demand recovering. Collections of taxes from domestic sales have also increased steadily. To mitigate the price pressures arising from higher energy costs, as well as shortages of agricultural products, especially fertilizers, several measures have been implemented in India, including a reduction in fuel taxes.

In Bangladesh and Nepal, domestic political uncertainties have waned, but private activity has been constrained by increased input costs and weaker investor sentiment. In these economies, the financial sector remains fragile, with subdued credit growth and deteriorating asset quality. In contrast, activity has recovered in Sri Lanka after the disruptions caused in late 2025 by Cyclone Ditwah, alongside a rise in private sector credit. Credit growth has also increased modestly in Bhutan, with enhanced regulatory frameworks and measures to support financial stability.

Outlook

Growth in SAR is expected to soften to 6.3 percent in 2026, mainly reflecting the adverse impact of the conflict in the Middle East, including higher energy prices, reduced supplies of oil and natural gas, and disruptions to remittances and tourism (table 2.9). Nevertheless, the growth forecast has been marginally upgraded since January, primarily because of more robust domestic demand and stronger export growth in several economies than previously expected. Improved access to major trading partners, as well as lower U.S. tariffs, is anticipated to contribute to the stronger export performance (World Bank 2026m). With conflict-related disruptions assumed to wane by the end of the year, growth in SAR is set to pick up to an average rate of 7 percent per year in 2027–28.

Growth in India is projected to moderate to 6.6 percent in fiscal year 2026/27 (April 2026 to March 2027), reflecting a slowdown in private demand growth owing to higher energy prices and other input costs, though a reduction in Goods and Services Tax rates should somewhat support consumer demand (table 2.10; World Bank 2026n). Reduced U.S. tariffs and the expected implementation of free trade agreements will likely mitigate the impact of weaker external demand due to the conflict, particularly on merchandise exports. Growth is then anticipated to rebound over the next two fiscal years, driven by firming domestic demand and a pickup in export growth.

Excluding India, growth in the region is forecast to increase to 4 percent in 2026 from 3.9 percent in 2025, reflecting some acceleration of growth in Bangladesh, driven by a gradual recovery in investment (World Bank 2026o). However, the growth projection has been downgraded by 1 percentage point since January, partly because of the weaker expansion of consumption and exports, as well as a rise in import costs. A recovery in external demand is expected to support growth in 2027–28.

In SAR, excluding Bangladesh and India, the projected softening of growth in 2026 partly reflects heightened uncertainty and higher input costs, which will weigh on investment, including in Nepal and Sri Lanka. Disruptions to tourism and higher energy prices are expected to contribute to a slowdown in Bhutan and Maldives. Over 2027–28, a rebound in growth is anticipated, supported by a return of tourist flows, increased remittances, and expansion of hydropower activity, including the construction of plants and electricity exports in Bhutan and Nepal (World Bank 2026p).

Fiscal balances in the region are set to deteriorate in 2026 (figure 2.7.A). In several economies, including Bangladesh, Bhutan, India, and Maldives, fiscal deficits are anticipated to rise, partly owing to increases in subsidies intended to counteract the surges in energy prices. Weaker revenues stemming from tax cuts and subdued tourism activity are also projected to erode fiscal balances, including in Bhutan and Maldives (World Bank 2026q). In India, reduced revenues due to tax reforms are forecast to be partly offset by slower capital expenditure growth and reductions in non-essential current spending. Revenue collection will likely remain strong in Sri Lanka, maintaining a primary surplus (World Bank 2026r).

External balances are also forecast to weaken in the region this year due to the impact of the conflict, including higher costs of energy imports, as well as declines in tourism revenues and remittances (figure 2.7.B). Over 2027–28, current account balances are projected to improve, on aggregate, supported by higher exports, reflecting a rebound in external demand. However, in Bhutan and Nepal, the worsening of current account balances will partly reflect increased imports for the construction of hydropower projects. Over the forecast horizon, trade agreements and structural reforms undertaken to improve the business environment are set to support foreign direct investment inflows in India. In contrast, despite the reform implementation, a tight business environment is expected to weigh on foreign investment inflows in Nepal.

FIGURE 2.7 SAR: Outlook

Growth in SAR is projected to slow in 2026, accompanied by a deterioration in fiscal and external balances. The expected decline in fiscal balances is partly due to measures intended to mitigate the adverse impact of the conflict in the Middle East, including increases in subsidies. Current account balances are also set to deteriorate, mainly reflecting higher import costs and declines in tourism revenues and remittances. Inflation is forecast to increase in 2026, before softening over 2027–28. The pace of poverty reduction will be slower than was expected in January, owing to the impact of the conflict.

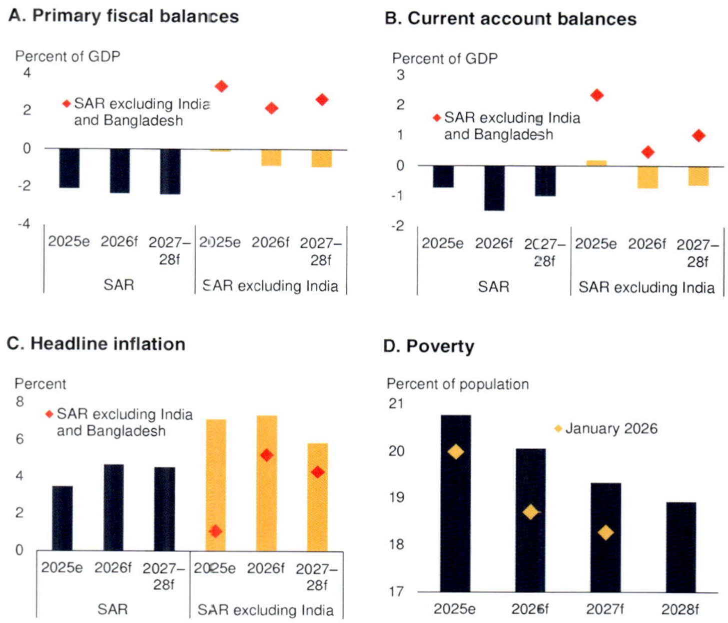

Source: World Bank.

Note: e = estimate; f = forecast. SAR = South Asia. Forecasts for 2027–28 are shown as averages over the two years.

A.B. Aggregates are calculated as weighted averages, using nominal GDP in U.S. dollars as weights.

C. Aggregates are calculated as weighted geometric averages, using nominal GDP in U.S. dollars as weights.

D. Poverty is defined using the lower-middle-income poverty threshold of 4.20 international dollars per day at 2021 purchasing power parity. Sample includes four countries (Bangladesh, Bhutan, Nepal, and Sri Lanka). Diamonds for January 2026 refer to rates computed with data in the January 2026 edition of the *Global Economic Prospects* report.

Inflation in the region is projected to rise in 2026, driven mainly by increases in energy and transport costs, though monetary policies are set to remain stable (figure 2.7.C). Over 2027–28, inflation is expected to soften in most countries, leading to monetary policy easing, which should boost demand.

With continuing per capita income growth, poverty in the region is anticipated to decline further (figure 2.7.D). However, the pace of decline will be slower than expected in January, mainly reflecting the adverse effects of higher energy and food prices on household welfare, agricultural income, and food security, as well as reduced remittances. In addition, job creation will remain subdued in the region, partly on account of regulatory and structural barriers, widespread informality, and skill mismatches.

TABLE 2.9 South Asia forecast summary

(Real GDP growth at market prices in percent, unless indicated otherwise)

	2023	2024	2025e	2026f	2027f	2028f	Percentage-point differences from January 2026 projections: 2026f	2027f
EMDE SAR, GDP [1]	**6.6**	**6.8**	**7.0**	**6.3**	**6.9**	**7.1**	**0.1**	**0.4**
GDP per capita (U.S. dollars)	5.6	5.8	6.1	5.3	6.0	6.2	0.1	0.4
(Average including economies that report expenditure components in national accounts) [2]								
EMDE SAR, GDP [2]	6.6	6.8	7.0	6.3	6.9	7.1	0.1	0.4
Private consumption	5.6	5.7	7.1	7.0	7.1	7.0	-0.1	0.1
Public consumption	2.0	4.9	5.6	6.4	7.3	7.1	1.1	-0.1
Fixed investment	6.6	6.1	6.9	6.5	6.6	6.8	-0.1	-0.2
Exports, GNFS	2.2	4.2	6.2	5.9	6.9	7.5	1.2	1.5
Imports, GNFS	-0.8	3.5	6.2	6.8	7.0	6.9	-0.8	-0.5
Net exports, contribution to growth	0.7	0.0	-0.3	-0.5	-0.3	-0.2	0.5	0.6
Memo items: GDP								
SAR excluding India	3.7	4.1	3.9	4.0	4.8	5.2	-1.0	-0.8
Excluding Bangladesh	-0.3	4.7	4.6	3.4	4.2	4.2	-0.2	0.6

Source: World Bank.

Note: e = estimate; f = forecast. EMDE = emerging market and developing economy; GNFS = goods and non-factor services; SAR = South Asia. World Bank forecasts are frequently updated based on new information and changing global circumstances. Consequently, projections presented here may differ from those in other World Bank documents, even if basic assessments of countries' prospects do not differ at any given moment in time.

1. GDP and expenditure components are measured in average 2010–19 prices and market exchange rates. Aggregates are presented in calendar-year terms.

2. Aggregate excludes Maldives.

TABLE 2.10 South Asia economy forecasts

(Real GDP growth at market prices in percent, unless indicated otherwise)

	2023	2024	2025e	2026f	2027f	2028f	Percentage-point differences from January 2026 projections: 2026f	2027f
Calendar-year basis								
Maldives	4.9	3.5	5.7	0.7	7.2	4.0	-3.2	3.2
Sri Lanka	-2.0	5.0	5.0	3.6	3.8	3.9	0.1	0.7
Fiscal-year basis [1]	2023/24	2024/25	2025/26e	2026/27f	2027/28f	2028/29f	2026/27f	2027/28f
India	7.2	7.1	7.7	6.6	7.2	7.0	0.1	0.6
	2022/23	2023/24	2024/25	2025/26e	2026/27f	2027/28f	2025/26e	2026/27f
Bangladesh	5.8	4.2	3.5	3.8	4.6	5.5	-0.8	-1.5
Bhutan	4.9	6.1	8.1	7.1	6.4	6.8	-0.2	0.3
Nepal	2.0	3.7	4.6	2.3	4.2	4.6	0.2	-0.5

Source: World Bank.

Note: e = estimate; f = forecast. World Bank forecasts are frequently updated based on new information and changing global circumstances. Consequently, projections presented here may differ from those in other World Bank documents, even if basic assessments of countries' prospects do not significantly differ at any given moment in time.

1. Fiscal year runs from April 1 to March 31 in India; from July 1 to June 30 in Bangladesh and Bhutan; and from July 16 to July 15 in Nepal.

Sub-Saharan Africa

Recent developments

Growth in SSA firmed to an estimated 4.1 percent in 2025. Growth and fiscal revenues were boosted by higher-than-expected commodity prices, particularly for precious metals, copper, and coffee, which drove robust exports. On the domestic side, headline and food disinflation, driven by improved agricultural output and currency appreciation across several economies, allowed a gradual easing of monetary policy, supporting domestic demand. Growth was also bolstered by progress on structural reforms across large economies, which increased investor confidence in the region, boosting private investment.

In early 2026, high-frequency survey indicators of economic activity in SSA showed initial signs of resilience despite higher energy prices and weaker external demand owing to the conflict in the Middle East (figure 2.8.A). The conflict is already impacting the region, and SSA governments have been more constrained in their policy responses than those in other regions, as highlighted by preliminary data indicating that the disinflation process may have stalled and that the annual headline consumer inflation rate reaccelerated in April. Nonetheless, some authorities have implemented measures to shield vulnerable households, including expanded or temporary fuel subsidies (for example, Ethiopia and Ghana), delays in planned subsidy reforms (for example, Angola), and adjustments in administered prices or transfers (for example, Senegal). Financial conditions tightened somewhat as sovereign bond yields and spreads temporarily rose, currencies depreciated slightly, and equity markets stagnated (figure 2.8.B). While oil exporters are benefiting from higher energy prices, most SSA economies are dependent on energy imports, contributing to deteriorating external and fiscal positions.

Other key developments included positive trade measures, notably the United States' extension of the African Growth and Opportunity Act to the end of 2026 and China's elimination of tariffs on all African imports, aimed at supporting the region's still-limited global trade integration. Additionally, in May 2026, the third-largest Ebola outbreak recorded globally was reported in eastern Democratic Republic of the Congo, with imported cases also confirmed in Uganda.

Outlook

Growth in SSA is forecast to edge down to 4 percent in 2026 and then recover to 4.4 percent on average in 2027–28 (figure 2.8.C). The growth forecast for 2026 has been revised down by 0.3 percentage point since January, with the negative impact of the conflict in the Middle East expected to outweigh existing growth drivers—including structural reforms and recent trade agreements that support investment and exports. The outlook assumes that the geopolitical environment stabilizes in the near term and that security improves in economies in FCS in the region.

Though the impact of the conflict in the Middle East, operating through higher commodity prices and weaker external demand, is expected to be overwhelmingly negative, it will be heterogeneous across SSA economies. Higher energy prices will benefit oil exporters, particularly Angola and Nigeria. Non-oil-exporting economies, on the other hand, will face higher fuel, fertilizer, and transport costs, driving up inflation, especially food prices (figure 2.8.D). Consequently, growth in non-oil-exporting economies is expected to be markedly lower than anticipated, as elevated consumer prices and input costs are set to dampen consumption and raise production costs.

Limited fiscal resources are restricting efforts to manage rising energy and food prices across many SSA economies, notwithstanding the improved fiscal positions and buffers in recent years. Expanding fuel subsidies are likely to increase deficits and borrowing, reducing support for vulnerable households and heightening macroeconomic risks. Monetary policy is expected to remain tight because of inflation concerns and limited scope to look through inflation shocks. Despite overall progress in improving fiscal credibility, high borrowing costs, reduced concessional financing, and declining ODA are also set to add to fiscal challenges in SSA, especially for economies that have been slower to improve policy frameworks.

Structural reforms and recent trade policy changes will only partly offset global headwinds. In South

FIGURE 2.8 SSA: Recent developments and outlook

Economic growth in SSA strengthened in 2025 and remained resilient in early 2026, despite the conflict in the Middle East raising energy costs and increasing uncertainty. Financial conditions tightened temporarily before resuming their easing trend. Recent reforms and strengthening investment and export growth support the outlook, and reform momentum remains an important domestic tailwind. The impact of higher energy prices on inflation is expected to be uneven across the region, putting the most upward pressure on food prices in import-dependent economies. Food insecurity remains elevated in the region.

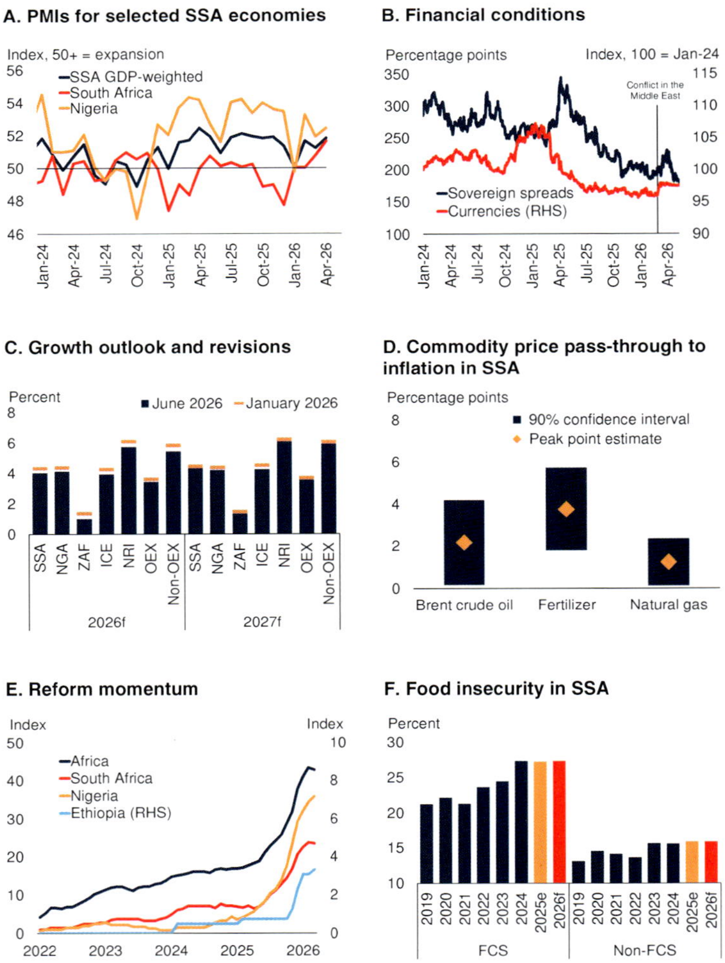

Sources: Google Trends; Haver Analytics; J.P. Morgan; World Bank; World Food Security Outlook (database).

Note: e = estimate; f = forecast. FCS = fragile and conflict-affected situations; GDP = gross domestic product; ICE = industrial commodity exporters excluding Nigeria, South Africa, and Sudan; NGA = Nigeria; NRI = non-resource-rich economies; OEX = oil exporters; non-OEX = non-oil-exporting economies; PMI = purchasing managers' index; RHS = right-hand scale; SSA = Sub-Saharan Africa; ZAF = South Africa.

A. GDP-weighted sample includes 7 SSA economies. Last observation is April 2026.

B. Blue line shows the median J.P. Morgan Emerging Markets Bond Index sovereign spread for 14 SSA economies. Red line shows the median currency index for 19 SSA economies. Last observation is May 28, 2026.

C. Aggregate growth rates are calculated using constant GDP weights at average 2010–19 prices and market exchange rates. Projected annual GDP growth by group from the current (bars) and January 2026 (orange) edition of the *Global Economic Prospects* report.

D. Figure shows the peak estimates (orange diamonds) of the cumulative impulse response function of a 1 percentage point shock to the commodity price indices on headline consumer inflation in SSA. Sample includes 44 SSA economies from 2000–25.

E. Twelve-month average of Google search index for "economic reform" for the relevant economy. Last observation is May 2026.

F. Blue bars represent SSA median of three-year centered average percentage of population subject to severe food insecurity. Orange bars show estimates, and red bars show forecasts. Sample includes 48 SSA economies.

Africa, reforms include improved energy availability, whereas in Ethiopia and Nigeria, they include exchange-rate liberalization, improvements in public financial management, and other business-friendly measures (figure 2.8.E). The deepening of intraregional trade through the African Continental Free Trade Area, along with tariff reductions from China and the United States, will also support export industries.

Though commodity prices are projected to increase significantly, weaker external demand and the impact of higher prices on consumption mean that growth for industrial commodity exporters will only edge up from 3.1 percent in 2025 to 3.2 percent in 2026, and an annual average of 3.5 percent in 2027–28. Indeed, the impact of the conflict in the Middle East has led to downward revisions, especially in Nigeria and South Africa, where structural constraints continue to limit growth. Non-resource-rich economies are expected to see growth slow from 6.4 percent in 2025 to 5.7 percent in 2026, and then average 6.2 percent over 2027–28, though still outpacing commodity exporters. Ethiopia's growth is expected to be driven by reforms in monetary policy and the financial sector, despite external challenges. Notably, growth forecasts have been lowered for Uganda as a result of oil project delays, for Senegal amid revelations of hidden debt and the subsequent freezing of funding from the International Monetary Fund (IMF), and for Côte d'Ivoire on account of falling cocoa prices.

Real per capita GDP growth in SSA is projected to remain at 1.6 percent in 2026, before firming to an average of 2 percent per year in 2027–28. Nonetheless, this pace is still insufficient to deliver substantial reductions in extreme poverty. Job creation in SSA is also expected to lag behind its growing labor force, projected to be the world's fastest-growing by 2030 (World Bank 2025b). Food insecurity in economies in FCS is set to remain at the highest levels since the early 2000s, while it is projected to increase in economies not in FCS (figure 2.8.F; World Bank 2026s). The decline in ODA is also likely to adversely affect living standards and deepen humanitarian and health crises, such as the recent Ebola outbreak (da Silva et al. 2026).

TABLE 2.11 Sub-Saharan Africa forecast summary

(Real GDP growth at market prices in percent, unless indicated otherwise)

	2023	2024	2025e	2026f	2027f	2028f	Percentage-point differences from January 2026 projections: 2026f	2027f
EMDE SSA, GDP [1]	**3.0**	**3.8**	**4.1**	**4.0**	**4.4**	**4.5**	**-0.3**	**-0.1**
GDP per capita (U.S. dollars)	0.5	1.3	1.6	1.6	1.9	2.1	-0.3	-0.1
(Average including economies that report expenditure components in national accounts) [2]								
EMDE SSA, GDP [2,3]	2.9	3.7	4.1	3.9	4.3	4.5	-0.3	-0.1
Private consumption	2.9	3.1	4.5	3.9	4.1	3.9	-0.2	0.0
Public consumption	2.5	3.8	4.0	-1.0	2.3	2.9	-4.3	0.0
Fixed investment	8.9	4.9	5.1	5.9	6.1	6.5	-0.5	-0.4
Exports, GNFS [4]	2.7	6.3	4.9	6.0	6.7	6.6	1.0	0.7
Imports, GNFS [4]	5.5	1.9	5.6	6.4	6.2	5.6	0.7	0.6
Net exports, contribution to growth	-1.0	1.1	-0.4	-0.4	-0.1	0.0	0.1	0.2
Memo items: GDP								
SSA excluding Nigeria and South Africa	3.7	4.8	5.2	5.0	5.3	5.4	-0.3	-0.2
Non-resource-rich countries [5]	5.9	5.9	6.4	5.7	6.2	6.2	-0.4	0.0
Industrial commodity exporters [6]	2.6	3.1	3.1	3.2	3.4	3.6	-0.3	-0.2
FCS [7]	3.0	4.2	4.8	4.7	4.8	4.8	-0.2	-0.1
Non-FCS [7]	3.1	3.4	3.6	3.4	4.0	4.2	-0.4	-0.1

Source: World Bank.

Note: e = estimate; f = forecast. EMDE = emerging market and developing economy. World Bank forecasts are frequently updated based on new information and changing global circumstances. Consequently, projections presented here may differ from those in other World Bank documents, even if basic assessments of countries' prospects do not differ at any given moment in time.

1. GDP and expenditure components are measured in average 2010–19 prices and market exchange rates.
2. Subregion aggregate excludes the Central African Republic, Eritrea, Guinea, Nigeria, São Tomé and Príncipe, the Federal Republic of Somalia, and South Sudan, for which data limitations prevent the forecasting of GDP components.
3. Subregion growth rates may differ from the most recent edition of Africa's Pulse (https://www.worldbank.org/en/publication/africa-pulse) because of data revisions.
4. Exports and imports of goods and nonfactor services (GNFS).
5. Non-resource-rich countries represent agricultural-commodity-exporting and commodity-importing countries.
6. Industrial commodity exporters are countries for which exports of metals, minerals, and/or energy account for a significant share of total goods exports as defined in table 1.2.
7. FCS refers to economies in fragile and conflict-affected situations; non-FCS includes all other economies.

TABLE 2.12 Sub-Saharan Africa economy forecasts[1]

(Real GDP growth at market prices in percent, unless indicated otherwise)

							Percentage-point differences from January 2026 projections	
	2023	2024	2025e	2026f	2027f	2028f	2026f	2027f
Angola	1.3	4.4	3.1	2.4	2.7	2.9	-0.2	-0.1
Benin	6.4	7.5	8.1	7.0	7.2	7.3	0.0	0.2
Botswana	3.2	-2.8	-0.7	2.7	3.2	3.1	0.4	-0.6
Burkina Faso	3.0	4.8	5.3	4.9	5.8	5.5	0.0	0.7
Burundi	2.7	4.1	4.0	4.1	4.8	4.9	-0.8	-0.7
Central African Republic	0.7	1.5	4.5	2.3	3.1	3.2	-0.7	0.0
Cabo Verde	4.8	7.2	6.3	4.8	5.0	5.1	-0.4	0.0
Cameroon	3.2	3.5	3.2	3.4	3.7	3.9	-0.3	-0.2
Chad	4.0	5.0	5.6	5.2	5.3	5.3	1.5	1.2
Comoros	3.2	3.3	3.8	4.1	4.3	3.9	0.4	0.5
Congo, Dem. Rep.	8.6	6.1	5.5	5.2	5.1	5.1	0.1	-0.2
Congo, Rep.	1.9	2.1	3.1	3.7	3.4	3.4	0.5	0.4
Côte d'Ivoire	6.6	6.0	6.3	5.8	6.5	7.0	-0.6	0.0
Equatorial Guinea	-7.4	0.4	-5.8	-3.5	-3.4	2.2	-3.9	-4.4
Eritrea	2.6	2.9	3.2	3.5	3.6	3.6	0.0	0.0
Eswatini	3.5	3.0	4.0	3.9	3.8	3.3	0.1	0.9
Ethiopia [2]	7.2	8.1	9.2	8.0	6.9	8.4	0.9	-0.8
Gabon	2.4	3.4	2.5	3.0	3.3	3.5	-0.7	-0.8
Gambia, The	5.9	5.6	5.9	5.3	5.2	5.2	-0.2	-0.1
Ghana	3.1	5.8	6.0	4.8	4.9	5.0	0.2	0.1
Guinea	5.5	5.4	7.4	8.8	11.6	10.7	-0.5	0.0
Guinea-Bissau	5.8	4.1	5.8	4.8	4.9	5.0	-0.4	-0.3
Kenya	5.7	4.7	4.6	4.4	5.0	5.0	-0.5	0.0
Lesotho	1.7	5.2	2.0	1.3	1.5	1.5	0.6	0.4
Liberia	4.7	4.0	5.1	5.0	5.4	5.6	-0.4	-0.2
Madagascar	4.2	4.3	3.0	3.8	4.5	4.4	-0.2	0.1
Malawi	1.9	1.7	1.9	2.3	2.7	3.0	-0.3	-0.4
Mali	4.5	4.7	4.1	5.0	5.2	5.3	0.0	0.2
Mauritania	6.8	6.3	4.0	4.4	4.5	4.8	-1.0	-1.4
Mauritius	4.7	4.9	3.2	2.5	4.6	3.1	-0.9	1.2
Mozambique	5.5	2.1	-0.5	0.9	1.6	2.5	-1.9	-1.9
Namibia	4.4	4.0	1.7	2.7	3.4	3.4	-0.8	-0.4
Niger	2.6	8.3	7.0	6.7	6.4	6.1	0.0	-0.2
Nigeria	3.3	4.1	4.0	4.1	4.2	4.3	-0.3	-0.2
Rwanda	8.6	7.2	9.4	7.2	7.6	7.3	0.0	0.0
São Tomé and Príncipe	0.4	1.1	2.1	2.9	3.9	3.3	-1.1	0.4
Senegal	4.3	6.1	6.7	2.2	2.6	3.0	-1.9	-1.7
Seychelles	5.2	3.4	5.8	1.1	4.5	3.1	-2.1	1.1
Sierra Leone	5.7	4.4	4.5	4.0	4.7	4.6	-0.4	0.1
Somalia, Fed. Rep.	4.2	4.1	3.0	2.8	3.1	3.5	-0.7	-0.4
South Africa	0.8	0.5	1.1	1.0	1.5	1.7	-0.4	0.0
South Sudan [2]	-1.3	-7.4	-7.7	20.3	2.4	2.9	-28.5	1.6
Sudan	-29.4	-14.0	3.1	5.5	4.4	2.6	0.4	0.7
Tanzania	5.1	5.5	5.9	6.1	6.4	6.5	-0.1	-0.1
Togo	6.2	6.5	5.9	5.0	5.8	6.2	-0.4	0.2
Uganda [2]	5.3	6.1	6.3	6.8	8.5	8.1	0.4	-1.3
Zambia	5.4	3.8	3.8	4.4	4.7	5.1	-1.4	-1.3
Zimbabwe	5.3	1.7	7.5	4.6	4.2	4.1	-0.4	-0.8

Source: World Bank.

Note: e = estimate; f = forecast. World Bank forecasts are frequently updated based on new information and changing global circumstances. Consequently, projections presented here may differ from those in other World Bank documents, even if basic assessments of countries' prospects do not significantly differ at any given moment in time.

1. Data are based on GDP measured in average 2010–19 prices and market exchange rates.

2. Fiscal-year-based numbers.

References

ACLED (database). Armed Conflict Location & Event Data Project. Accessed on May 29, 2026. https://acleddata.com/conflict-data/data-export-tool.

CDC (Centers for Disease Control and Prevention). 2026. *Ebola Outbreaks*. Atlanta, GA: CDC. https://cdc.gov/ebola/outbreaks/index.html. Accessed on May 29, 2026.

Chrimes, T., M. A. Kose, and K. Stamm. 2026. *The Global Jobs Challenge*. Washington, DC: World Bank.

da Silva, F. A., R. V. R. Anderle, G. Barreix Sibils, L. de O. F. de Sales, D. Pena, C. Monti, et al. 2026. "Impact of Two Decades of Humanitarian and Development Assistance and the Projected Mortality Consequences of Current Defunding to 2030: Retrospective Evaluation and Forecasting Analysis." *The Lancet Global Health*, published online February 2. https://thelancet.com/journals/langlo/article/PIIS2214-109X(26)00008-2/fulltext.

EM-DAT (Emergency Events Database) EM-DAT: The International Disaster Database. Centre for Research on the Epidemiology of Disasters (CRED), UCLouvain, Brussels. Accessed on June 2, 2026. https://emdat.be.

EBRD (European Bank for Reconstruction and Development). 2026. *Regional Economic Update in the EBRD Regions: Potential Economic Impact of the Conflict in the Middle East*. March. London: European Bank for Reconstruction and Development.

FAO, IFAD, UNICEF, WFP, and WHO. 2025. The State of Food Security and Nutrition in the World 2025: Addressing High Food Price Inflation for Food Security and Nutrition. Rome: Food and Agriculture Organization of the United Nations. https://doi.org/10.4060/cd6008en.

FAO (Food and Agriculture Organization of the United Nations) 2026. "Crop Prospects and Food Situation—Countries requiring external assistance for food, March 2026. Rome: FAO Global Information and Early Warning System (GIEWS)." https://fao.org/giews/country-analysis/external-assistance/en/.

FAO (Food and Agriculture Organization of the United Nations). 2025. FAOSTAT (database). Accessed on April 27, 2026. https://fao.org/faostat/en/#data/RL.

Fitzgerald, D., S. Haller, and Y. Yedid-Levi. 2024. "How Exporters Grow." *The Review of Economic Studies* 91 (4): 2276–306.

Gaulier, G., and S. Zignago. 2010. "BACI: International Trade Database at the Product-Level. The 1994–2007 Version." CEPII Working Paper 2010-23, Centre d'Études Prospectives et d'Informations Internationales, Paris.

Global Trade Alert. 2026. "Chokepoint: Tracking Trade Policy Responses to the Hormuz Crisis." https://globaltradealert.org/reports/chokepoint-tracking-the-hormuz-oil-shock.

IEA (International Energy Agency). 2025. Global Critical Minerals Outlook 2025. Paris: International Energy Agency. https://iea.org/reports/global-critical-minerals-outlook-2025.

Kohn, D., E. Luttini, M. Szkup, and S. Zhang. 2024. "International Trade Finance and Learning Dynamics." Working Paper 1031, Banco Central de Chile, Santiago.

Kose, M. A., S. Kurlat, F. Ohnsorge, and N. Sugawara. 2022. "A Cross-Country Database of Fiscal Space." *Journal of International Money and Finance* 128 (November): 102682.

Leepipatpiboon, P., C. Castrovillari, and T. Mineyama. 2023. "Macroeconomic Shocks and Conflict." IMF Working Paper 23/68, International Monetary Fund, Washington, DC.

Loungani, P., E. Luttini, and H. Pallan. 2025. "Buffering Recessions: Labor Market Asymmetries and the Role of Self-Employment." Policy Research Working Paper 11089, World Bank, Washington, DC.

Misra, A., J. Wang, S. McCullers, K. White, and J. L. Ferres. 2025. "Measuring AI Diffusion: A Population-Normalized Metric for Tracking Global AI Usage." https://arxiv.org/abs/2511.02781.

OECD (Organisation for Economic Co-operation and Development). 2025. "Cuts in Official Development Assistance: OECD Projections for 2025 and the Near Term." OECD Policy Brief, Organisation for Economic Co-operation and Development, Paris.

UNCTAD (United Nations Conference on Trade and Development). 2025. *Trade in Critical Minerals Shapes the Energy Transition and Digital Transformation.* UNCTAD SDG Pulse. Geneva: United Nations. Published June 26, 2025. https://sdgpulse.unctad.org/critical-minerals/index.htm .

UNU-CPR (United Nations University Centre for Policy Research). 2025. *Climate Change, Food Insecurity and Conflict.* New York: United Nations University. Published November 21, 2025. https://unu.edu/cpr/report/climate-change-food-insecurity-and-conflict .

World Bank. 2025a. *Jobs in A Changing Climate: Insights from World Bank Group Country Climate and Development Reports Covering 93 Economies.* November. Washington, DC: World Bank.

World Bank. 2025b. *Africa's Pulse: Pathways to Job Creation in Africa*. October. Washington, DC: World Bank.

World Bank. 2026a. *Commodity Markets Outlook.* April. Washington, DC: World Bank.

World Bank. 2026b. *East Asia and Pacific Economic Update: Industrial Policy in the Digital Age*. April. Washington, DC: World Bank.

World Bank. 2026c. *Africa Economic Update: Making Industrial Policy Work in Africa*. April. Washington, DC: World Bank.

World Bank. 2026d. *Global Economic Prospects.* January. Washington, DC: World Bank.

World Bank. 2026e. *Pacific Economic Update: The Pacific Jobs Pathway*. May. Washington, DC: World Bank.

World Bank. 2026f. *Europe and Central Asia: Industrial Policy*. April. Washington, DC: World Bank.

World Bank. 2026g. *Latin America and the Caribbean Economic Update: Revisiting Industrial Policy—Strategic Options for Today.* April. Washington, DC: World Bank.

World Bank. 2026h. *Economic Update on the West Bank and Gaza*. May. Washington, DC: World Bank.

World Bank. 2026i. *Challenges of Conflict and Industrial Policy for Development. Middle East, North Africa, Afghanistan & Pakistan Economic Update*. April. Washington, DC: World Bank.

World Bank. 2026j. *Djibouti Economic Monitor: Labor Market Structure and the School-to-Work Transition*. Spring. Washington, DC: World Bank.

World Bank. 2026k. *Afghanistan Development Update: The Private Sector in Afghanistan—Resilient but Constrained*. May. Washington, DC: World Bank.

World Bank. 2026l. *Yemen Economic Monitor: Pushing against the Tide*. Spring. Washington, DC: World Bank.

World Bank. 2026m. *South Asia Development Update: Working with Industrial Policy*. April. Washington, DC: World Bank.

World Bank. 2026n. *India Development Update*. April. Washington, DC: World Bank.

World Bank. 2026o. *Bangladesh Development Update: Special Focus—A Business Environment that Delivers Jobs*. April. Washington, DC: World Bank.

World Bank. 2026p. *Nepal Development Update: Growth under Pressure—Navigating Domestic and Global Shocks*. April. Washington, DC: World Bank.

World Bank. 2026q. *Bhutan Development Update: Special Focus—Transforming Bhutan's Agrifood System for More and Better Jobs*. Spring. Washington, DC: World Bank.

World Bank. 2026r. *Sri Lanka Development Update: Weathering the Storm*. May. Washington, DC: World Bank.

World Bank. 2026s. Quarterly food and nutrition security update. Issue 121 (March). Washington, DC: World Bank Group.

World Food Security Outlook (database). Accessed on May 12, 2026. World Bank. https://microdata.worldbank.org/catalog/6103.

WHO (World Health Organization). 2026. *Ebola disease caused by Bundibugyo virus, Democratic Republic of the Congo & Uganda*. Disease Outbreak News, May 29, 2026. Geneva: WHO. https://who.int/emergencies/disease-outbreak-news/item/2026-DON605.

CHAPTER 3

A RISING CHALLENGE

Sovereign Debt Levels and Interest Rates in EMDEs

Rising government debt poses a key challenge for emerging market and developing economies (EMDEs), as it leads to higher interest rates, higher debt-service payments, and a greater likelihood of debt distress. This chapter explores the impact of government debt on interest rates. It finds that debt levels are positively associated with dollar-denominated sovereign bond spreads and domestic-currency government bond yields. The estimated relationship with debt is non-linear: the increases in spreads or yields associated with increases in debt-to-GDP ratios are greater the higher the debt-to-GDP ratio. The rise in EMDE debt-to-GDP ratios since 2010 is associated with increases in sovereign spreads and domestic-currency yields of about 110 and 30 basis points, respectively. Rising debt in advanced economies, by pushing up yields in those economies, has added further to the upward pressure on EMDE interest rates. With EMDE government debt at historically high levels, additional borrowing may lead to progressively larger jumps in interest rates. The chapter also finds that rising debt has led to even larger increases in interest rates in countries with a history of default, low credit ratings, frontier market status, heavy reliance on short-term debt, and weak governance. These findings underscore the importance of strengthening fiscal positions. This can be achieved through stronger domestic revenue mobilization, more efficient public spending, improved debt management, support for domestic debt market development, and, where appropriate, debt-for-development swaps. By helping contain borrowing costs and preserve fiscal space, these measures can also support the infrastructure, services, and private investment needed for long-term growth and job creation.

Introduction

The rise in sovereign debt burdens ranks among the most pressing issues faced by governments around the world, especially in emerging market and developing economies (EMDEs). Aggregate government debt in EMDEs has increased from less than 40 percent of GDP in 2010 to over 70 percent, driven by both domestic policy measures and large external shocks (figure 3.1.A). Largely as a result, the cost of servicing government debt has risen, from 6 percent of government revenues in 2010 to an estimated 11 percent in 2025 (figure 3.1.B).

Mounting debt-service payments pose four critical challenges for many EMDEs. First, they may lead to a diversion of government resources from other priority uses such as investment in infrastructure, health and education, and support for social safety nets. This diversion can also weigh on the public investment, services, and reforms needed to raise productivity and support job creation. Second, high debt-service obligations may need to be financed by additional borrowing, causing debt to rise still higher. Third, rising sovereign debt costs increase the economy-wide cost of capital, limiting investment and private-sector growth. And fourth, this vicious cycle of rising debt and debt-service costs ultimately could trigger debt distress, default, and severe economic disruption.

Several developments since the advent of the COVID-19 pandemic have deepened the fiscal challenges facing EMDEs. Following the sharp runup in government debt during the previous decade, large pandemic-triggered fiscal deficits contributed to further increases in debt (Kose et al. 2021; World Bank 2022). Moreover, after a prolonged period of low borrowing costs, global interest rates rose sharply as central banks around the world attempted to suppress increased rates of inflation. And not only was there an associated rise in government borrowing costs, but GDP growth in EMDEs became more subdued than before the pandemic, slowing revenue growth and constraining these countries' debt-service capacity.

More recently, the conflict in the Middle East has disrupted energy markets, contributing to higher energy costs, renewed inflationary pressures, and slower economic growth. These developments may require governments to provide additional support to households, particularly vulnerable populations disproportionately affected by rising food and energy prices. In some countries, policy makers may also face pressure to expand targeted social assistance or protect essential public services to mitigate the broader economic and social consequences of the conflict. Meanwhile, the

Note: The chapter was prepared by Carlos Arteta, Steven Kamin, and Franz Ulrich Ruch, with contributions from Reina Eskimez and Jiwon Lee.

FIGURE 3.1 Implications of rising government debt in EMDEs

Government debt in EMDEs has increased significantly since the early 2010s. Rising debt levels and higher interest rates have resulted in a sharp increase in debt-service costs over that period. EMDEs with weaker credit ratings experienced much larger increases in spreads at the onset of the pandemic in 2020 and the Federal Reserve tightening cycle in 2022. The number of low- and middle-income EMDEs at high risk of or already in debt distress has doubled in the last decade.

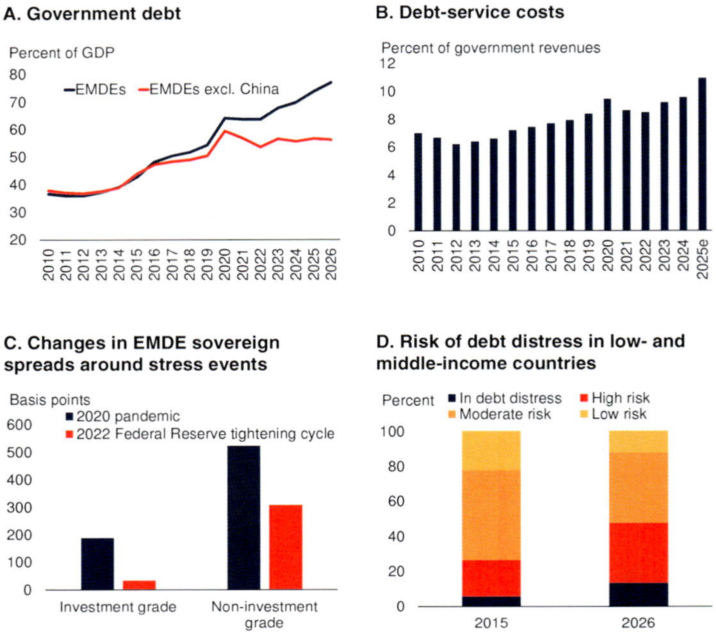

Sources: International Monetary Fund; J.P.Morgan; Kose et al. (2022); Moody's Analytics; World Bank; World Bank-IMF Debt Sustainability Framework.

Note: e = estimate; EMDEs = emerging market and developing economies; excl. = excluding.

A. Weighted average of government debt as share of GDP using GDP weights at average 2010–19 prices and market exchange rates since 2010. Sample includes 139 EMDEs.

B. Aggregates are computed as weighted averages, using government revenues in U.S. dollars as weights. Net interest payments are computed as differences between primary balances and overall fiscal balances. Data for 2025 are estimates. Sample includes up to 148 EMDEs.

C. Change in sovereign spread in EMDEs during the outbreak of the pandemic (February 2020–April 2020) and the onset of the Fed tightening cycle (January 2022–July 2022).

D. Sample covers economies where the Joint World Bank-International Monetary Fund Debt Sustainability Framework for Low-Income Countries is applied, as of end-March 2026, including up to 68 EMDEs.

recent increase in advanced economy bond yields has further tightened financing conditions, potentially raising borrowing costs for many governments already facing additional fiscal demands. This could make it more difficult for these governments to balance near-term support measures with concerns about debt sustainability and market confidence.

In all, these developments have exerted substantial pressure on the fiscal positions of many EMDEs. To be sure, EMDEs with strong credit ratings weathered the pandemic and subsequent rise in global interest rates relatively well, as indicated by the limited widening of their sovereign spreads—the difference between yields on foreign-currency bonds issued by their governments and those on the safest bonds, usually U.S. Treasuries (figure 3.1.C). However, EMDEs with weaker credit ratings experienced much larger increases in spreads, reflecting market expectations that these economies would face greater challenges servicing their bonds in an environment of higher debt loads, higher interest rates, and slower growth. In consequence, the share of low- and middle-income countries either in, or at high risk of, debt distress rose from 26 percent in 2015 to about 50 percent in 2026 (figure 3.1.D). Economies in fragile and conflict-affected situations (FCS) have become particularly vulnerable to debt distress.[1]

Increased debt may boost debt-service costs not only because interest rates are applied to a higher level of debt but also because the interest rates payable may be higher for governments with higher levels of debt, reflecting the increased risks of default, monetization, and inflation. Against this backdrop, this chapter explores the impact of rising government debt on the interest rates paid by EMDE governments, by addressing the following questions:

- By how much do increases in sovereign debt boost interest rates in EMDEs?
- How do government bond yields in advanced economies and increases in their public debt affect EMDE interest rates?
- How do domestic vulnerabilities and tight global financial conditions affect the impact of debt on EMDE interest rates?
- What are the policy implications?

[1] Debt distress refers to a situation where a borrower is unable, or at high risk of being unable, to meet its debt obligations, implying a high risk of default. For an analysis of debt distress in countries in fragile and conflict-affected situations, see Hill, Khadan, and Selcuk (2025).

While it is broadly understood that higher debt levels will raise interest rates, teasing out the exact relationship between them is far from straightforward. To begin with, interest rates in EMDEs are affected by a multiplicity of different macroeconomic factors, including inflation, monetary policy, economic growth, and global interest rates. As a result, average EMDE interest rates remained roughly range-bound for many years as declines in inflation, subdued U.S. interest rates (until 2021), and an increased tolerance for risk among global investors offset the boost to interest rates resulting from the persistent rise in debt levels.

But even abstracting from movements over time, the relationship between debt and interest rates is likely to be complex. First, governments with a greater reputation for good economic management and fiscal performance may be viewed as more creditworthy by investors; accordingly, such governments will be allowed both higher debt levels and lower interest rates. Second, investors might be unconcerned with increases in a country's debt as long as that debt stays within a relatively low range, and they may only start demanding higher rates when debt moves into a higher, more critical range.

Therefore, to estimate the effects of government debt accumulation on interest rates in EMDEs, the empirical analysis in this chapter controls for a wide range of variables, including measures of global financial conditions, domestic macroeconomic developments, and fiscal creditworthiness. In so doing, it builds on a large literature on the determinants of EMDE interest rates, updating earlier results with data from the pandemic years, improving on previous modeling, and considering the key policy implications of the new empirical findings. Both sovereign spreads over U.S. Treasury yields and yields on domestic-currency debt are examined. The questions considered include whether the relationship between government debt and interest rates in EMDEs is non-linear, whether and how increases in the government debt of advanced economies spill over to increases in interest rates in EMDEs, and how the domestic vulnerabilities of EMDEs, as well as global financial conditions, affect the relationship between EMDE debt and interest rates.

This chapter makes several contributions to the understanding of these critical issues. First, it updates and extends evidence on how higher government debt affects EMDE sovereign financing costs in both foreign-currency and domestic-currency bond markets. Second, it documents robust non-linearities in the debt–interest rate relationship using complementary methodologies. Third, it highlights the role of vulnerabilities in shaping the relationship between debt and borrowing costs. Fourth, the chapter quantifies how advanced economy government debt—through advanced economy bond yields—affects EMDE interest rates. Finally, to test the robustness of the findings, it incorporates forecast-based specifications to address endogeneity concerns.

Main findings. The chapter presents the following main findings:

First, the study confirms statistically and economically significant positive relationships in EMDEs between gross government debt-to-GDP ratios and both sovereign spreads and domestic-currency bond yields. Sovereign spreads appear considerably more sensitive to debt levels than domestic yields, perhaps reflecting a greater susceptibility of domestic yields to financial repression, monetization, or home bias in some EMDEs.

Second, the relationship between government debt and sovereign spreads is non-linear: the higher the initial debt level, the larger the effect of additional borrowing. For example, when debt is about 45 percent of GDP, a 1 percentage point increase in the debt-to-GDP ratio is associated with an 8 basis point rise in sovereign spreads; when debt is about 80 percent of GDP, the same increase adds about 26 basis points. Thus, reducing debt by 1 percentage point of GDP could lower annual interest costs by roughly 0.1-0.3 percent of GDP, depending on the starting debt level. Conversely, a 1 percentage point increase in the debt-to-GDP ratio raises yields on domestic-currency bonds by about 2 basis points when debt is about 45 percent of GDP, and by about 8 basis points when debt is about 80 percent. This implies that a 1 percentage point reduction in debt could generate annual interest savings of about 0.1 percent of GDP, with the exact gain depending on the initial debt ratio.[2] Overall, these results suggest that fiscal policy should be calibrated to the starting level of debt. At relatively low debt levels, additional borrowing may be justified to finance productive public investment. At much higher debt levels, however, fiscal consolidation becomes more important to contain borrowing costs, generate fiscal savings, and create space for private investment.

Third, these estimates suggest that rising EMDE government debt has contributed meaningfully to sovereign spreads and domestic-currency yields over the past decade and a half. Between 2010 and 2024, median EMDE debt rose by 20 percentage points of GDP. Based on the model estimates, this added 114 basis points to sovereign spreads and 31 basis points to domestic-currency yields. However, these effects were largely offset by other factors, including a more accommodative tone of global financial markets.

Fourth, advanced economy interest rates—and advanced economy government debt through its effect on those interest rates—play an important role in shaping EMDE borrowing costs. Based on previous studies of the effect of public debt on interest rates in advanced economies, the roughly 12 percentage point average increase in the debt-to-GDP ratios of the United States, the euro area, and Japan between 2010 and 2024 will have raised their weighted-average 10-year benchmark government bond yield by about 35 basis points (Gamber and Seliski 2019; Gruber and Kamin 2012; Laubach 2009). The estimates in this chapter suggest that this, in turn, would have increased EMDE dollar-denominated sovereign yields by 35 basis points and domestic-currency yields by 9 basis points.

Accounting jointly for the increases in domestic EMDE debt and advanced economy debt between 2010 and 2024, the estimates suggest that together they increased dollar-denominated sovereign yields by roughly 149 basis points and domestic-currency yields by 40 basis points. Looking ahead, continued increases in advanced economy debt would be expected to put further upward pressure on EMDE interest rates.

Finally, increases in debt are associated with larger increases in interest rates in economies that exhibit greater domestic vulnerabilities or that face a less favorable global financial environment. For sovereign spreads, domestic-currency yields, or both, the sensitivity to debt levels rises significantly in countries with previous defaults, weaker credit ratings, frontier market status, higher inflation, more short-term debt, and weaker governance. The incremental effect of debt on interest rates is also estimated to be larger during periods of tighter global financing conditions. These findings point to the importance of fundamentals, including fiscal discipline, stronger institutions, and policies that mobilize private capital and improve productivity.

Key trends in EMDE government debt and interest rates

Important features of EMDE government debt include its currency composition and the degree of concessionality. Although the share of EMDE public debt issued in foreign currencies has declined slightly since 2010, in part reflecting an expansion of domestic debt markets, it remains sizable at more than 40 percent of the total (figure 3.2.A). Therefore, the sovereign spreads examined in this chapter remain highly relevant to EMDE finances. The share of concessional debt has also declined, indicating that more public debt is being issued at the market-determined interest rates examined in this chapter.

With the exception of several surges, such as the one around the 2020 pandemic-related turmoil in financial markets, average EMDE sovereign spreads were broadly stable, at 300-400 basis points, over 2010–25 (figure 3.2.B). The effect on these spreads of rising public debt levels, especially for economies with better credit ratings, was offset, up to about 2021, by consistently low advanced economy interest rates and a generally accommodative global financing environment

[2] These two calculations of interest-payment savings from debt reduction assume that all of the debt is in the form of foreign-currency or of domestic-currency bonds, respectively, and that interest rates start at their sample average.

(figure 3.2.C). Since 2022, advanced economy interest rates have risen but U.S. corporate high-yield spreads—a barometer of the tone of global credit markets that is highly correlated with EMDE spreads—have declined to historically low levels.[3]

Average EMDE domestic-currency bond yields were similarly broadly stable, at 600-700 basis points, in the decade before the pandemic, again despite rising debt and reflecting low advanced economy interest rates and benign global financing conditions (figure 3.2.D). Interest rates plunged during the global pandemic recession of 2020 as both advanced economy and EMDE central banks cut policy rates aggressively and, in some cases, embarked on large-scale purchases of longer-term assets. This dip unwound rapidly in 2021-22 as inflation surged, central banks raised short-term policy rates, and risk aversion increased. Yields have since fallen back to their pre-pandemic range along with the declines in inflation and domestic policy rates, reduction of advanced economy interest rates, and improved conditions in global credit markets.

Impact of EMDE government debt on interest rates

A cursory inspection of summary data across countries and over time indicates that interest rates and government debt exhibit a positive association, albeit only at higher levels of debt (figures 3.3.A and 3.3.B). Stronger evidence of a positive relationship has been found in numerous studies for both advanced economies (Ardagna, Caselli and Lane, 2007; Engen and Hubbard, 2004; Gamber and Seliski, 2019; Gruber and Kamin, 2012) and EMDEs (Clements et al. 2023; Ferrucci 2003; Jaramillo and Weber 2013; Kennedy and Palerm 2014). This chapter builds on this literature, estimating panel regressions on quarterly data that take into account diverse

FIGURE 3.2 Key trends in EMDE government debt and interest rates

Although the share of EMDE public debt issued in foreign currencies has declined slightly since 2010, it remains sizable. With a few exceptions, average EMDE sovereign spreads remained range bound over the 2010–26 period. The impact on spreads of rising public debt levels over that period was offset by sustained low advanced economy interest rates (at least until 2022) and a generally accommodative global financing environment. Average EMDE domestic-currency bond yields remained similarly range bound over most of the period, with some exceptions—most notably, around the pandemic recession.

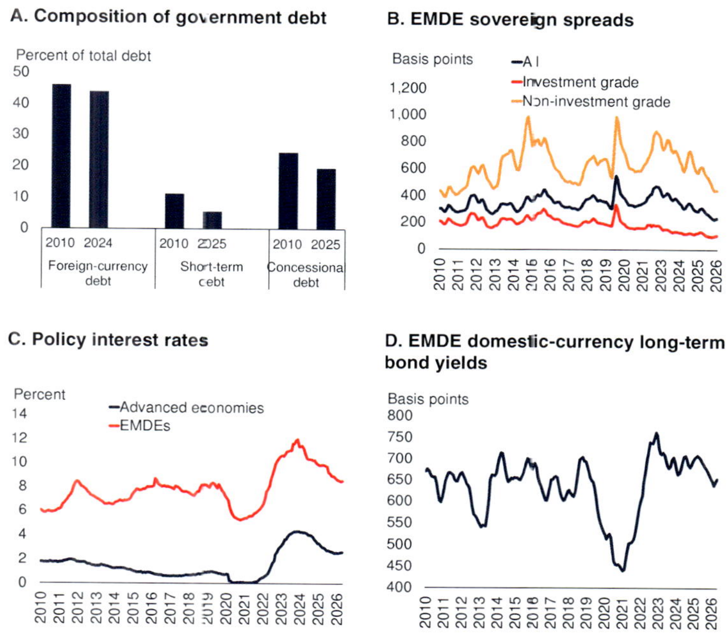

Sources: Haver Analytics; J.P.Morgan; World Bank.
Note: EMDEs = emerging market and developing economies.
A. Simple average based on up to 130 EMDEs.
B. Panel shows three-month moving average of monthly aggregate index of J.P.Morgan Emerging Markets Bond Index Global (EMBIG) spreads. Last observation is April 2026.
C. Panel shows the average monthly central bank policy rates across advanced economies and EMDEs. Sample includes 15 advanced economies and 57 EMDEs. Last observation is April 2026.
D. Panel shows three-month moving average of monthly J.P.Morgan Government Bond Index-Emerging Markets Diversified (GBI-EM Div) of domestic-currency bond yields. Last observation is April 2026.

characteristics of different economies; adding explanatory variables to control for other macroeconomic developments that may influence interest rates; and adding measures of U.S. financial conditions that may influence global and EMDE interest rates. (Results are presented in table 3.1; annex 3.1 describes the methodology and data.)

The analysis starts with estimation of a simple linear relationship between debt and interest rates, as in most of the earlier studies. The results show that increases in debt of 1 percentage point of

[3] Kamin and Aatman (2025) show that U.S. high yield spreads explained most of the variation in aggregate emerging market spreads over the past couple of decades, including the fall in emerging market spreads to very low levels in recent years.

FIGURE 3.3 Relationship between EMDE government debt and interest rates

Interest rates and government debt exhibit a positive association, especially at higher levels of debt. The relationship between sovereign spreads and debt is non-linear, with the marginal impact of additional debt rising at higher debt levels, likely reflecting progressively greater concern among investors about repayment as debt rises.

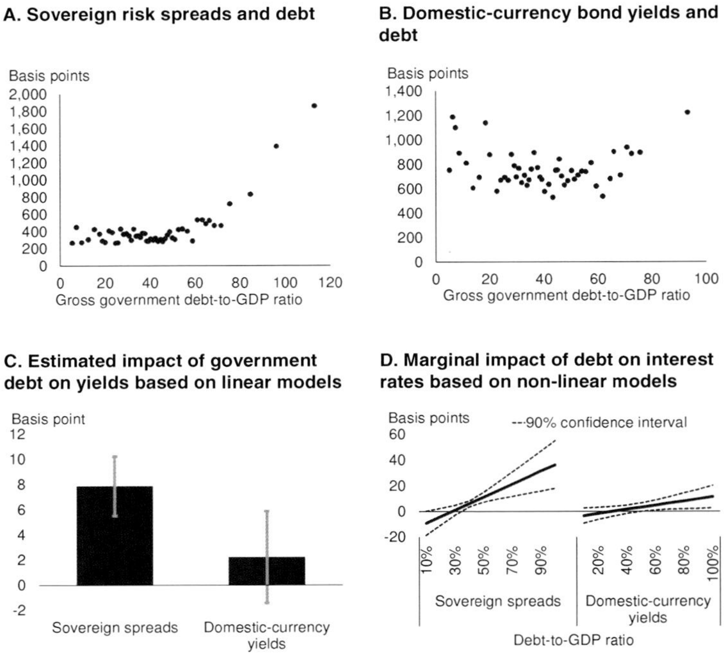

Sources: Haver Analytics; J.P.Morgan, World Bank.

Note: EMDEs = emerging market and developing economies.

A.B. Based on binscatter plots with 50 bins.

C. Based on regressions in table 3.1 columns (1) and (3). Whiskers reflect 90 percent confidence interval. Shows effect on interest rates of a 1 percentage point rise in the ratio of debt to GDP.

D. Based on regressions in table 3.1 columns (2) and (4). Shows effect on interest rates of a 1 percentage point rise in the ratio of debt to GDP at different initial levels of the debt ratio.

GDP have been associated with increases in sovereign spreads of about 8 basis points (table 3.1, column (1); figure 3.3.C). This estimate is considerably higher than most prior results, but quite similar to that found in one recent study (Clements et al. 2023). For domestic-currency bond yields, the estimates suggest an increase in yields of about 2 basis points for the same increase in debt, which is at the low end of the range of previous findings and not statistically significant; this is not surprising given that there is a wide range of debt levels where bond yields are essentially flat. This suggests that a non-linear model may better fit the data.

An alternative approach to evaluating the effect of debt on interest rates is to look at cases where estimated debt was revised upward as a result of more careful auditing or the discovery of previously hidden liabilities. As described in box 3.1, such revelations have generally been followed by increases in sovereign spreads, reinforcing the view that rising debt tends to be associated with rising market interest rates.

Non-linear relationship between debt and interest rates

Interest rates partly reflect the perceived likelihood of default, compensating an investor for the perceived risk of loss. When public debt is low, financial markets are more likely to view debt service as manageable and risks of default as low than when debt is high: as debt rises, concerns about servicing costs and the government's liquidity and solvency may increase, causing borrowing costs to rise increasingly sharply until eventually additional borrowing becomes infeasible.

As noted earlier, this non-linear relationship between debt and interest rates is apparent in a cursory examination of the data. And several previous studies have found econometric evidence of a non-linear relationship, including Ardagna et al. (2007), Baldacci and Kumar (2010), Matsuoka (2022), Sun (2023), and Ciżkowicz et al. (2025).[4] To identify a non-linear relationship between debt and interest rates, this chapter estimates a simple quadratic model, which adds the square of the debt-to-GDP ratio as an explanatory variable to the linear equation discussed above. (The methodology and estimation results for an alternative approach to estimating non-linearities—a "threshold" model—are described in annex 3.2).

Sovereign risk spreads

When the debt-squared term is included in the regression for sovereign spreads, its estimated coefficient is positive and highly statistically

[4] Similar non-linearities are found in the theoretical and empirical literature on default risk (e.g., Arellano, 2008; Cole and Kehoe, 2000; Bi, 2012; and Ghosh et al, 2013) and refinancing risks (e.g., Cole and Kehoe, 1996; Broner, Lorenzoni, and Schmukler, 2013; and Gennaioli, Martin and Rossi, 2018).

significant, providing clear evidence of a non-linear relationship (table 3.1, column (2)).[5] The coefficient on the debt ratio itself is negative, although it is not statistically significant. Taking both coefficients together, the estimates imply that increases in the debt-to-GDP ratio tend not to increase (indeed, tend to reduce) spreads until the ratio reaches about 30 percent, at which point further increases in the ratio do widen spreads, and by increasing amounts (figure 3.3.D).

The implied negative association between the debt-to-GDP ratio and spreads for ratios below 30 percent of GDP could merely be an artifact of the functional form of the quadratic specification, especially since the scatterplot of sovereign spreads and debt (shown in figure 3.3.A) indicates a generally flat relationship up to about 50 percent of GDP. Alternatively, it may be that countries with very small amounts of debt lack a record of borrowing and debt service, and that this is viewed by creditors as requiring higher risk premiums, or that at least in some cases low debt reflects poor creditworthiness in ways not captured by the control variables. In any event, none of these explanations imply that a government with an established record of debt-service risks raising its spreads if it reduces its debt.

To flesh out the implications of the estimates for the upward sloping part of the debt-spreads curve, the increase in spreads associated with a 1 percentage point increase in the debt-to-GDP ratio rises from about 8 basis points when the ratio is 45 percent to about 16 basis points at 60 percent and 26 basis points at 80 percent. This contrasts with the implication of the estimates for the linear model that a 1 percentage point increase in the debt-to-GDP ratio is associated with an 8 basis points increase in sovereign spreads at any level of the ratio. The estimate of the non-linear model thus clearly indicates that at the high levels of debt owed by the most indebted EMDEs, the marginal impact of debt is much higher than the estimate of the linear model suggests.

[5] The sample countries differ between baseline models for sovereign spreads and domestic-currency yields. If the sample countries are matched between the two regressions, so that sovereign spreads are estimated with a smaller sample, the impact of debt remains significant in both linear and non-linear models (refer to annex 3.2 for further details).

As noted above, the models also include various control variables intended to capture characteristics of EMDEs likely to affect spreads. The signs of the estimated coefficients are generally as expected. In particular, higher inflation is associated with wider spreads, whereas higher GDP growth is associated with narrower spreads. Higher bureaucratic quality (the institutional strength and quality of the civil service) is associated with narrower spreads, although this relationship is not statistically significant. Sovereign debt crises (a dummy variable equal to 1 if a country is facing a debt crisis) are, not surprisingly, associated with a substantial increase in spreads.[6] In addition to domestic control variables, the models include several measures of U.S. financial conditions. These are discussed in a separate section further below.

Domestic-currency bond yields

For domestic-currency yields, there is also evidence of a non-linear relationship with debt, but the impact of debt on yields is smaller and the non-linearity is less pronounced (table 3.1, column (4)). As with sovereign spreads, the association between debt and domestic-currency yields is found to be negative for debt-to-GDP ratios below about 30 percent, but it turns significantly positive for ratios above 50 percent (figure 3.3.D). The negative response may reflect, in addition to the factors cited above for sovereign spreads, the fact that, at relatively low levels of public debt, greater domestic issuance can contribute to the development and deepening of domestic bond markets, strengthen benchmark yield-curve formation, improve market liquidity, and reduce liquidity premiums. The increase in yields associated with a 1 percentage point increase in the debt-to-GDP ratio is estimated to be about 5 basis points when the ratio is 60 percent of GDP and about 8 basis points when the ratio is 80 percent.

[6] A debt crisis (sovereign default) is defined by Nguyen, Castro, and Wood (2022) as a situation where a country either fails to meet its interest and/or principal obligations by the due date or postpones its obligations through rescheduling or restructuring agreed with creditors but on terms less favorable to them than the original ones. By adding a control variable for crises, this allows the other parameters in the model to be interpreted as the effects on spreads during tranquil (noncrisis) periods.

BOX 3.1 The costs of hidden debt

Hidden government debt—liabilities that governments have already incurred but have not been fully disclosed—can undermine fiscal sustainability and is associated with significantly higher costs of borrowing. This box explores how emerging market and developing economy (EMDE) borrowing costs respond when hidden debts are revealed and assesses the associated policy implications. Hidden debt revelations are associated with large and significant increases in sovereign spreads. These hidden debt episodes also underscore the critical need to fill existing gaps in EMDE debt transparency practices.

Public debt is contracted in the name of a country's residents, who must pay off that debt through future taxes, reduced public services, and potentially higher inflation. When such debt is concealed, residents and their representatives are deprived of the information needed to assess tax and spending decisions, consent to the obligations of future generations, and hold elected representatives accountable. By the same token, creditors are deprived of the information needed to assess creditworthiness and charge appropriate interest rates. Greater data transparency is associated with lower sovereign borrowing costs (Choi and Hashimoto 2018; Kemoe and Zhan 2018). However, there is much more limited evidence about how revelations of previously undisclosed public debt—hidden debt—affect yields and sovereign financing conditions (Horn et al. 2024; Guler et al. 2025). These hidden debt revelations are partly the result of major gaps in the transparency of debt reporting (World Bank 2021, 2025).

As discussed in the main chapter, a key challenge in identifying the effects of public debt on interest rates is disentangling causal relationships from correlations with other macroeconomic, institutional, and financial factors that also influence borrowing costs. The analysis in the chapter seeks to isolate the impact of debt by controlling for observable determinants of interest rates that are plausibly correlated with debt levels, such as growth prospects, inflation dynamics, fiscal balances, and global financial conditions. An alternative identification strategy, which this box uses, exploits historical episodes in which previously hidden or off-balance-sheet liabilities were suddenly revealed. Because these disclosure events represent largely unanticipated debt, they allow for a more direct assessment of how markets reprice sovereign risk in response to unexpected increases in public indebtedness.[a]

Against this backdrop, this box explores seven country episodes and addresses the following questions:

- What is the relationship between hidden debt revelations and sovereign borrowing costs?
- How can policy makers improve debt transparency and minimize debt costs?

Hidden debt revelations: Selected country episodes

Public debt transparency plays a critical role in ensuring effective risk assessment to support sustainable borrowing and lending practices. By the same token, deficiencies in debt transparency frameworks—particularly in emerging market and developing economies (EMDEs)—can allow unreported obligations to accumulate, in some cases culminating in revelations of hidden debt that trigger a repricing of sovereign debt by financial markets. Debt stock revisions—measured as the difference between the most recent vintage and the first available vintage for a given country-year in the World Bank's International Debt Statistics—provide one proxy for hidden debt revelations (Horn et al. 2024).[b] Such revisions have been common and large in EMDEs over the past 50 years, and, on average, have been larger as a share of GDP in low-income countries.

This box focuses on seven of these hidden debt revelation episodes that occurred in the last two decades. The size of revelations varied significantly across the seven episodes, with some increasing reported government debt to GDP by double digits (figure B3.1.1.A). Each episode is dated based on the earliest

Note: This box was written by Reina Eskimez, Jiwon Lee, and Franz Ulrich Ruch.

a. Nevertheless, these events may also convey information about public sector transparency and institutional credibility, so the estimated effects should be interpreted as reflecting both debt stocks and broader confidence.

b. The World Bank's International Debt Statistics report external debt stocks for over 140 EMDEs once a year and is the most widely used source for EMDE external debt data. Reporting is mandatory for all countries with outstanding liabilities to the World Bank and failure to report risks losing eligibility for financial support. Ex post revisions to this data set likely reflect previously unreported loans.

BOX 3.1 The costs of hidden debt (*continued*)

FIGURE B3.1.1 Hidden debt revelation and market responses

The size of hidden debt revelations has varied significantly across the episodes examined, with some leading to large revisions to government debt stocks as a ratio to GDP. In Mozambique's case, the so-called tuna bond episode involved the revelation of about 9 percent of GDP in previously undisclosed non-concessional borrowing contracted during 2009–14, which coincided with a substantial rise in borrowing costs. More generally, when previously undisclosed liabilities become public, sovereign risk spreads rise materially and persistently, consistent with markets reassessing repayment risks.

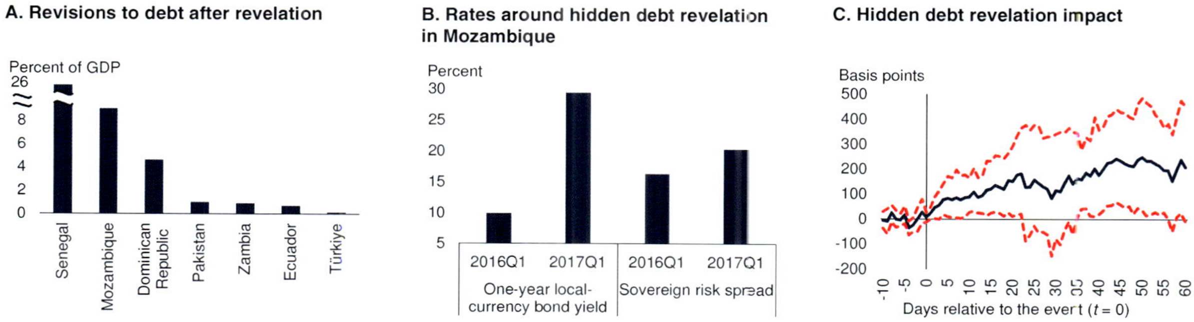

Sources: Haver Analytics; J.P.Morgan; Manger et al. (2025); World Bank.

Note: A. Bars show debt stock revisions associated with hidden debt revelations for seven country cases, measured as a percent of GDP.

B. Simple average of interest rates in Mozambique before and after hidden debt revelation. Bars report quarterly averages of Mozambique's rates in 2016Q1 (pre-revelation) and 2017Q1 (post-revelation).

C. Pooled event-level responses of residualized J.P.Morgan Emerging Market Bond Index Global (EMBIG) spread around hidden-debt revelation dates across seven countries. The solid line tracks mean of country specific spreads compared with its average level during the 10 days before the event (*t* = *0*), and dotted lines show 90 percent confidence intervals.

credible public disclosure of the existence and/or magnitude of the previously unreported debt using a combination of government audit reports, International Monetary Fund (IMF) documents, previous academic research, and international media coverage.[c] Among the identified episodes, the cases of Mozambique and Senegal are well documented and provide useful case studies on the impact of debt revelations (IMF-World Bank 2018; World Bank 2025).

Mozambique

The so-called tuna bond episode in Mozambique involved the revelation in April 2016 of about US$1.15 billion (9 percent of GDP) in previously undisclosed non-concessional borrowing.[d] At the time of the revelation, Mozambique was already burdened by severe fiscal challenges and extremely high borrowing costs; its sovereign risk spread (measured by the J.P.Morgan Emerging Markets Bond Index Global, or EMBIG) was 1100 basis points. The new information triggered a suspension of Mozambique's IMF program and a broader shock to confidence as investors reassessed the country's governance, transparency, and repayment risks. Access to external financing deteriorated sharply, and within three months, Mozambique's sovereign spread rose to a peak of nearly 1800 basis points, about 700 basis points higher than just before the revelation; yields on one-year local-currency domestic bonds also rose substantially (figure B3.1.1.B; World Bank 2017). These dynamics contributed to a marked slowdown in economic activity, with annual growth declining from an average of about 7.0 percent in the five years before the debt revelation to 3.6 percent in the three years after.

Senegal

Senegal's hidden-debt revelation was uncovered through audits of fiscal accounts commissioned by the new government after the March 2024 election (World Bank 2025). Concerns that debt would prove larger than previously reported led to the suspension of an

c. Countries and their identified hidden debt revelation dates are as follows: Dominican Republic (Feb 1, 2005); Ecuador (Apr 6, 2018); Mozambique (Apr 3, 2016); Pakistan (Mar 24, 2021); Senegal (Feb 12, 2025); Türkiye (Apr 26, 2005); and Zambia (Dec 19, 2013).

d. The episode is often called the "tuna bond" scandal, referring to a bond issued by a state-owned firm for a tuna fishing project that formed part of the undisclosed government debt.

BOX 3.1 The costs of hidden debt (*continued*)

IMF $1.8 billion credit facility in late 2024. The release of the audit in February 2025 led to abrupt revisions to the previously reported fiscal position, placing end-2023 central government debt at 111 percent of GDP (up from 73.8 percent) and the 2023 fiscal deficit at 13.4 percent of GDP (up from 4.9 percent). The disclosure prompted an immediate reassessment of repayment risk. Senegal's sovereign dollar bonds sold off immediately, and Eurobond prices dropped sharply. Senegal's sovereign risk spread rose from about 530 basis points prior to the revelation to a peak of about 940 basis points within two months.

Other episodes

Five additional episodes are identified, including in the Dominican Republic, Ecuador, Pakistan, Türkiye, and Zambia. In Ecuador in April 2018, as in Senegal, hidden debt was revealed following an audit by the national comptroller under the new government. The audit found that liabilities arising from advance payments received against future oil exports had been excluded from official public debt statistics (Contraloría General del Estado 2018).

The remaining four episodes of hidden-debt revelation were identified during IMF-supported program reviews.[e] In the Dominican Republic, the IMF Executive Board noted the contracting of previously undisclosed external debt by the public sector for 2003. In Pakistan, government guarantees had been underreported since 2016, amounting to about 1 percent of GDP. In Türkiye, expenditure levels reported in 2005 to assess the 2002 primary balance were slightly higher than previously assessed (by 0.13 percent of GDP). Zambia's case, in turn, reflected undisclosed external borrowing. The IMF learned that the government had contracted two external loans in late 2010 (about 0.9 percent of GDP) that had not been reported during program reviews.

Impact of hidden debt revelations

The market response to these seven episodes of the hidden debt disclosures is quantified using an event-study framework based on daily sovereign risk spreads (EMBIG). For each country, the event date (t = 0) is defined as the first public revelation of hidden debt. Given that spreads are influenced by global financial conditions, daily data are first adjusted to control for global risk and liquidity factors. The resulting country-specific sovereign spread component is then examined over a 60-trading-day window following the revelation, compared with its average level during the 10 trading days preceding the event.[f]

Results show that sovereign risk spreads rise materially and significantly following hidden debt revelations (figure B3.1.1.C). The rise takes place over several months, suggesting that markets may require time to fully process the information, reassess debt sustainability, and revise expectations about future financing conditions. Sovereign spreads rise by a cumulative 250 basis points over the two months since a debt revelation. About half of that increase happens in the first two weeks.

The material and significant rise in spreads associated with debt revelations is not driven by outliers, such as the large revelation that occurred in Mozambique. Excluding each country successively, one at a time, results in an increase of similar magnitude that remains statistically significant.

The increase in sovereign spreads reflects more than just a mechanical repricing of a larger debt stock: even in cases where the magnitude of newly revealed debt was modest, spreads rose substantially, reflecting that markets were also responding to revelations about the inadequacy of the borrowing country's governance and transparency. When hidden debt surfaces, investors reassess the credibility of reported fiscal accounts, penalizing not only the newly revealed debt but also the implied opacity of public finances. Greater uncertainty about sovereign indebtedness is associated with higher perceived default risk and lower bond prices, as creditors demand higher compensation (Horn et al., 2024). The persistence of elevated spreads after a revelation depends in part on how effectively this uncertainty is resolved. When authorities provide a prompt, credible, and comprehensive reconciliation of

e. The Dominican Republic case draws on IMF (2005a); the Pakistan case on IMF (2021); the Türkiye case on IMF (2005b) and table A1 in the IMF (2006); and the Zambia case on IMF (2013).

f. Specifically, daily EMBIG spreads are first regressed on the Chicago Board Options Exchange Volatility Index and the 10-year U.S. Treasury yield. The residuals—capturing country-specific movements—are then normalized by subtracting their average over the 10 trading days prior to the event and tracked over a 60-day post-event window. Confidence intervals for the mean response across the seven episodes are computed using the wild cluster bootstrap.

BOX 3.1 The costs of hidden debt (*continued*)

previously undisclosed obligations, uncertainty can be reduced and spreads may stabilize more quickly. By contrast, in cases involving confidentiality clauses or reliance on off-budget borrowing, uncertainty about the full scope of undisclosed obligations is more likely to persist, keeping spreads elevated for longer.

Policy implications

The incidence of hidden debt revelations in EMDEs and the substantial rise in sovereign risk spreads in response to such revelations point to key policy implications. Policy makers need to bolster debt transparency, focusing on accurate, comprehensive, and timely reporting of debt data (refer to World Bank, 2025, for an in-depth discussion on recommendations).

Borrowers should expand the coverage and improve the timeliness of public debt reports by ensuring that the full public sector—from central government to state-owned enterprises—is represented in debt statistics and by publishing quarterly debt updates. They should voluntarily agree to publish loan-level data and adopt legislative and regulatory reforms to enforce transparency in all loan contracts undertaken by the government. Within these loan contracts, borrowers should limit the use of confidentiality clauses and consent to creditors' disclosure of lending terms. Borrowers can also establish a centralized public debt registry, conduct and publish regular fiscal risk statements, and put in place controls to avoid off-budget borrowing. For domestic debt, governments should prioritize market-based issuing and restructuring mechanisms. Creditors should reconcile loan-level data with international organizations (such as the World Bank's Debtor Reporting System) and adopt standardized templates for reporting. They should include transparency requirements in bilateral debt restructurings and publish restructuring terms when agreed.

Policy makers should also better identify, quantify, and disclose contingent liabilities, which are distinct from hidden debt but can create similar fiscal risks. These may arise from guarantees to state-owned enterprises, revenue guarantees in public-private partnerships (PPPs), infrastructure contract termination payments, or implicit backstops for subnational borrowing. Digital and AI investments add new pressures because they often involve long-term service contracts and recurring operating costs that may not appear fully in debt statistics.

Whether estimated using linear models, as depicted in figure 3.3C, or non-linear models, as shown in figure 3.3D, the sensitivity to debt is found to be lower for domestic-currency yields than for sovereign spreads. The only other study that applies a similar methodology to estimate the relationships with debt of both sovereign spreads and domestic yields, IMF (2021), also finds lower sensitivities for domestic yields. There are various possible reasons for the difference in sensitivities. First, sovereign spreads are likely to be set at the margin by foreign investors comparing prospective returns and risks, including default risks, across countries, and this may make spreads more sensitive to changes in debt loads. Second, foreign-currency debt must be serviced and repaid in foreign exchange, which itself implies a higher default risk and sensitivity to debt loads than for domestic debt, which is serviced and repaid in domestic currency (*in extremis* through monetization). Third, domestic-currency debt is likely to be held by domestic banks and other financial institutions, which are likely to exhibit home bias and may be subject to financial repression in the form of capital controls and liquidity requirements. With demand for domestic-currency debt accordingly less sensitive to differences in risk and return than the demand for foreign-currency debt, an implication is that domestic-currency yields will be less sensitive to the volume of debt as well. Finally, domestic yields may be influenced by domestic monetary policy, as noted below, which could counterbalance the effects of rising debt.

Returning to the estimation results, the measured effect of control variables on domestic yields is generally as expected. Importantly, short-term domestic interest rates, which reflect the monetary

FIGURE 3.4 Contribution of rising government debt to EMDE interest rates

Between 2010 and 2024, according to the non-linear models, rising debt levels were associated with a cumulative 114 basis points to sovereign spreads and a cumulative 31 basis points to domestic-currency yields. A hypothetical scenario looks at a country that accumulates 10 percentage points of GDP in government debt starting from a level of 30 percent of GDP compared with one starting from a level of 60 percent; the non-linear models indicate the impact on interest rates to be significantly higher at higher debt levels, whereas the linear models predict the same rise in rates in either instance.

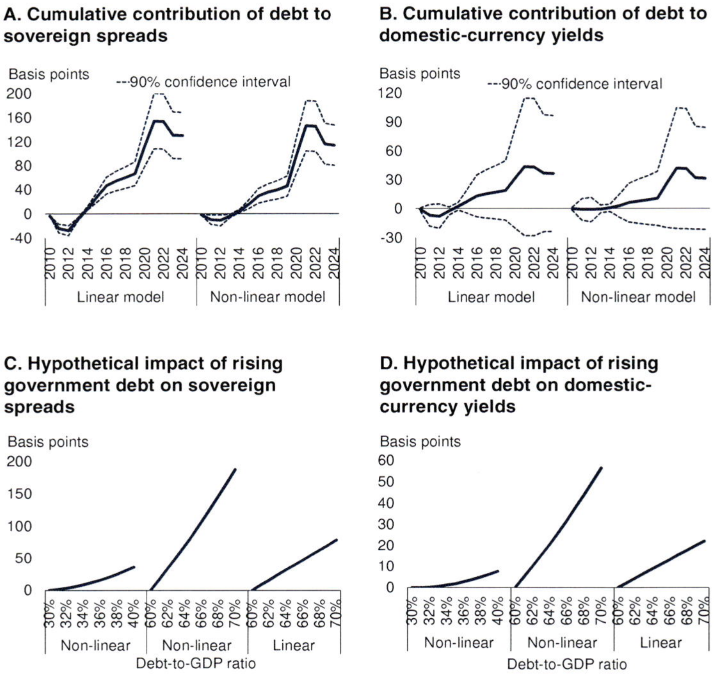

Sources: Haver Analytics; J.P.Morgan; World Bank.

Note: EMDEs = emerging market and developing economies.

A.B. Cumulative impact of the median rise in government debt between 2010 and 2024 in EMDEs based on the estimated relationships in table 3.1.

C.D. Panels reflect the impact of government debt rising by 10 percentage points of GDP in a hypothetical EMDE in which the increase occurs from a starting debt level of 30 percent of GDP and 60 percent of GDP.

policy stance and funding conditions, reprice the entire domestic yield curve upward, consistent with the idea that long-term interest rates are equal to an average of current and expected short-term interest rates and a term premium. Consequently, a 100 basis point increase in domestic short-term interest rates is associated with a 44-basis-point increase in 10-year interest rates.

Contribution of rising government debt to EMDE interest rates

The estimates described above were used to assess how much rising debt contributed to changes in sovereign spreads and domestic-currency yields in EMDEs in the period 2010–24. In this period, the median debt-to-GDP ratio in the sample rose from 34 percent to 54 percent. The estimate of the effect of increasing debt on sovereign spreads from the non-linear model implies that this rise, by itself, will have increased median spreads across EMDEs by 114 basis points (figure 3.4.A). The estimate of the linear model suggests a larger impact, of about 130 basis points: the levels of debt in the sample are sufficiently low that the net effect of the increases in the debt-to-GDP ratio and its square is less than the effect of the increase in the ratio in the linear model. The same calculation is done for domestic-currency bond yields (figure 3.4.B).[7] The estimate of the non-linear model suggests that between 2010 and 2024, rising debt contributed an increase of 31 basis points to domestic-currency yields—again, less than predicted by the linear model.

To highlight the importance of the non-linear relationship between debt and interest rates, a situation in which the debt-to-GDP ratio rises from 30 to 40 percent may be compared with a situation in which the ratio rises from 60 to 70 percent. The non-linear model suggests that spreads will rise in the first case by about 40 basis points, but in the second case by about 190 basis points—a substantial difference even though the increase in the ratio is 10 percentage points in both cases (figure 3.4.C). If the sensitivity of spreads to debt did not change with the level of debt, and the linear model applied, the implied increase in both cases would be about 80 basis points.

For domestic-currency yields, the estimate of the non-linear model implies that if the debt-to-GDP ratio increases from 30 to 40 percent, yields would increase by 8 basis points, but if the ratio rises from 60 to 70 percent, the increase in yields would be close to 60 basis points (figure 3.4.D).

[7] To ensure comparability across markets, the debt trajectory used in the domestic-currency estimate is constructed from the sovereign spread estimation sample. This ensures that differences in implied contributions reflect differences in pricing rather than differences in the underlying debt profile.

Potential fiscal savings from debt reduction

Another way to assess the impact of changing government debt on spreads and yields is to estimate the potential savings from debt reduction. A reduction in government debt will reduce the government's interest payments both because of the reduced volume of debt, at given spreads or yields, and because of the decline in spreads or yields associated with the reduction in debt. The resulting reduction in interest payments may be expressed as a ratio to, and thus as an annual rate of return on, the initial debt reduction. Importantly, the entire debt stock is assumed to be repriced when yields change; in practice, it would take time for declines in yields to filter through to interest payments as existing debt matures and is replaced by new lower-yielding debt.

The results show that the return to debt reduction rises with the level of debt for both sovereign spreads and domestic-currency yields (figure 3.5). At debt of 30 percent of GDP, the annual saving on debt service from reducing debt by 1 percentage point of GDP is only 0.04 percentage point of GDP for foreign-currency debt and 0.07 percentage point for domestic-currency debt. The implied rates of return are 4 percent and 7 percent, respectively. For debt at 60 percent of GDP, the annual savings are 0.12 percent of GDP for reducing foreign debt and 0.10 percentage point for reducing domestic-currency debt, so that the implied rates of return are 12 percent and 10 percent, respectively.

FIGURE 3.5 Potential fiscal savings from lowering debt

The return to deleveraging rises with the level of debt for both sovereign spreads and domestic-currency yields. At low debt levels, the return is modest and largely reflects the direct saving on the retired debt. However, as debt increases, the potential savings can be large.

A. Annual savings from debt reduction for sovereign spreads, by debt level

B. Annual savings from debt reduction for domestic-currency yields, by debt level

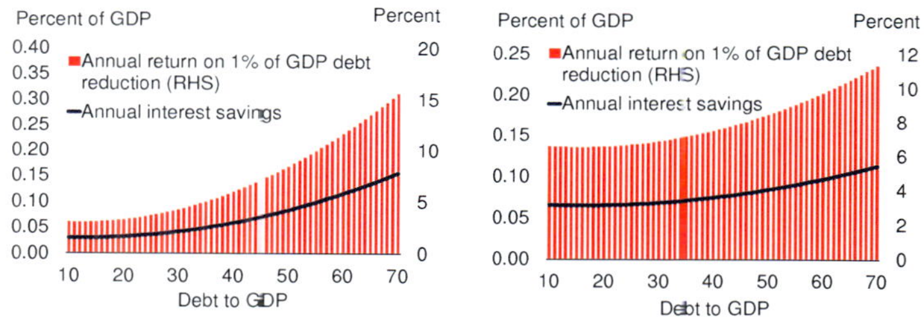

Source: World Bank.

Note: RHS = right-hand scale. Based on the annual reduction in interest costs from a decrease in interest rates assuming the entire debt stock reprices to the lower interest rate. The savings reflect savings on either foreign- or domestic-currency debt and do not reflect the fact that countries usually hold both types of debt. Initial level of sovereign spread and domestic-currency bond yield is at the sample mean of 3.6 and 6.9 percent, respectively, across all debt levels.

The role of advanced economy debt and bond yields

It is well understood that financial conditions in EMDEs are greatly influenced by global conditions (Arteta, Kamin, and Ruch 2025 provides a review). This study's estimates show EMDE sovereign spreads to be consistently and positively associated with U.S. high-yield corporate spreads and the Chicago Board Options Exchange Volatility Index (VIX), a measure of U.S. stock market volatility (table 3.1). Both of these indicators, though they relate to U.S. markets, may be considered reflective of global financial market conditions more generally (Kamin and Vakil, 2025). The estimates also indicate that advanced economy benchmark government bond yields have not exerted a large or statistically significant effect on spreads, perhaps partly because they are already reflected in U.S. corporate spreads and the VIX. However, advanced economy benchmark government bond yields are found to have had a consistently positive and statistically significant influence on EMDE domestic-currency yields, while corporate spreads and the VIX have not.[8]

Higher advanced economy yields influence EMDE interest rates in at least two ways. First, as discussed above, higher advanced economy yields lead to higher EMDE domestic-currency yields. Second, they pass one-for-one into the *yields* on EMDE foreign-currency-denominated sovereign bonds (since the EMDE *yield* equals the *spread* plus the advanced economy *yield*).

Because the level of advanced economy debt affects the level of advanced economy yields,

[8]The J.P.Morgan Emerging Markets Bond Index data used in this chapter's analysis is measured as spreads over U.S. Treasury yields. However, movements in these yields are well-correlated with those on bonds of other advanced economy governments. Therefore, debt-driven changes in advanced economy yields are likely to exert similar effects as U.S. Treasuries on EMDE yields.

FIGURE 3.6 Role of advanced economy debt

Between 2010 and 2024, advanced economy government debt increased by an average of about 12 percentage points of GDP. Accounting for the rise in domestic EMDE government debt and advanced economy debt on foreign-currency and domestic-currency bond yields implies a total rise in yields of 149 and 40 basis points, respectively.

A. Advanced economy government debt

B. Cumulative impact of EMDE and advanced economy debt on EMDE bond yield since 2010

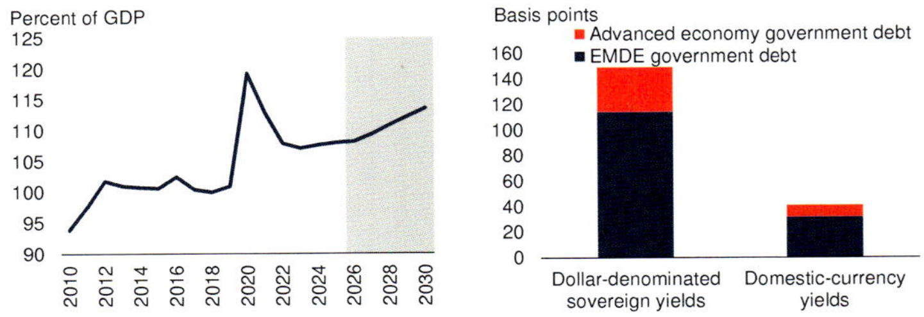

Sources: Haver Analytics; International Monetary Fund; J.P.Morgan; World Bank.
Note: EMDEs = emerging market and developing economies.
A. Based on the April 2026 *World Economic Outlook*.
B. Panel shows the cumulative impact of rising debt in EMDEs and advanced economies on EMDE interest rates.

advanced economy debt therefore exerts an indirect effect on EMDE interest rates. How important has the evolution of advanced economy debt been for EMDE interest rates compared with the growth of EMDE debt itself? In a back-of-the-envelope exercise, the analysis considers increases in both kinds of debt since 2010. Between 2010 and 2024, median EMDE debt rose by about 20 percentage points of GDP and advanced economy government debt by about 12 percentage points (figure 3.6.A).

As discussed in the previous section, the effect of the rise in EMDE debt on EMDE interest rates accounted for a rise since 2010 of 114 and 31 basis points for sovereign spreads and domestic-currency yields, respectively. Turning to the effects of rising advanced economy debt, estimates for the United States and other advanced economies indicate that a rise in government debt of 1 percent of GDP leads to a rise in benchmark yields of 2-5 basis points (Furceri, Goncalves, and Li 2025; Gruber and Kamin 2012; Laubach 2009; Neveu and Schafer 2024). Assuming an impact of 3 basis points, this implies that the 12 percentage point rise in advanced economy debt since 2010, holding all else constant, should have raised advanced economy yields by about 35 basis points, and thus raised the yields on EMDE foreign-currency debt by roughly the same extent. The rise in advanced economy yields would also have boosted domestic-currency bond yields by about 9 basis points (figure 3.6.B). The combined impact of EMDE and advanced economy debt implies a rise in spreads of 149 basis points and domestic-currency yields of 40 basis points. Given the mixing of different models using different assumptions and specifications, the exact magnitudes of these impacts should not be overemphasized, but in general terms the calculations suggest a meaningful boost to EMDE interest rates from rising debt.

Role of vulnerabilities in the impact of EMDE debt on interest rates

The models described above include a number of control variables—for example, inflation, GDP growth, and quality of governance—that are intended to capture determinants of a country's creditworthiness and which may therefore be expected to influence its international spreads and domestic financial yields. Such characteristics may affect EMDE interest rates not only directly but also by affecting the impact on interest rates of increases in government debt. Such state-contingent pricing may help to explain why some highly indebted countries are able to maintain lower borrowing costs than others. To shed further light on this issue, this section examines how government debt interacts with indicators of creditworthiness and financial vulnerability.[9] It also considers the effect of the global financing environment on the relationship between debt and interest rates.

History of past defaults

Defaults have long-lasting effects on investor confidence in a country's ability and willingness to

[9] The analysis is based on models assuming, for parsimony, a linear relationship between debt and interest rates. There are several possible sources of vulnerability and proxies for those vulnerabilities. This section focuses on key potential sources of vulnerability. Other sources, not explored in this section, include the share of debt held by private creditors, the share of non-Paris Club creditors, and other compositional changes in debt trends.

service and repay its debts (Arellano, 2008; Eaton and Gersovitz, 1981). Consequently, defaulters—especially serial defaulters—face lower credit ratings and persistently wider spreads, a phenomenon described as "debt intolerance" (Reinhart, Rogoff, and Savastano 2003). To assess the role of credit history, the model described above is augmented with a debt-crisis indicator which is equal to 1 when a country has experienced a debt crisis in the past 10 years (excluding the most recent year to avoid the inclusion of ongoing crises) and is otherwise zero.[10]

The estimates show that a history of debt crises is associated with an effect on spreads of increases in the government debt-to-GDP ratio that is roughly double the effect when there is no history of debt crises (figure 3.7.A). The estimated effect on domestic-currency yields of increases in debt is also higher in countries with prior histories of default, although the effect is smaller and not statistically significant. This is perhaps not surprising since outright defaults usually relate to foreign currency debt, as discussed earlier. It dovetails with the finding that debt sensitivities are greater for sovereign spreads than domestic-currency yields.

Credit ratings and frontier market status

Two possible approaches to gauging the effect of creditworthiness are comparing the effects of debt among economies with different credit ratings and making the same comparison between emerging markets and frontier markets, the latter being defined as EMDEs with meaningful but still-limited access to international financial markets.

For credit ratings, the average long-term sovereign foreign-currency debt ratings determined by Moody's, Standard & Poor's, and Fitch Ratings from Kose et al. (2022) are used. The results suggest that EMDEs with non-investment-grade ratings have spreads that are 50 percent more sensitive to additional debt than those with investment-grade ratings (figure 3.7.B). In the case of domestic-currency yields, the effect of rising debt does not significantly differ across ratings.

FIGURE 3.7 Role of vulnerabilities

EMDEs with a history of debt crises, as well as with weaker credit ratings or frontier market status, exhibit a greater sensitivity to a rise in government debt. Tighter global financing conditions also amplify the debt-spread relationship.

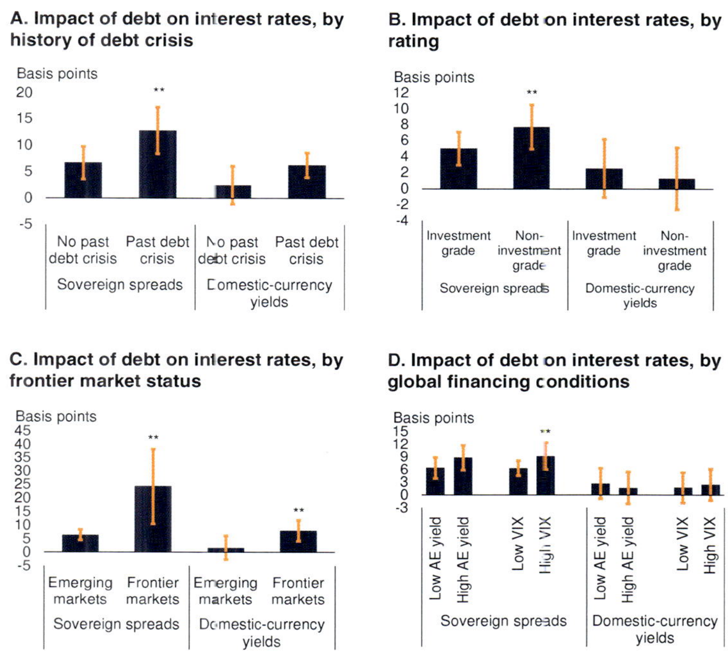

Sources: Haver Analytics; J.P.Morgan; Kose et al. (2022); MSCI; Nguyen, Castro, and Wood (2022); World Bank.

Note: AE = advanced economies; EMDEs = emerging market and developing economies; VIX = Chicago Board Options Exchange Volatility Index. Asterisks indicate whether the regimes are statistically significantly different from each other at a 10 percent level of significance.

A. Debt crisis equals 1 if a country experienced a crisis in the last 10 years, excluding the most recent year. Based on an updated debt crisis indicator in Nguyen, Castro, and Wood (2022).

B. Based on the average of foreign-currency long-term sovereign debt ratings by Moody's, Standard & Poor's, and Fitch Ratings from Kose et al. (2022).

C. Frontier classification based on 2026 MSCI market classification.

D. Low/high indicators reflect levels below and above the median.

The classification of EMDEs into emerging and frontier markets depends on the size, liquidity, and accessibility of their capital markets, including the stability of institutional frameworks.[11] The estimates show that rising interest rates are more strongly associated with rising debt levels in frontier markets than in emerging markets (figure 3.7.C). Specifically, for sovereign spreads, a 1 percentage point rise in the debt-to-GDP ratio is associated with a 24-basis-point increase in frontier markets, compared with just 6 basis points in emerging markets. Additionally, domestic-currency yields are nearly five times more sensitive

[10] The crisis indicator is updated through 2024 based on the definition in Nguyen, Castro, and Wood (2022).

[11] Frontier market status is based on MSCI market classification in 2026.

FIGURE 3.8 Role of vulnerabilities (cont'd)

Liquidity and rollover risks render interest rates more sensitive to additional debt. High inflation is associated with a stronger linkage between spreads and debt, whereas weaker governance increases the estimated sensitivity of domestic-currency bond yields to debt.

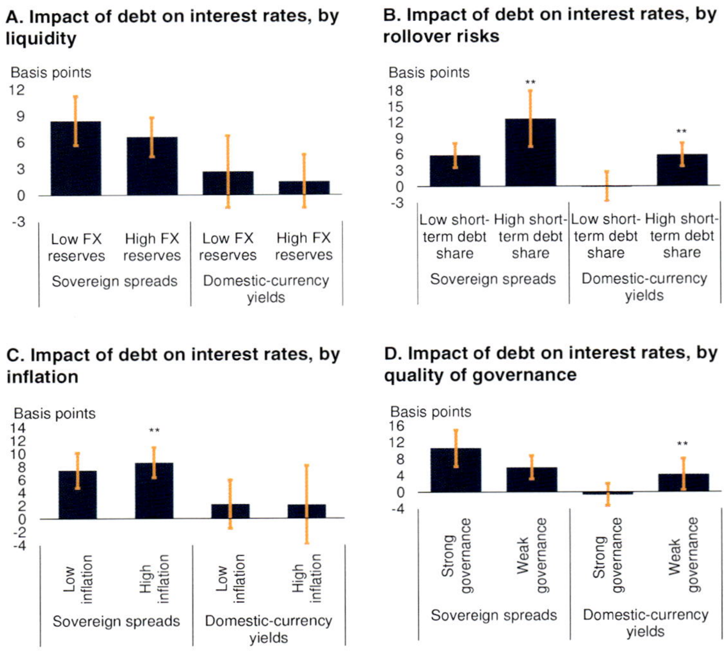

Sources: Haver Analytics; J.P.Morgan; PRS Group; World Bank.

Note: FX = foreign exchange. Asterisks indicate whether the regimes are statistically significantly different from each other at a 10 percent level of significance.

A.B.D. Low/high indicators reflect levels below and above the median.

C. Low/high inflation reflects inflation at 5 and 30 percent, respectively.

D. Based on International Country Risk Guide (ICRG) ratings of bureaucratic quality. Strong/Weak reflect levels above and below the median.

to increasing debt in frontier markets, with each 1 percentage point increase in the debt-to-GDP ratio raising yields by roughly 8 basis points.

Global financing environment

The direct effects of global financing conditions on EMDE interest rates and spreads have been discussed above. Do these conditions also affect the extent to which increases in debt boost interest rates in EMDEs? This issue is addressed by interacting government debt with advanced economy yields and the VIX. The estimates show that higher advanced economy yields and VIX readings (assumed to represent tighter global financing conditions) are associated with a greater sensitivity of sovereign spreads to debt (although the effect of advanced economy yields is not statistically significant). Thus, elevated global borrowing costs not only raise borrowing costs for EMDEs and narrow their fiscal space but also raise the marginal cost of additional external debt. However, the estimates show no difference in the sensitivity of domestic-currency yields to increases in debt when global financial conditions are tighter, suggesting that other factors—such as domestic monetary policy and financial market developments—are more important to the pricing of domestic-currency debt (figure 3.7.D).

Liquidity and rollover risk

Even solvent governments may default if they lack the liquidity to make interest payments and refinance maturing obligations, which is more likely to be the case when global financial conditions are unfavorable.

To examine the role of liquidity, the interaction between debt levels and two indicators of liquidity—holdings of foreign exchange reserves and the share of short-term debt—is examined (figures 3.8.A and 3.8.B). Larger foreign exchange reserves are associated with a slightly smaller sensitivity of both spreads and domestic-currency yields to debt. Conversely, higher shares of short-term debt are associated with substantial and statistically significant increases in debt sensitivity.

Inflation

In EMDEs, capital flight and currency depreciation have often stemmed from inflationary financing, which has contributed to concerns about policy credibility, repayment risk, and financial stability. To capture this effect, the analysis interacts public debt with the inflation rate. The estimates show that higher inflation is associated with a greater sensitivity of sovereign spreads to debt, but no difference in the sensitivity of domestic-currency yields, perhaps because these yields already fully discount expected inflation (figure 3.8.C).

Governance and institutional quality

Strong institutions enhance commitment to debt service and repayment, improve debt management, and reduce policy uncertainty, so that they can be expected to attenuate the sensitivity of interest rates to rising debt. Weak governance, by contrast, will tend to amplify concerns about fiscal indiscipline, fiscal dominance, and discretionary and destabilizing policy shifts, tending to steepen the debt–yield relationship. This is proxied by interacting public debt with the International Country Risk Guide's Bureaucratic Quality index. The estimates show that the sensitivity of domestic -currency yields to debt is significantly larger in countries with weaker governance, but that the debt-spreads relationship is unaffected (figure 3.8.D).

Country illustrations of debt-interest rate dynamics

The empirical results described above highlight the importance of three determinants of interest rates in EMDEs: public-sector debt levels, domestic economic conditions and vulnerabilities, and global financial market conditions. The country cases below, encompassing both emerging market and frontier market economies, illustrate how these have played out in different institutional and macroeconomic settings.

Debt distress and default. During the years preceding the pandemic, low advanced economy interest rates and highly accommodative global financial market conditions expanded EMDEs' access to global private credit markets and led to large increases in their debt, which were not always used productively; indeed, in some cases the easy borrowing enabled undisciplined macroeconomic policies. In Sri Lanka, years of large fiscal deficits, low tax revenues (just over 11 percent of GDP in 2018 before declining to near 7 percent of GDP in 2022), and rising reliance on commercial external borrowing eroded fiscal buffers (World Bank, 2022). As a result, the government debt-to-GDP ratio rose from about 79 percent in 2017 to over 119 percent in 2022 (figure 3.9.A). In Ghana, persistent fiscal deficits, rising energy-sector liabilities, and the legacy costs of financial-sector cleanup had already weakened debt dynamics before the pandemic, driving the public-debt-to-GDP ratio up from less than 40 percent in 2010 to nearly 100 percent in 2022. Zambia experienced an even sharper runup in debt, which peaked at over 140 percent of GDP in 2020 (figure 3.9.B). In all three countries, sovereign spreads widened as debt rose.

FIGURE 3.9 Country illustrations

Country episodes illustrate how fiscal slippage and rising public debt are associated with a deterioration in borrowing conditions. In frontier markets such as Sri Lanka and Zambia, rapid debt accumulation—often alongside weak fiscal frameworks and external vulnerabilities—has been followed by sharp increases in spreads and yields and culminated in default. In some emerging markets, such as the Arab Republic of Egypt and South Africa, gradual debt increases and repeated fiscal stress, compounded by increasing policy uncertainty, have been accompanied by rising borrowing costs, credit rating downgrades, and, in some cases, the loss of investment-grade status.

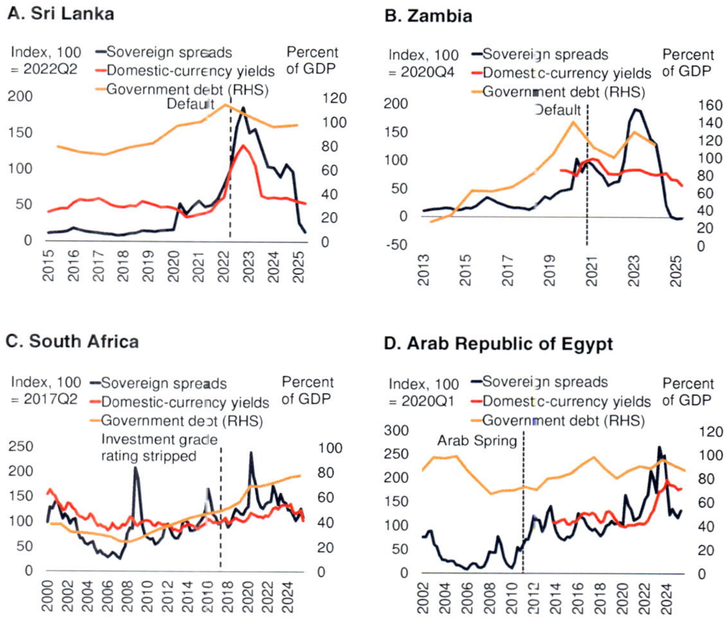

Sources: Bloomberg; Haver Analytics; J.P.Morgan.

Note: RHS = right-hand scale. Sovereign risk spreads based on J.P.Morgan's Emerging Markets Bond Index Global (EMBIG)

A. Sri Lanka announced a suspension of external debt servicing in April 2022.

B. Zambia missed Eurobond coupon payment in October 2020 and was downgraded to selective/restricted default by the rating agencies.

C. South Africa was downgraded to non-investment-grade on its foreign-currency sovereign debt in April 2017.

D. The "Arab Spring" reflected mass protests that resulted in political change in early 2011.

Like other economies, in the 2020s, Sri Lanka, Ghana, and Zambia suffered from the pandemic recession, the subsequent surge in global inflation and interest rates, and volatile commodity prices following Russia's invasion of Ukraine. But these economies' already-pronounced fiscal and financial vulnerabilities led to their being hit especially hard. Sri Lanka's sovereign spreads surged from their 300–500 basis point range to over 6,000 basis points in 2022, while domestic-currency bond yields rose from about 8 percent to nearly 29 percent. In April 2022, Sri Lanka suspended external debt service—its first sovereign default in modern history—and a sharp recession ensued. Ghanaian sovereign spreads surged to above 3,000 basis points in 2023 as the country lost access to international credit; a sharp depreciation, rise in inflation, and tightening of domestic financing conditions culminated in a domestic debt exchange in 2023 and external debt restructuring negotiations in the context of an IMF-supported policy program. Zambia defaulted in November 2020, but subsequent failure to conclude a restructuring agreement kept spreads in the thousands of basis points until 2023, when progress in restructuring allowed some improvement in market sentiment.

Since their respective debt crises, spreads and interest rates have declined in all three of these frontier market economies. These declines primarily reflect progress with debt restructuring and the adoption of IMF-supported policy programs that have reduced the likelihood of further default. Nevertheless, debt levels remain high and spreads remain elevated, reflecting continuing challenges to growth, stability, and fiscal stabilization.

Gradual debt accumulation, downgrade, and the cost of eroded credibility. Prior to the global financial crisis, South Africa's general government debt fell significantly, leading to a sharp decline in sovereign spreads (figure 3.9.C). Since then, however, debt has steadily climbed from 26 percent of GDP in 2009 to about 80 percent in 2025, driven by weak growth, elevated social protection commitments to address poverty and inequality, a structurally rigid and large public sector wage bill, and rising debt-service costs. Interest rates have trended up alongside rising debt, with EMBI spreads widening moderately from about 200 basis points initially to more than 400 basis points by 2022 (excluding the larger pandemic-driven spike in 2020), and 10-year domestic-currency yields moving up from 9 to 12 percent. The rise in interest rates was given further impetus in April 2017, when weakening policy credibility and institutional checks and balances (linked in part to a high-profile cabinet reshuffle) prompted a downgrade of South Africa's sovereign rating to sub-investment-grade, the first such grade since 2000. As a result, institutional investors with investment-grade mandates were forced to divest, amplifying funding pressures (World Bank 2017b).

Since 2022, spreads and interest rates have declined as a result of improvements in the fiscal accounts, some easing in global credit markets, and more recently a reduction in the central bank's inflation target. South Africa's sovereign risk spreads remain contained relative to many of its peers among EMDEs and Sub-Saharan Africa. Since mid–2024, the improvement has been further supported by enhanced electricity availability and continued reform momentum, which have helped strengthen investor sentiment. These developments attest to the scope for improved macroeconomic policies, credible reforms, and benign global conditions to offset some of the adverse effects of high debt. Nevertheless, debt and debt-service costs remain elevated, crowding out productive spending and leaving South Africa with limited fiscal room to absorb further shocks.

Repeated stress and the fragility of consolidation. Like South Africa, the Arab Republic of Egypt managed to lower its public debt levels during the early 2000s, leading to corresponding declines in sovereign spreads (figure 3.9.D). Since then, however, it has navigated two distinct waves of fiscal stress, each resolved through external financial support. Following the Arab Spring, large deficits driven by energy subsidies, a growing public wage bill, and weak revenues pushed public debt from 78 percent of GDP in June 2012 to over 100 percent by June 2017, boosted in part by a sharp exchange-rate depreciation that further inflated the foreign-currency stock of debt (World Bank 2017c). An IMF-supported adjustment program brought the primary balance into surplus and reduced debt to about 86 percent of GDP by June 2019. However, with the consolidation relying heavily on expenditure compression rather than durable revenue gains, fiscal austerity could not be maintained, especially in the face of the pandemic and the rise in commodity prices following Russia's invasion of Ukraine (World Bank 2024b). Spreads reached 1,200 basis points amid a resultant balance-of-payments crisis in 2022-23. They have since fallen back following the implementation of reforms, but debt remains elevated and rollover risks persist (World Bank 2024b).

Policy implications

A number of key policy implications follow from this chapter's analysis of public debt and interest rates in EMDEs. First, the analysis strengthens the pressing rationale for EMDE governments to maintain control over fiscal deficits and debts, especially for more highly indebted countries. Even if increases in debt were not accompanied by rising interest rates, it would still be necessary to restrain such increases, since they lead to higher debt-service burdens. But if increases in debt lead to higher interest rates, as shown by the analysis in this chapter, the effect of rising debt on debt-service burdens becomes even greater.

Second, the non-linearity of the relationship between debt and interest rates implies different tradeoffs between fiscal deficits and development objectives, depending on the extent of indebtedness. Governments with relatively low levels of debt can afford to increase that debt without substantially boosting interest rates and debt-service burdens; for these governments, it may be prudent to pursue growth-enhancing, high-return public investment projects financed through deficit spending. Indeed, the fiscal multiplier is higher in countries with lower debt. Conversely, for highly indebted governments, the rise in debt-service burdens associated with deficit spending may well exceed the return to even efficient public spending, arguing for a greater focus on deficit reduction and making the need to mobilize private investment to support growth and job creation even more urgent. These efforts can complement trade, diversification, and productivity-enhancing reforms.

For highly indebted governments, therefore, securing fiscal sustainability, including through appropriate fiscal consolidation, should be a key priority (Balasundharam et al. 2023). This requires both stronger domestic revenue mobilization and improvements in the efficiency of public spending. Government expenditures as a share of GDP in EMDEs have risen more than revenues since 2010 (figure 3.10.A). As a result, more than half of EMDEs have recorded fiscal deficits that increase public debt levels (or debt-increasing fiscal positions) in the past few years. This is more than double the share of such economies at the beginning of the 2000s, and it marks a faster pace of deterioration than in the advanced economies (figure 3.10.B). Broadening the tax base, strengthening tax administration capacity, reducing

FIGURE 3.10 Policy implications

Government revenues, relative to GDP, in the median EMDEs have changed little since the early 2000s, even as expenditures as a share of GDP have increased since 2010, underscoring the need for stronger revenue mobilization and spending discipline. As a result, more than half of EMDEs have experienced debt-increasing fiscal positions in the 2010s and early 2020s, highlighting the importance of fiscal consolidation. The share of EMDEs with fiscal rules has risen substantially, though it remains below that in advanced economies, pointing to scope for wider adoption. Fiscal rules tend to improve fiscal balances following adoption, particularly in EMDEs with strong institutional frameworks.

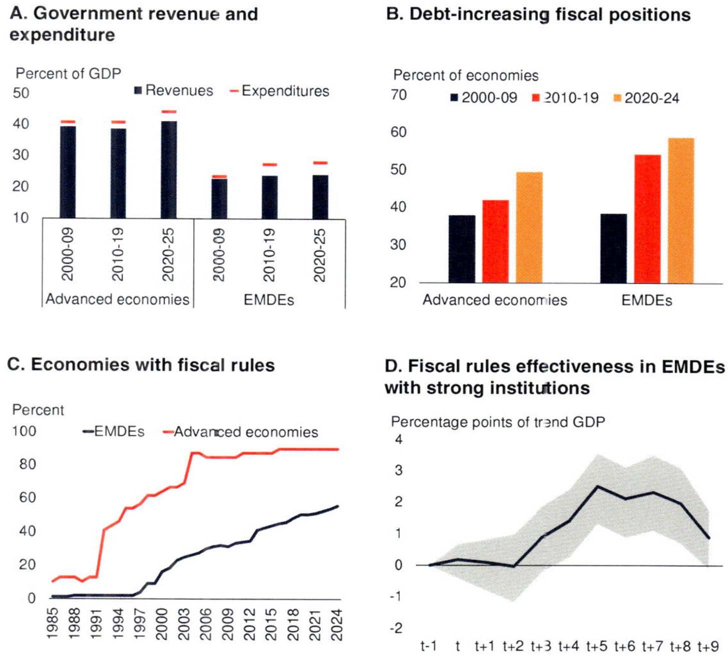

Sources: Gootjes, Mawejje, and Vorisek (2026); International Monetary Fund; Kose et al. (2022); World Bank.

Note: EMDEs = emerging market and developing economies.

A. Bars (dashes) represent period averages of median government revenue (expenditure) as percent of GDP in each group. Sample includes up to 39 advanced economies and 152 EMDEs.

B. Bars show the share of economies in each group with a primary balance sustainability gap of less than zero. The primary balance sustainability gap is calculated as the difference between the primary balance and the debt-stabilizing primary balance. Sample includes 34 advanced economies and 81 EMDEs.

C. Sample includes 153 EMDEs and 39 advanced economies.

D. Line shows the cumulative change in the cyclically adjusted primary balance (CAPB) as a percent of trend GDP in the years around fiscal rule adoption, compared with a counterfactual scenario of no rule adoption in year t (Gootjes, Mawejje, and Vorisek 2026). Shared areas show 90 percent confidence intervals. Institutional strength is measured using principal component analysis of *International Country Risk Guide* data. Results are based on a sample of 83 EMDEs with 33 cases of fiscal rule adoption between 1984 and 2015.

exemptions, and selectively increasing tax rates while minimizing distortions can help raise government revenues (IMF and World Bank 2024a). Reducing informality and supporting formal job creation could also expand the tax base and increase the fiscal multiplier. On the expenditure side, policy makers should seek to improve efficiency of government services and replace broad-based subsidies with better-targeted support for vulnerable populations. In some cases, debt-for-development swaps, which replace sovereign debt for commitments to support development objectives, can create fiscal space for investments in human capital and other growth-enhancing priorities while supporting debt sustainability (IMF and World Bank 2024b). For countries at high risk of, or already in, debt distress, the G20 Common Framework provides a multilateral pathway for debt restructuring. However, the process requires greater transparency, faster coordination, and enhanced information-sharing to secure sufficient and timely debt relief (Chen and Hart 2025; IMF, World Bank, and G20 Presidency 2026).

Medium-term budget frameworks, fiscal rules, and independent fiscal councils can help promote fiscal credibility and debt sustainability. EMDEs are now much better positioned than in the early 2000s, with the share of countries adopting fiscal rules increasing from about 15 percent in 2000 to 55 percent in 2024. Nevertheless, the prevalence of fiscal rules remains lower in EMDEs than in advanced economies (figure 3.10.C). Evidence suggests that fiscal balances typically improve following the adoption of fiscal rules (Gootjes, Mawejje, and Vorisek 2026). These gains are more durable when supported by a strong institutional environment, including transparent budget processes, democratic accountability, and the rule of law (figure 3.10.D).

Third, besides flattening the trajectory of government debt, the analysis in this chapter highlights the importance of strengthening the *structure* of public debt. Higher shares of short-term debt increase the sensitivity of borrowing costs to rising debt levels, as well as to increases in global and domestic interest rates. While EMDEs halved their share of short-term debt in the last two decades, the heightened sensitivity puts a premium on lengthening bond maturities to mute the effects of rising interest rates, reduce rollover risks, and improve resilience to domestic and external shocks.

The analysis also shows that increases in public debt lead to smaller increases in domestic-currency interest rates than in foreign-currency risk spreads, and those increases are less affected by the initial level of debt as well. To be sure, as discussed earlier in this chapter, not all the reasons for the lower debt-sensitivity of domestic currency yields reflect genuine financing advantages, as those yields may be more subject to financial repression, debt monetization, and mispricing than foreign-currency yields.

Moreover, domestic debt markets may pose risks for EMDEs and increase borrowing costs for private firms. Domestic debt markets are dominated by domestic banks and a narrow set of institutional investors, limiting secondary-market liquidity and reinforcing the sovereign–bank nexus. Domestic banks, on average, hold about 28 percent of their assets in domestic sovereign bonds—equivalent to many multiples of regulatory capital, implying substantial exposure to sovereign risk (World Bank 2024a). Private domestic firms are also disadvantaged by rising sovereign debt, with corporate yields increasing in tandem with sovereign yields. This implies that further sovereign debt increases disproportionately push up the economy-wide cost of capital (World Bank, forthcoming).

Even so, provided they are well-regulated, the benefits of domestic debt markets likely outweigh the costs, suggesting that governments should prioritize their development and draw on them to finance their deficit spending. Deep and efficient domestic government bond markets are vital for sustainable economic growth (Hashimoto et al. 2021; Meh and Schmukler 2025; OECD 2025). These markets can provide resilience to domestic and external shocks, mitigate the currency mismatch and risks from borrowing in foreign currency, foster private sector capital market development, help adequately price risk (when financial repression is absent), and empower central banks to effectively implement monetary policy. Key elements of domestic-currency bond market development include establishing a benchmark yield, maintaining secondary market liquidity, and expanding a retail investor base (IMF and World Bank 2020).

Finally, the analysis provides additional reasons for pursuing macroeconomic, financial, and structural reforms: they can strengthen fiscal sustainability while improving the conditions for investment and job creation. Higher growth stemming from structural reforms can flatten the trajectory of the debt-to-GDP ratio for a given path of nominal debt. Additionally, higher growth, lower inflation, and better governance lead directly to improved creditworthiness and lower EMDE interest rates. And lastly, better macroeconomic performance and stronger financial positions—such as higher foreign exchange reserves—attenuate the effect of rising debt levels on interest rates. Enumerating the many policies needed to achieve higher growth and greater resilience is beyond the scope of this chapter. However, such policies would typically include (besides fiscal restraint) prudent monetary policy and central bank independence, flexible exchange rates, the dismantling of overly restrictive regulations, promotion of competition, trade and diversification strategies, practical technology adoption in job-rich sectors, and careful supervision and regulation of the financial system.

ANNEX 3.1 Methodology and data

Linear models

The analysis first estimates linear panel data models similar to those used in the existing literature and in line with the theory of debt pricing. The models are of the form:

$$i_{jt} = \alpha_j + \beta \text{Debt}_{jt\text{-}1} + \Theta' X_{jt} + \varepsilon_{jt} \qquad \text{(A3.1.1)},$$

where $j = 1,2,\ldots, N$ represents countries, $t = 1,2, \ldots, T$ represents quarterly observations; i_{jt} is the domestic-currency 10-year bond yield or the EMBIG spread (between a hard-currency domestic bond and the U.S. bond yield; $i \in (i_t^l, i_t^*)$); Debt_{it} is gross government debt as a percent of GDP; X_{jt} is a set of control variables including growth, inflation, current account balance, debt crises, inflation volatility, and a control for governance; and α_j are country-fixed effects (and no time fixed effects in the baseline models). The model also includes measures of global financial conditions: the U.S. corporate high-yield spread, the VIX, and a weighted average of 10-year advanced economy government bond yields. For robustness, two other versions of these models are estimated. The first includes year-fixed effects to address common shocks. Second, the year-fixed effects are replaced with cross-sectional averages of interest rates and debt; this also implicitly controls for common shocks. The results of these two models, not reported here, are very similar to those in the baseline model. Standard errors are based on heteroskedasticity-robust variance estimators clustered at the country level because the interest rates are highly persistent and likely correlated across countries.

Non-linear models

The relationship between public debt and yields may be non-linear, with the sensitivity of yields rising with debt levels. There are several papers that address potential non-linearities. Ardagna, Caselli and Lane (2007), for example, use both a squared debt term and a threshold model (based on median debt levels in member countries of the Organisation for Economic Co-operation and Development) in their analysis. Baldacci and Kumar (2010) also add a squared debt term. More recently, Matsuoka (2022) looked at the impact of the composition of government debt on domestic-currency bond yields using a panel smooth transition regression. Ciżkowicz, Ledóchowski and Rzońca (2025) use an exponential model and interaction terms to identify the impact of debt on interest rates. This analysis provides updated estimates, improves on other aspects of their methodology, and explores the implications of the non-linearity in the debt relationship for the evolution of EMDE sovereign interest rates.

The analysis extends the linear model to a quadratic formulation linked to the idea of investors becoming more debt intolerant as countries reach fiscal limits. The quadratic model adds the square of the debt level as an explanatory variable. It thus assumes a smooth non-linear relationship between debt and interest rates: the higher the debt, the greater the sensitivity of interest rates to debt. The estimates described in the main text of this chapter are based on the quadratic model.

The quadratic model is estimated as:

$$i_{jt} = \alpha_j + \beta \text{Debt}_{jt\text{-}1} + \tau \text{Debt}^2_{jt\text{-}1} + \Theta' X_{jt} + \varepsilon_{jt} \text{ (A3.1.2)}.$$

To address the role of vulnerabilities and risks, the following model is estimated:

$$i_{jt} = \alpha_j + \beta \text{Debt}_{jt\text{-}1} + \rho(\text{Debt}_{jt\text{-}1} \times V_{it\text{-}1}) + \omega V_{it} + \Theta' X_{jt} + \varepsilon_{jt} \qquad \text{(A3.1.3)},$$

$(\text{Debt}_{jt\text{-}1} \times V_{it\text{-}1})$ reflect the interaction between debt and an indicator of vulnerability. The analysis looks at several indicators including past debt crises, global financial conditions, inflation and governance.

Data

The main interest rate variables are sovereign risk spreads (EMBIG) and 10-year domestic-currency bond yields. Sovereign risk spread (EMBIG) data are collected from J.P.Morgan for 83 EMDEs and are available from January 1994. The 10-year domestic-currency bond yields are collected from Haver Analytics. The data set is heavily unbalanced, however, with only 14 countries providing observations from 1994, 26 from 2000, and 40 from 2010. Data on 10-year domestic-currency yields are even more sparse, available for only 31 EMDEs. The sample only includes countries with at least 12 consecutive observations and exclude outliers in the 1st and 99th percentiles. Refer to table A3.1 for details on data, their sources, and transformations. The countries and samples used in the regressions are highlighted in table A3.2.

Quarterly data on gross government debt are drawn from Haver Analytics, and reference general government debt or, if that is not available, central government debt. As an alternative to lagged debt, the analysis also estimates the sensitivity of interest rates to two-year-ahead forecasts of gross government debt; these are drawn from the 2011 to 2024 edition of the International Monetary Fund's World Economic Outlook (WEO) database and are available on a semi-annual basis.

The main (domestic) control variables include real GDP growth, inflation, a debt crisis indicator, bureaucracy quality, and, in the case of domestic-currency yields, short-term interest rates. These variables help to control for repayment risk not captured by debt measures alone, and they also influence the demand for domestic-currency debt. Data for real GDP growth and consumer inflation are mainly sourced from two locations. First, actual quarterly data, mainly sourced from Haver Analytics, are collected as far back as possible. Second, two-year-ahead forecasts, used in alternative specifications described in annex 3.2, are collected from the IMF WEO database. To control for governance, the analysis uses the bureaucratic quality measure from the International Country Risk Guide (ICRG), which captures whether the civil service is free from political pressure, has sufficient administrative capacity and expertise, and can deliver services. It is measured from 0-4 with higher values indicating better bureaucratic quality. Finally, the analysis controls for sovereign debt default by including the debt crisis indicator of Nguyen, Castro, and Wood (2022); this indicator signals when a sovereign (1) fails to pay its interest and/or principal obligations when due or (2) postpones its obligations by rescheduling or restructuring debts with less favorable terms than the original ones.

Several global factors in line with theory (such as the expectations hypothesis of the term structure and interest rate parity) are included. To take into account the spillovers of financial conditions in advanced economies on EMDEs, the model includes the yield on advanced economy 10-year government bonds (the nominal-GDP weighted average of yields in the euro area, Japan, and the United States), the spread on U.S. high-yield corporate bonds over U.S. Treasuries, and the VIX (Arteta, Kamin, and Ruch 2025; Bräuning and Ivashina 2020; Cerutti et.al. 2023; Hoek, Kamin, and Yoldas 2022; Kamin and Vakil, 2025; Ozatay, Özmen, and Şahinbeyoğlu 2009).

For default risk, the analysis uses past debt crises as defined in Nguyen, Castro, and Wood (2022)—specifically, whether a country has experienced a debt crisis in the last 10 years excluding the most recent year to avoid the possibility of ongoing crises. For the exposure of the economy to liquidity risks, the analysis interacts debt with foreign exchange reserves to GDP and short-term debt to GDP (both defined as dummy variables with the median splitting the sample in two). For valuation, the analysis uses inflation in levels. Finally, for governance, the analysis uses the ICRG's bureaucratic quality index.

ANNEX 3.2 Alternative models

Threshold models

An alternative way investors may price debt is based on different regimes, assuming that below a certain debt-to-GDP threshold, there is one sensitivity of interest rates to debt, and above that threshold, a different sensitivity. This threshold model serves as a robustness test for the non-linearity of the debt-interest rate relationship, and estimation results are described below. In order to estimate this relationship, specifically implemented here as a continuous-threshold model (as in Hansen 2017), the analysis first identifies threshold levels of debt that reflect a break in the link between debt and interest rates. That is, it identifies the level of debt, if the sensitivity of interest rates to debt is allowed to differ at values of debt above and below that level, that minimizes the residual sum of squares for the model. This approach is applied separately for both sovereign spreads and domestic-currency yields.

The continuous-threshold model is expressed as:

$$i_{jt} = \alpha_j + \beta Debt_{jt-1} + \tau(Debt_{jt-1} - \gamma) + \Theta' X_{jt} + \varepsilon_{jt} \quad \text{(A3.2.1)},$$

where $(Debt_{jt-1} - \gamma) \equiv \max(0, Debt_{jt-1} - \gamma)$ is the kink term when gross general government debt to GDP is above a threshold of γ. Therefore, below that threshold, the response of interest rates to debt is captured by β; above that threshold, the response rises to $\beta + \tau$.

To identify the threshold, a grid search is performed over values of debt to minimize the residual sum of squares. To avoid choosing outliers as the threshold, the search is limited to to values between the 5th and 95th percentile of debt to GDP. While the exact distribution of debt differs between the data sets, this usually corresponds to between 9 and 76 percent of GDP, by 0.5 percentage point increments.

The fit of the equation is maximized when the debt threshold is set at roughly 70 percent of GDP for sovereign spreads and 30 percent of GDP for domestic-currency bond yields. About one in five economies with quarterly debt observations for 2024Q4 had debt levels above the 70 percent of GDP threshold for spreads, and four in five economies had debt above the 30 percent of GDP threshold for domestic-currency yields.

The estimation results for the threshold models show that debt has a small, positive and statistically significant impact on sovereign spreads below 70 percent of GDP (about 6 basis points per 1 percentage point of GDP increase in debt), but a much larger and significant impact above this threshold (36 basis points; table A3.3).

Turning to domestic-currency yields, below 30 percent of GDP, a 1 percentage point of GDP increase in debt is associated with a decrease in 10-year yields. This impact is not statistically different from zero. Above the 30 percent of GDP threshold, yields increase by 3 basis points for each incremental increase in debt; the difference above and below the threshold is statistically significant.

The exact level of the identified thresholds, as well as their implications for interest rates, are likely to be highly sensitive to model specification and sample composition. However, the results confirm the message of the quadratic models described in the main text of this chapter: as debt levels rise, the impact on interest rates of further increments to debt rises as well.

Models using forecast data

Because fiscal variables and other macroeconomic indicators may be endogenous with respect to interest rates, or because both may be influenced by third factors, an alternative approach uses forecast revisions—defined as changes in IMF WEO two-year-ahead debt projections across vintages—to capture unexpected shifts in the anticipated fiscal path of debt (similar approaches were implemented in Coibion and Gorodnichenko 2015 and Romer and Romer, 2010).[12] Forecast data are available from 2011 on a half-yearly basis. As a test of the robustness of the results described

[12] Forecast revisions do not fully resolve the endogeneity concern raised by the baseline specifications. Projected debt paths mechanically incorporate borrowing cost assumptions and broader macrofinancial developments that also influence the dependent variable.

above, this analysis replicates the model specifications reported in table A3.4, but using debt forecast revisions, and 2-year-ahead inflation and real GDP growth. The impact of debt on sovereign spreads and domestic-currency yields continues to be non-linear, with the quadratic relationship being statistically significant (table A3.3).

Models using other possible drivers of yields

A key challenge in identifying the effects of public debt on interest rates is disentangling causal relationships from correlations with other macroeconomic, institutional, and financial factors that also influence borrowing costs. One potential source of bias in the size of the impact of debt on interest rates comes from omitted variables. To address this concern, eight additional variables that may affect spreads and yields are included one at a time: fiscal policy uncertainty, inflation volatility, current account balance to GDP, foreign exchange reserves as a ratio to GDP, share of foreign-currency debt, real effective exchange rate, share of debt held by the central bank, and commodity prices.[13]

For sovereign spreads, none of the additional variables have a statistically significant impact and the non-linear relationship between debt and spreads remains. For domestic-currency yields, fiscal policy uncertainty has a statistically significant impact and raises yields. The non-linear impact of debt on yields remains significant in all but two regressions.

Sample coverage

Interest rate data in EMDEs vary substantially across countries and over time, reflecting differences in market development, instrument availability, and data continuity (refer to table A3.2 for details on the availability of sovereign spreads and domestic-currency yields used in regressions). This raises a potential concern that regression results are sensitive to samples. This concern is addressed in several ways. First, the sample of countries used to estimate the impact of debt on sovereign spreads is almost twice as large as for domestic-currency yields. Restricting the sample of countries for sovereign spreads to that of domestic-currency yields suggests that, based on the linear model, a 1 percent of GDP increase in debt is associated with a 6 basis point increase in spreads, compared with about 8 basis points in the baselines; both impacts are statistically significant. In the non-linear case, the initial level of debt continues to influence the sensitivity of sovereign spreads to debt but the impact is attenuated. When public debt is at 45 percent of GDP an incremental increase in debt is associated with a 5.5 basis point increase in spreads (about 8 from table 3.2) rising to 13 basis points when debt is at 80 percent (20 basis points in the baseline).

The smaller sample for sovereign spreads does affect the role of some vulnerability dimensions in the relationship between debt and spreads. A country with a history of defaults remains more sensitive to changes in debt; the sensitivity rises in the smaller sample. Speculative-grade EMDEs continue to be more sensitive to increases in debt, at least compared with the most highly-rated investment-grade EMDEs. Higher shares of short-term debt and higher inflation continue to significantly boost the sensitivity of spreads to debt. However, frontier market-status is not a clear driver of the sensitivity of spreads to debt in the smaller sample. Also, spreads continue to be sensitive to global financing conditions, but the impact is no longer significantly different.

Second, excluding one country at a time from the regressions does not change the significance of the non-linear relationship for sovereign spreads but does affect the significance of debt's impact on domestic-currency yields. For sovereign spreads, the coefficients on the debt squared term are within one standard deviation of the baseline results. For domestic-currency yields, the significance of the non-linear relationship weakens when 4 of the 19 countries are excluded from the sample.

[13] To control for inflation volatility, the analysis constructs a realized inflation volatility measure based on the conditional standard deviation from a Generalized Autoregressive Conditional Heteroskedastic (GARCH(1,1)) model estimated on monthly year-over-year consumer price index inflation. Fiscal policy uncertainty is based on Hong, Ke, and Nguyen (2025).

TABLE 3.1 Regressions of interest rates

	(1)	(2)	(3)	(4)
	Sovereign spreads		Domestic-currency yields	
Government debt-to-GDP ratio	7.866***	-9.006	2.217	-4.984
	[1.426]	[5.422]	[2.216]	[4.357]
Debt-to-GDP ratio squared		0.187***		0.0808*
		[0.0661]		[0.0442]
Consumer inflation	8.831***	7.540***	2.663	2.806
	[1.062]	[0.998]	[2.109]	[2.154]
Real GDP growth	-0.892*	-1.368**	0.283	0.184
	[0.446]	[0.513]	[0.335]	[0.351]
Debt crisis	164.9**	183.3**	30.29	66.68
	[76.61]	[71.83]	[39.83]	[56.48]
Bureaucracy quality	-68.04	-69.69	5.550	2.599
	[67.32]	[63.26]	[26.69]	[22.69]
U.S. high-yield corporate spread	20.13**	20.18**	3.020	1.864
	[8.112]	[8.012]	[4.443]	[4.241]
VIX	5.224**	4.606**	1.020	1.173
	[2.425]	[2.152]	[1.145]	[1.123]
Advanced economy 10-year treasury yield	8.665	10.51	29.01***	26.28***
	[10.19]	[9.843]	[8.039]	[7.623]
Short-term domestic interest rate			43.45***	43.79***
			[3.891]	[3.448]
Constant	-100.6	233.4	227.6**	376.1***
	[190.8]	[160.3]	[96.87]	[119.1]
Observations	2,084	2,084	1,101	1,101
R-squared	0.656	0.679	0.919	0.921
F stat	16.44	21.95	61.30	67.84
Country fixed effects	Yes	Yes	Yes	Yes
Number of countries	38	38	19	19

Source: World Bank staff estimates.
Note: Standard errors are based on heteroskedasticity-robust variance estimators clustered at the country level. Government debt data are lagged one quarter.

TABLE A3.1 Data

Variable	Description	Transformation	Unit	Source
Sovereign risk spread	Emerging Market Bond Index Global (EMBIG)	Level	Basis points	J.P.Morgan
10-year domestic-currency bond yield	Long-term domestic currency bond yields	Level	Basis points	Haver Analytics and OECD
Debt	Central or general government gross debt, seasonally adjusted	Percent of GDP	Percent of GDP	Haver Analytics
Inflation	Consumer price index, seasonally adjusted	Log first difference, annualized	Percent	Haver Analytics
Real GDP growth	Gross Domestic Product at constant prices in domestic currency, seasonally adjusted	Log first difference, annualized	Percent	Haver Analytics
VIX	Chicago Board Options Exchange's CBOE Volatility Index	Level	Index	Federal Reserve Bank of St. Louis
U.S. corporate high yield spread	ICE Bank of America U.S. High Yield Index Option-Adjusted Spread	Level	Spread	Federal Reserve Bank of St. Louis
10-year yield in advanced economies	Nominal GDP weighted average of 10-year bond yields in the euro area, Japan, and the United States	Level	Basis points	Haver Analytics
Short-term interest rate	3-month treasury bill or interbank rate	Level	Basis points	Haver Analytics and OECD
Debt crisis	Dummy equal to 1 when a country either: (1) fails to pay its interest and/or principal obligations by the due date or (2) postpones its obligations by rescheduling or restructuring debts with less favorable terms than the original ones. Interpolated to a quarterly frequency.	Dummy variable	Binary	Nguyen, Castro, and Wood (2022)
Bureaucratic quality	The institutional strength and quality of the civil service. High scores indicate an autonomous bureaucracy with the strength and expertise to govern without drastic changes in policy or interruptions in government services when governments change.	Level	Index	International Country Risk Guide, PRS Group
Real GDP forecast	Two-year-ahead forecasts of annual real GDP growth	Percent	Percent	IMF WEO
Inflation forecast	Two-year-ahead forecasts of annual CPI inflation	Percent	Percent	IMF WEO

Source: World Bank.

Note: ICE = Merrill Lynch Intercontinental Exchange; IMF = International Monetary Fund; OECD = Organisation for Economic Co-operation and Development; WEO = World Economic Outlook.

TABLE A3.2 Countries and sample used in regressions

Country	Sovereign spread	Domestic-currency yield	Country	Sovereign spread	Domestic-currency yield
Argentina	2012Q4–2025Q1	2014Q4–2018Q3	Morocco	2013Q1–2017Q4	2014Q4–2017Q4
Bahrain	2019Q1–2025Q1	—	Mexico	1994Q1–2025Q2	2001Q3–2025Q2
Belarus	2010Q4–2022Q1	—	Mongolia	2017Q4–2024Q2	—
Brazil	2009Q3–2025Q1	2009Q3–2025Q1	Malaysia	2005Q2–2025Q2	2005Q2–2025Q2
Chile	2002Q1–2025Q1	2004Q3–2025Q1	Peru	1999Q1–2025Q2	—
China	2014Q1–2025Q1	2014Q1–2025Q1	Philippines	1998Q2–2025Q2	2011Q3–2025Q2
Cameroon	2016Q1–2021Q3	—	Poland	1999Q4–2025Q1	2011Q4–2025Q1
Colombia	2000Q2–2025Q2	2008Q1–2025Q2	Paraguay	2013Q1–2024Q4	—
Costa Rica	2012Q3–2025Q2	—	Romania	2012Q1–2025Q1	2011Q2–2025Q1
Dominican Republic	2011Q1–2024Q4	—	Russia	2003Q1–2022Q2	2003Q1–2025Q1
Ecuador	2000Q4–2019Q1	—	Saudi Arabia	2019Q1–2025Q2	—
El Salvador	2002Q2–2025Q1	—	Serbia	2014Q1–2025Q2	—
Guatemala	2013Q4–2024Q4	—	Thailand	1997Q2–2006Q2	2001Q1–2025Q2
Honduras	2013Q2–2022Q1	—	Tunisia	2015Q1–2024Q3	—
Hungary	2005Q1–2025Q2	2005Q1–2025Q2	Türkiye	1998Q2–2025Q2	—
Indonesia	2012Q1–2024Q4	2012Q1–2024Q4	Ukraine	2010Q2–2023Q3	—
India	2012Q4–2025Q1	2001Q2–2024Q4	Uruguay	2019Q3–2024Q4	—
Jordan	2015Q4–2025Q1	—	South Africa	1995Q1–2025Q1	2000Q1–2025Q1
Kenya	2014Q3–2025Q1	2009Q2–2025Q1	Uganda	—	2020Q1–2025Q1
Sri Lanka	2014Q2–2025Q1	—			

Source: World Bank.

TABLE A3.3 Threshold models of interest rates based on quarterly data

	(1) Sovereign spreads	(2) Domestic-currency yield
Debt-to-GDP	5.939***	-4.046
	[1.139]	[2.535]
Debt-to-GDP above threshold	26.20**	7.406***
	[12.74]	[2.414]
Short-term domestic interest rate		43.28***
		[3.490]
Consumer inflation	7.957***	2.539
	[0.962]	[2.126]
Real GDP growth	-1.276**	0.247
	[0.568]	[0.333]
Debt crisis	176.6**	83.60
	[75.55]	[57.25]
Bureaucracy quality	-82.24	-3.137
	[56.90]	[24.94]
U.S. high yield corporate spread	21.16**	2.058
	[8.302]	[4.301]
VIX	4.364*	1.223
	[2.394]	[1.088]
Advanced economy 10-year treasury yield	11.52	26.36***
	[10.09]	[7.786]
Constant	2.431	410.0***
	[150.6]	[116.1]
Observations	2,084	1,101
R-squared	0.678	0.922
F stat	26.42	159.8
Country fixed effects	Yes	Yes
Number of countries	38	19

Source: World Bank staff estimates.
Note: Standard errors are based on heteroskedasticity-robust variance estimators clustered at the country level.

TABLE A3.4 Regressions using forecast data

	(1)	(2)	(3)	(4)
	Sovereign spreads		Domestic-currency yields	
2-year-ahead forecast revision to debt	2.934	1.978	-0.591	-1.383
	[2.194]	[2.089]	[0.955]	[0.998]
Debt forecast revision squared		0.235*		0.210**
		[0.128]		[0.0919]
2-year-ahead forecast of inflation	0.158	0.158	21.72***	21.49***
	[0.0957]	[0.0956]	[5.030]	[4.975]
2-year-ahead forecast of real GDP growth	-62.73***	-61.46***	-23.28**	-23.76**
	[21.51]	[20.78]	[9.991]	[9.855]
Debt crisis	680.2**	680.1**	-45.88	-45.11
	[286.9]	[286.5]	[96.58]	[97.08]
Bureaucracy quality	-37.80	-36.91	31.53	32.54
	[111.7]	[110.6]	[43.26]	[43.79]
U.S. high yield corporate spread	19.70*	19.07*	-7.844*	-7.358
	[11.29]	[11.11]	[4.560]	[4.570]
VIX	19.57***	18.90***	3.984*	3.753*
	[4.677]	[4.608]	[2.064]	[2.049]
Advanced economy 10-year treasury yield	82.19**	83.79**	12.21	12.75
	[32.89]	[32.61]	[11.43]	[11.29]
Short-term domestic interest rate			42.93***	42.87***
			[2.634]	[2.667]
Constant	129.9	125.6	463.3***	462.8***
	[257.8]	[251.1]	[129.1]	[130.9]
Observations	1,201	1,201	515	515
R-squared	0.569	0.572	0.966	0.967
F stat	280.3	237.6	52.94	70.64
Country fixed effects	Yes	Yes	Yes	Yes
Number of countries	65	65	25	25

Source: World Bank staff estimates
Note: Standard errors are based on heteroskedasticity-robust variance estimators clustered at the country level.

References

Ardagna, S., F. Caselli, and T. Lane. 2007. "Fiscal Discipline and the Cost of Public Debt Service: Some Estimates for OECD Countries." *The B.E. Journal of Macroeconomics* 7 (1): 1–35.

Arellano, C., 2008. Default Risk and Income Fluctuations in Emerging Economies. *American economic review*, 98(3), pp.690–712.

Arteta, C., S. B. Kamin, and F. U. Ruch. 2025. How Do Rising U.S. Interest Rates Affect Emerging and Developing Economies? It Depends. *Journal of Money, Credit, and Banking*.

Balasundharam, V., O. Basdevant, D. Benicio, A. Ceber, Y. Kim, L. Mazzone, H. Selim, and Y. Yang. 2023. Fiscal Consolidation: Taking Stock of Success Factors, Impact, and Design. International Monetary Fund.

Baldacci, E. and M. Kumar. 2010. Fiscal Deficits, Public Debt, and Sovereign Bond Yields. International Monetary Fund, WP/10/184, August.

Bi, H. 2012. Sovereign Default Risk Premia, Fiscal Limits, and Fiscal Policy. *European Economic Review*, 56(3), pp.389–410.

Blomquist, J., and J. Westerlund. 2013. "Testing Slope Homogeneity in Large Panels with Serial Correlation." *Economics Letters*, 121(3), pp.374–78.

Bräuning, F. and V. Ivashina. 2020. "U.S. Monetary Policy and Emerging Market Credit Cycles." *Journal of Monetary Economics*, 112, pp.57–76.

Broner, F. A., G. Lorenzoni, S. L. and Schmukler. 2013. Why Do Emerging Economies Borrow Short Term?. *Journal of the European Economic Association*, 11(suppl_1), pp.67–100.

Chen, Y., and T. Hart. 2025. "Common Framework, Uncommon Challenges: Lessons from the Post-COVID Debt Restructuring Architecture." ODI Global Insight (blog). February 21. 2025. https://odi.org/en/insights.

Choi, S., and Y. Hashimoto. 2018. "Does Transparency Pay? Evidence from IMF Data Transparency Policy Reforms and Emerging Market Sovereign Bond Spread." *Journal of International Money and Finance*, 88, 171–190.

Ciżkowicz, P., M. Ledóchowski, and A. Rzońca. 2025. Fiscal Policy and Government Bond Yields: New Evidence from the EU. *Economic Modelling*, 147, p.107054.

Clements, B., S. Gupta, J. Jalles, and B. Adrogue. 2023. Climate Change and Government Borrowing, Center for Global Development, Working Paper 660, October.

Coibion, O., and Y. Gorodnichenko. 2015. "Information Rigidity and the Expectations Formation Process: a Simple Framework and New Facts." *American Economic Review*, 105(8), pp.2644–78.

Cole, H. L. and T. J. Kehoe. 1996. A Self-Fulfilling Model of Mexico's 1994–1995 Debt Crisis. *Journal of international Economics*, 41(3–4), pp.309–30.

Cole, H. L. and T. J. Kehoe. 2000. Self-fulfilling Debt Crises. *Review of Economic Studies*, 67(1), pp.91–116.

Contraloría General del Estado (Ecuador). 2017. Examen Especial a la Legalidad, Fuentes y Usos de la Deuda Pública Interna y Externa en el Ministerio de Economía y Finanzas (Informe DNA3-0007-2018). Retrieved February 24, 2026, from https://contraloria.gob.ec/WFDescarga.aspx?id=52076&tipo=inf.

Curcuru, S.E., S.B. Kamin, C. Li, and M. Rodriguez. 2023. International Spillovers of Monetary Policy: Conventional Policy vs. Quantitative Easing. *International Journal of Central Banking*, Vol. 19, 1, March.

Eaton, J., and M. Gersovitz. 1981. Debt with Potential Repudiation: Theoretical and Empirical Analysis. *The Review of Economic Studies*, 48(2), pp.289–309.

Engen, E. M. and R. G. Hubbard. 2004. Federal Government Debt and Interest Rates. *NBER Macroeconomics Annual*, Vol. 19, pp. 83–138.

Ferrucci, G. 2003. "Empirical Determinants of Emerging Market Economies' Sovereign Bond Spreads." Bank of England Working Paper 205.

Furceri, D., C. Goncalves, and H. Li. 2025. "The Impact of Debt and Deficits on Long-Term Interest Rates in the US." IMF Working Paper 25/142, International Monetary Fund, Washington, DC.

Gamber, E., and J, Seliski. 2019. "The Effect of Government Debt on Interest Rates." Congressional Budget Office.

Gennaioli, N., A. Martin, and S. Rossi. 2018. Banks, Government Bonds, and Default: What Do the Data Say?. *Journal of Monetary Economics*, 98, pp.98–113.

Ghosh, A. R., J. I. Kim, E. G. Mendoza, J. D. Ostry, and M. S. Qureshi. 2013. Fiscal Fatigue, Fiscal Space and Debt Sustainability in Advanced Economies. *Economic Journal*, 123(566), pp.F4–F30.

Gootjes, B., J. Mawejje, and D. Vorisek. 2026. "Rebuilding Fiscal Space: The Case for Fiscal Rules." In *Global Economic Prospects, January 2026*. Washington, DC: World Bank.

Gruber, J. and S. B. Kamin. 2012. Fiscal Positions and Government Bond Yields in OECD Countries. *Journal of Money, Credit and Banking*, 2012, vol. 44, issue 8, 1563–87.

Guler, B., Y. K. Önder, and T. Taskin. 2025. "Sovereign Debt Disclosure." *Journal of International Economics*: 104118.

Hansen, B. E., 2017. Regression Kink with an Unknown Threshold. *Journal of Business & Economic Statistics*, 35(2), pp.228–40.

Hashimoto, H., Y. Mooi, G. Pedras, A. Roy, K Chung, T. Galeza, M. G. Papaioannou, et al. 2021. Developing Government Local Currency Bond Markets. International Monetary Fund and World Bank Guidance Note, 1.

Hill, S., J. Khadan, and P. M. Selcuk. 2025. Fragile and Conflict-Affected Situations: Intertwined crises, Multiple vulnerabilities (No. 11210). Washington, DC: World Bank.

Hoek, J., S. Kamin, and E. Yoldas. 2022. "Are Higher U.S. Interest Rates Always Bad News for Emerging Markets?" *Journal of International Economics* 137 (July): 103585.

Hong, G.H., S. Ke, and A. D. M. Nguyen. 2025. The Macroeconomic Effects of Fiscal Policy Uncertainty around the World. In *AEA Papers and Proceedings* (Vol. 115, pp. 182–87). 2014 Broadway, Suite 305, Nashville, TN 37203: American Economic Association.

Horn, S., D. Mihalyi, P. Nickol, and C. Sosa-Padilla. 2024. "Hidden Debt Revelations." World Bank Policy Working Paper 10907, World Bank, Washington, DC.

IMF (International Monetary Fund). 2005a. "Press Release: IMF Executive Board Reviews Noncomplying Purchase by the Dominican Republic." February 1, 2005.

IMF (International Monetary Fund). 2005b. "Press Release: IMF Executive Board Approves US$10 Billion Stand-By Arrangement for Turkey." May 11, 2005.

IMF (International Monetary Fund). 2006. "Making the Misreporting Policies Less Onerous in De Minimis Cases." Washington, DC, International Monetary Fund.

IMF (International Monetary Fund). 2013. "Press Release: IMF Executive Board Reviews Noncomplying Disbursements and Recommendation for Waiver of Nonobservance of a Performance Criterion." December 19, 2013.

IMF (International Monetary Fund). 2021. "IMF Fiscal Monitor, Chapter 2: Strengthening the Credibility of Public Finances," International Monetary Fund, Washington, DC, October.

IMF (International Monetary Fund). 2021. "Press Release: IMF Executive Board Reviews Pakistan's Remedial Actions, Data Revision Linked to Noncomplying Purchase." March 24, 2021.

IMF (International Monetary Fund) and World Bank. 2018. "G-20 Notes on Strengthening Public Debt Transparency."

IMF (International Monetary Fund) and World Bank. 2020. "Staff Note for the G20 International Financial Architecture Working Group: Recent Developments on Local Currency Bond Markets in Emerging Economies." World Bank, Washington, DC.

IMF (International Monetary Fund) and World Bank. 2024a. Debt for Development Swaps: An Approach Framework. International Monetary Fund.

IMF (International Monetary Fund) and World Bank. 2024b. "Stepping Up Domestic Resource Mobilization: A New Joint Initiative from the IMF and WB." International Monetary Fund, Washington, DC.

IMF (International Monetary Fund), World Bank, and G20 Presidency. 2026. *Global Sovereign Debt Roundtable—6th Co-Chairs Progress Report.* April 15, 2026. IMF Press Release 26/121, International Monetary Fund, Washington, DC.

Jaramillo, L., and A. Weber. 2013. Global Spillovers into Domestic Bond Markets in Emerging Market Economies. IMF Working Paper No. 13/264, December.

Kamin, S. B., and A. Vakil. 2025. "Why Emerging Markets Weathered Federal Reserve Tightening So Well." American Enterprise Institute Working Paper, May.

Kemoe, L., and Z. Zhan. Fiscal Transparency, Borrowing Costs, and Foreign Holdings of Sovereign debt. International Monetary Fund, 2018.

Kennedy, M. and A. Palerm. "Emerging Market Bond Spreads: the Role of Global and Domestic Factors from 2002 to 2011." *Journal of International Money and Finance*, 43: (2014), pp. 70–87.

Kose, M. A., S. Kurlat, F. Ohnsorge, and N. Sugawara. 2022. A Cross-Country Database of Fiscal Space. *Journal of International Money and Finance*, 128, p.102682.

Kose, M. A., P. Nagle, F. Ohnsorge, and N. Sugawara. 2021. *Global Waves of Debt: Causes and Consequences*. Washington, DC: World Bank.

Laubach, T. 2009. "New Evidence on the Interest Rate Effects of Budget Deficits and Debt." *Journal of the European Economic Association* 7 (4): 858–85.

Manger, M. S., D. Mihalyi, U. Panizza, N. Rescia, C. Trebesch, and K. L. Wong. 2025. Africa's Domestic Debt Boom: Evidence from the African Debt Database (No. 2303). Kiel Working Paper.

Matsuoka, H., 2022. Debt Intolerance: Threshold Level and Composition. *Oxford Bulletin of Economics and Statistics*, 84(4), pp.894–932.

Meh, C. A., and S. L. Schmukler, eds. 2025. *Financing Firm Growth: The Role of Capital Markets in Low- and Middle-Income Countries.* International Finance Corporation Research Series. Washington, DC: World Bank.

Neveu, A. R., and J. Schafer. 2024. "Revisiting the Relationship Between Debt and Long-Term Interest Rates." Washington, DC: Congressional Budget Office.

Nguyen, T. C., V. Castro, and J. Wood. 2022. A New Comprehensive Database of Financial Crises: Identification, Frequency, and Duration. *Economic Modelling*, 108, p.105770.

OECD (Organisation for Economic Co-operation and Development). 2025. *Global Debt Report 2025: Financing Growth in a Challenging Debt Market Environment*. Paris: OECD.

Reinhart C., K. Rogoff, and M. Savastano. 2003. Debt Intolerance, NBER Working Paper, vol. 9908, National Bureau of Economic Research, Cambridge, Mass.

Romer, C. D., and D. H. Romer. 2010. "The Macroeconomic Effects of Tax Changes: Estimates Based on a New Measure of Fiscal Shocks." *American Economic Review*, 100(3), pp.763–801.

Shiller, R. J. and J. H. McCulloch. 1990. The Term Structure of Interest Rates. *Handbook of Monetary Economics*, 1, pp.627–722.

Sun, L., 2023. Debt and Real Interest Rates: Evidence from G20 countries. *Review of International Economics*, 31(4), pp.1528–51.

U.S. Census Bureau (2016). X-13ARIMA-SEATS Reference Manual.

World Bank. 2017. *Mozambique Economic Update: Making the Most of Demographic Change.* Washington, DC: World Bank.

World Bank. 2021. *Global Waves of Debt: Causes and Consequences.* Washington, DC: World Bank.

World Bank. 2022. *Global Economic Prospects.* January. Washington, DC: World Bank.

World Bank. 2024a. *Finance and Prosperity 2024.* Washington, DC: World Bank.

World Bank. 2024b. *Egypt: Generating Resilience, Opportunities, and Welfare for a Thriving Egypt (GROWTH) Development Policy Financing.* Washington, DC: World Bank.

World Bank. 2025. *Radical [Debt] Transparency.* Washington, DC: World Bank.

World Bank. Forthcoming. *Curbing the Cost of Borrowing for Businesses in LMICS: The Role of Bond Markets.* Washington, DC: World Bank.

CHAPTER 4

NAVIGATING VOLATILITY

Fiscal Policy and Commodity Price Swings

Large commodity market disruptions—most recently triggered by the conflict in the Middle East—have brought renewed attention to the persistent fiscal challenges faced by commodity-exporting emerging market and developing economies (EMDEs). Since 2000, fiscal positions in these economies have generally been weaker than those in other EMDEs, reflecting lower and more volatile revenues, commodity price swings, and limited buffer accumulation in good times. Government debt across EMDEs has risen since the global financial crisis, but commodity exporters are especially vulnerable. A 1 percent increase in commodity prices raises both revenues and primary spending in commodity exporters by about 0.4 percent after five years, suggesting that revenue windfalls are gradually spent rather than saved. Fiscal positions over commodity price cycles vary across exporters of different commodities. Primary balances in energy and metal exporters strengthen during booms and worsen in slumps, mainly as a result of revenue swings, while primary spending remains broadly contained; debt ratios fall in booms and rise in slumps. In contrast, agricultural exporters increase spending in booms, offsetting revenue gains and leading to more lasting debt accumulation. Although sovereign wealth funds (SWFs) and fiscal rules have helped smooth spending over commodity cycles in some countries, they offer limited protection amid intensifying spending pressures after commodity shocks. Policy implications point to an integrated approach combining credible fiscal rules, well-governed SWFs, independent fiscal councils, strengthened debt management, revenue diversification, and robust institutions. Together, such reforms are critical to enhancing fiscal resilience, reducing volatility, supporting sustainable and inclusive growth, and boosting job creation.

Introduction

The conflict in the Middle East has generated historically large disruptions in global commodity markets (World Bank 2026a). During March and April 2026, energy prices averaged about 45 percent above their 2025 average while fertilizer prices were more than 30 percent higher. The latest turmoil follows a sequence of major shocks that have buffeted commodity markets in this decade, testing the fiscal frameworks of emerging market and developing economies (EMDEs)—both commodity exporters and commodity importers (figure 4.1.A). Among commodity exporters, the burden of the ongoing commodity market disruptions falls most acutely on energy exporters in the Gulf region. Fiscal dependence on the commodity sector is especially high in energy exporters: commodity revenues have averaged more than half of total fiscal revenues since 2000, far exceeding the shares in metal and agricultural exporters (figure 4.1.B). Meanwhile, many agricultural exporters face both revenue gains from higher food prices and acute cost pressures from the surge in fertilizer prices, complicating fiscal planning on multiple fronts.

The recent shocks follow a characteristic pattern of large fluctuations in commodity prices—a stark reminder that fiscal policy management in commodity-exporting EMDEs remains an enduring challenge (figure 4.1.C). What makes the current episode particularly challenging for policy makers is that conflict-related shocks are inherently unpredictable in duration and trajectory, making it difficult to distinguish a temporary windfall requiring buffer accumulation from a structural shift.

Natural resource abundance can act as an economic asset, generating fiscal and export revenues that support growth and development (Gill et al. 2014; Lederman and Maloney 2007). However, it also presents challenges, as dependence on commodity revenues exposes countries to price volatility and fiscal fragility. Large swings in commodity prices significantly impact fiscal policy in many EMDEs, as commodities are a critical source of revenues for about two-thirds of these economies and nearly 90 percent of low-income countries (LICs) (figure 4.1.D). About 25 percent of EMDEs are classified as agricultural commodity exporters, 23 percent as energy exporters, and 16 percent as metal exporters.

Dependence on commodities makes fiscal management challenging in both the short and longer run. In the short run, reliance on commodity revenues in commodity-exporting EMDEs—especially for economies exporting a limited range of commodity products—means that swings in commodity prices often translate into volatile

Note: This chapter was prepared by Francisco Arroyo Marioli, Bram Gootjes, and Garima Vasishtha.

FIGURE 4.1 Commodity prices and EMDE commodity dependence

Commodity prices have been buffeted by repeated shocks since the beginning of this decade, most recently by significant disruptions caused by the conflict in the Middle East. These overlapping shocks are part of a characteristic pattern of large fluctuations in commodity prices. Fiscal dependence on the commodity sector is especially high in energy exporters where commodity revenues have averaged more than half of total fiscal revenues since 2000, far exceeding the shares in metal and agricultural exporters. Overall, commodities are critical sources of revenue for about two-thirds of EMDEs, particularly low-income countries and economies in FCS.

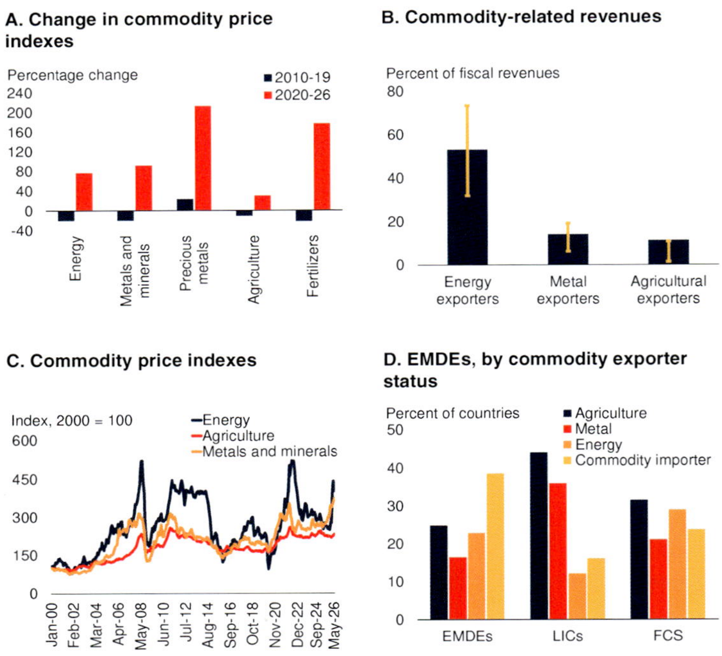

Sources: United Nations University World Institute for Development Economics Research (UNU-WIDER); World Bank.

Note: EMDEs = emerging market and developing economies; FCS = fragile and conflict-affected situations; LICs = low-income countries.

A. Panel shows percentage changes in price indexes (2010 = 100) for commodity groups over 2010–19 and 2020–26. Last observation is May 2026.

B. Bars show the unweighted average of commodity-related revenues as a percentage of fiscal revenues for EMDE commodity exporters: 32 for energy, 15 for metals, and 12 for agricultural commodities. Whiskers show the interquartile range. Data are for the 2000–23 period.

C. Panel shows the aggregate monthly indexes for energy, agriculture, and metals and minerals (excluding precious metals) from the World Bank's Commodity Price Data ("Pink Sheet"). Last observation is May 2026.

D. Panel shows the shares, as of 2025, of EMDEs, LICs, and FCS that are classified as agricultural, metal, and energy exporters, and commodity importers.

fiscal revenues (figure 4.2.A). Over longer horizons, limited diversification keeps fiscal revenues tied to commodity markets, while spending pressures often persist longer than revenues. Indeed, fiscal policy in commodity exporters is both more volatile and more procyclical than in other EMDEs (Arroyo Marioli and Végh 2026; Arroyo Marioli, Fatás, and Vasishtha 2024; World Bank 2024a). Fiscal positions in these economies often deteriorate markedly when commodity prices fall, and the buffers accumulated during booms—if they are accumulated at all—typically fail to cushion the subsequent downswing in commodity prices. Swings in commodity prices are also correlated with the business cycle in commodity-exporting EMDEs and are associated with high investment and consumption volatility (figure 4.2.B).

The consequences of fiscal procyclicality and volatility for macroeconomic conditions are material: they amplify business cycles, dampen growth, and reduce policy space for sustained public investment. These effects can also weaken labor market outcomes, primarily by discouraging private investment, which serves as the proximate driver of job creation in developing economies (World Bank 2013). In EMDEs in which formal labor markets are often thin and social safety nets limited, the employment consequences of fiscal volatility manifest less through rising open unemployment and more through a transition toward informality, declining real wages, and deteriorating job quality (Loayza and Rigolini 2011; World Bank 2013). These labor market dynamics are particularly persistent: workers displaced into informal employment during downturns rarely return to equivalent formal positions once conditions recover, reinforcing structural informality over time (Bosch and Maloney 2010). Fiscal procyclicality in commodity exporters therefore not only drives output volatility but can also create a structural impediment to the sustained private investment on which durable, quality job creation depends.

Beyond these effects, procyclical fiscal policies can cause government deficits and debt positions to ratchet up and deteriorate over time. Elevated public debt and borrowing costs limit fiscal space and pose significant challenges to EMDEs—particularly those with weak credit ratings—seeking to improve fiscal sustainability. They also reduce policy space for critical infrastructure development and reforms that countries need to support private sector growth. These vulnerabilities are reflected in more pronounced downgrades in long-term sovereign debt ratings for commodity exporters compared with those for commodity importers over the past decade (figure 4.2.C). In tandem, debt vulnerabilities have worsened markedly in commodity exporters: the share of countries in, or at high risk of, debt distress more than doubled, from about 20 percent in 2015 to nearly 49 percent in 2026, based on the joint 'World Bank–IMF Debt Sustainability Framework for Low-Income Countries' (figure 4.2.D). Among commodity importers, the share fell sharply after the pandemic to 45 percent in 2026, still about 3 percentage points above its 2015 level.

Fiscal vulnerabilities in commodity-exporting EMDEs are often compounded by spending rigidities and risks that accumulate outside the general government budget. In many of these economies, poorly targeted subsidies—frequently introduced or expanded during commodity price spikes to insulate consumers from price pressures—become entrenched and potentially crowd out productive spending. These pressures are further magnified when public investment bears the brunt of fiscal consolidation during downturns. Furthermore, fiscal risks can build up through state-owned enterprises (SOEs) exposed to commodity market fluctuations and contingent liabilities, including those arising from government guarantees. Heightened commodity price volatility in recent years has exacerbated these weaknesses, putting existing fiscal frameworks to the test.

Against this backdrop, this chapter presents a comprehensive assessment of the implications of commodity price volatility for the conduct of fiscal policy in commodity-exporting EMDEs. The analysis is particularly timely given the scale and cross-commodity implications of the disruptions triggered by the conflict in the Middle East in 2026. It begins by taking stock of the evolution of fiscal positions in these economies over the past quarter century. It then uses a range of empirical tools to analyze how fiscal policy responds to commodity price shocks and how this compares with its response over episodes of commodity price booms and slumps. Further, it examines how fiscal frameworks in commodity exporters have evolved over time, focusing on identifying where existing frameworks have helped commodity exporters build resilience and where policy makers need to strengthen them to better navigate commodity-related fiscal challenges.

FIGURE 4.2 Commodity prices, fiscal revenues, and public debt sustainability

Fiscal revenues and growth in commodity-exporting EMDEs move closely with global commodity prices, reflecting the exposure of these economies to commodity price fluctuations. Since 2000, sovereign debt ratings in commodity exporters have consistently been weaker than those of other EMDEs. The share of low-income commodity exporters facing elevated debt distress risk has risen markedly in recent years, highlighting their accumulated fiscal vulnerabilities.

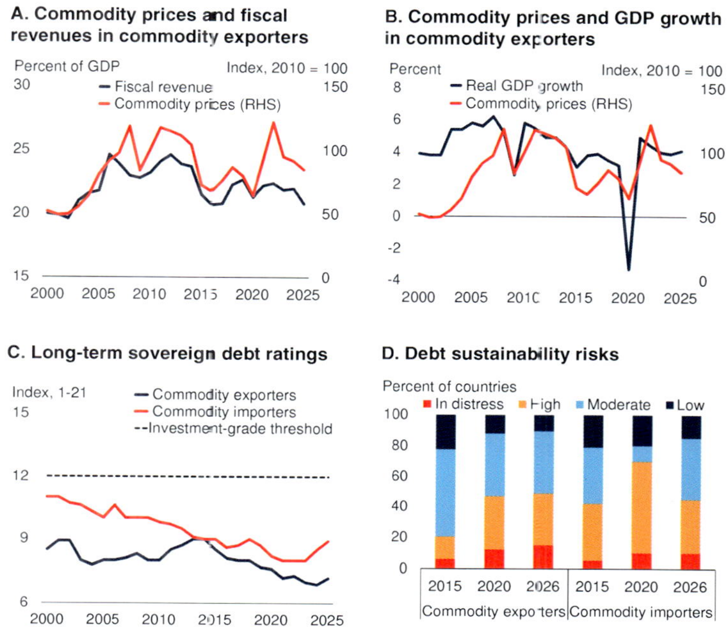

Sources: International Monetary Fund; World Bank.

Note: EMDEs = emerging market and developing economies; RHS = right-hand scale.

A. Panel shows median fiscal revenue in commodity-exporting EMDEs and the World Bank's aggregate commodity price index in nominal U.S. dollars (2010 = 100). Sample includes 94 commodity exporters.

B. Panel shows the median real GDP growth rate for EMDE commodity exporters and the World Bank's aggregate commodity price index in constant 2010 U.S. dollars (2010 = 100). Sample includes 94 commodity exporters.

C. Panel shows medians of foreign-currency long-term sovereign debt ratings. Sovereign debt ratings are converted to a numerical scale ranging from 1–21, with a higher value indicating a better rating. The horizontal line (at 12) indicates an investment-grade rating. Sample includes up to 72 EMDE commodity exporters and 41 commodity importers.

D. Percent of countries in, or at risk of, debt distress, based on the joint World Bank–International Monetary Fund Debt Sustainability Framework for Low-Income Countries (LIC DSF). Risk assessments for 2026 are as reported in March 2026. The information is available for up to 49 commodity exporters and up to 20 commodity importers.

Specifically, this chapter addresses the following questions:

- How have fiscal policy and debt dynamics evolved in commodity-exporting EMDEs since the turn of the century?
- How does fiscal policy in commodity exporters respond to commodity price shocks?

- How does fiscal policy in commodity exporters comove with commodity price booms and slumps?
- How do fiscal frameworks and institutions affect countries' ability to manage commodity-related fiscal pressures?

Contributions. This chapter makes the following main contributions to the literature.

Systematic documentation of how fiscal policy and debt dynamics have evolved in commodity-exporting EMDEs since the turn of the century. The chapter draws attention to heterogeneity across energy, metal, and agricultural exporters, highlighting how sensitivity to commodity price movements differs across these exporter groups. Additionally, it contrasts the evolution of fiscal outcomes in commodity exporters with that in other EMDEs. The analysis draws on a large sample of up to 94 commodity exporters and 59 commodity importers (table 4.1).

Examination of comovement between commodity price cycles and fiscal indicators in commodity-exporting economies using multiple empirical approaches. For these commodity exporters, the volatility of fiscal revenues is primarily influenced by commodity price movements rather than the output cycle, making price swings a key challenge. Although there is sizable literature on the cyclicality of fiscal policy with respect to output cycles in EMDEs, few studies have analyzed fiscal indicators over commodity price booms (a trough-to-peak rise in commodity prices) and slumps (a peak-to-trough decline in commodity prices) for such a large and diverse sample of countries.

Analysis distinguishing fiscal dynamics over commodity price cycles from year-to-year dynamics around commodity price shocks. Using local projections, the chapter quantifies the effects of commodity price shocks by tracing the response of revenue and primary spending over time. It then analyzes fiscal dynamics over commodity price cycles to examine whether commodity-exporting EMDEs build buffers in booms to stabilize primary spending in slumps.

Assessment of how fiscal frameworks and institutions shape fiscal outcomes in commodity exporters. Specifically, the chapter empirically examines whether fiscal rules and sovereign wealth funds (SWFs) help contain procyclical fiscal responses to commodity price shocks and improve fiscal management over commodity price cycles.

Rich menu of policy options for strengthening fiscal resilience in commodity-exporting EMDEs. Building on its empirical findings, the chapter distills policy options centered on stronger fiscal rules, better-governed SWFs, wider use of fiscal councils, improved public debt management, stronger non-resource revenue mobilization, and longer-term economic diversification. It also distinguishes policy priorities across energy, metal, and agricultural exporters, linking differences in fiscal exposure and the institutional environment to a more tailored policy agenda.

Main findings. The chapter presents the following main findings.

Fiscal positions in commodity-exporting EMDEs have generally been weaker than in other EMDEs since 2000, reflecting lower and more volatile revenues, as well as the impacts of repeated commodity price shocks. Over 2000–25, both median fiscal revenues and primary expenditures averaged about 3 percentage points of GDP below those in other EMDEs. These patterns have contributed to rising debt vulnerabilities since the global financial crisis, even though average debt levels as a share of GDP remain somewhat below those of other EMDEs. Beneath these aggregate trends, there is substantial heterogeneity across commodity exporters: energy exporters are the most dependent on resource revenues and therefore the most exposed to commodity price swings, followed by metal exporters. Agricultural exporters tend to face chronically weak revenues and the least favorable debt dynamics, generally holding the highest debt-ratios among commodity exporters.

Fiscal policy tends to respond to commodity price shocks gradually. On average, a 1 percent increase in the commodity price index raises government revenues by about 0.3 percent on impact and 0.4 percent after five years. Primary spending rises only modestly at first but increases cumulatively by about 0.4 percent over the same horizon, suggesting that the revenue windfall is gradually spent over time. The spending response is strongest in energy exporters, where it reaches 0.5 percent after five years, compared with 0.4 percent for agricultural exporters and 0.3 percent for metal exporters.

Fiscal dynamics over commodity price booms and slumps differ from short-run responses to commodity price shocks. In energy exporters, the median primary balance strengthens by about 0.9 percentage point of GDP per year in booms and weakens by about 1.1 percentage points in slumps, while debt falls by 2.8 percentage points of GDP per year in booms and rises by 1.3 percentage points in slumps. Metal exporters display a similar but less pronounced pattern. By contrast, primary balances in agricultural exporters do not differ significantly across booms and slumps as expenditure growth accelerates in booms and slows in slumps, offsetting revenue gains and contributing to less favorable debt dynamics.

Fiscal policy frameworks in commodity exporters have generally strengthened since 2000, driven in part by the increasing adoption of SWFs and fiscal rules. While these frameworks can support fiscal management over the commodity cycle, their effectiveness varies across instruments and commodity exporters. Among energy exporters, SWFs are associated with more contained spending growth during commodity price booms: in a typical boom year, primary spending growth averaged 2.9 percent per year in countries with SWFs, compared with 5.8 percent in those without. Among metal exporters, fiscal rules appear to act as a medium-run anchor: spending growth was more restrained during booms, at 3.1 percent per year, while rising to 5.8 percent during slumps, consistent with some degree of buffer accumulation in upturns and support in downturns.

The effectiveness of fiscal frameworks appears more limited when viewed through the lens of spending responses triggered by commodity price shocks. On average, SWFs and fiscal rules do not appear to contain spending responses to price shocks. Formal frameworks may support buffer accumulation and fiscal discipline over the cycle, but they seem to offer little protection when commodity prices move sharply. This exposes a critical gap between adoption and effectiveness, likely reflecting the importance of framework design, credible enforcement, transparency, and the broader institutional environment. Indeed, institutional strength appears decisive: stronger public institutions are closely associated with more dampened spending responses to commodity price shocks, particularly in energy exporters.

Strengthening fiscal resilience requires a broad policy agenda centered on stronger fiscal frameworks, greater domestic revenue mobilization, and economic diversification. Recent commodity market volatility is putting existing fiscal frameworks in commodity-exporting EMDEs under renewed pressure. Design of fiscal rule frameworks can be strengthened to contain spending pressures during windfall shocks while preserving well-defined space for support during shortfalls. SWFs can benefit from stronger safeguards to prevent excessive withdrawals and mandates that more clearly link volatile revenues to savings and stabilization objectives, especially in agricultural exporters. Wider adoption of fiscal councils and stronger public debt management frameworks can reinforce both instruments by improving transparency, oversight, and accountability. At the same time, commodity exporters, especially energy exporters, need to broaden their tax effort and expand more stable sources of revenue to reduce reliance on volatile resource revenues. Over time, targeted diversification policies can help reduce exposure to commodity-driven boom-bust cycles.

Fiscal indicators in commodity exporters since 2000

Since 2000, commodity exporters have generally faced greater fiscal challenges than commodity importers, as their public finances tend to be more heavily exposed to swings in commodity prices. During commodity booms, higher tax and non-tax revenues, stronger nominal GDP growth, and easier financing conditions tend to improve fiscal positions; in downturns, these gains are often quickly reversed (Ocampo 2017; Rosnick and Weisbrot 2014). Commodity importers, by contrast, typically rely on broader and more stable tax bases, making their fiscal revenues relatively less volatile.

FIGURE 4.3 Fiscal revenues

Commodity-exporting EMDEs have been characterized by lower and more volatile fiscal revenues, as well as weaker non-resource tax collection compared with other EMDEs. Among commodity exporters, fiscal revenues fluctuate with commodity prices to varying degrees: energy exporters are much more reliant on resource revenues than exporters of non-energy commodities. Agricultural exporters have been marked more by chronically weak revenue performance than by commodity revenue swings.

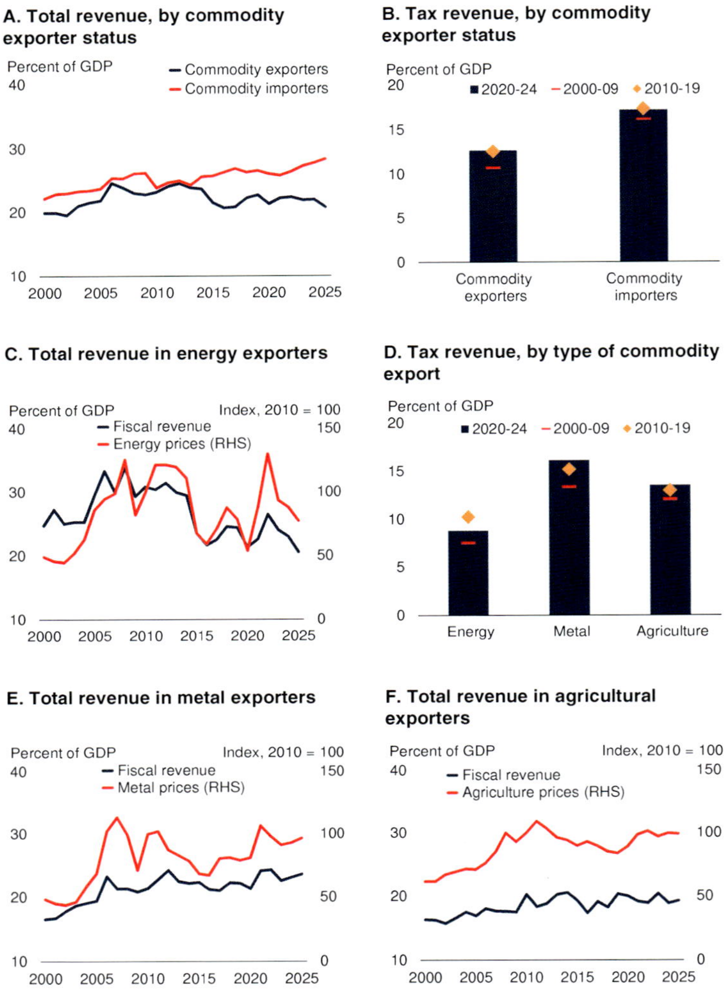

Sources: International Monetary Fund; World Bank.

Note: EMDEs = emerging market and developing economies; RHS = right-hand scale. Panels show median fiscal revenue (percent of GDP) and median tax revenue (percent of GDP) for the respective country groups.

A.B. Samples include up to 94 EMDE commodity exporters and 59 EMDE commodity importers in panel A, and up to 92 EMDE commodity exporters and 55 EMDE commodity importers in panel B.

C. Panel shows the World Bank energy price index in constant 2010 U.S. dollars. Sample includes up to 35 EMDE energy exporters.

D. Sample includes up to 34 EMDE agricultural exporters, 23 metal exporters, and 35 energy exporters.

E. Panel shows the World Bank metal price index, in constant 2010 U.S. dollars. Sample includes up to 25 EMDE metal exporters.

F. Panel shows the World Bank agriculture price index, in constant 2010 U.S. dollars. Sample includes up to 35 EMDE agricultural exporters.

Commodity exporters are, however, far from uniform. Reliance on commodities for fiscal and export revenues varies substantially across countries. Energy exporters have experienced the largest fiscal booms and busts, metal exporters have generally been somewhat more resilient, and agricultural exporters have faced the most persistent structural fiscal weaknesses. These differences reflect various factors, including variation in governments' dependence on commodity revenues, the extent to which commodity prices comove with economic conditions, and non-resource revenue mobilization.

Fiscal revenues

In the early 2000s, rising commodity prices worked in favor of commodity-exporting EMDEs, contributing to strong global growth and revenues. In the median commodity exporter, revenue increased from about 20 percent of GDP in 2000 to 25 percent of GDP in 2006 (figure 4.3.A). By comparison, median revenue in commodity importers rose more modestly over the same period, from 22 to 25 percent of GDP.

As the global financial crisis hit, commodity exporters faced an abrupt reversal of fiscal fortunes because weakening global demand and falling commodity prices caused revenues to drop sharply. The recovery in the early 2010s was only partial, and subsequent shocks—notably the 2014–16 oil price collapse—kept revenues under pressure. That weakness persisted into the 2020s. Even the surge in commodity prices in 2022 did not generate a strong rebound in revenues as a share of GDP, likely reflecting weak post-pandemic recoveries outside the resource sector, persistently weak non-resource tax mobilization, and denominator effects from higher nominal GDP.

Revenues in commodity importers have followed a steadier, upward path since the turn of the century, notwithstanding adverse global shocks. Over 2000–25, median fiscal revenue in commodity importers averaged about 25 percent of GDP, compared with 22 percent in commodity exporters; by 2025, the gap had widened further, as median revenue in commodity importers increased to 29 percent of GDP, while that in commodity exporters stood at about 22 percent. A comparison of tax revenue mobilization between commodity importers and exporters reinforces this contrast: in commodity importers, the tax-to-GDP ratio has hovered at about an average of 16 to 17 percent since 2000, while in commodity exporters it edged up from 12 percent in 2000–09 to 13 percent in 2020–24 (figure 4.3.B).

Revenue dynamics differed considerably across commodity exporters. Energy exporters are the most dependent on resource income, which accounted for about 53 percent of government receipts over 2000–25, with fiscal revenues averaging 27 percent of GDP—the highest among commodity exporters.[1] This dependence generated large windfalls during energy price booms but it also left public finances highly exposed to price swings. Revenues rose sharply during the 2000s boom, then fell abruptly during the global financial crisis, when oil prices dropped from about $97 per barrel in 2008 to about $62 in 2009. They declined again during the 2014–16 oil price collapse, laying bare the risks of reliance on a single volatile revenue source (figure 4.3.C). Weak domestic tax mobilization further amplifies this vulnerability: between 2000 and 2024, median tax revenue averaged only about 9 percent of GDP, substantially lower than that in metal and agricultural exporters, with little sign of a durable strengthening of the non-resource tax base (figure 4.3.D).

Metal exporters have experienced a more moderate version of the pattern observed in energy exporters. Their revenues averaged about 21 percent of GDP over 2000–25, and commodity income made up a much smaller share of total revenue than in energy exporters. Revenue performance was strong during the commodity boom of the 2000s, with revenues in the median economy rising from 17 percent of GDP in 2000 to 24 percent in 2006 (figure 4.3.E). Although revenues weakened during the global financial crisis, this was largely reversed as prices recovered. After some softness in the early 2010s, stronger metal prices starting in the mid-2010s helped support revenues. Since the pandemic, prices have remained relatively firm, supported in part by energy-transition demand and supply constraints, although precious metal prices have surged in recent years. Non-resource tax mobilization also helped cushion these shocks: median tax revenue rose from an average of 13 percent of GDP in 2000–09 to 16 percent in 2020–24, reflecting a generally broader and more durable revenue base than in energy exporters.

Agricultural exporters, by contrast, have faced chronically weak revenues rather than pronounced boom-bust swings. Their fiscal revenues averaged about 19 percent of GDP over 2000–25, of which commodity revenues accounted for less than 10 percent. Revenue performance improved only gradually over time. Unlike energy and metal exporters, they benefited less from the commodity boom of the early 2000s, as agricultural prices increased more modestly. And while these prices also fell less sharply during the global financial crisis, this relative stability did not translate into lasting fiscal strength. Once they peaked in the early 2010s, revenue growth stalled, and in the mid-2010s and early 2020s, these economies again proved fragile in the face of falling prices and overlapping shocks (figure 4.3.F). Median tax revenue increased only marginally—from about 12 percent of GDP in 2000–09 to 13 percent in 2020–24.

Fiscal expenditure and balances

Revenue differences between commodity exporters and importers, as well as among exporter groups, translate into distinct spending patterns and fiscal outcomes. Since 2000, median primary expenditure has trended up in both commodity-exporting and commodity-importing EMDEs, reflecting growing development needs and crisis-related support (figure 4.4.A). In commodity exporters, spending broadly tracked rising revenues during the commodity price boom of the 2000s, allowing expenditures to expand while fiscal balances improved. As a result, the median primary balance strengthened from a surplus of 0.4 percent of GDP in 2000 to 2.7 percent in 2006 (figure 4.4.B). This aggregate pattern was shaped above all

[1] This reflects larger economic rents generated by energy extraction and export, global demand, and higher prices compared with many metals and agricultural commodities (Gelb 2012). Moreover, energy exporters tend to have less diversified economic linkages outside the resource sector, which makes energy revenues critical for government finances and economic activity.

FIGURE 4.4 Fiscal expenditures and fiscal balances

Since 2000, primary-expenditure-to-GDP ratios in commodity exporters have been lower than those in other EMDEs, consistent with the gap in revenues. Primary expenditures in these economies tend to comove with commodity prices, with limited buffer building during booms shrinking the room for maneuver during downturns, albeit to varying degrees across exporter groups. Energy exporters have historically recorded higher expenditure-to-GDP ratios than agricultural and metal exporters, but the gap between the two has narrowed substantially in the post-pandemic period. Primary balances in EMDEs improved in the first half of the 2000s—especially among commodity exporters, led by energy exporters. This progress was reversed following the global financial crisis, leading to persistent and often widening primary deficits in commodity exporters throughout the 2010s.

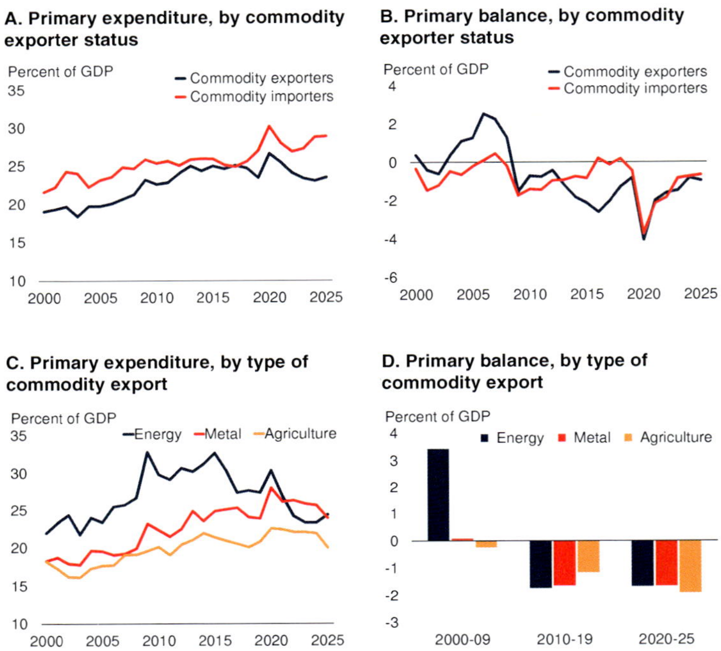

Sources: International Monetary Fund; World Bank.

Note: EMDEs = emerging market and developing economies.

A.B. Panels show median primary government expenditure (percent of GDP) and primary balance (percent of GDP), respectively, for EMDE commodity exporters and commodity importers. Sample includes up to 92 commodity exporters and 56 commodity importers.

C. Panel shows median primary government expenditure (percent of GDP). Sample includes up to 34 EMDE agricultural exporters, 24 metal exporters, and 34 energy exporters.

D. Panel shows the simple average of annual median primary balances (percent of GDP) over the indicated periods. Sample includes up to 34 agricultural exporters, 24 metal exporters, and 34 energy exporters.

by energy exporters, where revenue windfalls fueled rapid primary expenditure growth without eroding surpluses; in metal and agricultural exporters, spending increased more moderately (figure 4.4.C).

The pattern reversed during the global financial crisis, when revenues fell sharply but spending often rose or remained elevated in response to the downturn, causing primary balances in commodity exporters to deteriorate markedly in 2009 and the early 2010s. Again, the deterioration was most pronounced in energy exporters, where spending adjusted only partially to the revenue collapse, resulting in widening deficits through much of the 2010s (figure 4.4.D). In metal exporters, and even more so in agricultural exporters, smaller revenue losses meant a more moderate weakening in primary balances. Commodity importers also saw fiscal balances worsen, owing to stimulus measures, weaker activity, and lower revenues.

As commodity prices softened and revenue mobilization weakened, spending pressures remained in place. Primary balances deteriorated more sharply in exporters than in importers between 2015 and 2019. During the pandemic, spending again rose sharply in both groups, reaching about 26 percent of GDP in commodity exporters and 30 percent in importers, before easing somewhat thereafter. Agricultural exporters stood out as limited fiscal space afforded them less room to provide fiscal stimulus. Thereafter, spending patterns across exporter groups converged, and median primary expenditure settled at about 24 percent of GDP. The gap with commodity importers, however, widened again in recent years: after narrowing in the mid-2010s, it reached about 5 percentage points by 2025, with spending in importers rising to an estimated 29 percent of GDP.

Public debt

Debt dynamics mirror the trends in fiscal policy. Government debt fell sharply in the 2000s, especially in commodity exporters, where median debt declined from 56 percent of GDP in 2000 to 25 percent in 2008 (figure 4.5.A). Beyond improved fiscal balances, debt reduction in EMDEs was also supported by debt relief initiatives—notably the Heavily Indebted Poor Countries (HIPC) initiative and the Multilateral Debt Relief Initiative (MDRI)—and strengthened public debt management institutions (Huidrom, Kose, and Ohnsorge 2016). After the global financial crisis, however, debt levels resumed their upward trajectory, particularly in commodity exporters during the subsequent commodity price downturn. The pandemic resulted in further debt accumulation in EMDEs. By 2025, median government debt had risen to an estimated 51 percent of GDP in commodity exporters and 59 percent in other EMDEs.

Across commodity exporter groups, debt dynamics have been comparable: debt as a share of GDP fell steeply before the global financial crisis and rose rapidly thereafter, including during the pandemic (figure 4.5.B). Since then, debt in energy and metal exporters has returned to pre-pandemic levels, whereas it remained elevated in agricultural exporters. Throughout much of the past 25 years, debt was lowest in energy exporters and highest in agricultural exporters. By 2025, median public debt stood at 41 percent of GDP in energy exporters, 48 percent in metal exporters, and 57 percent in agricultural exporters.

The weakening of fiscal balances and the buildup of public debt increasingly translate into higher debt-service pressures. Across EMDEs, net interest payments declined through much of the 2010s amid historically low global interest rates. However, this trend reversed in recent years as tighter financial conditions raised borrowing costs (figure 4.5.C). By 2025, net interest payments had reached 6 percent of total expenditure in commodity exporters and 7 percent in commodity importers, where interest burdens were higher even before the pandemic as a result of earlier debt buildup. Differences between commodity exporters are also notable. Energy exporters faced the lowest interest burden in 2025, at 6 percent of total expenditure, although net interest payments have risen sharply since the 2010s (figure 4.5.D). Interest payments in metal exporters stood in the middle, at 7 percent in 2025. Agricultural exporters faced the greatest strain and saw interest payments rise to 10 percent of expenditure by 2025 after accelerating in the post-pandemic period.

FIGURE 4.5 Public debt and interest payments

Government debt in commodity-exporting EMDEs has followed a U-shaped trajectory since 2000, declining sharply during the commodity boom before rising rapidly in the subsequent decade. Agricultural exporters tend to carry the highest debt burdens and face acute interest rate pressures, with rising debt service increasingly crowding out productive expenditure.

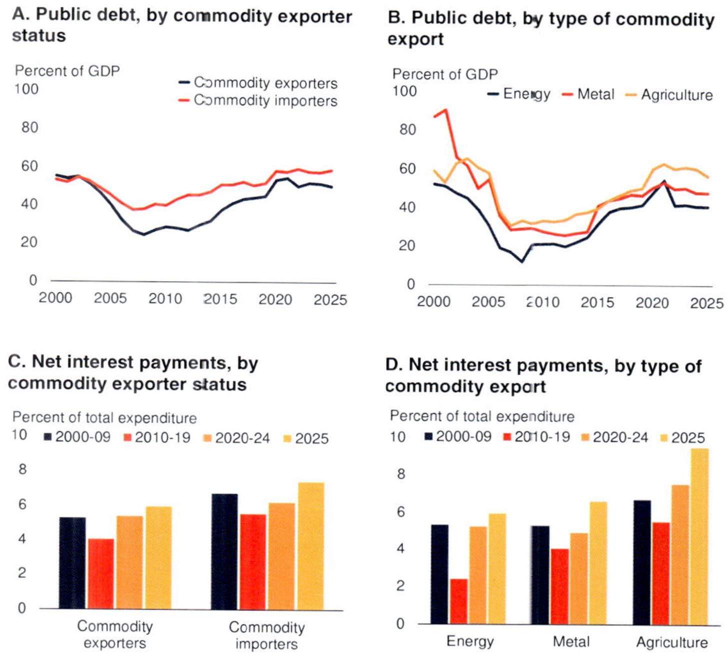

Sources: International Monetary Fund; World Bank.

Note: EMDEs = emerging market and developing economies.

A. Panel shows median government debt (percent of GDP) for up to 92 EMDE commodity exporters and 58 EMDE commodity importers.

B. Panel shows median government debt (percent of GDP) for EMDE commodity exporters. Sample includes up to 35 agricultural exporters, 24 metal exporters, and 33 energy exporters.

C.D. Net interest spending is defined as the difference between the primary balance and the overall balance. Bars show simple averages of annual median values over the indicated periods; bars for 2025 show the median values. Sample includes up to 56 EMDE commodity importers and 92 commodity exporters, including up to 34 agricultural exporters, 24 metal exporters, and 34 energy exporters.

Fiscal policy volatility in commodity exporters

Broad trends in fiscal balances, debt, and interest burdens do not capture the degree of unpredictability in fiscal policy—the extent to which government spending deviates from a systematic path from year to year. This unpredictability, or fiscal policy volatility, is a key dimension of fiscal performance that bears directly on private investment decisions and long-run growth outcomes, and it proves particularly relevant in resource-rich economies where revenue streams remain inherently unstable.

Fiscal policy volatility is measured by estimating a fiscal policy reaction function and computing the standard deviation of the resulting country-specific residuals (Arroyo Marioli, Fatás, and Vasishtha 2024). It captures the discretionary component of spending that is not explained by systematic policy responses to economic conditions (annex 4.1).[2]

[2] Other recent studies based on this approach include World Bank (2024a).

FIGURE 4.6 Fiscal policy volatility and procyclicality

Energy exporters exhibit the highest spending volatility among commodity-exporting EMDEs, though the main driver of volatility across all groups is the degree of commodity dependence rather than the type of commodity exported. Overall, fiscal policy in commodity-exporting EMDEs is substantially more volatile than that in advanced economies, with the widest gaps in SSA and MNA. Fiscal procyclicality is substantially higher in EMDEs than in advanced economies, which have an acyclical fiscal stance on average. Among EMDEs, fiscal policy in commodity exporters is significantly more procyclical than that in commodity importers. This procyclical tendency is most pronounced among energy exporters.

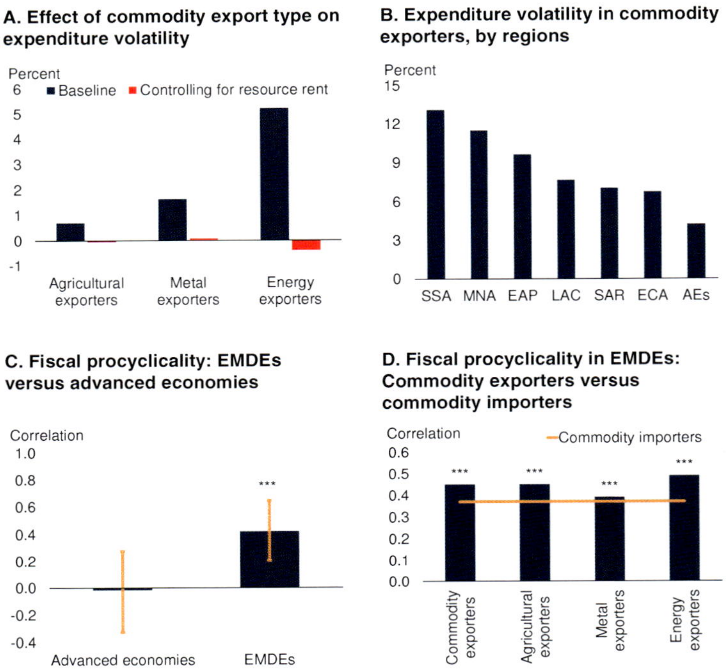

Sources: Arroyo Marioli, Fatás, and Vasishtha (2024); International Monetary Fund; World Bank.

Note: AEs = advanced economies; EAP = East Asia and Pacific; ECA = Europe and Central Asia; EMDEs = emerging market and developing economies; LAC = Latin America and the Caribbean; MNA = Middle East, North Africa, Afghanistan, and Pakistan; SAR = South Asia; SSA = Sub-Saharan Africa.

A. Panel shows the coefficient estimates obtained from the regression specified in equation A4.1.1 (annex 4.1). The dependent variable is the measure of fiscal expenditure volatility. The blue bars represent the coefficients on the dummy variables representing the three major commodity exporter groups in the baseline regressions (not controlling for resource rents). The red bars represent the corresponding coefficient estimates when resource rents are included as explanatory variables.

B. Panel shows the average (unweighted) volatility in commodity exporters in each country group (annex 4.1 provides details).

C.D. Bars show average country-level correlation between the (Hodrick-Prescott-filtered) cyclical components of real GDP and real government spending within groups. The sample period is 1980–2024. Panel C is based on 36 advanced economies and 146 EMDEs; whiskers show the 25th and 75th percentiles. Panel D is based on 87 commodity-exporting EMDEs—including 38 agricultural, 21 metal, and 31 energy exporters—and 59 commodity-importing EMDEs.

*** indicates that the difference relative to the comparator group (advanced economies in panel C and commodity importers in panel D) is statistically significant at the 10 percent level or better.

Annual data are used for the 1990–2024 period for 184 countries, including 148 EMDEs and 36 advanced economies.

This approach indicates that fiscal expenditure volatility in commodity-exporting EMDEs is primarily associated with the degree of commodity dependence rather than by the type of commodity exported. When resource rents are accounted for, differences in expenditure volatility across exporter types narrow considerably (figure 4.6.A). Baseline results, which do not control for resource rents, illustrate how this dependence manifests across groups. Energy exporters, where commodity revenues average more than half of total fiscal receipts, exhibit the highest expenditure volatility—about 5.2 percentage points higher than in commodity importers. This gap reflects both the scale and concentration of energy revenue flows, which are highly sensitive to global price swings and prove relatively easy to capture through SOEs or sector-specific taxation. Metal exporters display a more moderate volatility gap of about 1.6 percentage points relative to commodity importers. This partly reflects a lower share of commodity revenues in total fiscal receipts, averaging about 14 percent, and higher non-resource revenue mobilization, which can help offset commodity price-driven revenue shortfalls. In agricultural exporters, where commodity revenues represent about 11 percent of total receipts, expenditure volatility is not significantly different from that in commodity importers.

Regional patterns reinforce this heterogeneity. Fiscal expenditure volatility is highest among commodity exporters in Sub-Saharan Africa and the Middle East, North Africa, Afghanistan, and Pakistan—at about 13 and 12 percent, respectively—followed by East Asia and Pacific at roughly 10 percent. Latin America and the Caribbean and South Asia display more moderate levels, while Europe and Central Asia is closest to the advanced-economy average of about 4 percent (figure 4.6.B).

Taken together, these patterns suggest that spending volatility in commodity exporters likely reflects deep-seated structural characteristics stemming from commodity dependence. Other important factors that have a bearing on fiscal volatility include institutional quality and policy frameworks (World Bank 2024a). Fiscal policy volatility can amplify downturns by driving abrupt fiscal tightening when revenues fall, and fueling fiscal expansions during booms that are hard to unwind. Such policy volatility is detrimental to growth due largely to its impact on output volatility (Arroyo Marioli, Fatás, and Vasishtha 2024). Additionally, higher spending volatility may increase tax rate volatility or raise uncertainty about future tax rates, in turn dampening investment and growth even further.

Fiscal procyclicality in commodity exporters

Fiscal policy in commodity-exporting economies tends to be highly volatile, complicating macroeconomic stabilization. In principle, allowing fiscal balances to move with the cycle can support stability, provided debt remains sustainable and borrowing constraints do not bind. Optimal fiscal policy therefore calls for a countercyclical stance: tightening in good times and providing support in bad times. In practice, however, fiscal policy in EMDEs—especially in commodity exporters—tends to be procyclical, amplifying rather than dampening business cycle fluctuations (Gavin and Perotti 1997; Kaminsky, Reinhart, and Végh 2004; World Bank 2024a).

Measuring fiscal procyclicality

One common approach to measuring fiscal procyclicality traces the fiscal stance through the correlation between the cyclical components of real primary government spending and real GDP at an annual frequency (Arroyo Marioli and Végh 2026). A positive correlation indicates that spending rises when the economy expands and falls when it contracts—that is, procyclical behavior relative to the output cycle. By construction, this approach captures the responsiveness of fiscal policy to year-to-year fluctuations in economic activity, regardless of where the economy stands in the broader commodity cycle.

By this measure, fiscal policy in EMDEs was procyclical from 1980–2024, while that in advanced economies was acyclical, on average (figure 4.6.C). Among EMDEs, fiscal policy in commodity exporters proved significantly more procyclical than in other EMDEs. The average correlation between the cyclical components of real government spending and real GDP is about 0.46 for commodity exporters, compared with 0.37 for commodity importers (figure 4.6.D).

Energy and agricultural exporters display the highest procyclicality, with a correlation of 0.49 and 0.45, respectively, compared with 0.39 for metal exporters. The differences across exporter types are more modest than the gap with importers, suggesting that the procyclical bias is a shared feature of commodity dependence rather than a characteristic of any particular export sector. Nonetheless, the comparatively higher correlation among energy exporters aligns with the greater magnitude and concentration of commodity revenue flows in this group, which amplify the transmission of commodity price shocks to the budget.

Several theoretical explanations have been proposed to explain the persistence of fiscal procyclicality in commodity-exporting EMDEs. The first explanation points to imperfections in international capital markets. Specifically, during commodity price downturns, falling revenues restrict access to external financing and raise borrowing costs, leaving governments with limited capacity to sustain expenditure when they most need it. A second explanation is the "voracity effect," whereby multiple fiscal entities, such as ministries and subnational governments, compete to appropriate revenue windfalls during booms without internalizing the costs to others, driving spending increases that exceed the windfall itself (Tornell and Lane 1999).

An alternative argument posits that running surpluses during good times generates intense lobbying pressure to spend those resources. Anticipating this, fiscal authorities may instead reduce taxes and expand expenditure procyclically to forestall even more wasteful outcomes (Talvi and Végh 2005). A fourth explanation relies on the notion of "starving the beast" (Alesina, Campante, and Tabellini 2008). In environments with weak governance, voters rationally demand higher public spending or lower taxes during booms to prevent officials from misappropriating windfall revenues, thus perpetuating procyclical fiscal outcomes. Fiscal procyclicality in commodity-exporting EMDEs can also be shaped by optimism bias in official growth and revenue forecasts, particularly during booms. Overly optimistic projections can create a false sense of fiscal space, delaying adjustment and weakening buffer accumulation, thereby reinforcing fiscal procyclicality (Frankel and Schreger 2013).

Output cycles versus commodity price movements

Much of the evidence on fiscal procyclicality comes from estimating average responses of government spending or cyclically adjusted fiscal balances with respect to economic activity. But output and commodity price cycles do not fully coincide, and commodity price movements are often sharp. As a result, the degree of fiscal procyclicality can look quite different depending on how it is measured or assessed. Evidence suggests that once fiscal responses are conditioned on changes in global commodity prices, the picture becomes more nuanced—and in some cases, procyclicality is lower than standard estimates suggest (Céspedes and Velasco 2014; Petrella, Juvenal, and Di Pace 2025).

Fiscal policy makers in commodity-exporting EMDEs must contend with two sets of challenges, at varying frequencies, arising from commodity price fluctuations: short-term swings in prices and longer-lasting commodity price cycles. Both of these challenges are defining features of commodity markets. In the face of abrupt swings in commodity prices, governments in commodity exporters often need to manage acute fiscal pressures. Over commodity price cycles, however, the task is different. It requires managing policy in a way that builds buffers in booms and protects priority spending in slumps. Hence, what appears to be a general tendency toward fiscal procyclicality may look stronger or weaker depending on whether fiscal behavior is viewed through the lens of short-term shock responses or more medium-term commodity price cycle management.

To reconcile these perspectives, the fiscal responses to commodity price shocks are studied, and these responses are compared with broader fiscal patterns over price booms and slumps. This helps assess whether fiscal policy responses to commodity price fluctuations differ when examined as short- to medium-run reactions to shocks rather than as trends that unfold over the full commodity cycle. In doing so, the chapter complements the broader literature on fiscal procyclicality by focusing more closely on the commodity price channel and disentangling the different time horizons over which commodity-related fiscal pressures play out.

Dynamic fiscal response to commodity price shocks

Commodity prices are highly volatile and can often experience surges or sharp declines. Such swings can place fiscal policy under intense pressure, and the nature of the challenge differs depending on whether prices rise or fall. A priori, it is not obvious that the tendency of fiscal policy to act procyclical maps directly onto governments' responses to large shocks. Procyclicality may become more pronounced when financing constraints or political pressures intensify, but it may also weaken—or even give way to countercyclical responses—for instance, as a result of automatic stabilizers or governments facing stronger incentives to save prudently in booms and cushion slumps.

To investigate this, the dynamic response of fiscal policy to a commodity price shock is estimated using a local projections framework (Jordà 2005). The analysis focuses on the behavior of primary spending as the policy instrument rather than on outcomes such as fiscal balances and public debt, which are shaped to a greater extent by economic conditions. Revenue dynamics serve as a benchmark to help gauge how the shock transmits through fiscal policy. The empirical approach covers 88 commodity-exporting EMDEs and links cumulative changes in spending to shocks in global commodity prices, measured using the World Bank's real commodity price indexes (annex 4.2 provides details).[3] The effects are traced over a five-year horizon, intended to capture both immediate and medium-term fiscal responses.

The analysis controls for key macro-fiscal factors, such as primary balances, public debt, growth, and inflation (all in lagged terms). It also includes fiscal policy frameworks—fiscal rules, SWFs, and fiscal councils—and measures of institutional quality. Country-fixed effects are included along with year dummies for the global financial crisis and the

[3] The results, available on request, are robust to using the IMF's commodity terms-of-trade index as an alternative measure of commodity prices.

COVID-19 pandemic. Finally, the model incorporates leads and lags of the shock. Including leads isolates the response to the contemporaneous commodity price shock conditional on the subsequent path of commodity prices. This helps separate the effect of the initial price innovation from later price movements, regardless of whether the current shock is transitory or persistent.

The results show that commodity price shocks boost government revenues but translate into higher spending more gradually. On average, a 1 percent increase (decline) in the commodity price index is associated with a 0.3 percent rise (fall) in government revenues on impact, which increases marginally to 0.4 percent five years after the shock. Primary spending responds only modestly in the year of the shock, consistent with the notion that fiscal policy takes time to move from planning to implementation (figure 4.7.A). Over time, however, the average response becomes clearly procyclical: a 1 percent change in the commodity price index is associated with a cumulative change in government spending of about 0.4 percent after five years following the initial shock.[4] Hence, the results indicate that much of the revenue windfall is absorbed by higher spending over the medium run, while revenue shortfalls are met with expenditure cuts.[5]

This pattern is broadly similar across exporter groups, although the magnitude of the response varies. In energy exporters, the associated revenue windfall is larger, especially on impact. Spending then rises steadily, with a 1 percent increase in the energy price index corresponding to a 0.5 percent increase in spending after five years (figure 4.7.B). Agricultural exporters display a similar pattern: a 1 percent increase in the agriculture price index is associated with a 0.4 percent increase in spending after five years (figure 4.7.C). Metal exporters also exhibit a qualitatively similar response, though more muted: a 1 percent increase in the metal price index is associated with a 0.3 percent higher spending after five years (figure 4.7.D). However, despite differences in magnitude, spending largely tracks the revenue gains and losses resulting from commodity price shocks across all three groups. This suggests that differences in spending responses mainly reflect differences in revenue exposure rather than systematically different fiscal behavior, reinforcing the familiar pattern of fiscal procyclicality in commodity exporters.

FIGURE 4.7 Responses of revenue and primary spending to commodity price shocks

Primary spending in commodity exporters responds procyclically to commodity price shocks. This pattern is strongest among energy exporters, where revenue and spending elasticities to commodity prices are highest, but it is also sizable among agricultural and metal exporters—suggesting that windfalls are often gradually spent rather than saved.

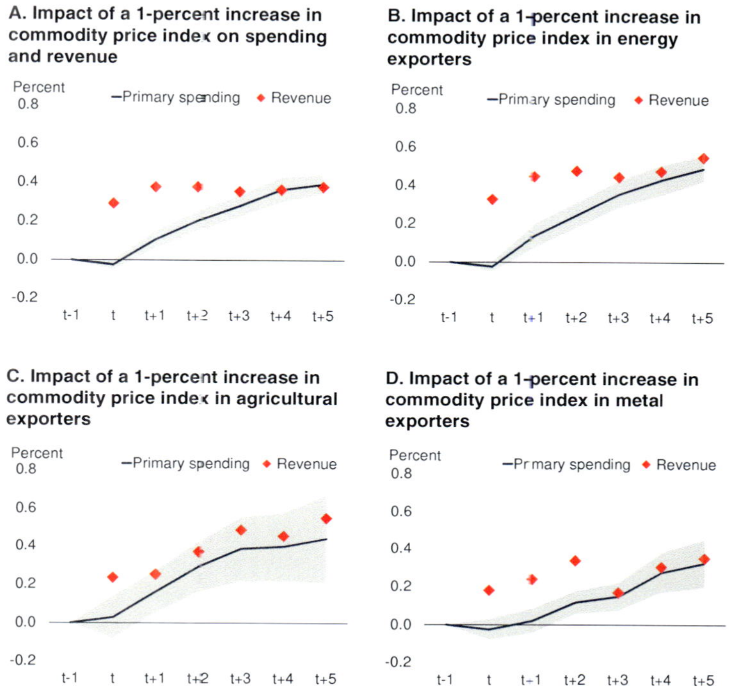

Sources: International Monetary Fund; World Bank.

Note: EMDEs = emerging market and developing economies. Results are derived from a local projections framework. Technical details are provided in annex 4.2. Panel A shows the responses of revenues and primary spending to a shock (relative to a no-shock trajectory) to a pooled commodity price index, which uses the World Bank's energy price index for energy exporters, the metal price index for metal exporters, and the agricultural price index for agricultural exporters. Panels B, C, and D are based on shocks to the commodity price indexes for the respective commodity classification. Lines show the cumulative change in primary expenditure (in percent) in the years following a shock, and diamonds show the corresponding change in revenues. Shaded areas show 90 percent confidence intervals. Results are based on a sample of 88 commodity-exporting EMDEs (31 energy exporters, 24 metal exporters, and 33 agricultural exporters).

[4] This result is broadly in line with earlier research, which estimated that each additional dollar of commodity revenue raises public spending by about $0.25, on average, with the marginal propensity to spend commodity revenues varying with country characteristics (Mendes and Pennings 2025).

[5] This overall pattern is not driven solely by either positive or negative shocks (refer to figures A4.2.1.A and A4.2.1.B). The evidence therefore points against a one-sided explanation, be it liquidity constraints in downswings or profligate spending in upswings.

These spending responses may reflect several interacting channels. Revenue windfalls can intensify political pressure to expand transfers, public wages, and other current spending, especially where fiscal institutions do not sufficiently insulate temporary gains from competing distributional claims (Tornell and Lane 1999). Also, social transfers in EMDEs are generally smaller and less countercyclical than in advanced economies, limiting their stabilizing role in downturns and leaving EMDEs more vulnerable to cuts when revenues fall (Michaud and Rothert 2018). Energy-related subsidies can further amplify procyclicality. Together, these channels align with a gradual but sizable pass-through from commodity price shocks to public spending over the medium term.

Fiscal management over commodity price cycles

Policy makers rarely know in real time whether a commodity price shock will prove temporary or persistent. This uncertainty highlights the importance of fiscal responses that save windfalls until their durability is clearer, prevent temporary revenue gains from financing permanent spending commitments, and preserve fiscal space to respond if negative shocks become prolonged.

Yet, commodity-related fiscal challenges extend beyond discrete shocks. When commodity price movements persist, they can become part of multi-year booms or slumps—a typical feature of commodity markets. During booms, governments should continue to limit procyclical spending and build buffers, but a sustained improvement in revenues may also create space for growth-enhancing investment or measures to promote economic diversification. During slumps, accumulated buffers can help protect essential services, social spending, and high-quality public investment. However, they cannot indefinitely substitute for adjustment if lower prices persist, as this may eventually jeopardize fiscal sustainability. Longer-lasting commodity cycles therefore require a more strategic medium-term approach, not just short-term shock responses. Fiscal behavior over commodity cycles may consequently differ from the responses observed after discrete commodity price shocks.

In this context, the analysis next examines fiscal outcomes during booms and slumps in commodity prices, complementing the standard literature on fiscal cyclicality, which typically focusses on fiscal dynamics over the business cycle. To identify commodity price cycles, the analysis applies well-established techniques to examine business cycles to real commodity price indexes (Balatti, forthcoming; annex 4.3 provides details). A *boom* in commodity markets is defined as a trough-to-peak rise in commodity prices; a *slump* is a peak-to-trough decline. Booms and slumps in energy, metal, and agricultural prices are identified using the corresponding monthly price indexes for January 1970–April 2026. The identified cycles indicate broad synchronization of peaks and troughs in prices across commodity groups, alongside shorter and more volatile cycles in recent years (World Bank 2025).

Fiscal dynamics over booms and slumps are assessed using real changes in primary expenditures and revenues, which filters out trend components and fluctuations driven by large swings in nominal output. However, this does not filter out all effects directly related to commodity price swings. Although the responsiveness of government spending and revenues to the output cycle is well documented and commonly used for constructing cyclically adjusted fiscal measures, the sensitivity of fiscal variables to commodity price movements is much less explored and generally only available for specific countries. As a result, in cross-country studies, it is challenging to distinguish between the effects of automatic stabilizers and those stemming from discretionary fiscal measures when analyzing the impact of commodity price changes. Therefore, the analysis is intended to be descriptive rather than causal. As in the literature, primary balances and public debt are expressed as a share of GDP. The analysis is based on the post-2000 period, in line with the sample period used in the preceding analysis, and covers 92 commodity-exporting EMDEs.

Energy exporters

Fiscal outcomes in energy exporters move closely with commodity price cycles. The median primary balance improves by about 0.9 percentage point of

GDP per year during booms and deteriorates by about 1.1 percentage points during slumps (figure 4.8.A). A non-parametric *k*-sample test confirms that the distributions of primary balance changes differ significantly across boom and slump episodes.[6] Beyond the mechanical boost from faster nominal GDP growth during booms, these dynamics reflect pronounced revenue swings: real revenues grow by 9.4 percent in boom years and shrink by about 0.6 percent in slumps (figure 4.8.B). Expenditure dynamics also help explain the pattern, but mainly because they do not seem to amplify the cycle. Median primary expenditure growth remains relatively stable, with no statistically significant difference between booms and slumps (figure 4.8.C). This suggests that, on average, energy exporters exercise some degree of spending restraint during booms, allowing higher revenue growth to translate into improved primary balances and helping preserve space to sustain spending during slumps. Public debt dynamics align with these patterns: median debt-to-GDP declines by about 2.8 percentage points per year during booms and rises by 1.3 percentage points per year during slumps (figure 4.8.D).[7]

Metal exporters

Fiscal outcomes in metal exporters display a similar boom-slump pattern, though the underlying dynamics differ. The median primary balance improves by about 0.4 percentage point of GDP during booms and weakens by about 0.3 percentage point during slumps—smaller swings compared with energy exporters, but still highly statistically significant. As with energy exporters, median primary balance fluctuations appear to be driven in part by revenues, which are tightly linked to the commodity cycle. The key difference is on the spending side. In metal exporters,

FIGURE 4.8 Fiscal positions over commodity price cycles

Fiscal indicators in commodity-exporting EMDEs tend to comove with commodity price cycles, albeit to varying degrees across countries. In energy exporters, the median primary balance (as a share of GDP) typically strengthens during booms and weakens during slumps, reflecting sizable swings in revenue growth. Metal exporters display similar, although relatively less pronounced, trends in primary balances, with spending remaining relatively contained during booms. In contrast, revenue gains in agricultural exporters during booms are offset by accelerating expenditure growth, leaving primary balances broadly unchanged over the cycle. As a result, agricultural exporters reduce debt less during booms and accumulate more of it during slumps, likely pointing to structural fiscal vulnerabilities.

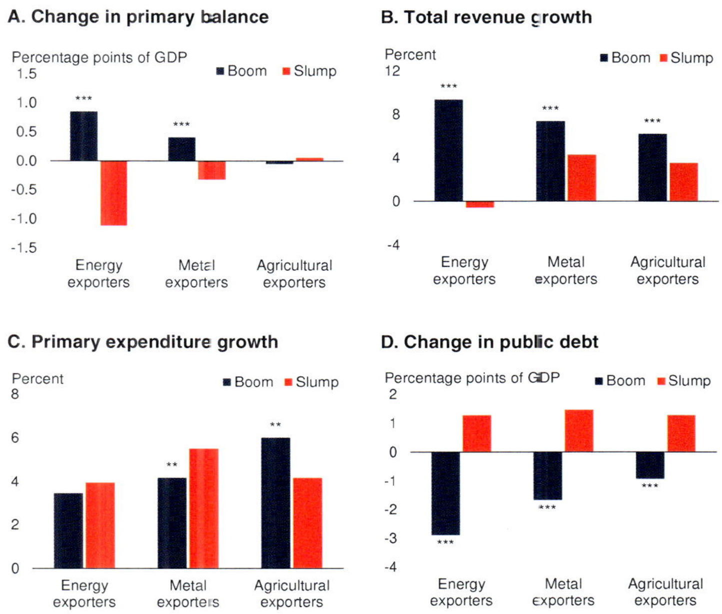

Sources: International Monetary Fund; World Bank.

Note: EMDEs = emerging market and developing economies. Panels show median changes in fiscal variables during commodity price booms and slumps.

***, **, and * denote differences between boom and slump episodes that are statistically significant at the 1, 5, and 10 percent levels, respectively, based on a non-parametric *k*-sample test.

A.-D. Samples include 34 energy exporters in panels A and B (33 in panels C and D), 25 metal exporters, and 37 agricultural exporters in panels A and C (38 in panels B and D).

primary expenditure growth is significantly higher during slumps than during booms—5.5 percent compared with 4.2 percent—suggesting countercyclical spending behavior. Overall, improved primary balances in booms help stabilize debt dynamics: public debt as a share of GDP declines during booms, by about 1.7 percentage points per year, and increases by 1.5 percentage points per year during slumps.

Agricultural exporters

Primary balances in agricultural exporters do not differ significantly between booms and slumps.

[6] Paired *t*-tests based on within-country differences—which compare changes in country-level fiscal variables between booms and slumps—yield similar results for primary balances and the other fiscal indicators considered (Gootjes and Vasishtha, forthcoming).

[7] These median responses should be interpreted with some caution, as they may obscure episodes in which debt rises sharply or primary balances deteriorate rapidly during large commodity price declines—developments that are not always fully captured by comparisons across broad boom and slump phases. For example, the plunge in oil prices in 2014–16 led to a sharp increase in government debt ratios and a widening of fiscal sustainability gaps in many oil-exporting EMDEs (IMF 2017; World Bank 2018).

However, this apparent stability conceals offsetting movements in revenues and expenditures. Unlike energy exporters, where spending is broadly smoothed over the cycle, and metal exporters, where spending growth increases during slumps, agricultural exporters display a more procyclical expenditure pattern. Median primary expenditure growth accelerates from 4.2 percent in slumps to 6.0 percent in booms, suggesting that revenue gains are partly absorbed by higher spending rather than translated into stronger balances. Debt dynamics are correspondingly less favorable. Median debt declines by about 0.9 percentage point of GDP per year during booms and rises by 1.3 percentage points during slumps, making agricultural exporters more vulnerable to debt accumulation over commodity cycles.

Policy frameworks for fiscal management

Commodity price shocks do not translate one-for-one into medium-run management over commodity price cycles. Energy and metal exporters appear to act procyclically in response to large shocks, yet practice more prudence on average over the cycle. Agricultural exporters, by contrast, display procyclical behavior both in response to shocks and over the cycle. These results provide a more nuanced understanding of fiscal procyclicality across commodity exporters, by showing more clearly where in the fiscal process such procyclicality tends to arise.

These patterns may partly reflect the policy frameworks and institutional arrangements that commodity exporters have adopted over time. In these economies, stabilizing fiscal policy in the face of repeated price booms and slumps requires more than discretionary policy action; it depends on durable fiscal anchors, savings mechanisms, and strong institutions. Stronger economic frameworks and better public institutions tend, on average, to reduce fiscal procyclicality in these economies (Arroyo Marioli and Végh 2026; World Bank 2024a). Moreover, countries with stronger policy and institutional fundamentals tend to achieve better macroeconomic and growth outcomes (Arezki and Bruckner 2010; Arezki, Hamilton, and Kazimov 2011; van der Ploeg 2011).

Against this backdrop, this section examines the evolution of policy instruments—fiscal rules, SWFs, and independent fiscal councils—and tests whether they help (1) mitigate procyclical responses to commodity price shocks, and (2) improve fiscal management over the broader commodity price cycle. Fiscal rules set numerical limits on key fiscal variables—such as the fiscal balance, public debt, or government expenditure—to strengthen fiscal discipline and safeguard sustainable public finances (Alonso et al. 2025). In addition to serving as a commitment device for governments, they provide clear benchmarks for stakeholders, including financial markets, to assess fiscal policy developments (Kelemen and Teo 2014).

SWFs are state-owned investment funds set up to manage public assets for macroeconomic goals, including budget stabilization, intergenerational savings, more efficient reserve investment, development financing, and pension support (IMF 2008). In commodity-exporting countries, a key purpose of SWFs is to save windfall revenues so governments can smooth public spending over time and strengthen the management of public wealth (Elbadawi, Soto, and Youssef 2018). Fiscal councils operate as independent technical bodies tasked with monitoring and assessing fiscal policy (IMF 2013). Their independent analysis helps reduce the opacity that often surrounds public debate on government budgets, including questions about the adequacy of the fiscal stance and the sustainability of public finances (Beetsma et al. 2019).

Evolution of fiscal policy frameworks

Since 2000, commodity-exporting EMDEs have strengthened their fiscal policy frameworks considerably. The number of commodity exporters with at least one fiscal rule rose from 16 in 2000 to 50 by 2024, while the number of countries with an operational SWF tripled over the same period, from 18 to 54 by 2024. By contrast, the spread of independent fiscal councils has been much slower, increasing from just 1 country in 2000 to 12 in 2024. A notable trend across all groups is the shift from reliance on a single instrument toward combinations of frameworks, reflecting a growing recognition that no single tool is likely to be sufficient to manage the full complexity of commodity revenue volatility. However, the pace and type of adoption, as well as the mix of frameworks introduced, vary by exporter groups.

Energy exporters

In energy exporters, policy frameworks have been reinforced primarily by the adoption of SWFs. By 2024, 83 percent of energy exporters had established such a fund, up from about 37 percent in 2000, the highest adoption rate of any exporter group (figure 4.9.A). Fiscal rules have also become more prevalent among energy exporters, with adoption rising from only 6 percent in 2000 to 46 percent in 2024. The primacy of SWFs reflects the scale and concentration of energy revenues: by channeling windfall receipts into a dedicated fund, governments can insulate the budget from the immediate spending pressures that large price swings generate. Independent fiscal councils, by contrast, remain relatively uncommon, with only 9 percent of energy exporters maintaining one in 2024.

Metal exporters

Among metal exporters, policy frameworks have been strengthened primarily through the adoption of fiscal rules, which were in place in nearly 60 percent of countries by 2024, up from about 16 percent in 2000 (figure 4.9.B). SWF adoption has also grown significantly, reaching 40 percent. Independent fiscal councils have gained some ground in recent years, with 16 percent of metal exporters having established one by 2024. Even so, adoption has been gradual: no metal exporter had an independent fiscal council until after 2012.

Agricultural exporters

Compared with other exporter groups, agricultural exporters trail in progress on strengthening fiscal frameworks (figure 4.9.C). Fiscal rules are the most common instrument, with adoption having doubled since 2000 to 53 percent of countries by 2024. SWF adoption also increased from zero in 2000 but remains lower than that in other exporter groups; only 29 percent of agricultural exporters had a SWF in 2024. Independent fiscal councils remain the least

FIGURE 4.9 Fiscal rules, SWFs, and fiscal councils

The adoption of fiscal policy frameworks has expanded considerably across commodity-exporting EMDEs since 2000, though the pace of adoption has varied by commodity exporter type. Energy exporters have led in SWF adoption, increasingly combining SWFs with fiscal rules. Metal exporters have adopted fiscal rules as their primary anchor, whereas agricultural exporters lag in adopting these frameworks. The combination of multiple instruments has become more common across all groups, reflecting growing recognition that no single tool is sufficient to manage commodity revenue volatility. However, only a few commodity exporters have established independent fiscal councils, and uptake in regard to such councils has been slower than in commodity importers.

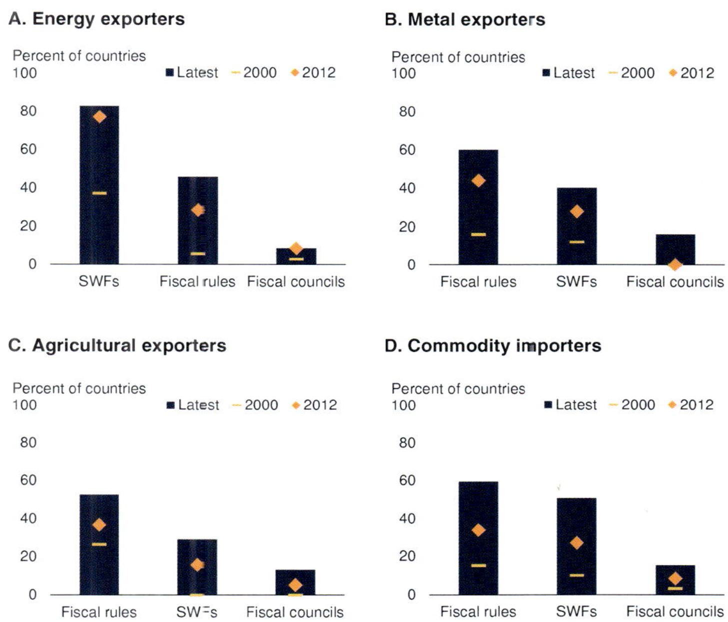

Sources: Alonso et al. (2025); Global SWF (database); International Monetary Fund; World Bank.
Note: EMDEs = emerging market and developing economies; SWF = sovereign wealth fund. Panels show the share of countries that have adopted SWFs, fiscal rules, and fiscal councils.
A.-D. Samples include 35 energy-exporting EMDEs, 25 metal-exporting EMDEs, 38 agricultural-exporting EMDEs, and 59 commodity-importing EMDEs, respectively.

prevalent framework, increasing from zero in 2000 to just 13 percent in 2024.

Other EMDEs

Commodity-importing EMDEs present a useful comparator for the evolution of fiscal policy frameworks. Their adoption of fiscal rules has broadly kept pace with that of commodity exporters: by 2024, 59 percent of importers had at least one rule in place, a share comparable to metal exporters and above that of energy and agricultural exporters (figure 4.9.D). SWF adoption among importers, at 51 percent, exceeds that of metal and agricultural exporters but remains well below that of energy exporters. Independent fiscal councils remain relatively rare among importers as well, but their adoption started earlier. The share of countries with fiscal councils rose from 3 percent in 2000 to 15 percent in 2024.

Effectiveness of policy frameworks in mitigating the impact of commodity price shocks

The strengthening of fiscal policy frameworks is encouraging, but it may not necessarily translate into more prudent fiscal management of commodity price shocks. Local projections are used to assess whether fiscal rules and SWFs help dampen the spending response to such shocks.[8] However, framework adoption is likely related to institutional capacity and fiscal prudence: countries that adopt fiscal rules or establish SWFs may already be more fiscally prudent, institutionally capable, or better equipped to smooth commodity revenue volatility. To address this potential endogeneity, the local projections employ augmented inverse probability weighting (AIPW). In the first stage, the model estimates the probability that a fiscal rule or SWF exists, conditional on predetermined fiscal, institutional, macroeconomic, and commodity-sector characteristics. The model then combines the resulting propensity scores with an outcome model in an augmented local projections framework, making framework and non-framework observations more comparable (annex 4.2 provides further details).

The results point to only limited stabilizing effects in the face of commodity price shocks. SWFs are linked to a more contained spending response in the year of a commodity price shock, especially among energy exporters. A 1 percent increase in the energy price index is associated with a 0.1 percent decline in primary spending among energy exporters with SWFs, compared with a 0.1 percent increase in those without SWFs (figure 4.10.A). The difference between the two responses is statistically significant, suggesting that SWFs are associated with a more muted immediate fiscal response to energy price shocks. This pattern aligns with SWFs helping to decouple government spending from revenue windfalls by channeling part of the gains into savings vehicles rather than the budget. For metal exporters, and to a lesser extent agricultural exporters, the estimated responses point in a similar direction, but the estimates do not differ significantly from those of countries without SWFs.

This mitigating role appears short-lived. While SWFs may help dampen immediate spending pressures after commodity price shocks, particularly in energy exporters, they do not appear to prevent spending increases over the medium term as revenue windfalls fully materialize. The evidence is even weaker for fiscal rules. Across all exporter groups, impulse responses of primary spending to commodity price shocks do not differ materially based on whether fiscal rules are in place (figure 4.10.B). In agricultural exporters with fiscal rules, spending responses appear relatively contained, but the estimates are highly uncertain and not significantly different from those for countries without such frameworks. A similar pattern emerges for SWFs. As a result, little can be concluded about the medium-term stabilizing role of either SWFs or fiscal rules in agricultural exporters.

The limited ability of SWFs and fiscal rules to smooth spending across the commodity cycle may reflect several factors. First, the environment in which these frameworks operate is exceedingly demanding. Commodity prices are highly volatile, and revenue windfalls can create strong political pressure to spend. Resisting those pressures can be difficult, and at times politically costly, especially when social and investment needs are large. Second, the effectiveness of fiscal frameworks often depends critically on their design, calibration, and enforcement. In the case of SWFs, they may differ in size, funding structure, and core mandate, all of which can result in different levels of efficiency. Clear restrictions on how to make use of the funds are important and need to be intertemporally consistent. In some cases, governments use SWFs for spending needs that are not temporary—or are only temporary in appearance—raising the risk of depleting funds

[8] Independent fiscal councils are not assessed because, although their adoption is rising, in many countries they remain too recent to allow for a robust assessment.

over time. Additionally, in other cases, SWFs are well designed but lack both an adequate political incentive scheme and institutional structure, rendering their boundaries weak and resulting in leaks that can build over time.

Similar considerations apply to fiscal rules. Proper calibration and sound design are widely recognized as important determinants of their effectiveness in promoting fiscal discipline (Caselli and Reynaud 2020; Gootjes, de Haan, and Jong-A-Pin 2021). That fiscal rules do little to dampen spending responses to commodity price shocks may reflect a basic design problem: such shocks do not always cause fiscal constraints to bind when they are most needed. When rules target the fiscal balance, for example, a positive commodity price shock can expand fiscal space and move governments further away from the constraint. Unless the rule is adjusted over the economic or commodity price cycle, as under Chile's structural balance rule introduced in 2001, the resulting revenue windfall may remain largely unprotected. Likewise, rigid rules may constrain fiscal support when a negative shock hits, especially where windfall revenues from earlier booms were not saved and the subsequent revenue shortfall caused constraints to bind quickly. International capital markets may reinforce this dynamic, insofar as fiscal rules credibly shape perceptions of fiscal sustainability (Kelemen and Teo 2014). When investors view binding fiscal constraints as a sign of heightened risk, they may demand higher risk premiums.

The challenge, therefore, is not only to adopt fiscal frameworks but to design them so that they bind when windfalls arrive, preserve buffers when pressures to spend are strong, and provide support when commodity revenues fall.[9] Still, even well-designed SWFs and fiscal rules may not be sufficient on their own. Their effectiveness often

[9] The analysis in the chapter is structured according to commodity-exporter groups—energy, metals, and agriculture—to capture potential differences in revenue exposure and shock transmission across a diverse group of countries. This limits the extent to which fiscal frameworks can be disaggregated by design features, as such granular analysis would at best be based on only small subsets of countries with specific rule types, SWF mandates, funding structures, or withdrawal rules. The resulting estimates would therefore be difficult to interpret and would not provide a sufficiently robust basis for conclusions.

FIGURE 4.10 Role of fiscal rules, SWFs, and institutions during commodity price shocks

The primary expenditure response to commodity price shocks varies across policy settings. In energy exporters, SWFs are typically associated with a countercyclical response in the year of a shock, but this effect fades over the medium term. The presence of fiscal rules does not appear to materially affect the expenditure response across exporter groups. Spending responses vary more markedly depending on the quality of public institutions. Among energy exporters, in particular, countries with strong institutions display a more contained and countercyclical spending response in the short run, followed by only mild procyclicality over the medium run. In countries with weaker institutions, the response of spending is strongly procyclical, amplifying the effects of commodity price shocks.

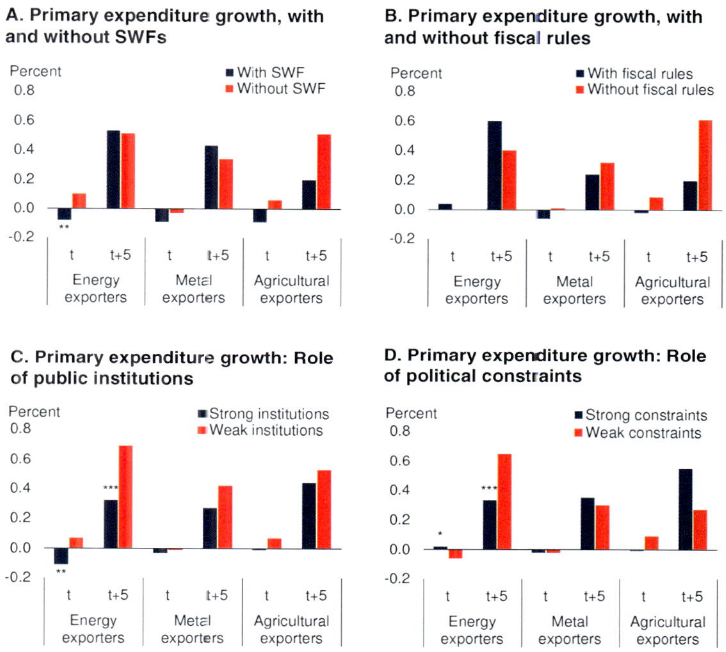

Sources: Alonso et al. (2025); Global SWF (database); Henisz (2000); International Monetary Fund; World Bank.

Note: EMDEs = emerging market and developing economies; SWF = sovereign wealth fund. Results are derived from local projection regressions. Technical details are provided in annex 4.2. Bars show the cumulative change in primary expenditure (in percent) in the years following a shock (relative to a no-shock trajectory) to a pooled commodity price index, which uses the World Bank's energy price index for energy exporters, the metal price index for metal exporters, and the agricultural price index for agricultural exporters.

***, **, and * denote statistically significant differences in spending responses between groups at the 1, 5, and 10 percent levels, respectively. Results are based on a sample of 88 commodity-exporting EMDEs (31 energy exporters, 24 metal exporters, and 33 agricultural exporters). Institutions quality is taken from the World Bank's Worldwide Governance Indicators, and the indicator of political constraints is from the Political Constraint Index (Henisz 2000).

C. Commodity exporters with "strong (weak) institutions" are defined as those with values of the institutional quality indicator above (below) the sample median.

D. Commodity exporters with "strong (weak) constraints" are defined as those with values of the indicator of political constraints above (below) the sample median.

depends heavily on the broader institutional environment (Arroyo Marioli and Vasishtha 2025). Indeed, the literature identifies institutional quality as an important—if not the key—determinant of fiscal procyclicality.[10] The contrast between fiscal cyclicality in advanced economies and EMDEs is likewise often attributed to differences in institutional strength (Calderón, Duncan, and Schmidt-Hebbel 2016).

To examine this channel, the analysis distinguishes countries by institutional quality, using a simple average of indicators of the rule of law, regulatory quality, control of corruption, government effectiveness, voice and accountability, and political stability. Countries above the sample median are classified as having stronger public institutions, while those below the median are classified as having weaker public institutions. Results point to a strong association between institutional quality and spending dynamics. In energy exporters with stronger institutions, the short-run spending response to energy price shocks is clearly contained, and the medium-term response is milder: a 1 percent increase in the energy price index is associated with a cumulative 0.3 percent increase in spending (figure 4.10.C). In energy exporters with weaker institutions, by contrast, spending comoves even on impact following the shock, and the medium-term response is significantly stronger, reaching 0.7 percent.

This pattern is consistent with stronger public institutions helping to limit the pass-through of commodity windfalls into government spending, both in the short and medium run. Among energy exporters, the more constrained response—particularly at longer horizons—also appears positively correlated with stronger checks and balances on political actors (figure 4.10.D). Metal and agricultural exporters do not display similar patterns. This may reflect their lower reliance on commodity exports and fiscal revenues, which could make the broader institutional environment less decisive in shaping spending responses to commodity price shocks.

[10] Refer to Arroyo Marioli and Végh (2026); Bova, Carcenac, and Guerguil (2014); Bova, Medas, and Poghosyan (2018); Frankel, Végh, and Vuletin (2013); World Bank (2024a).

Effectiveness of policy frameworks over commodity price cycles

The evidence on the ability of formal fiscal frameworks to manage commodity price shocks is limited. SWFs can help dampen short-run spending responses, but fully restraining the resulting spending pressures following a commodity price shock is much harder in the medium run. Stronger public institutions—especially among energy exporters—are associated with more restrained spending behavior, both on impact and over the medium term. Beyond sound fiscal framework design, an important precondition for prudent fiscal management therefore appears to be a broader institutional environment that supports disciplined fiscal policy making.

Yet these results do not necessarily imply that formal fiscal frameworks have been largely ineffective in managing commodity-related fiscal challenges. Commodity price shocks often create acute fiscal pressures, but as noted earlier, commodity prices also tend to move in prolonged booms and slumps that persist for years. For commodity exporters, the relevant test of fiscal policy is therefore broader than its response to contemporaneous commodity price (or output) fluctuations; it also depends on how fiscal variables behave over the full commodity cycle (Céspedes and Velasco 2014). A key consideration is whether governments can accumulate sufficient buffers during booms to sustain spending during slumps (Basdevant, Hooley, and Imamoglu 2021). This pertains to medium-run fiscal planning rather than only short-run shock absorption. Viewed through this lens, policy instruments that appear to have limited traction in the immediate aftermath of commodity price shocks may still matter over the broader cycle. The results presented below support this interpretation: the more prudent spending management observed over commodity price cycles—particularly among metal exporters, and, to a lesser extent, energy exporters—is associated with the presence of fiscal rules and SWFs in these countries.

Energy exporters

Many energy exporters have adopted SWFs over time, and their presence is associated with more disciplined expenditure management over commodity cycles (figure 4.11.A). In countries with SWFs, spending growth tends to slow significantly during booms, allowing it to hold up better during slumps. When such funds are absent, by contrast, primary spending tends to be more procyclical—accelerating in booms and weakening in slumps. The contrast is especially stark during boom years, when median spending growth reaches 5.8 percent in energy exporters without SWFs, compared with just 2.9 percent in those with SWFs. This pattern suggests that SWFs can help insulate budgets from sustained revenue increases during commodity price booms, supporting countercyclical behavior. By contrast, fiscal rules do not appear to materially shape fiscal dynamics over the commodity cycle in energy exporters (figure 4.11.B).

Metal exporters

In metal exporters, SWFs show little systematic association with spending dynamics over the commodity cycle, but fiscal rules appear to provide a more effective stabilizing anchor (figures 4.11.C and 4.11.D). In countries with fiscal rules, spending growth is relatively restrained during booms—about 3.1 percent—and rises to 5.8 percent during slumps, consistent with building buffers in good times and greater support when conditions deteriorate. By contrast, metal exporters without fiscal rules show a less varied spending pattern over the cycle, suggesting less saving during booms and weaker stabilization during slumps. These results indicate that the countercyclical pattern documented for metal exporters is concentrated among countries that have adopted fiscal rules. Fiscal rules therefore appear to be associated with improved spending discipline during booms, supporting stronger primary balances and fiscal sustainability.

Agricultural exporters

Fiscal policy frameworks appear to be less effective at offsetting fiscal pressures across agricultural exporters. Primary spending displays similar procyclical tendencies in countries with and without SWFs (figure 4.11.E). The lack of a statistically significant difference in spending

FIGURE 4.11 Primary expenditure growth during commodity booms and slumps

Primary expenditure growth over commodity cycles differs significantly depending on the fiscal frameworks in place. In energy exporters, SWFs are associated with spending restraint during booms, allowing more expenditure stabilization during slumps. Fiscal rules are associated with more countercyclical expenditure in metal exporters, where spending is restrained during booms and rises during slumps. Among agricultural exporters, by contrast, fiscal rules and SWFs show relatively limited stabilizing effects.

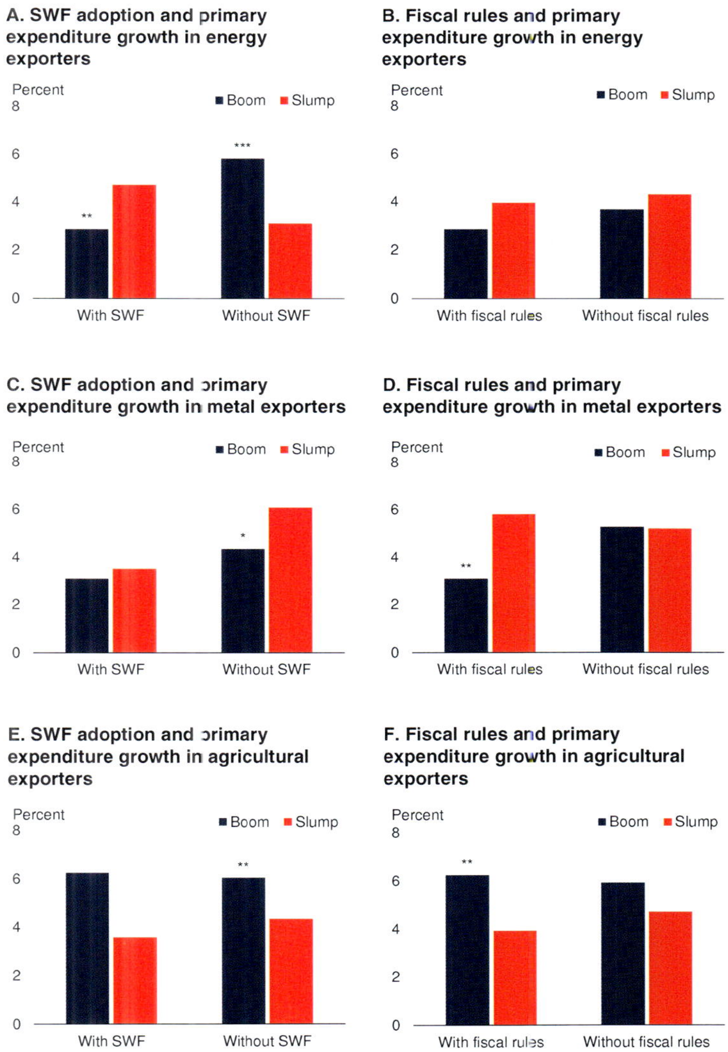

Sources: Alonso et al. (2025); Global SWF (database); International Monetary Fund; World Bank.

Note: EMDEs = emerging market and developing economies; SWF = sovereign wealth fund. Panels show median changes in primary expenditure during commodity price booms and slumps.

***, **, and * denote statistically significant differences between boom and slump episodes at the 1, 5, and 10 percent levels, respectively, based on a non-parametric *k*-sample test. Results distinguish between commodity exporters with and without SWFs (panels A, C, and E) and fiscal rules (panels B, D, and F).

A.–F. Samples include 33 energy-exporting EMDEs (panels A–B), 25 metal-exporting EMDEs (panels C–D), and 37 agricultural-exporting EMDEs (panels E–F).

across booms and slumps in countries with SWFs is therefore more likely to reflect limited SWF adoption and small-sample uncertainty than to reflect evidence that SWFs improve stabilization in this group. Fiscal rules—the primary instruments adopted by agricultural exporters—also show little association with fiscal stabilization. In fact, they coincide with a sharper slowdown in spending during slumps, reinforcing rather than dampening fiscal pressures. In countries with fiscal rules, spending growth rises by about 6.2 percent in boom years but slows to 3.9 percent in slumps (figure 4.11.F). That fiscal rules have not translated into meaningful fiscal stabilization likely reflects the broader structural constraints facing many of these countries. Weak public institutions, narrow revenue bases, and limited enforcement capacity can reduce the effectiveness of fiscal rules regardless of their formal design.

Policy priorities

Commodity prices have been buffeted by repeated shocks since the beginning of this decade, most recently by the significant disruptions caused by the conflict in the Middle East. At the same time, commodity price swings have intensified in the 2020s, with price cycles becoming shorter and booms more pronounced than in the past (World Bank 2025). These shifts reflect both short-term shocks—including the pandemic, geopolitical tensions, conflicts, and extreme weather events—and longer-term forces related to the energy transition, climate-related supply risks, and rising geoeconomic fragmentation. The high frequency of commodity market disruptions in recent years has exerted renewed pressure on existing fiscal frameworks in commodity-exporting EMDEs. Evidence in this chapter suggests that while these frameworks can support fiscal management over commodity cycles, their effectiveness is often more limited when governments face acute spending pressures from large price shocks. Policy action is therefore needed to place countries on a firmer footing to manage the fiscal implications of future swings in commodity prices.

Need for policy action

Commodity price volatility complicates revenue and debt management and hinders the accumulation of fiscal buffers. When commodity prices rise, the incentives to spend are often strong and immediate, while the costs of doing so—such as rising debt and reduced fiscal space—accumulate gradually and often become evident only when prices fall. Breaking this cycle is a key policy challenge. It requires policy makers to make difficult choices during cyclical upswings, resist the temptation to translate temporary windfalls into permanent spending commitments, and design budgets that can withstand downturns without forcing cuts to essential spending. Preserving fiscal space through buffer accumulation can help smooth adjustment during downturns, limiting the need for abrupt fiscal consolidation that often reduces employment and wages, and increases inequality.

A related challenge is the pronounced procyclicality of fiscal policy in commodity exporters. Instead of smoothing the economic cycle, fiscal policy in these economies tends to amplify it, fueling expansions during booms and deepening contractions during slumps. This is not simply a consequence of revenue volatility; it also reflects weak institutional frameworks that fail to constrain discretionary spending during revenue windfalls. The empirical analysis in the chapter reinforces this pattern of procyclicality in commodity exporters: in the face of commodity price shocks, revenue windfalls tend to be absorbed through higher spending over time, while revenue shortfalls are met with expenditure cuts.

These spending responses reflect a combination of distinct constraints that operate differently across phases of the commodity price cycle. During booms, the binding constraints are often political and institutional rather than financial: windfall revenues intensify distributional pressures from multiple competing groups, and weak institutional checks allow transfers, public wages, and other current spending to expand rapidly, consistent with the voracity effect documented in resource-rich economies (Tornell and Lane 1999). During busts, by contrast, fiscal adjustment is typically shaped by financial constraints, as falling revenues coincide with tighter access to external financing and rising sovereign risk premiums. This may force procyclical consolidation episodes, often with public investment bearing a disproportionate share of the adjustment (Ardanaz et al. 2021).

Another dimension of fiscal fragility lies in the accumulation of spending rigidities arising from poorly targeted subsidies and hidden fiscal liabilities. Energy subsidies and price controls remain a significant drag on fiscal space in commodity-exporting EMDEs, diverting resources away from pressing development needs and increasing debt sustainability risks. These subsidies and price controls are frequently expanded when energy prices spike—such as following the oil price surge in late 2020 and 2022—to shield domestic consumers from price pressures or to distribute resource wealth broadly (Akcura 2025). These measures, however, tend to become entrenched and are politically and administratively costly to reverse when fiscal conditions deteriorate, potentially weakening debt management over time. In Argentina, for example, the use of commodity windfalls to finance increasingly rigid expenditures, notably energy subsidies, has emerged as a significant fiscal concern, contributing to recurrent difficulties in public debt management (IMF 2024b; World Bank 2024a).

Beyond subsidies, fiscal space can also be constrained by contingent liabilities resulting from the exposure of SOEs to the commodity export sector, especially in highly commodity-dependent countries. A negative commodity price shock can directly impact fiscal positions through lower tax revenues, dividends, and growing needs for financial support—notably through budgeted and unbudgeted transfers, debt servicing on account of SOEs, and recapitalization needs.

Underlying all of these challenges is a structural dependence on commodity revenues that leaves fiscal positions inherently fragile, constrains fiscal room for maneuver, and increases volatility in growth and employment outcomes. Commodity-exporting EMDEs lag other EMDEs in domestic revenue mobilization, generally reflecting weak tax administration and reliance on volatile resource revenues. They also collect a smaller share of total revenues from more stable non-tax revenues, such as social contributions, than other EMDEs. These patterns also reflect some commodity-specific characteristics. For example, revenues in agricultural exporters are often harder to tax, reflecting diffuse production structures and relatively large informal sectors. Limited revenue predictability and weak tax collection restrict fiscal space, hinder countercyclical policy, and heighten vulnerability to commodity price swings. Moreover, declining external aid further underscores the need to strengthen domestic revenue mobilization for LICs in particular.

In light of these challenges, commodity-exporting EMDEs have multiple policy options to manage the short- and long-term fiscal implications of commodity price swings. While priorities will vary depending on country-specific circumstances, strengthening fiscal resilience requires targeted policy action along three interrelated pillars: bolstering fiscal policy frameworks, strengthening non-resource revenue mobilization, and promoting economic diversification to reduce commodity reliance over the long run.

Bolstering fiscal policy frameworks

Fiscal rules

Fiscal rules are an important tool for strengthening fiscal governance and preserving fiscal space (World Bank 2024a). This is particularly relevant for commodity-exporting EMDEs, where fiscal space is key to macroeconomic stabilization and safeguarding employment, allowing governments to cushion shocks and avoid procyclical cuts when aggregate demand and labor markets are weak. The presence of fiscal rules has been linked to improvements in fiscal sustainability, including stronger fiscal balances and lower sovereign risk premiums (Caselli and Reynaud 2020; Islamaj, Samano, and Sommers 2024). The chapter finds similar evidence for commodity exporters: fiscal rules are associated with more prudent fiscal management, particularly in metal exporters, where they help smooth public spending over commodity price cycles. These rules, however, appear to be less effective at curbing spending pressures following commodity price shocks. This contrast highlights a central challenge for commodity exporters: designing fiscal rules that can withstand the uncertainty and volatility of

FIGURE 4.12 Characteristics of fiscal rules in EMDEs

The adoption of fiscal rules varies widely across commodity-exporting EMDEs. Metal and energy exporters rely more heavily on debt rules, whereas deficit rules are more prevalent in agricultural exporters. Although fiscal rules in commodity exporters are often well anchored in legislation, such rules' coverage of the public sector remains weaker than in other EMDEs. Many commodity exporters have also adopted enforcement provisions for implementing rules, but only a few complement these provisions with formal correction mechanisms. Flexibility provisions also vary widely across commodity exporter groups.

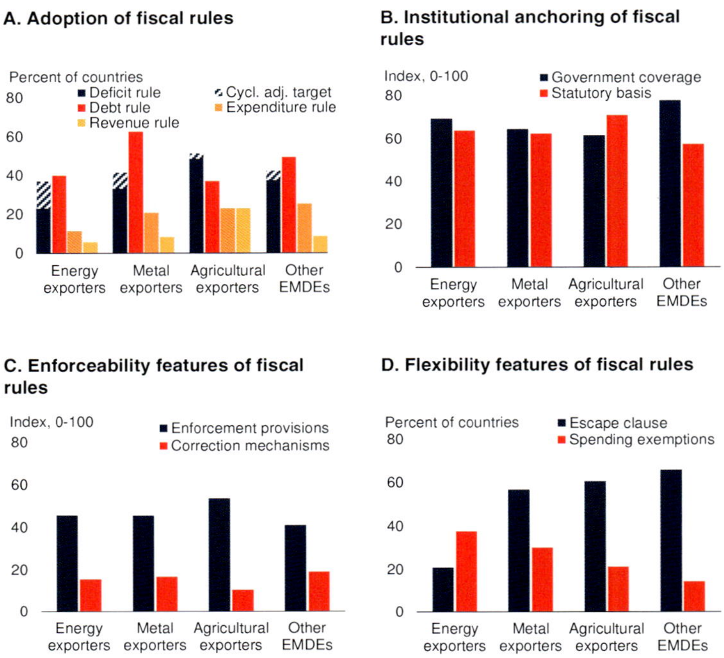

Sources: Alonso et al. (2025); International Monetary Fund; World Bank.

Note: Cycl. adj. target = Deficit rule with cyclically-adjusted constraint. EMDEs = emerging market and developing economies. Data are for 2024.

A. Sample includes 35 energy-exporting EMDEs, 24 metal-exporting EMDEs, 35 agricultural-exporting EMDEs, and 59 other EMDEs.

B.C. Sample includes 16 energy-exporting EMDEs, 15 metal-exporting EMDEs, 19 agricultural-exporting EMDEs, and 35 other EMDEs. Bars show average index scores of fiscal rule design features, derived from Alonso et al. (2025) and normalized on a 0–100 scale (100 = best). Higher values indicate greater use or sophistication of each feature.

B. Statutory basis measures the legal foundation of the fiscal rule(s) in place. The index captures the legal basis of fiscal rules, ranging from political commitment and coalition agreement to statutory law, international treaty, and constitutional provision. It is normalized on a 0–100 scale, with higher values indicating a stronger legal basis. Where multiple legal bases apply, including cases involving both national and supranational rules, the highest applicable basis is selected.

D. Sample includes 16 energy-exporting EMDEs, 15 metal-exporting EMDEs, 19 agricultural-exporting EMDEs, and 35 other EMDEs.

commodity revenues, and rapid changes in the macroeconomic environment (Gootjes and Vasishtha forthcoming).

Effectively managing the impact of commodity price volatility through fiscal rules requires a framework that provides clear guidance for policy. The choice of rule—or combination of rules—therefore matters. Deficit rules have generally proven more effective than other types of rules in promoting fiscal discipline, in part because they can link short-term policy decisions to longer-term sustainability (World Bank 2026b). Yet many commodity exporters—especially metal exporters—rely more heavily on debt rules, even though these rules offer more limited guidance for routine fiscal management (figure 4.12.A). To promote fiscal sustainability, debt rules can be made more effective when paired with an operational rule that guides annual policy and, in commodity exporters, is aligned with the commodity cycle.

Calibration of fiscal constraints is central. Fiscal rules that adjust for cyclical conditions, including commodity price fluctuations, can make fiscal constraints more binding when economic performance is robust, strengthening the incentives to build fiscal buffers. They can also allow greater flexibility during downturns, supporting countercyclical policy and helping insulate the budget from large and persistent shocks (Eyraud, Gbohoui, and Medas 2023).

By contrast, rigid rules can be poorly timed: too loose to restrain spending during commodity booms and too tight when prices collapse, forcing procyclical spending patterns. Chile's structural balance rule remains the benchmark example of a commodity-linked framework because it adjusts fiscal targets for the economic cycle and long-run copper prices. Some countries have even adopted non-resource or non-oil fiscal targets that exclude volatile resource revenues and focus policy on the underlying fiscal stance. Examples include Azerbaijan, Ecuador, and Papua New Guinea (Alonso et al. 2025). However, these approaches remain relatively rare, with only 38 percent of energy exporters, 20 percent of metal exporters, and 5 percent of agricultural exporters adjusting fiscal constraints for cyclical conditions. The limited use partly reflects the demands of establishing such rules: reliable data, credible revenue estimates, and strong technical and administrative capacity are essential.

Sound design features can further strengthen rule effectiveness. Although fiscal rules in commodity exporters are often well anchored in legislation, their coverage of the public sector is lower than in other EMDEs (figure 4.12.B). Broad public-sector coverage can be important because it reduces the scope for shifting deficits across levels of government or outside of the government's perimeter, thereby reducing the risk that fiscal pressures and contingent liabilities accumulate beyond the reach of the rule. Many commodity exporters have also adopted enforcement provisions to strengthen compliance (figure 4.12.C). These provisions specify the adjustments required under binding constraints and establish procedures for monitoring adherence to fiscal rules. However, only a small share of commodity exporters complements these provisions with formal correction mechanisms, which trigger automatic corrective actions when fiscal rules are breached and fiscal adjustment proves insufficient. These mechanisms are present in 16 percent of energy exporters, 17 percent of metal exporters, and 11 percent of agricultural exporters. In countries where correction mechanisms are introduced within the broader rule framework, a reduction in sovereign spreads tends to follow (Acalin, Martinez, and Roch 2025).

Flexibility provisions are also important, but they must be implemented with appropriate discipline. Escape clauses allow for temporary deviations during major shocks, which can be crucial for creating fiscal space in times of crisis, as seen during the COVID-19 pandemic. However, escape clauses need clear activation criteria and a credible path back to the rule (World Bank 2026b). These clauses remain unevenly used: only 21 percent of energy exporters include escape clauses in their fiscal rule frameworks (figure 4.12.D). Fiscal rules can also protect priority spending, including public investment, from excessive cuts during commodity price slumps. Investment carve-outs remain uncommon, especially among agricultural exporters. When well designed, these provisions can preserve growth-enhancing expenditure during fiscal consolidation episodes (Ardanaz et al. 2021). However, spending exemptions must be narrowly defined and backed by transparent fiscal reporting to prevent abuse and safeguard long-term fiscal sustainability (World Bank 2026b).[11]

For commodity exporters with fiscal rules, the policy priority is not simply to add more design features but to make rules fit for purpose. Frameworks need to be strong enough to bind during booms, flexible enough to accommodate severe downturns, broad enough to limit circumvention, and simple enough to monitor and enforce. Greater sophistication can improve stabilization where data, forecasting capacity, and institutions are strong. Where these foundations are weaker, however, overly complex rules may reduce transparency and credibility. International templates are therefore unlikely to work without adaptation to domestic fiscal challenges, technical and administrative capacity, and the structure of commodity dependence (World Bank 2026b).

Where fiscal rules are absent, commodity exporters may benefit from adopting them, but establishing credibility is essential. Credibility, in turn, depends not only on sound design but also on the adoption environment. The first years after adoption are especially important because political commitment is still being tested and consensus around the rule may remain fragile. The economic and political context at adoption can therefore act as either a tailwind or a headwind, shaping early performance in ways that may have lasting effects on the credibility and effectiveness of the rule (Fatás, Gootjes, and Mawejje 2026). Complementary institutions also play an important role. For instance, fiscal councils can strengthen monitoring, enhance transparency, and support rule implementation. Embedding fiscal rules in a medium-term fiscal framework can further boost compliance and strengthen credibility by aligning annual budgets with medium-term fiscal planning. However, building and sustaining these institutions often requires strong state capacity—a foundation that may be lacking in many commodity-exporting EMDEs, especially LICs.

Sovereign wealth funds

SWFs can be effective instruments for fiscal stabilization, especially for energy-exporting

[11] Exemptions from fiscal constraints can create scope for creative accounting. In practice, the boundary between investment and consumption spending is often blurred, leaving room for governments to reclassify expenditures and circumvent the rule. This risk is material: spending exemptions are associated with a significantly lower likelihood that fiscal rules trigger fiscal adjustment (World Bank 2026b). Strong fiscal transparency is therefore essential to prevent misuse and ensure that fiscal rule design continues to support credible adjustment (Gootjes and de Haan 2022; Milesi-Ferretti 2004).

EMDEs. By channeling windfall revenues into a dedicated savings vehicle, governments can insulate the budget from immediate spending pressures and accumulate buffers to sustain expenditure during downturns. As commodity markets become more exposed to larger shocks and more volatile price cycles, well-designed SWFs may become increasingly important for managing the fiscal risks associated with commodity dependence.

SWF effectiveness depends critically on the quality of the institutional environment in which they operate—an environment that can support the credibility of withdrawal rules, the transparency of fund management, and the degree of political insulation from spending pressures (Çiçekçi and Gaygısız 2023). For energy exporters, where SWFs are most prevalent, the priority is to strengthen the fiscal institutions that support their operation and integrate SWFs more closely into the broader fiscal policy framework. For example, about 40 percent of energy exporters had established a mix of fiscal rules and SWFs by 2024 (figure 4.13.A).

For metal exporters, the results suggest that fiscal rules have been an effective sustainability anchor, so the case for SWFs should be evaluated against institutional capacity and the scale of commodity-related fiscal revenues. Where metal exporters have adopted SWFs, most funds are explicitly designed to smooth commodity revenues for stabilization purposes (figure 4.13.B). For agricultural exporters, the case is more limited. Compared with energy and metal exporters, existing funds in these economies are linked far more often to general budget savings than to commodity flows, and their core mandates tend to emphasize strategic investment rather than savings or stabilization objectives. Where feasible, these countries could seek to progressively link a share of commodity windfall revenues to existing funds or stabilization mechanisms.

Commodity exporters' experiences illustrate why design and institutional discipline matter. SWFs can help contain spending pressures during commodity price shocks, though these stabilizing effects may not persist over the medium term if withdrawal rules are frequently bypassed or funds are used to finance persistent expenditure commitments. The experience of Timor-Leste, for example, illustrates these challenges. The country established its Petroleum Fund in 2005 to manage oil and gas revenues, with a rule designed to limit annual withdrawals to a sustainable share of total petroleum wealth. Early on, the framework worked as intended: transfers to the budget remained below the ceiling, and the fund accumulated rapidly. Beginning in 2009, however, repeated excess withdrawals were made to finance large infrastructure projects and recurrent expenditures. Expenditures became closely tied to oil price movements, undermining the fund's stabilizing function and raising concerns about depletion given the limited expected remaining lifetime of the country's oil fields (World Bank 2024a).

Timor-Leste's experience underscores that even well-designed SWFs lose effectiveness if escape clauses are frequently invoked and institutional safeguards cannot prevent procyclical drawdowns. By contrast, Chile's experience has been more favorable (World Bank 2024a). During the 2008–09 global financial crisis, Chile was able to respond to the sharp contraction in economic activity and the decline in export prices by deploying resources from its stabilization fund to support fiscal expansion (IMF 2009). This policy space reflected prudent saving during the preceding commodity price boom. Between 2003 and 2008, Chile's Economic and Social Stabilization Fund accumulated more than $20 billion, which was subsequently drawn down to finance countercyclical measures. As a result, fiscal policy was able to cushion the downturn without undermining debt sustainability.

Fiscal councils

Commodity-exporting EMDEs would benefit from wider use of fiscal councils. The primary role of fiscal councils is to reduce the opacity surrounding public finances, strengthen accountability, and raise the reputational cost of deviations from stated fiscal objectives (Beetsma et al. 2019). By providing independent, nonpartisan assessments of the fiscal stance, debt sustainability, and compliance with fiscal rules, fiscal councils can make policy slippages harder to justify and improve the credibility of the broader fiscal framework (Alonso et al. 2025). Fiscal councils can also scrutinize the forecasts underlying the budget, thereby helping to reduce the risk that budgets are built on optimistic projections.

Despite their benefits, independent fiscal councils remain relatively uncommon among commodity-exporting EMDEs. Adoption has increased since 2000, but it has done so from a very low base and at a slower pace than in commodity importers. In energy exporters, in particular, fiscal councils remain rare despite the sophistication of fiscal frameworks in some of these countries. Beyond capacity constraints, this limited adoption may reflect the political economy of fiscal transparency. Independent fiscal councils can reduce information asymmetries between voters and policy makers, helping voters assess fiscal competence and discouraging opportunistic fiscal behavior (Beetsma, Debrun, and Sloof 2022). This makes political support for fiscal councils conditional: where voters place less weight on fiscal competence or where incumbents enjoy strong political advantages, governments may have little incentive to create institutions that expose policy choices to independent scrutiny.

This mechanism is particularly relevant for commodity exporters. Resource revenues are volatile, uncertain, and often politically valuable because they give governments discretion over windfall spending. A fiscal council that scrutinizes commodity-price assumptions, production forecasts, and resource-revenue projections can make temporary windfalls harder to present as permanent fiscal space. That strengthens accountability, but it also raises the political cost of discretionary control over resource revenues.

Political incentives may also shape the design of fiscal councils where they are adopted. Fiscal councils differ in their mandate, responsibilities, instruments, and accountability. If governments face pressure to demonstrate commitment to fiscal discipline but are reluctant to subject policy choices to meaningful independent scrutiny, they may establish councils with limited resources, weak legal mandates, or insufficient access to information (Beetsma, Debrun, and Sloof 2022). This concern is particularly relevant for commodity exporters: compared with other EMDEs,

FIGURE 4.13 Fiscal frameworks, revenue dependence, and structural vulnerabilities

Many commodity exporters have strengthened their fiscal frameworks by adopting a combination of fiscal rules, SWFs, and fiscal councils. The mix of frameworks and their characteristics vary across countries. Boosting domestic non-resource revenue mobilization is a key priority—particularly in energy exporters. Reforming poorly targeted subsidies is crucial in many commodity-exporting EMDEs for bolstering public finances. Furthermore, achieving economic diversification remains a challenge, especially for energy exporters.

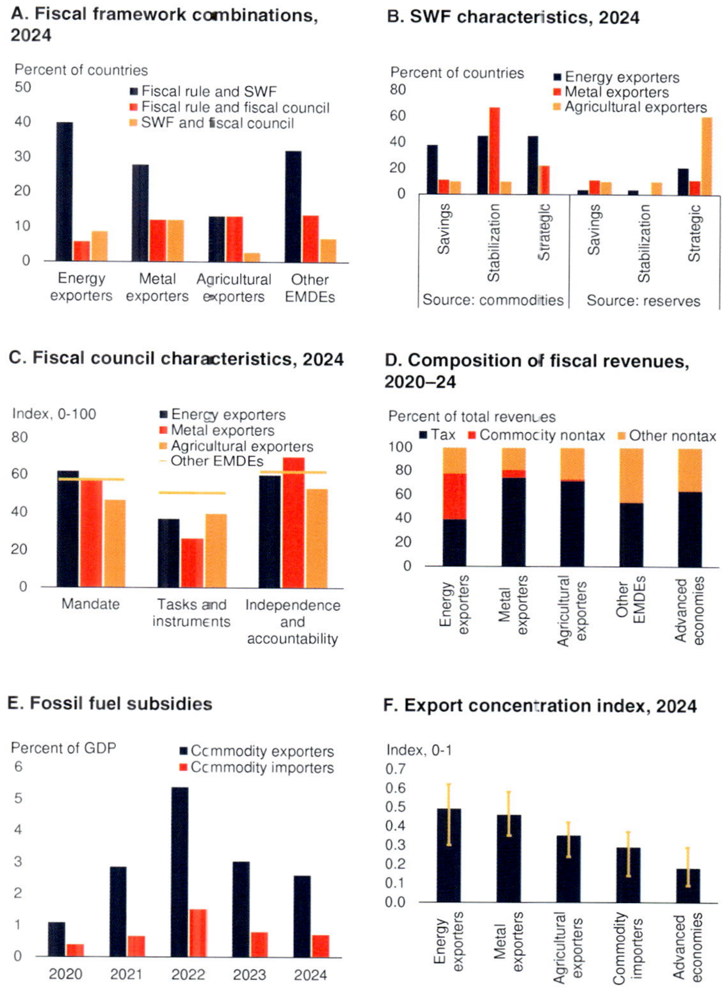

Sources: Alonso et al. (2025); Fossil Fuel Subsidy Tracker; Global SWF (database); International Monetary Fund; UN Trade and Development (UNCTAD); World Bank.

Note: EMDEs = emerging market and developing economies; SWF = sovereign wealth fund.

A. Sample of EMDEs includes 35 energy exporters, 24 metal exporters, 35 agricultural exporters, and 59 other EMDEs.

B. EMDE sample includes 23 energy exporters, 9 metal exporters, and 10 agricultural exporters. SWFs are distinguished by their core mandate—savings (or future-generation) funds, stabilization (or "rainy-day") funds, and strategic (or development) funds—as well as their main source of funding: commodity revenues and excess foreign exchange reserves.

C. EMDE sample includes 3 energy exporters, 4 metal exporters, 5 agricultural exporters, and 8 other EMDEs. Higher values of the index indicate stronger institutional features. Details can be found in Alonso et al. (2025).

D. Sample includes 90 commodity-exporting EMDEs (34 for energy, 22 for metals, 34 for agriculture), 58 other EMDEs, and 38 advanced economies. Commodity nontax revenues include direct revenue from extractive activities. Other nontax revenues include social contributions, grants, and other miscellaneous types of revenue.

E. Bars show the weighted average of fossil fuel subsidies as a percent of GDP. Sample includes 91 commodity-exporting EMDEs and 54 commodity importers.

F. Bars show the unweighted average of the product concentration index of exports. A larger value denotes a higher concentration of exports. Sample includes 35 energy-exporting EMDEs, 24 metal-exporting EMDEs, 38 agricultural-exporting EMDEs, 59 commodity-importing EMDEs, and 38 advanced economies. Whiskers indicate the interquartile range.

commodity exporters score noticeably lower on the tasks-and-instruments dimension, which captures councils' ability to inform the public and influence the budget process through public reports, media visibility, and a formal role in budget preparation (figure 4.13.C).

The experience of Chile suggests that when independent oversight is credible and integrated into the fiscal framework, it can strengthen discipline during booms and preserve fiscal space during downturns. Even before the establishment of a formal fiscal council, the country's structural balance rule implemented in 2001 was supported by relatively strong institutional arrangements. Independent expert committees used transparent methodologies to estimate potential GDP and long-run copper prices, helping anchor the rule's credibility and reduce fiscal procyclicality (Barreix et al. 2019). In 2006, Chile further strengthened its framework through a fiscal responsibility law that formally established a SWF. This framework helped support prudent fiscal management during the 2000s commodity boom: Chile saved a large share of copper-related windfalls and built substantial buffers, which were later deployed after copper prices collapsed in 2008 without undermining fiscal sustainability (Céspedes, Parrado, and Velasco 2014). More recently, however, fiscal performance has weakened, with repeated deviations from structural targets and more limited buffer replenishment following the pandemic, highlighting the challenges of sustaining discipline and preserving fiscal space over time. Chile's experience thus illustrates both the potential benefits and the limits of comprehensive fiscal frameworks in commodity-exporting economies, underscoring the importance of strong institutions not only for framework design but also for effective and sustained implementation.

Public debt management frameworks

While fiscal rules may set limits on fiscal aggregates and help constrain the debt path, public debt management (PDM) frameworks govern the structure and risk profile of the borrowing used to finance that path. They comprise the legal, institutional, and operational arrangements through which governments meet financing needs while managing the cost and risk of the public debt portfolio. Effective PDM frameworks require a clear legal mandate, transparent accountability, a medium-term debt management strategy, reliable debt recording and reporting, and coordination with fiscal and monetary policy (IMF and World Bank 2014; Jonasson and Papaioannou 2018). Active monitoring of risks—including those related to refinancing, interest rates, currency movements, liquidity, and operational vulnerabilities—is also essential.

PDM frameworks are especially important for commodity exporters because commodity price downturns can weaken revenues, raise financing needs, and tighten market access simultaneously. In this context, debt management should go beyond securing low-cost financing and place greater weight on balance sheet resilience. A medium-term debt management strategy should incorporate adverse commodity price scenarios, smooth redemption profiles, limit exposure to excessive exchange rate movements, and coordinate borrowing plans with cash buffers and SWFs (IMF and World Bank 2019). Peru provides a useful example of how stronger debt management—by lengthening maturities, developing local-currency debt markets, and reducing exchange-rate risk—preserved market access and strengthened resilience to commodity shocks (IMF 2024a).

In addition, PDM frameworks should support the monitoring and disclosure of contingent liabilities, particularly those linked to SOEs, guarantees, public-private partnerships, and resource-backed borrowing (chapter 3, box 3.1). This helps ensure that debt-related risks outside the general government perimeter are transparently recorded and incorporated into broader fiscal risk assessments. In Mexico, for instance, the major state-owned oil enterprise, Pemex, has emerged as a significant contingent liability for the central government (IMF 2025). Finally, PDM frameworks can also help anchor expenditure discipline. In many EMDEs, commodity windfalls have been accompanied by an expansion of rigid spending programs, which become difficult to reverse once favorable price conditions fade and can give rise to debt vulnerabilities over time. Energy subsidies are a common example.

Strengthening non-resource revenue mobilization

In addition to bolstering fiscal frameworks, diversification of revenue sources beyond commodity exports is essential for fiscal sustainability in commodity exporters. This is particularly important for energy exporters, where resource revenues have historically substituted for broader tax effort (figure 4.13.D). Increased and more stable domestic revenues provide fiscal room for maneuver, enabling higher investment in infrastructure, healthcare, and education, which boosts medium-term growth. In addition, more stable sources of revenue can reduce volatility in public spending and help avoid procyclical fiscal policies.

Policies to boost domestic revenue mobilization rest on four interrelated pillars: the tax base, tax administration, subsidy schemes, and institutions and governance frameworks. Concrete measures to broaden the tax base include eliminating exemptions, deductions, and loopholes that erode revenues. However, even where tax policy frameworks are well designed, collection often falls short of potential. Investing in modernizing tax administration through digitalization can help address this issue. Reforms to poorly targeted subsidies in many commodity-exporting EMDEs can help make their economies and public finances more resilient to commodity price fluctuations (figure 4.13.E). For example, many energy exporters undertook energy subsidy reforms following the 2014–16 oil price plunge to discourage wasteful energy consumption, reallocate spending to programs better targeted to the poor, and restore fiscal space (IMF 2017; World Bank 2020a; World Bank 2020b). Finally, improving governance and institutions is critical: stronger institutions, better rule of law, and reduced corruption are all associated with improved tax compliance and more effective tax collection.

Promoting economic diversification

The implications of the conflict in the Middle East have reinforced the need for energy exporters to promote economic diversification over the long run. As of 2024, energy-exporting EMDEs exhibited a higher degree of export concentration than both other commodity exporters and commodity-importing EMDEs (figure 4.13.F). More broadly, EMDEs that are heavily reliant on commodity production are vulnerable to instability in export earnings and fiscal revenues. Reducing commodity reliance over time can mitigate the macroeconomic volatility induced by commodity fluctuations and help strengthen fiscal resilience. Evidence from cross-country analyses indicates that diversifying exports and government revenue streams away from commodities enhances long-term growth prospects and bolsters resilience to external shocks (Hesse 2008; Papageorgiou and Spatafora 2012; World Bank 2018). Yet despite its apparent economic benefits, achieving diversification remains a challenge (Diop, Marotta, and de Melo 2012).[12]

For fossil fuel exporters, the form that diversification takes matters considerably. Traditional diversification involves moving from fossil fuel extraction to add value in domestic fuel processing and fuel-intensive manufacturing (Peszko et al. 2020). Although such diversification strategies help to hedge against cyclical risks in commodity markets, they also heighten structural vulnerabilities to the low-carbon transition by deepening economic dependence on traditional carbon-intensive industries. By contrast, asset diversification focuses on diversifying the underlying wealth—a broader portfolio of physical, human, and natural capital (Gill et al. 2014). It involves investing resource rents in education, innovation, and renewable energy and represents a more robust long-term strategy for fossil-fuel exporters (Peszko et al. 2020). Insights from the World Bank's Country Climate and Development Reports indicate that countries where fossil fuels dominate export revenues (such as Angola, Azerbaijan, Colombia, and Iraq) face particularly acute risks related to the low-carbon transition, underscoring the urgency of expanding into manufacturing, services, and clean energy (World Bank 2024c).

[12] Moreover, the academic literature offers little guidance. For oil-exporting countries, efforts to identify factors associated with success and failure in diversification have been constrained by substantial data gaps (Ross 2017).

Multiple policy levers can facilitate economic diversification (World Bank 2022). A strong starting point is implementing regulatory reforms to improve the business climate and attract investment into alternative sectors, gradually scaling up productive capacity over time. Beyond the investment climate, policies can encourage firms to undertake multiple stages of production—vertical diversification—as well as broaden their output mix through horizontal diversification, with an emphasis on innovation and technological upgrading (Cherif and Hasanov 2014). Furthermore, managing resource rents in ways that support productive-capacity building and infrastructure development can help reduce trade costs and enable participation in regional and global value chains. In high-income Gulf Cooperation Council countries, SWFs are being increasingly used to promote domestic diversification, including by financing sectors such as green energy and tourism (World Bank 2026c). These efforts can be further underpinned by investment in education and skills development, with a focus on learning outcomes that equip the workforce to support a more diversified economy, thereby boosting employment and growth.

Examples of relatively successful diversification experiences reveal diverse, context-specific pathways rather than a "one-size-fits-all" approach, while also highlighting the role of natural endowments as well as external factors. One such example is Indonesia. Plummeting oil prices in the 1980s provided an opportunity for economic reforms that ignited growth in the non-resource sector. Major policy changes included banking sector reforms to ease entry barriers and remove credit subsidies, accompanied by a gradual reduction in import tariffs and the dismantling of non-tariff barriers (Temple 2003). These changes boosted manufacturing export growth and productivity in the sector. The country's size, large domestic market, natural endowments for agribusiness and labor-intensive manufacturing, and favorable demographics supported economic diversification (Lashitew, Ross, and Werker 2021). The experience of Indonesia suggests that active diversification policies can yield results under favorable conditions, including access to markets and foreign technologies.

Oman's diversification experience over the past five decades presents a less successful example. Although the manufacturing sector has registered robust growth in nominal terms since the 1980s, structural transformation remains an ambition. The manufacturing sector's share of GDP has remained under 10 percent, largely because much of its growth was driven by resource-based processed goods such as petrochemicals rather than new industries. When oil prices collapsed in 2014–16, the fiscal deficit exceeded 20 percent of GDP, illustrating that the underlying fiscal structure had changed little despite decades of reform effort, and fiscal revenues and exports remained tied to oil market developments (World Bank 2019, 2024b). Oman has lagged its high-income peers in R&D expenditure, credit access, new firm entry rates, and tertiary education enrollment—all of which are essential enabling factors for diversification (Lashitew, Ross, and Werker 2021). To mitigate the vulnerabilities related to reliance on hydrocarbon exports, Oman has implemented various structural reforms under its Vision 2040 (Chattha et al. 2025). These include diversifying export markets, developing logistics and port infrastructure, encouraging private-sector investment, and promoting tourism.

TABLE 4.1 Economies in the sample

Commodity exporters	
Agriculture	Argentina; Belize; Benin; Brazil; Burundi; Cabo Verde; Chad; Comoros; Costa Rica; Côte d'Ivoire; Ethiopia; Fiji; Gambia, The; Greenland; Guatemala; Guinea-Bissau; Honduras; Kenya; Lao PDR; Madagascar; Malawi; Mali; Nicaragua; Paraguay; Rwanda; São Tomé and Príncipe*; Senegal; Seychelles; Solomon Islands; Sudan; Tajikistan; Tanzania; Togo; Uganda; Ukraine; Uruguay; Uzbekistan; West Bank and Gaza*; Zimbabwe.
Metals	Armenia; Bhutan; Botswana; Burkina Faso; Central African Republic; Chile; Congo, Dem. Rep.; Eritrea; Guinea; Kosovo; Kyrgyz Republic; Liberia; Mauritania; Mongolia; Mozambique; Namibia; Niger; Papua New Guinea; Peru; Sierra Leone; South Africa; Sudan; Suriname; Tajikistan; Zambia.
Energy	Algeria; Angola; Azerbaijan; Bahrain; Bhutan; Bolivia; Brunei Darussalam; Cameroon; Chad; Colombia; Congo, Rep.; Ecuador; Equatorial Guinea; Gabon; Ghana; Guyana; Indonesia; Iran, Islamic Rep.; Iraq; Kazakhstan; Kuwait; Libya*; Myanmar; Nigeria; Oman; Qatar; Russian Federation; Saudi Arabia; South Sudan; Timor-Leste; Trinidad and Tobago; Turkmenistan*; United Arab Emirates; Venezuela, RB*; Yemen, Rep.*
Commodity importers	
Afghanistan; Albania; Antigua and Barbuda; Bahamas, The; Bangladesh; Barbados; Belarus; Bosnia and Herzegovina; Cambodia; China; Djibouti; Dominica; Dominican Republic; Egypt, Arab Rep.; El Salvador; Eswatini; Georgia; Grenada; Haiti; Hungary; India; Jamaica; Jordan; Kiribati; Lebanon; Lesotho; Malaysia; Maldives; Malta; Marshall Islands; Mauritius; Mexico; Micronesia, Fed. Sts.; Moldova; Montenegro; Morocco; Nauru; Nepal; North Macedonia; Pakistan; Palau; Panama; Philippines; Poland; Romania; Samoa; Serbia; Sri Lanka; St. Kitts and Nevis; St. Vincent and the Grenadines; Syrian Arab Republic; Thailand; Tonga; Tunisia; Türkiye; Tuvalu; Vanuatu; Viet Nam.	

Source: World Bank.

Note: Economies that are not included in the local projection regressions are marked with asterisks. An economy is defined as a commodity exporter when, on average in 2017–19, either (1) total commodities exports accounted for 30 percent or more of its total exports, or (2) exports of any single commodity accounted for 20 percent or more of its total exports. Economies for which these thresholds were met as a result of re-exports were excluded. When data were not available, judgment was used. This taxonomy results in the classification of some well-diversified economies as importers, even if they are exporters of certain commodities (for example, Mexico). Commodity export patterns can change over time, which may require recategorization. Commodity importers are EMDEs not classified as commodity exporters.

ANNEX 4.1 Fiscal policy volatility

The framework used to estimate fiscal policy volatility is based on the approach of Fatás and Mihov (2013), which involves estimating a fiscal policy reaction function of the following form:

$$FiscalPolicy_t = \alpha + \beta EconomicActivity_t + \epsilon_t, \quad \text{(A4.1.1)}$$

where *Fiscal Policy* is a variable that captures the stance of fiscal policy, which in this case refers to primary expenditures. *Economic Activity* denotes the cyclical stance of the economy and is represented by annual GDP growth.

β summarizes the cyclical behavior of fiscal policy and indicates whether fiscal policy is countercyclical or procyclical. It is composed of both automatic stabilizers and the discretionary response of governments to economic fluctuations. The residual, ϵ, captures changes in fiscal policy that are unrelated to the business cycle or to the control variables. These decisions can be the result of political decisions (such as changes in tax rates or spending associated with the political cycle) or policy errors (such as mismeasurement of the output gap). The uncertainty associated with the residual can be seen as generating excessive volatility in GDP and, possibly, reduced long-term growth. Following Fatás and Mihov (2013), the volatility of fiscal policy is measured as the standard deviation of the residual in the fiscal policy reaction function (σ_i^ϵ).

Figure 4.6.A shows the estimates when the measure of fiscal policy volatility (σ_i^ϵ) is regressed on dummy variables for commodity exporter type, both with and without resource rents as a control variable.

ANNEX 4.2 Local projections

The dynamic response of government spending to a commodity price shock is estimated using a local projections framework (Jordà 2005):

$$\Delta_h y_{i,t+h} = \beta^h shock_{i,t} + \sum_{p=1}^{2} \phi_p^h shock_{i,t-p} + \sum_{j=1}^{h} k_j^h shock_{i,t+j} + \lambda^h X_{i,t} + \alpha_i^h + \varepsilon_{i,t+h};$$
$$h = 0,1,\ldots,5 \quad \text{(A4.2.1)}$$

where $\Delta_h y_{i,t+h} \equiv y_{i,t+h} - y_{i,t-1}$ is the long difference in the logarithm of real primary spending in country i, year t; α_i^h are country fixed effects; $shock_{i,t}$ is the commodity price shock; $X_{i,t}$ is a vector of controls; and $\varepsilon_{i,t+h}$ is the error term.

The commodity price shock is measured as the change (in logarithms) in the global commodity price index from the World Bank's commodity prices database. The price index, however, varies by exporter group: the global real energy price index is used for energy exporters in the sample, the real metal price index for metal exporters, and the real agricultural price index for agricultural exporters. Year dummies for the global financial crisis (2009) and the COVID-19 outbreak (2020) are included to control for common global fiscal dynamics.[13] Leads of the shock are included to purge the effect of future shock realizations embedded in long-difference outcomes, following the Teulings-Zubanov (2014) correction, while lags account for persistence in spending dynamics. The control vector $X_{i,t}$ includes lagged primary balances (as a share of GDP), the public-debt-to-GDP ratio, real GDP growth, and inflation (IMF

[13] Year fixed effects are not included in the baseline. Including a full set of year fixed effects would absorb much of the common time-series variation in the commodity price shocks, since the price index varies only by exporter group and year. Full time fixed effects would absorb much of the common global variation in these shocks—especially in group-specific estimations—and would shift identification away from the average fiscal response to global commodity price movements. Instead, the specification controls for major global recession episodes and includes lagged real GDP per capita growth to account for domestic cyclical conditions. Results are nonetheless robust to including time fixed effects, which helps address concerns that the estimates are driven by broader global trends. However, the preferred specification better matches the object of interest: the fiscal response of commodity exporters to global commodity price shocks.

2026). Moreover, it includes indicators for the presence of fiscal rules and councils (Alonso et al. 2025a, 2025b), SWFs (Global SWF database), and a composite measure of the quality of public institutions (Worldwide Governance Indicators database).

The estimation sample is restricted to commodity-exporting EMDEs over 2000–20, with responses traced over horizons $h = 0,\ldots,5$. The upper limit of 2020 ensures that future outcomes and future shock realizations required for the five-year horizon remain available. Driscoll-Kraay standard errors are computed, which are robust to heteroskedasticity, serial correlation, and cross-sectional dependence.

To examine whether the fiscal response differs by the type of commodity exported, the baseline specification is extended by allowing the effect of the commodity price shock to vary across energy, metal, and agricultural exporters. Specifically, for each exporter group, a binary indicator is constructed that identifies whether a commodity-exporting EMDE belongs to that group. The local projection is then re-estimated separately for each group comparison by interacting the contemporaneous commodity price shock, its two lags, and its future leads with the relevant group indicator. This yields separate impulse responses for, for example, energy exporters and non-energy-commodity exporters, metal exporters and non-metal-commodity exporters, and agricultural exporters and non-agricultural-commodity exporters.

The specification is further extended to assess whether formal fiscal frameworks—fiscal rules and SWFs—shape the spending response to commodity price shocks. For each exporter type—energy, metal, and agriculture—the shock, its lags, and its future leads are interacted with both an indicator for the relevant exporter group and an indicator for whether a formal fiscal framework is in place. This triple-interaction specification yields separate impulse responses for exporters with and without fiscal frameworks within each commodity group. The comparison is designed to assess whether fiscal frameworks are associated with a more muted spending response to commodity price shocks and whether this association differs across energy, metal, and agricultural exporters.

FIGURE A4.2.1 Fiscal impacts of asymmetric commodity price shocks

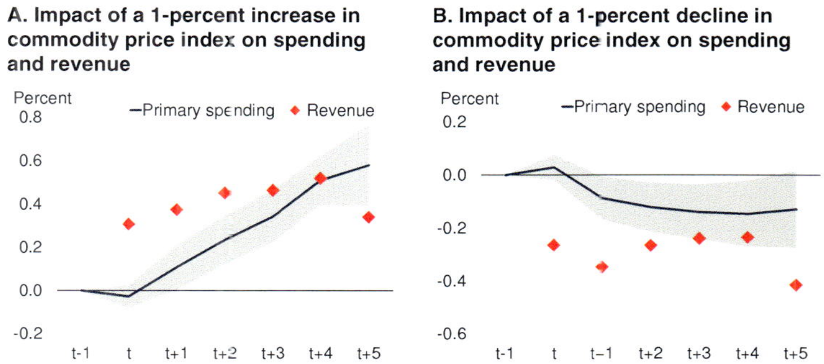

Sources: International Monetary Fund; World Bank.

Note: EMDEs = emerging market and developing economies. Results are from local projection regressions. Technical details are provided in annex 4.2. Lines show the cumulative change in primary expenditure (in percent) in the years following a shock (relative to a no-shock trajectory) to a pooled commodity price index, which uses the World Bank's energy price index for energy exporters, the metal price index for metal exporters, and the agricultural price index for agricultural exporters. To estimate asymmetric effects, the index is split into two components: a positive-shock measure, in which negative values are set to zero, and a negative-shock measure, in which positive values are set to zero. Shaded areas show 90 percent confidence intervals. Results are based on a sample of 88 commodity-exporting EMDEs (31 energy exporters, 24 metal exporters, and 33 agricultural exporters).

To improve comparability between countries with and without fiscal frameworks, the triple-interaction local projections are estimated using an augmented inverse-probability-weighted (AIPW) approach. Following the doubly robust logic, this approach combines inverse-propensity-score weighting with regression adjustment in the local projection (Jordà and Taylor 2025). These weights are based on the predicted probability of having a fiscal framework, estimated from a first-stage probit model that includes macroeconomic controls, exporter-type indicators, and region fixed effects. Countries with fiscal frameworks (fiscal rules, SWFs) receive weights equal to the inverse of the predicted probability of framework adoption, while countries without fiscal frameworks receive weights equal to the inverse of one minus that probability.[14] The weighted local projection then includes the same control vector as that used in the baseline specification. This procedure helps ensure that differences in impulse responses between framework and non-framework countries are not driven mechanically by observable differences in the likelihood of having adopted a fiscal framework.

[14] To limit the influence of observations with extreme predicted probabilities, weights are capped at 10.

ANNEX 4.3 Commodity price cycles

Following the literature, turning points in commodity price series are identified using the algorithm proposed by Balatti (forthcoming), which is based on well-established techniques for dating business cycles. Earlier work by Cashin, McDermott, and Scott (2002), Harding and Pagan (2002), and the World Bank (2022) has extended the methodology to analyze commodity price cycles. Peaks (troughs) in series are identified whenever $\{y_t >(<) y_{t+k}\}$, where $k = 1,\ldots,K$, and $K = 12$, in line with Cashin, McDermott, and Scott (2002). The minimum cycle length is 36 months. After the turning points—peaks and troughs—are identified, the intervals between these points are classified as boom and slump phases.

To identify turning points, the original Bry–Boschan algorithm is modified to account for peculiarities of commodity prices, following Balatti (forthcoming), and building on Cashin, McDermott, and Scott (2002) and Harding and Pagan (2002). Specifically, (1) a phase (peak to trough or trough to peak) must be at least 12 months long, owing to the dominance of the annual production process in many agricultural commodities; (2) a cycle (peak-to-peak or trough-to-trough) must be at least 36 months, which is the minimum time needed to encompass at least two harvests for annual crops; (3) smoothing is not applied to the original price series; (4) the algorithm is applied to the actual level of prices (deflated by the consumer price index), rather than to trend-adjusted price series; and (5) an explicit amplitude restriction is incorporated to prevent the identification of negligible fluctuations as "regular" cycles and to distinguish between boom and slump phases accurately. Calibrated at a 15 percent threshold, this criterion addresses limitations observed in previous methodologies, ensuring that only relevant price movements are classified as cycles.

Balatti (forthcoming) conducted a battery of robustness checks, including alternative model specifications and variations in key assumptions, to ensure that the results are not driven by specific modeling choices. Most notably, alternative minimum-amplitude thresholds for identifying commodity cycles were tested; across these specifications, the identified cycle durations remain consistent. Additionally, for this chapter, the sensitivity of the results to the use of nominal prices to identify commodity-price booms and slumps was tested. The identified turning points and the fiscal dynamics over commodity price cycles remain unchanged.

References

Acalin, J., L. Martinez, and F. Roch. 2025. "Fiscal Rules, Robust Correction Mechanisms, and Sovereign Spreads." IMF Working Paper 25/195, International Monetary Fund, Washington, DC.

Akcura, E. 2025. "Global Stock-Take of Fuel Subsidies and Pricing Policies." Policy Research Working Paper 11154, World Bank, Washington, DC.

Alesina, A., F. Campante, and G. Tabellini. 2008. "Why Is Fiscal Policy Often Procyclical?" *Journal of the European Economic Association* 6 (5): 1006–36.

Alonso, V., C. Arroyo, O. Aydin, V. Balasundharam, H. R. Davoodi, G. Hegab, A. M. Nguyen, N. Salazar Ferro, G. Sher, A. Solovyeva, and N. Tchelishvili. 2025. "Fiscal Rules and Fiscal Councils: Recent Trends and Revisions since the Pandemic." IMF Working Paper 25/198, International Monetary Fund, Washington, DC.

Ardanaz, M., E. Cavallo, A. Izquierdo, and J. Puig. 2021. "Growth-Friendly Fiscal Rules? Safeguarding Public Investment from Budget Cuts Through Fiscal Rule Design." *Journal of International Money and Finance* 111 (March): 102319.

Arezki, R., and M. Bruckner. 2010. "Commodity Windfalls, Polarization, and Net Foreign Assets: Panel Data Evidence on the Voracity Effect." IMF Working Paper 10/209, International Monetary Fund, Washington, DC.

Arezki, R., K. Hamilton, and K. Kazimov. 2011. "Resource Windfalls, Macroeconomic Stability and Economic Growth." IMF Working Paper 11/142, International Monetary Fund, Washington, DC.

Arroyo Marioli, F., A. Fatás, and G. Vasishtha. 2024. "Fiscal Policy Volatility and Growth in Emerging Markets and Developing Economies." *International Review of Economics and Finance* 92 (April): 758–77.

Arroyo Marioli, F., and G. Vasishtha. 2025. "Fiscal Policy Procyclicality and Volatility in Commodity-Exporting Emerging and Developing Economies: Determinants and Implications for Growth." Policy Research Working Paper 11037, World Bank, Washington, DC.

Arroyo Marioli, F., and C. A. Végh. 2026. "Fiscal Procyclicality in Commodity Exporting Countries: How Much Does It Pour and Why?" *American Economic Journal: Economic Policy* 18 (2): 309–45.

Balatti, M. Forthcoming. "Cracking Commodity Cycles: Uncovering the Hidden Clock and Decoding the Drivers." Unpublished.

Barreix, A. D., L. F. Corrales, J. C. Benitez, C. Garcimartín, M. Ardanaz, S. Díaz, R. Cerda, et al. 2019. *Resilient Fiscal Rules in Latin America.* Washington, DC: Inter-American Development Bank.

Basdevant, O., J. Hooley, and E. Imamoglu. 2021. "How to Design a Fiscal Strategy in a Resource-Rich Country." IMF How To Note 2021/01, International Monetary Fund, Washington, DC.

Beetsma, R., X. Debrun, X. Fang, Y. Kim, V. Lledó, S. Mbaye, and X. Zang. 2019. "Independent Fiscal Councils: Recent Trends and Performance." *European Journal of Political Economy* 57 (March): 53–69.

Beetsma, R., X. Debrun, and R. Sloof. 2022. "The Political Economy of Fiscal Transparency and Independent Fiscal Councils." *European Economic Review* 145 (June): 104118.

Bosch, M., and W. F. Maloney. 2010. "Comparative Analysis of Labor Market Dynamics Using Markov Processes: An Application to Informality." *Labour Economics* 17 (4): 621–31.

Bova, M. E., N. Carcenac, and M. M. Guerguil. 2014. "Fiscal Rules and the Procyclicality of Fiscal Policy in the Developing World." IMF Working Paper 14/122, International Monetary Fund, Washington, DC.

Bova, E., P. Medas, and T. Poghosyan. 2018. "Macroeconomic Stability in Resource-Rich Countries: The Role of Fiscal Policy." *Journal of Banking and Financial Economics* 1: 103–22.

Calderón, C., R. Duncan, and K. Schmidt-Hebbel. 2016. "Do Good Institutions Promote Countercyclical Macroeconomic Policies?" *Oxford Bulletin of Economics and Statistics* 78 (5): 650–70.

Caselli, F., and J. Reynaud. 2020. "Do Fiscal Rules Cause Better Fiscal Balances? A New Instrumental Variable Strategy." *European Journal of Political Economy* 63 (June): 101873.

Cashin, P., C. J. McDermott, and A. Scott. 2002. "Booms and Slumps in World Commodity Prices." *Journal of Development Economics* 69 (1): 277–96.

Céspedes, L. F., E. Parrado, and A. Velasco. 2014. "Fiscal Rules and The Management of Natural Resource Revenues: The Case of Chile." *Annual Review of Resource Economics* 6 (1): 105–32.

Céspedes, L. F., and A. Velasco. 2014. "Was This Time Different? Fiscal Policy in Commodity Republics." *Journal of Development Economics* 106: 92–106.

Chattha, M. K., A. N. Maseeh, Z. Luan, M. Thelejane, O. Ftomova, H. Youssef, T. S. Kawalec, O. Yacine, X. Wang, and Z. Bogetic. 2025. *Gulf Economic Update: Smart Spending, Stronger Outcomes – Fiscal Policy for a Thriving GCC (English).* Gulf Economic Update. Washington, DC: World Bank.

Cherif, R., and F. Hasanov. 2014. "Soaring of the Gulf Falcons: Diversification in the GCC Oil Exporters in Seven Propositions." IMF Working Paper 14/177, International Monetary Fund, Washington, DC.

Çiçekçi, C., and E. Gaygısız. 2023. "Procyclicality of Fiscal Policy in Oil-rich Countries: Roles of Resource Funds and Institutional Quality." *Resource Policy* 85 (August): 103675.

Diop, N., D. Marotta, and J. de Melo, eds. 2012. *Natural Resource Abundance, Growth, and Diversification in the Middle East and North Africa: The Effects of Natural Resources and the Role of Policies.* Washington, DC: World Bank.

Elbadawi, I., R. Soto, and H. Youssef. 2018. "Sovereign Wealth Funds and Macroeconomic Stabilization in the Home Economy." Economic Research Forum Working Paper 1175, Cairo.

Eyraud, L., W. Gbohoui, and P. A. Medas. 2023. "A New Fiscal Framework for Resource-Rich Countries." IMF Working Paper 23/230, International Monetary Fund, Washington, DC.

Fatás, A., B. Gootjes, and J. Mawejje. 2026. "Dynamic Effects of Fiscal Rules: Do Initial Conditions Matter?" *Journal of International Money and Finance* 161 (February): 103499.

Fatás, A., and I. Mihov. 2013. "Policy Volatility, Institutions, and Economic Growth." *The Review of Economics and Statistics* 95 (2): 362–76.

Frankel, J., and J. Schreger. 2013. "Over-optimistic Official Forecasts and Fiscal Rules in the Eurozone." *Review of World Economics* 149 (2): 247–72.

Frankel, J. A., C. A. Végh, and G. Vuletin. 2013. "On Graduation from Fiscal Procyclicality." *Journal of Development Economics* 100 (1): 32–47.

Gavin, M., and R. Perotti. 1997. "Fiscal Policy in Latin America." *NBER Macroeconomics Annual* 12: 11–61.

Gelb, A. H. 2012. "Economic Diversification in Resource-Rich Countries." In *Beyond the Curse; Policies to Harness the Power of Natural Resources*, edited by R. Arezki, T. Gylfason, and A. Sy, Chapter 4. Washington, DC: International Monetary Fund.

Gill, I. S., I. Izvorski, W. Van Eeghen, and D. De Rosa. 2014. *Diversified Development: Making the Most of Natural Resources in Eurasia*. Washington, DC: World Bank.

Global SWF (database). Global SWF, Singapore. Accessed on December 13, 2024. http://globalswf.com.

Gootjes, B., and J. de Haan. 2022. "Do Fiscal Rules Need Budget Transparency to Be Effective?" *European Journal of Political Economy* 75 (December): 102210.

Gootjes, B., J. de Haan, and R. Jong-A-Pin. 2021. "Do Fiscal Rules Constrain Political Budget Cycles?" *Public Choice* 188 (July): 1–30.

Gootjes, B. and G. Vasishtha. Forthcoming. "Fiscal Policy Amidst Commodity Price Volatility: Trends and Challenges." Unpublished.

Harding, D., and A. Pagan. 2002. "Dissecting the Cycle: A Methodological Investigation." *Journal of Monetary Economics* 49 (2): 365–81.

Hesse, H. 2008. "Export Diversification and Economic Growth." Commission on Growth and Development Working Paper 21, World Bank, Washington, DC.

Huidrom, R., M. A. Kose, and F. Ohnsorge. 2016. "Challenges of Fiscal Policy in Emerging and Developing Economies." Policy Research Working Paper 7725, World Bank, Washington, DC.

IMF (International Monetary Fund). 2008. *Sovereign Wealth Funds: A Work Agenda.* Washington, DC: International Monetary Fund.

IMF (International Monetary Fund). 2009. *Chile: 2009 Article IV Consultation—Press Release; Staff Report; and Statement by the Executive Director for Chile.* IMF Country Report 09/271. Washington, DC: International Monetary Fund.

IMF (International Monetary Fund). 2013. *The Function and Impacts of Fiscal Councils.* Washington, DC: International Monetary Fund.

IMF (International Monetary Fund). 2017. *Fiscal Monitor. Achieving More with Less.* April. Washington, DC: International Monetary Fund.

IMF (International Monetary Fund). 2024a. *Peru: 2024 Article IV Consultation—Press Release; Staff Report; and Statement by the Executive Director for Peru.* IMF Country Report 24/133. Washington, DC: International Monetary Fund.

IMF (International Monetary Fund). 2024b. *Argentina: Seventh Review Under the Extended Arrangement Under the Extended Fund Facility.* IMF Country Report 24/37. Washington, DC: International Monetary Fund.

IMF (International Monetary Fund). 2025. *Mexico: 2025 Article IV Consultation—Press Release; Staff Report; and Statement by the Executive Director for Mexico.* IMF Country Report 25/286. Washington, DC: International Monetary Fund.

IMF (International Monetary Fund). 2026. *World Economic Outlook: Global Economy in the Shadow of War.* April. Washington, DC: International Monetary Fund.

IMF (International Monetary Fund) and World Bank. 2014. *Revised Guidelines for Public Debt Management.* Washington, DC: International Monetary Fund and World Bank.

IMF (International Monetary Fund) and World Bank. 2019. *Developing a Medium-Term Debt Management Strategy Framework (MTDS): Updated Guidance Note for Country Authorities.* Washington, DC: International Monetary Fund and World Bank.

Islamaj, E., A. S. Penaloza, and S. Sommers. 2024. "The Sovereign Spread Compressing Effect of Fiscal Rules during Global Crises." Policy Research Working Paper 10741, World Bank, Washington, DC.

Jonasson, T., and M. G. Papaioannou. 2018. "A Primer on Managing Sovereign Debt-Portfolio Risks." IMF Working Paper 18/74, International Monetary Fund, Washington, DC.

Jordà, Ò. 2005. "Estimation and Inference of Impulse Responses by Local Projections." *American Economic Review* 95 (1): 161–82.

Kaminsky, G. L., C. M. Reinhart, and C. A. Vegh. 2004. "When it Rains, It Pours: Procyclical Capital Flows and Macroeconomic Policies." *NBER Macroeconomics Annual* 19: 11–53.

Kelemen, R. D., and T. K. Teo. 2014. "Law, Focal Points, and Fiscal Discipline in the United States and the European Union." *American Political Science Review* 108 (2): 355–70.

Lam, R. W., Y. Cao, A. Lagerborg, and A. Scipioni. 2023. "Chile Technical Assistance Report—Fiscal Considerations in Managing Stabilization Funds." IMF Country Report 23/249, International Monetary Fund, Washington, DC.

Lashitew, A. A., M. L. Ross, and E. Werker. 2021. "What Drives Successful Economic Diversification in Resource-Rich Countries?" The World Bank Research Observer 36 (2): 164–96.

Lederman, D., and W. F. Maloney. 2007. "Neither Curse nor Destiny: Introduction to Natural Resources and Development." In *Natural Resources: Neither Curse nor Destiny*, edited by D. Lederman and W. F. Maloney, 1–12. Washington, DC: World Bank.

Loayza, N. V., and J. Rigolini. 2011. "Informal Employment: Safety Net or Growth Engine?" World Development 39 (9): 1503–15.

Mendes, A., and S. Pennings. 2025. "One Rule Fits All? Heterogeneous Fiscal Rules for Commodity Exporters When Price Shocks Can Be Persistent: Theory and Evidence." *Review of Economic Dynamics* 55 (January): 101239.

Michaud, A., and J. Rothert. 2018. "Redistributive Fiscal Policies and Business Cycles in Emerging Economies." *Journal of International Economics* 112 (May): 123–33.

Milesi-Ferretti, G. M. 2004. "Good, Bad or Ugly? On the Effects of Fiscal Rules with Creative Accounting." *Journal of Public Economics* 88 (1–2): 377–94.

Ocampo, J. A. 2017. "Commodity-Led Development in Latin America." In *Alternative Pathways to Sustainable Development: Lessons from Latin America*, edited by G. Carbonnier, H. Campodónico, and S. Tezanos Vázquez, 51–76. Boston: Brill | Nijhoff.

Papageorgiou, C., and N. Spatafora. 2012. "Economic Diversification in LICs: Stylized Facts and Macroeconomic Implications." IMF Staff Discussion Note 12/13, International Monetary Fund, Washington, DC.

Peszko, G., D. van der Mensbrugghe, A. Golub, J. Ward, D. Zenghelis, C. Marijs, A. Schopp, J. A. Rogers, and A. Midgley. 2020. *Diversification and Cooperation in a Decarbonizing World: Climate Strategies for Fossil Fuel–Dependent Countries. Climate Change and Development*. Washington, DC: World Bank.

Petrella, I., L. Juvenal, and F. Di Pace. 2025. "Commodity Prices and Fiscal (Pro)Cyclicality." IDB Working Paper Series 14347, Inter-American Development Bank, Washington, DC.

Rosnick, D., and M. Weisbrot. 2014. "Latin American Growth in the 21st Century: The 'Commodities Boom' That Wasn't." CEPR Reports and Issue Briefs 2014–09, Center for Economic and Policy Research.

Ross, M. L. 2017. "What Do We Know about Economic Diversification in Oil-producing Countries?" https://ssrn.com/abstract=3048585.

Talvi, E., and C. A. Végh. 2005. "Tax Base Variability and Procyclical Fiscal Policy in Developing Countries." *Journal of Development Economics* 78 (1): 156–90.

Temple, J. 2003. "Growing into Trouble: Indonesia after 1966." In *In Search of Prosperity: Analytic Narratives on Economic Growth*, edited by D. Rodrik. Princeton: Princeton University Press.

Teulings, C. N., and N. Zubanov. 2014. "Is Economic Recovery a Myth? Robust Estimation of Impulse Responses." *Journal of Applied Econometrics* 29 (3): 497–514.

Tornell, A., and P. R. Lane. 1999. "The Voracity Effect." *American Economic Review* 89 (1): 22–46.

van der Ploeg, F. 2011. "Natural Resources: Curse or Blessing?" Journal of Economic Literature 49 (2): 366–420.

World Bank. 2013. *World Development Report 2013: Jobs.* Washington, DC: World Bank.

World Bank. 2018. *Broad-Based Upturn, but for How Long?* January. Washington, DC: World Bank.

World Bank. 2019. Macro Poverty Outlook. April. Washington, DC: World Bank.

World Bank. 2020a. *Global Economic Prospects: Slow Growth, Policy Challenges.* January. Washington, DC: World Bank.

World Bank. 2020b. *Commodity Markets Outlook: Implications of COVID-19 for Commodities.* April. Washington, DC: World Bank.

World Bank. 2022. *Global Economic Prospects.* January. Washington, DC: World Bank.

World Bank. 2024a. *Global Economic Prospects.* January. Washington, DC: World Bank.

World Bank. 2024b. Oman: Macro Poverty Outlook. October. Washington, DC: World Bank.

World Bank. 2024c. *People in a Changing Climate: From Vulnerability to Action–Insights from World Bank Group Country Climate and Development Reports Covering 72 Economies.* Washington, DC: World Bank.

World Bank. 2025. *Commodity Markets Outlook.* April. Washington, DC: World Bank.

World Bank. 2026a. *Commodity Markets Outlook.* April. Washington, DC: World Bank.

World Bank. 2026b. *Global Economic Prospects.* January. Washington, DC: World Bank.

World Bank. 2026c. *Challenges of Conflict and Industrial Policy for Development.* Middle East, North Africa, Afghanistan & Pakistan Economic Update. Washington, DC: World Bank.

STATISTICAL APPENDIX

Real GDP growth

	Annual estimates and forecasts [1] (Percent change)						Quarterly estimates [2] (Percent change, year-on-year)					
	2023	2024	2025e	2026f	2027f	2028f	24Q4	25Q1	25Q2	25Q3	25Q4	26Q1e
World	**2.8**	**2.9**	**2.9**	**2.5**	**2.8**	**2.8**	**3.1**	**3.0**	**2.9**	..	..	..
Advanced economies	**1.6**	**1.8**	**1.8**	**1.5**	**1.8**	**1.7**	**1.9**	**2.0**	**1.8**	**1.9**	**1.7**	..
United States	2.9	2.8	2.1	2.2	2.1	2.0	2.4	2.0	2.1	2.3	2.0	2.6
Euro area	0.5	1.0	1.4	0.8	1.3	1.3	1.4	1.7	1.6	1.4	1.2	0.3
Japan	0.7	-0.2	1.1	0.7	0.9	0.8	0.7	1.5	1.8	0.5	0.4	0.4
Emerging market and developing economies	**4.3**	**4.4**	**4.4**	**3.6**	**4.2**	**4.1**	**4.8**	**4.5**	**4.4**	..	..	..
East Asia and Pacific	**5.2**	**5.0**	**5.0**	**4.2**	**4.4**	**4.3**	**5.4**	**5.3**	**5.2**	**4.8**	**4.6**	**5.0**
Cambodia	5.0	6.0	5.3	3.9	4.9	5.1	..	..	..	..	..	..
China	5.4	5.0	5.0	4.2	4.3	4.2	5.4	5.4	5.2	4.8	4.5	5.0
Fiji	9.4	3.5	3.2	2.7	3.2	3.3	..	..	..	..	..	..
Indonesia	5.0	5.0	5.1	5.0	5.2	5.2	5.0	4.9	5.1	5.0	5.4	5.6
Kiribati	3.3	4.6	4.3	3.1	2.4	2.2	..	..	..	..	..	..
Lao PDR	3.7	4.1	4.8	3.8	3.7	3.7	4.3	4.9	4.8	4.3	5.4	5.5
Malaysia	3.5	5.1	5.2	4.4	4.4	4.1	5.0	4.4	4.6	5.3	6.2	5.4
Marshall Islands [3]	-4.0	3.0	2.5	2.0	2.4	1.9	..	..	..	..	..	..
Micronesia, Fed. Sts. [3]	1.1	2.3	1.1	0.8	1.3	1.4	..	..	..	..	..	..
Mongolia	7.2	5.1	6.9	5.0	5.5	5.5	5.5	2.5	8.5	6.3	9.2	8.0
Myanmar [3 4]	1.0	-1.0	-2.0	2.0	..	..	..	..	..	..	..	..
Nauru [3]	0.6	1.6	2.1	1.9	1.9	1.8	..	..	..	..	..	..
Palau [3]	1.2	12.0	6.7	3.0	2.7	2.6	..	..	..	..	..	..
Papua New Guinea	3.8	3.9	5.6	3.8	3.8	3.1	..	..	..	..	..	..
Philippines	5.5	5.7	4.4	3.7	5.6	5.6	5.3	5.4	5.4	4.0	3.0	2.8
Samoa [3]	15.2	4.8	4.2	4.0	3.3	2.4	..	..	..	..	..	..
Solomon Islands	2.8	3.0	3.6	2.9	3.2	3.2	..	..	..	..	..	..
Thailand	2.2	2.9	2.4	1.7	2.1	2.4	3.7	3.1	2.8	1.2	2.5	2.8
Timor-Leste [5]	2.4	4.3	4.5	4.1	4.0	4.0	..	..	..	..	..	..
Tonga [3]	2.1	2.1	2.7	2.0	1.8	1.5	..	..	..	..	..	..
Tuvalu	4.0	3.1	3.0	2.5	2.7	2.3	..	..	..	..	..	..
Vanuatu	2.1	0.9	1.7	2.3	2.7	2.3	..	..	..	..	..	..
Viet Nam	5.0	7.0	8.0	6.8	7.1	7.4	7.5	6.4	8.2	8.3	8.5	7.8
Europe and Central Asia	**3.6**	**3.9**	**2.5**	**2.1**	**2.3**	**2.6**	**4.0**	**2.1**	**2.7**	**2.4**	**2.4**	..
Albania	4.0	4.0	3.8	3.4	3.7	3.6	4.4	3.8	3.6	3.9	3.8	..
Armenia	8.3	5.9	7.1	5.3	5.1	5.0	4.1	5.4	6.4	6.3	9.3	4.0
Azerbaijan	1.4	4.2	1.4	2.0	1.8	1.8	..	..	..	..	..	..
Belarus	4.1	4.3	1.3	1.1	0.8	0.7	3.0	3.3	1.0	0.8	0.3	..
Bosnia and Herzegovina [5]	2.0	3.2	2.1	2.5	3.0	3.2	2.8	1.9	2.2	2.3	2.1	..
Bulgaria	1.7	3.4	3.1	2.6	2.9	3.0	4.6	2.8	3.5	3.0	3.1	2.7
Croatia	3.8	3.8	3.4	2.4	2.3	2.3	3.8	3.6	3.8	2.6	3.9	2.2
Georgia	7.8	9.7	7.5	5.0	5.5	5.0	8.5	9.9	7.4	6.4	6.7	..
Kazakhstan	5.1	5.0	6.5	4.6	3.9	3.5	7.9	5.4	7.9	5.5	7.0	3.0
Kosovo	4.1	4.6	3.6	3.7	3.9	4.0	..	..	..	..	..	..
Kyrgyz Republic	9.0	11.5	11.1	6.1	5.8	6.1	..	..	..	..	..	..
Moldova	1.2	0.3	2.4	1.9	2.9	3.2	-1.1	-1.3	1.1	5.1	3.6	..
Montenegro	6.5	3.2	2.7	2.9	3.1	3.1	2.5	2.8	3.5	3.1	1.5	2.6
North Macedonia	2.6	3.0	3.5	2.9	3.0	3.0	4.3	2.9	3.5	3.8	3.8	..
Poland	0.2	3.2	3.6	3.1	2.6	2.9	3.7	3.2	3.3	3.8	4.1	3.5
Romania	2.3	0.9	0.7	0.0	1.7	2.0	0.8	0.6	2.5	1.3	-1.2	-2.1
Russian Federation	4.1	4.9	1.0	0.8	0.7	0.7	5.2	1.3	1.0	0.8	1.0	-0.2
Serbia	3.7	3.9	2.0	2.7	3.0	4.0	3.5	1.8	2.0	2.0	2.2	3.2
Tajikistan	8.3	8.4	8.4	6.5	5.0	4.8	..	..	..	..	..	..
Türkiye	5.0	3.3	3.6	2.8	3.7	4.3	3.2	2.5	4.7	3.8	3.4	2.5
Turkmenistan [4]	6.3	6.3	6.3	..	..	..						
Ukraine	5.5	3.2	1.8	1.2	4.0	4.5	0.3	0.8	0.9	2.4	2.8	-0.5
Uzbekistan	6.3	6.7	7.7	6.4	6.7	6.8	..	..	..	..	..	..

Real GDP growth (*continued*)

	Annual estimates and forecasts[1] (Percent change)						Quarterly estimates[2] (Percent change, year-on-year)					
	2023	2024	2025e	2026f	2027f	2028f	24Q4	25Q1	25Q2	25Q3	25Q4	26Q1e
Latin America and the Caribbean	**2.3**	**2.3**	**2.3**	**2.2**	**2.5**	**2.6**	**2.8**	**2.8**	**2.3**	**2.0**	**..**	**..**
Argentina	-1.9	-1.3	4.4	3.6	3.7	3.5	2.6	5.8	6.4	3.3	2.1	..
Bahamas, The	3.0	3.4	2.8	2.2	1.9	1.8	7.6	..	..	..	..	..
Barbados	1.8	3.4	2.7	2.7	3.0	3.1	..	..	..	..	..	..
Belize	0.5	3.5	1.5	2.4	2.2	2.2	2.1	-1.9	1.4	7.8	4.7	..
Bolivia	2.5	-1.1	-1.6	-3.2	4.0	3.2	-1.7	-1.7	-2.8	-0.7	-1.1	..
Brazil	3.2	3.4	2.3	1.9	2.0	2.2	3.6	3.1	2.4	1.8	1.8	1.8
Chile	0.7	2.8	2.5	2.1	2.5	2.3	4.1	2.9	3.7	1.7	1.6	-0.5
Colombia	0.8	1.5	2.6	2.3	2.4	2.7	2.6	2.5	1.9	3.8	2.1	2.2
Costa Rica	4.8	4.1	4.6	3.5	3.6	3.7	4.1	4.1	4.3	5.4	4.5	4.0
Dominica	3.7	2.1	3.1	2.8	2.9	2.8	..	..	..	..	..	..
Dominican Republic	2.2	5.0	2.1	3.6	4.4	4.5	4.1	2.7	2.0	1.8	1.9	..
Ecuador[2]	2.0	-2.0	3.7	2.5	2.5	2.5	-1.0	3.4	3.5	3.0	5.0	..
El Salvador	3.4	2.6	3.9	3.2	3.0	3.1	3.1	2.7	3.7	5.1	4.0	..
Grenada	4.5	3.3	4.5	3.1	3.0	2.9	..	..	..	..	..	..
Guatemala	3.5	3.7	4.2	3.7	3.8	3.8	4.5	3.8	4.0	4.5	4.8	..
Guyana	33.8	43.8	15.4	16.3	23.5	21.2	36.2	6.2	9.0	26.7	34.7	..
Haiti[3]	-1.9	-4.2	-2.7	0.6	1.9	2.2	..	..	..	..	..	..
Honduras	3.6	3.6	3.8	3.4	3.7	3.8	3.6	4.4	4.1	3.7	2.9	..
Jamaica[2]	2.7	-0.5	-0.4	-1.0	3.2	1.6	-0.5	1.1	1.7	5.1	-7.1	..
Mexico	3.1	1.4	0.6	1.3	1.7	1.9	0.4	0.6	-0.1	-0.2	1.7	0.2
Nicaragua	4.4	3.6	4.9	3.4	3.4	3.3	3.4	2.8	4.7	6.1	6.0	..
Panama	7.4	2.9	4.4	3.9	4.1	4.1	4.8	5.2	3.4	3.9	4.8	..
Paraguay	5.3	4.7	6.6	4.4	4.2	4.0	4.0	7.0	6.7	6.7	6.2	..
Peru	-0.4	3.5	3.4	2.7	2.8	2.8	4.4	4.1	2.8	3.8	3.2	3.5
St. Lucia	3.3	4.7	1.3	1.9	1.8	1.7	..	..	..	..	..	..
St. Vincent and the Grenadines	5.3	4.1	3.6	3.0	3.1	2.9	..	..	..	..	..	..
Suriname	2.4	1.7	1.8	4.0	4.5	20.5	..	..	..	..	..	..
Trinidad and Tobago	1.5	2.5	0.8	0.7	3.2	3.5	3.4	-2.1	2.6	0.1	..	..
Uruguay	0.8	3.3	1.8	1.6	1.9	2.1	4.1	4.0	2.3	1.0	0.1	..
Middle East, North Africa, Afghanistan, and Pakistan	**2.0**	**2.9**	**4.0**	**1.6**	**5.0**	**4.0**	**3.9**	**3.4**	**3.8**	**..**	**..**	**..**
Afghanistan[3]	2.3	1.9	4.8	4.0	3.9	3.8	..	..	..	..	..	..
Algeria[2]	4.1	3.7	3.8	3.7	3.1	3.1	4.2	4.3	3.9	..	..	..
Bahrain	3.9	2.9	3.5	1.3	2.8	3.1	3.9	2.7	2.5	4.0	4.6	..
Djibouti	6.8	7.0	6.5	5.9	6.3	6.5	..	..	..	..	..	..
Egypt, Arab Rep.[3]	3.8	2.4	4.4	4.6	4.0	4.6	4.3	4.8	5.0	5.3	5.3	5.0
Iran, Islamic Rep.[3,4]	5.3	3.7	-2.8	..	..	..	4.2	3.1	-2.5	0.6	2.2	..
Iraq[2,5]	0.5	-1.5	-2.2	-8.9	12.2	3.5	-0.6	-1.7	-3.7	-0.9	-2.3	..
Jordan	3.1	2.6	2.8	2.7	2.9	3.0	2.6	2.7	2.8	2.8	3.0	..
Kuwait	-1.6	-1.5	2.6	-6.4	13.5	2.8	0.5	1.8	2.0	4.7	2.4	..
Lebanon[4]	-0.5	-5.2	4.2	..	..	..	-8.7	..	..	..	..	..
Libya	10.2	1.9	13.4	4.5	4.0	6.0	..	..	..	..	..	..
Morocco[2]	3.7	3.8	4.7	4.2	4.0	4.3	4.2	4.8	5.5	4.0	4.1	5.0
Oman	1.2	1.7	2.6	2.4	3.0	3.4	2.0	2.4	2.1	2.0	2.3	..
Pakistan[2,3,5]	-0.2	2.6	3.1	3.0	3.2	3.7	2.5	2.6	6.1	3.9	4.1	4.0
Qatar	1.2	3.0	3.0	-5.7	5.7	6.4	6.4	4.9	1.9	2.8	2.0	..
Saudi Arabia	0.5	2.6	4.5	3.1	4.9	3.7	5.2	3.7	4.5	4.8	5.0	2.8
Syrian Arab Republic[4]	0.3	0.9	2.0	..	..	..	..	..	..	..	..	..
Tunisia[2]	0.2	1.6	2.5	2.5	2.3	2.3	2.5	1.6	3.2	2.4	2.7	2.6
United Arab Emirates	4.3	6.6	6.2	2.4	4.1	4.2	5.0	3.9	4.5	6.8	..	..
West Bank and Gaza	-1.0	-22.9	4.1	4.5	11.3	9.1	4.4	9.9	3.2	1.4	3.2	..
Yemen, Rep.[4]	-2.0	-1.5	-1.5	-0.5	1.6	..	..	..	..	..	..	..

Real GDP growth (*continued*)

	Annual estimates and forecasts [1] (Percent change)						Quarterly estimates [2] (Percent change, year-on-year)					
	2023	2024	2025e	2026f	2027f	2028f	24Q4	25Q1	25Q2	25Q3	25Q4	26Q1e
South Asia	**6.6**	**6.8**	**7.0**	**6.3**	**6.9**	**7.1**	**6.9**	**6.7**	**6.3**	**7.8**	**7.4**	**..**
Bangladesh [3]	5.8	4.2	3.5	3.8	4.6	5.5	3.5	4.5	2.1	5.0	3.0	..
Bhutan [3]	4.9	6.1	8.1	7.1	6.4	6.8	9.1	7.8	9.2	6.5	8.8	..
India [3]	7.2	7.1	7.7	6.6	7.2	7.0	7.4	7.0	6.8	8.3	8.0	7.8
Maldives	4.9	3.5	5.7	0.7	7.2	4.0	2.2	3.4	7.5	7.4	7.3	..
Nepal [2,3]	2.0	3.7	4.6	2.3	4.2	4.6	3.8	4.2	4.7	3.2	4.1	..
Sri Lanka	-2.0	5.0	5.0	3.6	3.8	3.9	5.5	4.7	5.0	5.3	4.8	..
Sub-Saharan Africa	**3.0**	**3.8**	**4.1**	**4.0**	**4.4**	**4.5**	**3.3**	**3.5**	**3.3**	**..**	**..**	**..**
Angola	1.3	4.4	3.1	2.4	2.7	2.9	3.3	4.3	1.5	1.7	5.1	5.3
Benin	6.4	7.5	8.1	7.0	7.2	7.3	9.2	7.4	7.7	8.8	8.2	..
Botswana	3.2	-2.8	-0.7	2.7	3.2	3.1	-1.9	-0.3	-5.2	8.2	-5.4	..
Burkina Faso	3.0	4.8	5.3	4.9	5.8	5.5	..	..	..	..	..	..
Burundi	2.7	4.1	4.0	4.1	4.8	4.9	3.3	4.1	5.2	4.0	3.7	..
Cabo Verde	4.8	7.2	6.3	4.8	5.0	5.1	..	..	..	..	..	..
Cameroon	3.2	3.5	3.2	3.4	3.7	3.9	1.1	6.7	3.9	3.5	..	..
Central African Republic	0.7	1.5	4.5	2.3	3.1	3.2	..	..	..	..	..	..
Chad	4.0	5.0	5.6	5.2	5.3	5.3	..	1.8	4.4	6.1	5.5	..
Comoros	3.2	3.3	3.8	4.1	4.3	3.9	..	..	..	..	..	..
Congo, Dem. Rep.	8.6	6.1	5.5	5.2	5.1	5.1	..	..	..	..	..	..
Congo, Rep.	1.9	2.1	3.1	3.7	3.4	3.4	3.3	2.7	3.1	..	..	..
Côte d'Ivoire	6.6	6.0	6.3	5.8	6.5	7.0	..	..	..	..	..	..
Equatorial Guinea	-7.4	0.4	-5.8	-3.5	-3.4	2.2	..	..	..	..	..	..
Eritrea	2.6	2.9	3.2	3.5	3.6	3.6	..	..	..	..	..	..
Eswatini	3.5	3.0	4.0	3.9	3.8	3.3	..	..	..	..	..	..
Ethiopia [3]	7.2	8.1	9.2	8.0	6.9	8.4	..	..	..	..	..	..
Gabon	2.4	3.4	2.5	3.0	3.3	3.5	..	..	..	..	..	..
Gambia, The	5.9	5.6	5.9	5.3	5.2	5.2	..	..	..	..	..	..
Ghana	3.1	5.8	6.0	4.8	4.9	5.0	4.0	6.2	6.6	5.3	5.8	..
Guinea	5.5	5.4	7.4	8.8	11.6	10.7	8.0	8.7	7.7	7.0	6.2	..
Guinea-Bissau	5.8	4.1	5.8	4.8	4.9	5.0	..	..	..	..	..	..
Kenya	5.7	4.7	4.6	4.4	5.0	5.0	5.4	4.9	4.9	4.8	4.0	..
Lesotho	1.7	5.2	2.0	1.3	1.5	1.5	5.7	2.9	5.2	3.6	..	..
Liberia	4.7	4.0	5.1	5.0	5.4	5.6	..	..	..	..	..	..
Madagascar	4.2	4.3	3.0	3.8	4.5	4.4	..	..	..	..	..	..
Malawi	1.9	1.7	1.9	2.3	2.7	3.0	..	..	..	..	..	..
Mali	4.5	4.7	4.1	5.0	5.2	5.3	6.6	3.0	6.4	6.8	4.9	..
Mauritania	6.8	6.3	4.0	4.4	4.5	4.8	..	..	..	..	..	..
Mauritius	4.7	4.9	3.2	2.5	4.6	3.1	5.1	3.4	3.2	3.3	2.7	..
Mozambique	5.5	2.1	-0.5	0.9	1.6	2.5	-5.7	-3.9	-0.9	-0.8	4.7	..
Namibia	4.4	4.0	1.7	2.7	3.4	3.4	4.2	3.1	1.9	2.6	-0.5	..
Niger	2.6	8.3	7.0	6.7	6.4	6.1	..	..	..	..	..	..
Nigeria	3.3	4.1	4.0	4.1	4.2	4.3	4.2	3.8	4.1	4.2	4.0	3.9
Rwanda	8.6	7.2	9.4	7.2	7.6	7.3	4.2	6.5	7.8	11.8	11.2	..
São Tomé and Príncipe	0.4	1.1	2.1	2.9	3.9	3.3	..	..	..	..	..	..
Senegal	4.3	6.1	6.7	2.2	2.6	3.0	..	..	..	..	..	..
Seychelles	5.2	3.4	5.8	1.1	4.5	3.1	2.1	7.2	3.2	4.1	8.8	..
Sierra Leone	5.7	4.4	4.5	4.0	4.7	4.6	..	..	..	..	..	..

Real GDP growth (*continued*)

	Annual estimates and forecasts[1] (Percent change)						Quarterly estimates[2] (Percent change, year-on-year)					
	2023	2024	2025e	2026f	2027f	2028f	24Q4	25Q1	25Q2	25Q3	25Q4	26Q1e
Sub-Saharan Africa (*continued*)												
Somalia, Fed. Rep.	4.2	4.1	3.0	2.8	3.1	3.5	..	..	..	..	..	..
South Africa	0.8	0.5	1.1	1.0	1.5	1.7	0.8	0.9	0.7	2.1	0.8	..
South Sudan [3]	-1.3	-7.4	-7.7	20.3	2.4	2.9	..	..	..	..	..	..
Sudan	-29.4	-14.0	3.1	5.5	4.4	2.6	..	..	..	..	..	..
Tanzania	5.1	5.5	5.9	6.1	6.4	6.5	..	..	..	..	..	..
Togo	6.2	6.5	5.9	5.0	5.8	6.2	..	..	..	..	..	..
Uganda [3]	5.3	6.1	6.3	6.8	8.5	8.1	5.4	8.4	5.5	4.8	8.5	..
Zambia	5.4	3.8	3.8	4.4	4.7	5.1	8.3	4.6	5.5	3.7	1.6	..
Zimbabwe	5.3	1.7	7.5	4.6	4.2	4.1	..	..	..	..	..	..

Sources: Haver Analytics; World Bank.

Note: e = estimate; f = forecast.

1. Aggregate growth rates calculated using GDP weights at average 2010-19 prices and market exchange rates.

2. Quarterly estimates are based on non-seasonally-adjusted real GDP, except for advanced economies, as well as Algeria, Ecuador, Morocco, and Tunisia. In some instances, quarterly growth paths may not align to annual growth estimates, owing to the timing of GDP releases. Quarterly data for Iraq, Jamaica, Nepal, and Pakistan are gross value added.

Regional averages are calculated based on data from the following economies.

East Asia and Pacific: China, Indonesia, the Lao People's Democratic Republic, Malaysia, Mongolia, the Philippines, Thailand, and Viet Nam.

Europe and Central Asia: Albania, Armenia, Belarus, Bosnia and Herzegovina, Georgia, Hungary, Kazakhstan, Moldova, Montenegro, North Macedonia, Poland, Romania, the Russian Federation, Serbia, Türkiye, and Ukraine.

Latin America and the Caribbean: Argentina, Belize, Bolivia, Brazil, Chile, Colombia, Costa Rica, the Dominican Republic, Ecuador, El Salvador, Guatemala, Guyana, Honduras, Jamaica, Mexico, Nicaragua, Panama, Paraguay, Peru, Trinidad and Tobago, and Uruguay.

Middle East, North Africa, Afghanistan, and Pakistan: Algeria, Bahrain, the Arab Republic of Egypt, Iraq, Jordan, Kuwait, Morocco, Oman, Pakistan, Qatar, Saudi Arabia, Tunisia, the United Arab Emirates, and West Bank and Gaza.

South Asia: Bangladesh, Bhutan, India, Maldives, Nepal, and Sri Lanka.

Sub-Saharan Africa: Angola, Benin, Botswana, Burundi, Cameroon, the Republic of Congo, Ghana, Guinea, Kenya, Lesotho, Mali, Mauritius, Mozambique, Namibia, Nigeria, Rwanda, the Seychelles, South Africa, Uganda, and Zambia.

3. Annual GDP is on fiscal-year basis, as per reporting practice in the country. For Bangladesh, Bhutan, the Arab Republic of Egypt, Ethiopia, Nepal, South Sudan, Pakistan, and Uganda, the column for 2023 refers to FY2022/23. For Afghanistan, India, and the Islamic Republic of Iran, the column for 2023 refers to FY2023/24.

4. Data for the Islamic Republic of Iran (beyond FY2025/26), Lebanon (beyond 2025), Myanmar (beyond 2026), the Syrian Arab Republic (beyond 2025), and the Republic of Yemen (beyond 2027) are excluded because of a high degree of uncertainty. Macroeconomic projections for Turkmenistan are not currently included, pending further alignment of data with international statistical practices. In the Syrian Arab Republic, growth estimate for 2025 ranges between 2.0 and 4.0 percent.

5. Data for Bosnia and Herzegovina are from the production approach. Annual data for Iraq and Pakistan are based on factor cost. Data for Timor-Leste represent non-oil GDP.

Data and Forecast Conventions

The macroeconomic forecasts presented in this report are prepared by staff of the Prospects Group of the Development Economics Vice Presidency, in coordination with staff from the Fiscal Policy and Growth of the Prosperity Vice Presidency and from regional and country offices, and with input from regional Chief Economist offices. They are the result of an iterative process that incorporates data, macroeconometric models, and judgment.

Data. Data used to prepare country forecasts come from a variety of sources. National Income Accounts (NIA), Balance of Payments (BOP), and fiscal data are from Haver Analytics; the World Development Indicators by the World Bank; the *World Economic Outlook*, *Balance of Payments Statistics*, and *International Financial Statistics* by the International Monetary Fund. Population data and forecasts are from the United Nations World Population Prospects. Country- and lending-group classifications are from the World Bank. The Prospects Group's internal databases include high-frequency indicators such as industrial production, consumer price indexes, the J.P.Morgan Emerging Markets Bond Index (EMBI), exchange rates, exports, imports, policy rates, and stock market indexes, based on data from Bloomberg, Haver Analytics, IMF *Balance of Payments Statistics*, IMF *International Financial Statistics*, and J.P.Morgan.

Aggregations. Aggregate growth rates for the world and all subgroups of countries (such as regions and income groups) are weighted averages of country-specific growth rates, calculated using GDP weights at average 2010-19 prices and market exchange rates. Income groups are defined as in the World Bank's classification of country groups.

Output growth forecast process. The process starts with initial assumptions about advanced-economy growth and commodity price forecasts. These are used as conditioning assumptions for the first set of growth forecasts for EMDEs, which are produced using macroeconometric models, accounting frameworks to ensure national account identities and global consistency, estimates of spillovers from major economies, and high-frequency indicators. These forecasts are then evaluated to ensure consistency of treatment across similar EMDEs. This is followed by extensive discussions with World Bank country teams, who conduct continuous macroeconomic monitoring and dialogue with country authorities and finalize growth forecasts for EMDEs. The Prospects Group prepares advanced economy and commodity price forecasts. Throughout the forecasting process, staff use macroeconometric models that allow the combination of judgment and consistency with model-based insights.

Global trade growth forecast process. Global trade growth is calculated as the percentage change in the average of global exports and imports of goods and nonfactor services, both measured in real U.S. dollars. Forecasts for global exports and imports are derived from a bottom-up approach, using country-level forecasts for real exports and imports produced during the forecasting process as described above.

Global Economic Prospects: Selected Topics, 2015-26

Growth and business cycles		
Growth prospects		
	How much will AI affect global growth?	June 2026, box 1.1
	Global recovery: Surprisingly strong, disappointingly uneven	January 2026, box 1.1
	Frontier market economies: Promise, performance, and prospects	January 2026, chapter 4
	From tailwinds to headwinds: Emerging and developing economies in the twenty-first century	January 2025, chapter 3
	Falling graduation prospects: Low-income countries in the twenty-first century	January 2025, chapter 4
	Low-income growth accelerations: Lessons from country case studies	January 2025, box 4.1
	Small states: Overlapping crises, multiple challenges	January 2023, chapter 4
	Global growth scenarios	January 2021, box 1.4
	Scenarios of possible global growth outcomes	June 2020, box 1.3
	Growth in low-income countries: Evolution, prospects, and policies	June 2019, special focus 2.1
	Long-term growth prospects: Downgraded no more?	June 2018, box 1.1
	Quantifying uncertainties in global growth forecasts	June 2016, special focus 2
Potential growth		
	Global economy: Heading into a decade of disappointments?	January 2021, chapter 3
	How do deep recessions affect potential output in EMDEs?	June 2020, box 3.1
	Building solid foundations: How to promote potential growth	January 2018, chapter 3
	What is potential growth?	January 2018, box 3.1
	Understanding the recent productivity slowdown: Facts and explanations	January 2018, box 3.2
	Moving together? Investment and potential output	January 2018, box 3.3
	The long shadow of contractions over potential output	January 2018, box 3.4
	Productivity and investment growth during reforms	January 2018, box 3.5
Global output gap		
	Is the global economy turning the corner?	January 2018, box 1.1
Productivity		
	How do disasters affect productivity?	June 2020, box 3.2
	Fading promise: How to rekindle productivity growth	January 2020, chapter 3
	EMDE regional productivity trends and bottlenecks	January 2020, box 3.1
	Sectoral sources of productivity growth	January 2020, box 3.2
	Patterns of total factor productivity: A firm perspective	January 2020, box 3.3
	Debt, financial crises, and productivity	January 2020, box 3.4
Investment		
	Unlocking private investment	June 2026, box 1.2
	Harnessing the benefits of public investment	June 2024, chapter 3
	Public investment dynamics around adverse events	June 2024, box 3.1
	Macroeconomic impacts of public investment: A literature review	June 2024, box 3.2
	The magic of investment accelerations	January 2024, chapter 3
	Sparking investment accelerations: Lessons from country case studies	January 2024, box 3.1
	Investment growth after the pandemic	January 2023, chapter 3
	Investment: Subdued prospects, strong needs	June 2019, special focus 1.1
	Weak investment in uncertain times: Causes, implications, and policy responses	January 2017, chapter 3
	Investment-less credit booms	January 2017, box 3.1
	Implications of rising uncertainty for investment in EMDEs	January 2017, box 3.2
	Investment slowdown in China	January 2017, box 3.3
	Interactions between public and private investment	January 2017, box 3.4
Capital flows and financial conditions		
	Incidence and drivers of surges and stops in capital inflows	January 2026, box 4.2
	The global financial cycle: Asset prices and credit growth	January 2026, box 4.3
	Foreign direct investment in retreat: Policies to turn the tide	June 2025, chapter 3
	Dynamics of FDI around adverse events	June 2025, box 3.1
	Impact of FDI on economic growth: Heterogeneous PVAR analysis	June 2025, box 3.2

Global Economic Prospects: Selected Topics, 2015-26

Growth and business cycles (*continued*)		
Cross-border spillovers		
	Who catches a cold when emerging markets sneeze?	January 2016, chapter 3
	Sources of the growth slowdown in BRICS	January 2016, box 3.1
	Understanding cross-border growth spillovers	January 2016, box 3.2
	Within-region spillovers	January 2016, box 3.3
	Linkages between China and Sub-Saharan Africa	June 2015, box 2.1
	What does a slowdown in China mean for Latin America and the Caribbean?	January 2015, box 2.2
Inflation		
	Global stagflation	June 2022, special focus 1
	Emerging inflation pressures: Cause for alarm?	June 2021, chapter 4
	Low for how much longer? Inflation in low-income countries	January 2020, special focus 2
	Currency depreciation, inflation, and central bank independence	June 2019, special focus 1.2
	The great disinflation	January 2019, box 1.1
Economics of pandemics		
	Impact of COVID-19 on global income inequality	January 2022, chapter 4
	Lasting scars of the COVID-19 pandemic	June 2020, chapter 3
	Adding fuel to the fire: Cheap oil during the pandemic	June 2020, chapter 4
	Regional macroeconomic implications of COVID-19	June 2020, special focus
	How deep will the COVID-19 recession be?	June 2020, box 1.1
	Scenarios of possible global growth outcomes	June 2020, box 1.3
	How does informality aggravate the impact of COVID-19?	June 2020, box 1.4
	The impact of COVID-19 on global value chains	June 2020, box SF1
	How do deep recessions affect potential output?	June 2020, box 3.1
	How do disasters affect productivity?	June 2020, box 3.2
	Reforms after the 2014-16 oil price plunge	June 2020, box 4.1
	The macroeconomic effects of pandemics and epidemics: A literature review	June 2020, annex 3.1
Informality		
	How does informality aggravate the impact of COVID-19?	June 2020, box 1.4
	Growing in the shadow: Challenges of informality	January 2019, chapter 3
	Linkages between formal and informal sectors	January 2019, box 3.1
	Regional dimensions of informality: An overview	January 2019, box 3.2
	Casting a shadow: Productivity in formal and informal firms	January 2019, box 3.3
	Under the magnifying glass: How do policies affect informality?	January 2019, box 3.4
Other topics		
	Fragile and conflict-affected situations: Intertwined crises, multiple vulnerabilities	June 2025, chapter 4
	Post-conflict recoveries: Lessons from country experiences	June 2025, box 4.1
	Education demographics and global inequality	January 2018, special focus 2
	Recent developments in emerging and developing country labor markets	June 2015, box 1.3
	What does weak growth mean for poverty in the future?	January 2015, box 1.1

Debt, fiscal policy, and fiscal space	
A rising challenge: Sovereign debt levels and interest rates in EMDEs	June 2026, chapter 3
The costs of hidden debt	June 2026, box 3.1
Navigating volatility: fiscal policy and commodity price swings	June 2026, chapter 4
Rebuilding fiscal space: The case for fiscal rules	January 2026, chapter 3
Fiscal challenges in small states: Weathering storms, rebuilding resilience	June 2024, chapter 4
Fiscal policy in commodity exporters: An enduring challenge	January 2024, chapter 4
How does procyclical fiscal policy affect output growth?	January 2024, box 4.1
Do fiscal rules and sovereign wealth funds make a difference? Lessons from country case studies	January 2024, box 4.2
Fiscal policy challenges in low-income countries	June 2023, chapter 4
Resolving high debt after the pandemic: lessons from past episodes of debt relief	January 2022, special focus
How has the pandemic made the fourth wave of debt more dangerous?	January 2021, box 1.1

Global Economic Prospects: Selected Topics, 2015-26

Debt, fiscal policy, and fiscal space (*continued*)	
The fourth wave: Rapid debt buildup	January 2020, chapter 4
Debt: No free lunch	June 2019, box 1.1
Debt in low-income countries: Evolution, implications, and remedies	January 2019, chapter 4
Debt dynamics in emerging market and developing economies: Time to act?	June 2017, special focus 1
Revenue mobilization in South Asia: Policy challenges and recommendations	January 2015, box 2.3
Having fiscal space and using it: Fiscal challenges in developing economies	January 2015, chapter 3
Revenue mobilization in South Asia: Policy challenges and recommendations	January 2015, box 2.3
Fiscal policy in low-income countries	January 2015, box 3.1
What affects the size of fiscal multipliers?	January 2015, box 3.2
Chile's fiscal rule—an example of success	January 2015, box 3.3
Narrow fiscal space and the risk of a debt crisis	January 2015, box 3.4

Commodity markets	
Russia's invasion of Ukraine: Implications for energy markets and activity	June 2022, special focus 2
Commodity price cycles: Underlying drivers and policy options	January 2022, chapter 3
Reforms after the 2014-16 oil price plunge	June 2020, box 4.1
Adding fuel to the fire: Cheap oil in the pandemic	June 2020, chapter 4
The role of major emerging markets in global commodity demand	June 2018, special focus 1
The role of the EM7 in commodity production	June 2018, SF1, box SF1.1
Commodity consumption: Implications of government policies	June 2018, SF1, box SF1.2
With the benefit of hindsight: The impact of the 2014–16 oil price collapse	January 2018, special focus 1
From commodity discovery to production: Vulnerabilities and policies in LICs	January 2016, special focus
After the commodities boom: What next for low-income countries?	June 2015, special focus 2
Low oil prices in perspective	June 2015, box 1.2
Understanding the plunge in oil prices: Sources and implications	January 2015, chapter 4
What do we know about the impact of oil prices on output and inflation? A brief survey	January 2015, box 4.1

Monetary and exchange rate policies	
Financial spillovers of rising U.S. interest rates	June 2023, chapter 3
Asset purchases in emerging markets: Unconventional policies, unconventional times	January 2021, chapter 4
The fourth wave: Rapid debt buildup	January 2020, chapter 4
Price controls: Good intentions, bad outcomes	January 2020, special focus 1
Low for how much longer? Inflation in low-income countries	January 2020, special focus 2
Currency depreciation, inflation, and central bank independence	June 2019, special focus 1.2
The great disinflation	January 2019, box 1.1
Corporate debt: Financial stability and investment implications	June 2018, special focus 2
Recent credit surge in historical context	June 2016, special focus 1
Peg and control? The links between exchange rate regimes and capital account policies	January 2016, chapter 4
Negative interest rates in Europe: A glance at their causes and implications	June 2015, box 1.1
Hoping for the best, preparing for the worst: Risks around U.S. rate liftoff and policy options	June 2015, special focus 1
Countercyclical monetary policy in emerging markets: Review and evidence	January 2015, box 1.2

Global Economic Prospects: Selected Topics, 2015-26

Globalization of trade and financial flows	
Regional aspects of integration	January 2025, box 3.1
Transmission channels of integration	January 2025, box 3.2
High trade costs: causes and remedies	June 2021, chapter 3
The impact of COVID-19 on global value chains	June 2020, box SF1
Poverty impact of food price shocks and policies	January 2019, chapter 4
Arm's-length trade: A source of post-crisis trade weakness	June 2017, special focus 2
The U.S. economy and the world	January 2017, special focus
Potential macroeconomic implications of the Trans-Pacific Partnership Agreement	January 2016, chapter 4
Regulatory convergence in mega-regional trade agreements	January 2016, box 4.1.1
China's integration in global supply chains: Review and implications	January 2015, box 2.1
Can remittances help promote consumption stability?	January 2015, chapter 4
What lies behind the global trade slowdown?	January 2015, chapter 4

Prospects Group: Selected Other Publications on the Global Economy, 2015-26

Commodity Markets Outlook	
New shocks, old tools: Revisiting international commodity agreements in a fragmented world	October 2025
Post-pandemic commodity cycles: A new era?	April 2025
Commodity price synchronization: A new era?	October 2024
Forecasting industrial commodity prices: An assessment	April 2024
Potential near-term implications of the conflict in the Middle East for commodity markets: A preliminary assessment	October 2023
Forecasting industrial commodity prices	April 2023
Pandemic, war, recession: Drivers of aluminum and copper prices	October 2022
The impact of the war in Ukraine on commodity markets	April 2022
Urbanization and commodity demand	October 2021
Causes and consequences of metal price shocks	April 2021
Persistence of commodity shocks	October 2020
Food price shocks: Channels and implications	April 2019
The implications of tariffs for commodity markets	October 2018, box
The changing of the guard: Shifts in industrial commodity demand	October 2018
Oil exporters: Policies and challenges	April 2018
Investment weakness in commodity exporters	January 2017
OPEC in historical context: Commodity agreements and market fundamentals	October 2016
From energy prices to food prices: Moving in tandem?	July 2016
Resource development in an era of cheap commodities	April 2016
Weak growth in emerging market economies: What does it imply for commodity markets?	January 2016
Understanding El Niño: What does it mean for commodity markets?	October 2015
How important are China and India in global commodity consumption?	July 2015
Anatomy of the last four oil price crashes	April 2015
Putting the recent plunge in oil prices in perspective	January 2015

Accelerating Investment: Challenges and Policies	
Investment in emerging and developing economies	Overview
Investment trends, structure, and drivers in EMDEs	Chapter 1
The magic of investment accelerations	Chapter 2
Public investment as a catalyst of economic growth	Chapter 3
Reinvigorating private investment: Policy options	Chapter 4
Foreign direct investment in retreat: Policies to turn the tide	Chapter 5

Prospects Group: Selected Other Publications on the Global Economy, 2015-26

Prospects Group: Selected Other Publications on the Global Economy, 2015-26

Global Productivity: Trends, Drivers, and Policies	
Global productivity trends	Chapter 1
What explains productivity growth	Chapter 2
What happens to productivity during major adverse events?	Chapter 3
Productivity convergence: Is anyone catching up?	Chapter 4
Regional dimensions of productivity: Trends, explanations, and policies	Chapter 5
Productivity: Technology, demand, and employment trade-offs	Chapter 6
Sectoral sources of productivity growth	Chapter 7

Global Waves of Debt: Causes and Consequences	
Debt: Evolution, causes, and consequences	Chapter 1
Benefits and costs of debt: The dose makes the poison	Chapter 2
Global waves of debt: What goes up must come down?	Chapter 3
The fourth wave: Ripple or tsunami?	Chapter 4
Debt and financial crises: From euphoria to distress	Chapter 5
Policies: Turning mistakes into experience	Chapter 6

A Decade After the Global Recession: Lessons and Challenges for Emerging and Developing Economies	
A decade after the global recession: Lessons and challenges	Chapter 1
What happens during global recessions?	Chapter 2
Macroeconomic developments	Chapter 3
Financial market developments	Chapter 4
Macroeconomic and financial sector policies	Chapter 5
Prospects, risks, and vulnerabilities	Chapter 6
Policy challenges	Chapter 7
The role of the World Bank Group	Chapter 8

Inflation in Emerging and Developing Economies: Evolution, Drivers, and Policies	
Inflation: Concepts, evolution, and correlates	Chapter 1
Understanding global inflation synchronization	Chapter 2
Sources of inflation: Global and domestic drivers	Chapter 3
Inflation expectations: Review and evidence	Chapter 4
Inflation and exchange rate pass-through	Chapter 5
Inflation in low-income countries	Chapter 6
Poverty impact of food price shocks and policies	Chapter 7

High-frequency monitoring
Global Monthly newsletter